I'M GLAD I LIVED

By

ERNEST E. HOLBROOK

authorHOUSE

1663 Liberty Drive, Suite 200
Bloomington, Indiana 47403
(800) 839-8640
www.authorhouse.com

First published by AuthorHouse 07/02/04

ISBN: 1-4184-0696-1 (e)
ISBN: 1-4184-0695-3 (sc)

Library of Congress Control Number: 2004093242

Printed in the United States of America
Bloomington, Indiana

This book is printed on acid-free paper.

ABOUT THE BOOK

The occurrences listed herein are real life incidents and accidents that happened to or were caused by the author. They cover childhood to adulthood. Read about:

- A rat trap that caught something besides rats
- The pumpkin that exploded
- The 6-year old "school teacher" (no kidding!)
- The 8-year old race-car driver and tricycle rider
- The cure-all tiny pills
- The truck-driver, cattle rancher, airplane fighter pilot
- The "Berry-Pickin' Boys from Florida"
- Near-tragedy at a U.S. air force base
- The Prodigal Son's return
- Restitution time
- Sermon number one versus sermon number two
- A fall from grace – right in the pulpit!
- Grits in the pot, on the plate, and in the face
- A tent revival with 200 people inside and 400 outside
- A baptismal candidate that could not swim
- A brand new car and 50 cents worth of gas
- A watch-dog named "Barko"
- The "ghost" of Easter
- A churchyard full of dynamite
- A place where everyone is a Christian (on another planet)
- A "shootout" – at midnight! At the church!
- Stuck on an elevator

ACKNOWLEDGEMENTS

This autobiography could not have been accomplished and completed without the help of my soul-mate, my darling wife, Junell. Also, my daughters, Sandra Waldron and Sharon Franklin and my granddaughter, Farrah Moore, did the typing for me and were assisted by Polly Herrin. My daughter, Phyllis Conner, as well as my son-in-law, Phillip Waldron, participated in the proof-reading of the manuscript. Phil and Sandra also did the photo editing for the book.

There were also many others who helped recall incidents that had slipped my memory. To all these I owe a debt of sincere gratitude.

Ernest Holbrook

DEDICATION

This book is dedicated with love and affection to my wife, Junell, for her undying faithfulness and support throughout my life and ministry.

To our three daughters, Sandra, Sharon and Phyllis, and their families who have so enriched our lives with theirs.

To my parents and grandparents, who pioneered the Christian way before me.

To Robert and Charles Raburn, who were there in the beginning to provide companionship in the ministry.

To the wonderful family of God, who is the salt of the earth and the light of the world.

And most of all, to God Almighty and His Christ, who created, planned for and provided our present and eternal salvation.

This autobiography could not have been accomplished and completed without the help and presence of the above named persons and the inspiration of the Holy Spirit.

Ernest Holbrook

TABLE OF CONTENTS

FOREWORD
By Terry Raburn

It is said that every life has a story. Actually, every life *is* a story! And, in truth, the story of a single life is the combination of the multi-faceted intersections, overlaps, joinings and parallels of the many lives of the many individuals it touched, worked with, helped and loved. The wonder of our living is that each life is separate while no life stands alone.

These pages present the story of Ernest and Junell Holbrook. It is written in the experience of normal lives responding to a higher calling. Every life suffers lows and enjoys highs, weeps and giggles, celebrates wins and endures defeats, while lives all around are going through similar experiences. The distinctive of this story is much more than just the living. It is the reason behind the living. That reason is God, His call upon two people, their response and faithfulness over the years, and His blessings in return. That makes this more than just *a* story. That makes this *the best story* lives can produce!

It has been my joy to know these lives all of mine. Ernest and my father are cousins and, more, were boyhood friends. They extended their camaraderie by answering the call to preach the Gospel of Jesus Christ together and evangelized throughout the southeastern United States. They met and married their God given wives, Junell and Merle, in the same frame of time and, soon after, I entered the world as one of the first of the next generation.

Ernest and Junell have been constant encouragers and powerful examples to me and countless others. They have exemplified the best traditions of the church while always being aggressive in using the newest and most effective tools of media, music and ministry. They have pastored successful congregations and pioneered new ones. They have written outstanding songs, sheet music and musical scores. They have cared for the lives the Lord put under their leadership. They produced three beautiful, intelligent, lovely and valuable daughters. They improved themselves through education and made significant contributions to their neighborhoods and communities. They are loved and respected in the church world, the civic arena and the classroom.

Now, they start new chapters of their story. They are mentoring grandchildren and, as you will read, writing the lessons of their lives into a book, which will benefit all its readers. We, the readers, will be better because they shared with us. And, as we read, we will interpret the story in light of our own living and, therefore, may see it a bit differently than another. However, in the end, we will agree in appreciation, gratitude and inspiration. It is a great story and we can all be thankful it touched each of us in a positive and productive way.

Terry Raburn
Superintendent
Peninsular Florida District Council
Assemblies of God

For to me, to live is Christ, and to die is gain.

Philippians 1:21

PREFACE

For years I have contemplated writing a book. Conversations with relatives and friends often evoke memories of incidents, blunders and numerous other things I have experienced. Unless they are transcribed they will be forgotten, either by me, or by my loved ones in a generation or two. Therefore, I have taken upon myself the task of recording many of these happenings as I remember them.

Of course, God has a process of record-keeping, too, on His gigantic computer in the sky. According to the Scriptures, He has the ways and means to log everything about everyone, including the very thoughts and intents of the heart. But I am very grateful that He also has a big eraser for sins forgiven, which are blotted out, never to be remembered again, when we trust Him.

The book title, "I'm Glad I Lived," comes from a very special person in my life, my grandfather, the late Reverend J. J. Holbrook. I do not know if the phrase was original with him, but I've heard him use it many times in his sermons and testimonies. Implicit in the statement is his genuine thankfulness to the Lord for allowing him the privilege of life itself, which he took on vigorously. Another saying of his was, "The sun rises too late and sets too soon."

Even more than just the opportunity to live, move and have his being, was my granddad's gratefulness to God for having life in the knowledge and love of the saving grace of Christ, which enabled him to serve the kingdom of God for most of his life.

It is easy to contrast his eternally meaningful and productive life with countless others who live as if they haven't the slightest idea why they were born, or what life is really all about. Or with those who expend the major portion of their time, talent and energies pursuing the pleasures of sin for a season. My granddad, like Moses, refused these in favor of things that truly count for time and eternity.

While it is true that everyone encounters trials, tribulations and disappointments in life, this is no excuse to abhor the gift of life. An existence lived in the realms of Christ's salvation and presence can find divine assistance in making stepping stones out of the stumbling blocks of life. Instead of being overcome by the vicissitudes of life, believers are made over-comers through Christ who ever lives to make intercession for His own. Such a person can spread joy instead of misery, both of which has a profound effect upon every other life they touch.

Christ's abiding presence makes life well worth living and can cause a testimony during life and at the end of life that loudly proclaims: "I'm Glad I Lived!"

It is my understanding that a person on his deathbed will not tell a lie. Since many lives end today under heavy sedation, we do not have the dying testimonies we once had. Based on some we do have, it is very interesting to note the great differences between the last words of atheists, skeptics and other unbelievers and those who died in the faith of Jesus Christ.

"I am about to take a fearful leap in the dark," is said to be the renowned atheist Hobbs' last words.* Voltaire parted this life stating, "I am abandoned by God and man."* How uniquely dissimilar the concluding words of John Wesley: "The best of all, God is with us,"* or those of Dwight L. Moody: "This is my triumph; this is my coronation day! It is glorious!"* It isn't difficult from these to determine who could have stated, "I am glad I lived," and who couldn't.

The plan of God and Christ for mankind's deliverance from sin and self is universal. "Whosoever will" means precisely that. None is excluded except "whosoever won't." Peter affirms that the Lord is longsuffering to us and not willing that any should perish, but that all should come to repentance. (II Peter 3:9) May we, with Joshua of old say: "As for me and my house, we will serve the Lord." (Joshua 24:15)

Like my grandfather, I, too, am glad I lived! And I hope many others who might come across the following pages of the story of my life will not only enjoy the many comical happenings, but also learn and profit from my "fortunes" and "misfortunes." And most of all, live the Christ life and be able to say now and at the crossing over: "I'm Glad I Lived!"

Ernest E. Holbrook

(Footnotes)
* Knights Master Book of Illustrations, pages 158-160.

INTRODUCTION

*For this reason a man will leave his father and mother
and be united with his wife, and they will become one flesh. Genesis 2:24*

The time had finally arrived! I could hardly believe it wasn't a dream. I was actually on my way to my wedding! Since about age 14, I had given much thought to this very important milestone in my life. Who knows how many hours of the day and night I had spent looking, hoping, fantasizing about a future companion. Second to my relationship with God, this occasion which I had long considered, dated and planned for, had surely arrived. To be driving to my own marriage ceremony seemed too good to be true. But it was!

There had always been girlfriends! At age five, it was the cutest five year-old in the Hopewell community. I had been embarrassed beyond words at her fifth birthday party. We were playing, "pin the tail on the donkey." When the blindfold was removed from my eyes, I had attached the tail right under the donkey's neck amid roaring laughter from my peers. She was laughing too, and my face grew redder by the moment.

My family's occupation was truck farming and consequently we moved every four years or so, seeking better farmland and home situations. At every new school I attended, Cork, Winston and Trapnell Elementary, and at Turkey Creek High School, I would quickly observe the "crop" of girls. As the upper teen years came, the search became more serious than ever.

When I fully surrendered to the Lord, and a call to preach the gospel of Jesus Christ, seeking out a spouse became a sincere matter of prayer. I would want a Christian girl who was truly dedicated to Christ and the ministry. Again, there were several prospects. What a confusing time! In the church circles, where I diligently began to search, many promising young ladies already had several suitors. It became a time of competition with fellas near my age. Plus, there was no scarcity of adult advice from parents, relatives and church members. Matchmakers seemed to be everywhere.

Finally, it was settled! We had selected each other! We were now both ready to say "I do." And so we did! And no, the Lord had not returned before we could get married, as we had feared! We both had grown up having heard it preached constantly that the Lord was coming soon, even any minute. Not that we didn't want Him to return! We just hoped and prayed He would delay His coming until our nuptials had been said! He did!

I shall never forget my first date with Junell. I was on top of the world, perhaps even higher, like cloud nine. By now, I definitely knew I had been called to be a gospel preacher. I had already conducted several revival meetings with my first cousin, Robert Raburn. The services were well attended and there were numerous converts to Christ, giving reassurance to our entering the ministry.

The night of that first date, I was to speak at the midweek service at my home church, Mt. Zion Assembly of God, located just west of Plant City, Florida, on the Thonotosassa road. It would be a great opportunity for me to make a good first impression on the beautiful, talented young lady that I had recently met at one of the Saturday night youth rallies.

Three local groups of Pentecostal churches, the Assemblies of God, Church of God and Pentecostal Holiness, had formed a Saturday evening fellowship meeting which rotated from church to church and placed strong emphasis on the young people. The meetings were designed to provide a spiritual alternative to a possible "worldly" Saturday night for teenagers.

Each church represented would present a song and testimony and the host church would select a speaker, usually a pastor or perhaps an aspiring young minister.

I was with a group of upper teens from our church at this particular service being held at the Dover Pentecostal Holiness church. All of a sudden, there she was, singing with her mother and father. It was as if she had angelic qualities. It seemed a glow emanated from her face and I even envisioned a halo above her head. I absolutely could not keep my eyes off her the rest of the service.

The speaker was a young Pentecostal Holiness evangelist. I thought he would never stop preaching. I was anxious to make some inquiries of the young lady who had left me spellbound. Finally, the long sermon ended with an invitation and a responsive gathering around the altar, mostly young people.

Certainly I believe in prayers, rededication and renewed commitments to Christ as per the sermon challenge. But there is a time for all things and it seemed it was time for me to meet, if possible, that certain someone. I could always pray later. But she, too, was at prayer, on her knees and I had to wait.

In the meantime, the pastor of Plant City's First Assembly of God was nearby, so I asked him about the special singers that had upstaged all the rest. "They are," he said, "the Reverend and Mrs. J. M. Player, recently moved from Marianna, Florida, and the newly elected pastors at the Assembly of God at Lithia, Florida." "And what about their daughter?" I asked. "Oh, she is engaged to be married to the young evangelist who preached tonight." My heart sank!

No matter, I still made it my business to meet her, introduce myself, tell her I was a minister, and inform her of how inspirational her singing had been. At later rallies, I would see her and her parents, but I never saw her "fiancée" again. She was not wearing an engagement ring, but in those days many of the holiness people did not even wear wedding bands. Upon further questioning from some of the people who knew her, I found she was not engaged. I immediately made my move!

"Hi, so nice to see you and hear you sing again. How are you? I am to preach at Mt. Zion next Wednesday night and I wondered if I might come and get you for the occasion?" I was startled when she, without hesitation, said, "Yes, I'd like that!" Inwardly, my heart did somersaults, or something like that. Accompanying chills ran up and down my spine! I learned her name was Junell, which I also liked from the very first. I could hardly wait for 4 days to transpire!

Wednesday evening did finally arrive. From my home near Lakeland, Florida, where I worked in our dairy between revival meetings I was conducting, to her house at Lithia was some 20 miles, then another 15 miles back to Mt. Zion. My elation was interrupted when I discovered the bridge across the Alafia River was out. I took the detour back through Durant and over to Bloomingdale, and on unfamiliar roads searched for a route to Lithia.

Arriving late and additionally nervous, I knocked on her front door. She came out and announced that her friend from Hawaii, who had been a schoolmate in Sevierville, Tennessee, had arrived for an unexpected visit and would like to accompany us. I agreed it would be fine, even though my spirits dropped further. I thought, "Of all times for her to visit! My first date!"

We three headed back via the long detour route to Mt. Zion. The anxiousness of the first date, the unexpected detour and "three's a crowd," all contributed, I'm sure, to an unwelcome call of nature. I stopped at a corner farm supply store in the Turkey Creek community, went in and asked for the you know what, was directed right back out the front door in full view of my two passengers, and around back of the building. I could only imagine what the girls might be thinking.

The only plus I could come up with was the fact that with three people in the front seat of the car, at least I was sitting very close to the girl of my dreams. Had I known what next was to befall me, I might have found an excuse to turn around, take the girls back home and then hunt a place to hide for the next several days.

Fortunately, for the late arrivers, the song and testimony service, in which most everyone sang (and preached), was still in progress 40 minutes after starting time. One could only expect all eyes to turn to the front door as Ernest, Junell and her school-mate entered. Since this would be the first time that some of our church folks had seen Junell, I was overly excited about "showing her off." My concern, however, was what reaction, if any, to expect from an all-white congregation to our beautiful, but very dark-skinned Hawaiian guest.

But soon I would be in the pulpit ready to display my God-given preaching ability. That, I assured myself, would allay the concerns of my fellow members and hopefully delight my new-found girlfriend. With nearly one hundred people present, the pastor stood to announce the young, home-town, local church, fire-ball evangelist, the Reverend Ernest Holbrook. Little did I consider at the moment the scripture that says in Proverbs 16:18, "Pride goes before destruction and a haughty spirit before a fall!"

The podium area of old Mt. Zion was an elevated platform some two feet above the floor level and was enclosed front and sides with a decorative railing. It was constructed of 2 X 4's and draped with a beautiful cloth covering. Being boisterous in the pulpit in those days in our church circles was a sure divine indication of God's approval and anointing. Commotion and emotion, combined with fast, loud oratory, gained audience approval and evoked responsive "Amens!"

I took my cue and engaged in the accepted ritual of abundant exuberance. With this supposed unction from the Holy One, I was past the scripture reading, subject announcement and introduction, and well into my sermon when it happened!

What the Holy One, or no one else had told me, was that the pulpit railing had been removed for the Christmas program and had only been temporarily propped up until a more convenient moment when it would be re-anchored. I abruptly moved from behind the lectern, and leaned heavily against the railing while endeavoring to rail home my first point. The next moment, in humpty-dumpty fashion, down came the railing, Ernest, and all.

When I came to my wits I realized I was hanging in midair across the railing which had fallen to the platform floor by the lectern, but was still standing full height at the corner. I couldn't reach the floor forwards, or backwards. But before help arrived, I had managed to rock back and forth until I regained my footing.

Amidst shock, giggles and apologies from those responsible for the temporariness of the rail situation, I could sense my face was very flushed and my sermon gone! It was only through the sympathy of several congregants with their "Amens" that I was able to regroup and begin again. With the rail re-propped, I started hammering away again and almost repeated the catastrophe. One man exclaimed, "Be careful, it (the rail) could fall again!" I calmed down and was able to finish the message.

I was wondering if my ministry was at an end, and I surely felt Junell would never want to see me again. How in this world could something so humiliating happen to a promising young clergyman like me? From a high, high, I had gone to a low, low and was fully ready for the world to come to an end, then and there! Once again I was surrounded with apologies and given encouraging words regarding my sermon. None of which helped my feelings very much.

I took the girls back to Lithia and on the way not a word was mentioned about the great fall by either of them, and certainly not by me. I walked the young ladies to the door and before I bade them goodnight, asked Junell if I might call on her again. And once again the answer was "yes." The "ego-buster" incident apparently hadn't ended our relationship and I started feeling better that very moment.

I think I learned some very important lessons that night. One, that I was still very human, even while ministering God's Word. Two, that the law of gravity is a reality in the pulpit as well as out of it. I should also have considered that an overabundance of physical movement and emotionalism is not necessarily indicative of anointed preaching.

Our dating continued and our attraction to each other kept growing. We both had some others who were nice and interesting prospects as we faced the major decision of choosing a companion for life. But it was soon very evident that each of us was narrowing the field down to us!

Some months after that devastating plunge over the rail, I finally got the nerve to ask Junell her reaction since she had never mentioned it. She responded, "It was really funny, seeing your big rear-end rocking back and forth over that rail." I suppose I shouldn't have revisited the issue after all.

Among our church circles a Christian marriage was considered essential. "Be not unequally yoked together with unbelievers," (II Cor. 6:14) to us, meant we were not to marry an unbeliever. This is why we both were searching out a dedicated Christian for a future mate.

As a minister, it was paramount that a wife must sense the calling as well. This is one thing that so attracted me to Junell. She was a Christian from age 8, even as I, and she was brought up in church all her life. The fact that she was beautiful, could play a piano and accordion, could sing wonderfully, and had a pleasant personality, didn't hurt, either.

I was fully convinced it had to be her, perhaps a little sooner than she, but I prevailed. The availability of other young ladies and young men perhaps delayed the decision for a short time but on June 24, 1949, she became my bride!

What a wonderful marriage we have had! Three precious, lovely daughters, three very outstanding sons-in-law, several top-notch grandchildren, (Would you like to see a picture of them?), and lives lived with multiplied blessings and few regrets. Christian ministry has been priority number one for us. Traveling as evangelists for some four years and pastoring four different churches over a period of 44 years has proven to be very rewarding.

To God and His Christ be all the glory for every convert, for every person we may have helped along life's pathway and for the lasting friendships we have made across the years. We apparently have now arrived at the point where we "dream dreams" while the young converts are "seeing visions." (Joel 2:28) We are most grateful to have been a very small part of the Kingdom of Heaven, on earth.

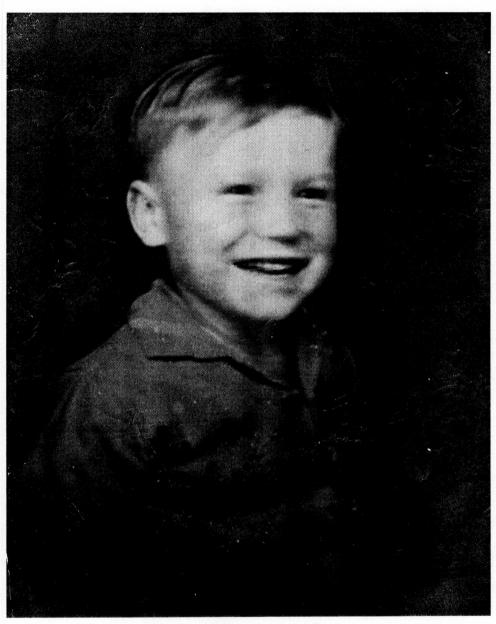

Ernest Holbrook at age four

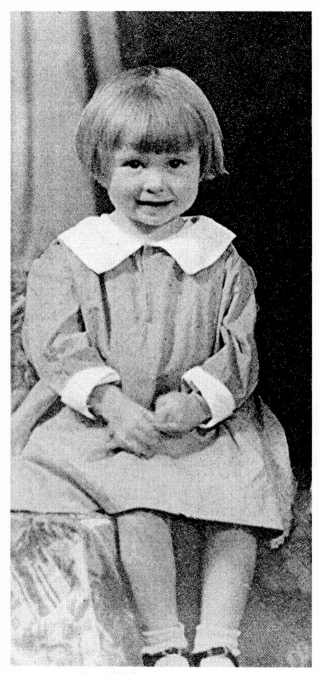

Junell Player at age three

Courting couple at parsonage in Lithia, Florida

At Hillsborough River State Park just before marriage

Ernest and Junell in the 1980's

ONE

THE GENESIS YEARS

In the beginning God created the Heavens and the earth.
Then God said, "Let us make man in our image, in our likeness..."
Genesis 1:1, 26a

Plant City, Florida, USA, my hometown, is a small municipality whose size reminds me of the description of Bethlehem, in Judah of Israel, given by the prophet Micah in Chapter 5, verse 2: "small among the clans of Judah..." There are some major differences, however. The two towns are oceans apart, both in geography and culture. And Bethlehem is the birthplace of the one who is destined and predestined to rule Heaven and earth, and all the inhabitants thereof. (Revelation 19:6b)

The other, Plant City, probably has its greatest claim to fame, not necessarily by who was born here, but in the title: "World's Winter Strawberry Capital." I was born here, almost in a strawberry patch, on March 8, 1929, the same year the stock market crashed. So, Plant City is not a very geographically important place and 1929 is not a particularly great year to recall.

I learned later that I came into this world in one of the largest countries on earth, one of millions of people stateside and over a billion worldwide. As of this writing the world population is approaching 7 billion and in my opinion, no one anywhere, anytime has been born with the acclaim given that special child in Bethlehem, Judea, about two thousand years ago. (Dr. Luke 2:11-14)

And yet I live in awe of the fact that I am the center of the earth and universe. Or at least it so appears, since all the scenes of life and the world come to me through my eyes, as well as my perception and interpretation of them. This is self-centeredness and is a powerful privilege and blessing on one hand, but can be disastrous both for now and eternity. If one never moves from this normal carnal state to Christ-centeredness and the humble

1

admission that there are billions of other human beings, he or she is in for a very narrow life.

My predecessors migrated from England and Ireland to Virginia, then North Carolina, North Georgia, South Georgia, Frostproof, Florida, (which, incidentally, isn't really frost-proof) and finally to Plant City, the year before I was born.

My grandfather-to-be, Jessup Jasper Holbrook, of Ducktown, some fifty miles north, northeast of Atlanta, Georgia, and about five miles west of Cumming, was a rural dirt-farmer. He had eloped with my grandmother-to-be, Emma Lou Nora Bramblett, since her father was a medical doctor and objected to their marriage. The societal difference had developed when my great-grandfather Bramblett moved up the ladder from a country farmer to M.D. Thus Jessup Jasper, still of peon status, had to steal Lou Nora from the upstairs window of the doctor's house (except she was most willing to be stolen)!

A neighbor girl had come to spend the night with Lou Nora, to cover for her. While the doctor was making a house call that evening, up went J. J.'s ladder to her second story bedroom window and down came Lou Nora. Off they went in his horse and buggy limousine! Lou Nora's heart was pounding, not only from the utter daring and excitement of the hopefully covert escape from the house, but also for fear that on the very narrow lane leading to and from her house she and Jessup might meet the doctor returning from his house call. Fortunately for all three, it did not happen.

The get-a-way trip would last the rest of the night and they arrived at Alpharetta, Georgia, at the crack of dawn. They stopped in front of the Methodist parsonage, awakened the sleeping minister, and he, with his wife as a witness, came buggy-side in their night clothes and tied the Holbrook-Bramblett knot. The union apparently eased the social gap between the families. Later, there would be other marriages across the family lines.

Jessup and Lou Nora would be farmers with the two principle crops, tobacco and little Holbrooks, eleven, all total. Once, when the two first-born children, Bessie and Curtis, were very small, the first snowfall of winter had come. This meant a prime opportunity for hunting jack-rabbits, since they were easily tracked by their give-a-way foot prints in the snow. Jessup, and his brothers, would be out at daylight for the big event.

Emma Lou Nora was to arise long before daybreak to fix a hearty breakfast for Jessup in preparation for the rabbit chase. With the children ill and fretful, she, very reluctantly, got out of a warm bed, then purposely stalled for time hoping the delay might make Jessup change his mind. It didn't! Instead, she later told me, she heard a movement behind her, felt a swift kick and was propelled all the way across the kitchen.

She said she then finished breakfast in record-breaking time which Jessup hastily consumed and was out and gone! No goodbye! No parting kiss! No "I'll be back at what time." No nothing! For her, with such a tumultuous beginning, two crying young ones, a bruised hip and a hurting heart, the day seemed almost endless. Dark came and no Jessup. Time dragged on but finally about 10 p.m., the jack-rabbit hunter returned. He asked, "Did you think I wasn't coming back?" With that question she said, "I just busted!" The flowing tears and fond embrace brought a happy ending to the several hour separation.

This Emma Lou Nora Bramblett Holbrook was a fascinating woman. Her memory was amazing and she could recall incidents in her early life from age five. Her story-telling could easily capture your attention and paint pictures in one's mind par-excellent.

One day while visiting her, she said, "I'd like to go back and visit Ducktown in North Georgia and see the place and my relatives. None of my children will take me because they say I'm too old to make the trip. It's been 50 years since I left and I've never been back!" I said, "Grandma, Junell and I will take you!" She was thrilled no end!

We set out on what would become a very interesting trip. She kept us entertained the entire way talking about her upbringing and elopement. She told of a cold, wintry morning when she was five years old. Outside the house everything was frozen, including the iron water pump on the back porch. An older brother dared her to touch her tongue to the iron surface and she pulled it loose leaving some of the skin on the pump. A lesson learned the hard way! And a very mean brother!

As we approached Alpharetta, then still just a small town, she asked me to slow down. She showed us the very spot where she got married. The brick church building was still there.

Soon we arrived in Cumming and as we turned west toward Ducktown we passed a store building with Holbrook Hardware in bold letters across the upper front. Five miles later we turned northward up the country road leading to our long anticipated destination. I was in awe at the numerous mailboxes in front of the houses with Holbrook and Bramblett written on them. "Here's the house, stop here," Lou Nora exclaimed.

Grandmother's niece and some other relatives burst out the front door as we entered their yard. After highly emotional greetings, inside we went and a few phone calls brought relatives from all around. Junell and I were utterly amazed at how our grandmother, after 50 years, recognized most of them and called them by name. And we were elevated to hero status for having brought her to see all of them.

After the long, drawn out daytime kinfolk's fest, too much food and darkness setting in, we were more than ready for bedtime. No such luck! Other relatives, who had been at work during the day began coming in. Weary and exhausted, we welcomed the departing of the night-comers, who along with the others promised, "We'll see you again tomorrow!"

Finally, we were shown the bedroom which was the big front room where we were to sleep. It was a huge old frame house and I had already noticed cracks between the boards in the floor wide enough to see some three feet beneath to the ground. I was glad they had shown us the stack of quilts near to the bed since the November night cold was creeping through those cracks. We kept adding quilts, one by one, until about eight of them were keeping us warm but weighted down.

The next morning a second cousin invited us to stay with her and her husband. It was a modern brick house that was centrally heated. We gladly stayed there the balance of our trip.

Of Grandmother Holbrook's four brothers, three had become doctors. They were Rader, Cicero, and Thad. Rader's son, Rupert, also became a physician and is now retired. At the time of our visit, her other brother, Corbett, was the only one still living and he was staying with Grandmother's sister, "Nett." I don't know if "Nett" was a short for "Nettie" or something else. I never heard her referred to by any other name. Her house was several miles away and since they couldn't come to see us we went to their house.

On the way I couldn't help wondering why my folks would want to move from such beautiful, country. Despite the bleakness of an approaching winter, the hills and valleys were attractive and awe-inspiring. I thought of where the Psalmist in 121:1 & 2 said, "I will lift up my eyes to the hills – from whence comes my help? My help comes from the Lord, who made heaven and earth."

Our visit was cordial and I learned a little more about the early days of my great uncle and aunt. We were invited and visited several other relatives. They discovered we sang so we had some music and singing. We were told about the "Holbrook Camp Ground" and on Wednesday night we sang and I preached at the nearby Pleasant Grove Methodist church. Adjacent was a cemetery filled with Holbrooks and some Brambletts. It seemed strange to see so many headstones with our family names inscribed.

I learned my great uncle we had visited there passed away soon after that as did my grandmother. But up to her death she never stopped talking about and thanking us for the trip back to her upbringings. One day, as I often did, I was bringing her some fish. I had traded cars and my new Oldsmobile had an automatic trunk opener. She was sitting on the front porch as I drove up. The frozen fish were in a pan in the trunk so I pushed the trunk-opener button as I began to stop. The trunk-lid flew up and she jumped up and exclaimed, "Your car is flying all to pieces!" What a grand, grandmother!

So why did my family migrate from the splendor of the north Georgia region, the geographical area of four distinct seasons, rich and fertile clay-type soil, snowy winters, flourishing green springs and summers and spine-tingling multicolored autumns? I will tell you why!

I really think that North Georgia as a permanent home for grandfather Jessup was never a question until a Methodist evangelist, preaching at the Holbrook campground tabernacle, condemned not only the use of tobacco but the growing and selling of it as well. Strongly convicted and feeling he could not support his family otherwise, Jessup moved his family to South Georgia a few miles east of Ashburn where cotton, corn, peanuts, potatoes, hogs and cows and a host of other things could produce a livelihood without depending on tobacco.

And this was where my father, Virgil Ernest Holbrook, the third child of Jessup and Lou Nora, met, courted and married my mother, Minnie Julia Payne. Living only a few miles apart, Dad would walk to the Payne house after work and court Mom sitting on the front porch. The date was always fully chaperoned by an adult and the curfew was 8 p.m., exactly! No exceptions!

My dad, having a tenth-grade education, taught school there during the absence of a qualified teacher. It was a one-room, grades one through eight country school, and the position gave him some prestige in the Live Oak community. This resulted in some jealousy among his peers, especially the ones who were also interested in one Minnie Julia Payne. Two of them plotted to stop his dating my mom to be.

One evening, after going to see Julia, Dad was walking home in the darkness. As he approached the Live Oak cemetery, he heard weird noises coming from the graveyard. He looked and made out two ghost-like figures faintly glowing amidst the tombstones, inside the fenced area. His first thought was to run as fast as he could. Instead, he calmly walked along the downhill graded road and suddenly his knees touched a rope stretched from tree to tree across the road. Had he been running, great would have been the summersaults thereof, and possible injuries which was what was intended by the two suitors of Minnie Julia.

My grandfather, James Thomas Payne, who didn't care much for my dad anyway, especially disliked the fact that my dad was courting his 13 year-young daughter, Julia. One evening, when Dad overstayed his visit, Granddad Payne angrily stormed out of the house threatening and swinging his walking stick. Dad ran to his motorcycle, which he had recently acquired, but of all times it wouldn't start. He tried talking his future father-in-law out of hitting him while he frantically cranked away. Fortunately, two of my mom's brothers restrained my grandfather which helped save my dad from being clobbered.

The Live Oak community where the Paynes, Holbrooks and other farming families lived, worked and played, had three churches: Baptist, Methodist and Wesleyan Methodist, the latter of which was founded by my grandmother Payne. The respective preachers were circuit riders, each coming one Sunday a month and serving other churches elsewhere on the other Sundays. The local church services were set on three different Sundays of the month, thus affording many families the opportunity to attend each other's churches.

I'm told it wasn't unusual for the Baptists to lower the boom on the Methodists and Wesleyan Methodists. And reciprocation followed the next two Sundays. The Methodists preached sanctification in addition to the new birth and were, they insisted, advanced spiritually over the Baptists. The Baptists were eternally secure and were happy they couldn't fall from grace like the Methodists.

The Wesleyan Methodists, of which my mother's mother was a lay preacher, preached "Holiness unto the Lord" as a cardinal doctrine and thus claimed the right to lambaste both the Baptists and Methodists for their "unholiness"! I remember my mother recalling the times my grandmother Payne referred to the regular Methodists as, "them old M. E.'s, that don't have a dab of real religion!"

After a few years in Turner County, Georgia, where my older sister Louise and brother Ralph were born, several members of the Payne and Holbrook families got the yearning to move to Florida, land of sunshine, lakes and orange trees; flatlands, palm trees and beaches (as well as alligators, snakes, mosquitoes, sandspurs and tropical hurricanes)! Frostproof, Florida, would become home for some of the Paynes to this day. But the still-wandering Holbrooks followed Jessup to Plant City, "World Winter Strawberry Capital."

I was born soon after; in the old Dickson house (now gone) just north of the Thonotosassa road and west of what is now Chitty Road. The house sat on a small hill among huge oak trees. It was located about three or four miles from downtown. We moved several times from one farm to another all around Plant City and three times in Polk County, west of Lakeland. My younger sister Joann was born at Hopewell and Linda at Trapnell. We were truck farmers (major crop was strawberries) and eventually got into the cattle and dairy business.

My earliest memories date back to when I was age three or four when we lived near the intersection of Thonotosassa and Cork roads. I'll never forget when my older brother Ralph and I were going to the strawberry field early one foggy winter morning. We encountered an awful odor. Bad would hardly describe it. "What do we smell?" I asked Ralph. "A polecat" was his reply. In my young mind I imagined a cat dragging a pole attached to it, which, no doubt was causing such a stench. We never saw the kitty but Ralph warned me to stay as far away from one as I could.

My weaknesses were candy, cold drinks and ice cream. Fortunately for me, or perhaps unfortunately, there was a country grocery and gas station right across the road. The nickels and dimes were hard to come by during those depression years, though I didn't know what the depression really was or just how poor we were. All I knew was that ten cents would buy a candy bar and a big Nehi orange or grape soda, my favorites.

One day when I asked for a dime and got none, I found a ticket on a fertilizer bag that somewhat resembled a dollar bill, what with all the fancy writing on it. I detached it, took it to the store, ordered a cold drink and Baby

Ruth and promptly presented the ticket to the store owner for payment. He accepted it and I waited for some change (which I didn't get). He later told my dad, who paid him and spanked me! I never tried to use counterfeit money again.

Another desire of mine was to get in the car and go! Anywhere! And I never wanted to come home. I would, when sensing we were headed home, suggest we turn on this road, or that, anywhere but home. Going, seeing and doing things away from home always seemed better than hum-drum home-life. My motto was, "Let's go!"

One day I heard Dad say he had to go to town. At this time we were living some five miles south of Plant City. My mom reminded Dad to take the milk jar. During the time our cow was dry, we purchased milk from a neighbor up the road a piece. Often we would leave the empty jar on the way to town and pick it up on the way home all filled up.

I put in on Dad this day to let me go with him. He said, "No, I've got to tend to some business and you would be in the way." I begged again but the "no" was final. Or was it? A bright idea came to my five year-young mind. I would hide in the back foot of the car and go anyway. While Dad was making preparations, I went around the car, opened the back door, got in, crouched down and gently shut the door.

Ere long Dad got in, cranked up our model A Ford, and away we went! I was trying to figure the best way to let my presence be known, since there wasn't much to see from the back floorboard. But the issue resolved itself much sooner than I expected. We had only gone a short distance when Dad pulled over and stopped. I heard the neighbor greet my dad. Then the back door opened and I, along with the milk jar I hadn't noticed, was in plain view of him and my dad.

Three people were very surprised at the revelation. I'm not sure who was most. Dad said nothing, gave the milk man the milk jar, closed the door and made an abrupt u-turn. Back home, he administered Proverbs 22:15 in good fashion. Had it been today, I probably could have sued for child abuse!

Listening to records on the old graphonola (graphophone), and my older brother and sister play the guitar and sing, I learned to sing at a very early age. Dad worked Saturdays as a meat cutter at Rogers and Middlebrooks, a combined grocery and department store in downtown Plant City. In those days, Saturday was "go to town day" for most everyone. From everywhere people came to shop, visit and stock up on supplies for the coming week. They would put me on a counter in the department part of the store and my singing would soon draw a crowd.

One Saturday night one of the owners emptied a large matchbox and used it to take a collection for my singing. When I got home I counted the money and thought I was rich. There was a one dollar bill, some fifty cents coins, quarters, dimes, nickels and pennies, nearly six dollars. I would have spent it all for candy and drinks on Monday (all the stores were closed on Sundays) if my folks had allowed me. They tried to teach me how to properly manage my money so it would last. I didn't care for any such instructions. I wanted to enjoy "the pleasures of sin for a season," now! (Heb. 11:25)

I got a jump-start in school, enrolling at age five, at Hopewell Elementary School, which encompassed grades one through nine. It was an exciting new world, but one I didn't always relish because it curtailed my freedom. I was used to playing, not sitting in class all day.

My brother Ralph and I used to walk the mile or so to school. One morning I wasn't feeling very well and upon arriving at school decided I would go into the ninth grade classroom with Ralph. Ralph and the teacher, who was also school principal, tried to persuade me to go to my first grade class. I was reluctant, so they agreed to walk with me. They left me at my classroom door. I waited until they were out of sight, then I left the school and hit the road for home. A preacher, who lived just past where we did, had carried his school teacher wife to school and was headed back home. He stopped, inquired why I was leaving school, and finally offered me a ride home.

I angrily refused to either speak to him or ride with him. I kept on walking! Mom soon discovered I had fever and later our doctor diagnosed my sickness as diphtheria. I was a miserable wreck not knowing why I wasn't feeling good or able to play. My folks brought me candy, which didn't taste right. When I finally recovered I remember how great I felt, learning somewhat to appreciate good health. Since I was only five years old, the family decided to wait until the following year to send me back to school.

Being well again, my five year-old energy level returned. So did the privilege to play all day, since I now was no longer in school. There also was more time for me to get in trouble.

Mom and Dad were old-fashioned and religious enough to believe Proverbs 22:6. They administered discipline in the forms of spankings and restrictions of things I wanted most to do. I preferred Mom's chastisements over Dad's, because they were tempered with much more mercy than his.

If these weren't enough, add my oldest sister, Louise, to the surveillance corps. She took it upon herself to enact the punishment Mom or Dad had overlooked. Once, she grabbed me by the shoulders and shook me so hard I couldn't hold my teeth together. As they clattered and the pain intensified, I thought surely she would stop. She didn't! She kept on until her strength subsided which I felt saved me from a sure death.

Mom always read from the Bible to us each evening after supper. Then, we would have family prayer before retiring to bed. We did not have a utility room or barn in which to keep the sack of feed for our cow, so it was kept inside the house beside the back door. My favorite sitting spot during these devotions was on the feed sack.

One night during the prayer, I decided to reach into the sack and run my hand into the feed. "Ka-whap!" The huge rat trap placed in the feed sack to catch rats, caught me instead. My scream disrupted the prayer as all the family rushed to my rescue. I pulled my hand out with the trap securely attached. I surely thought my hand was broken, but it was only bruised and sore for a couple of days. I never felt inside the feed sack again.

Louise and Ralph had an altercation one night just before supper. A neighbor had given me a huge pumpkin, and said to tell my mother to bake the family a pie. A few weeks had passed and the pumpkin was still sitting in the corner of the kitchen floor. Louise grabbed it and threw it at Ralph. He ducked and it hit the facing on the door that divided the kitchen and dining room.

The pumpkin, which by then was rotten, exploded and filled both rooms with its obnoxious odor and mushy content. We had pumpkin alright, but certainly not in the form of a pie. Both Ralph and Louise were ordered to clean up the mess. The stains and smell lingered for awhile.

Louise was a beauty, as were all my sisters. She had many suitors and I liked a certain one best because he always gave me money to leave the room where they were courting. I could count on loading my pockets with nickels, dimes and sometimes even a quarter when he came.

By the time I was to begin school again, we had gone to a new location. The grass always looks greener elsewhere and we moved to another farm northwest of Plant City on the Sam Allen Road near the Cork community. Cork Elementary School had a primer, a class which precedes the first grade, and to my disappointment, this is where I was placed. In a few days, our teacher discovered I could read all the words and do all the numbers. She divided the class and let me teach letters of the alphabet and simple words, as well as addition and subtraction, while she took the rest of the class outside.

I couldn't wait to get home and tell Mom and Dad I "taught" that day! Unfortunately, I got spanked for lying! Mom later apologized when she learned it was true, but that didn't undo the undeserved chastisement. Both my pride and my backside had been injured.

My glory was short-lived, however, because the next week I was moved to first grade. I soon learned our teacher was someone to be reckoned with. Word had it that she was the "meanest" teacher at school. She caught a student cheating one day. He sat two seats in front of me. She grabbed his paper, wadded it up and threw it into the woodpile, which was stacked in the corner of the room for heating on cold days. Then she jerked him up, dragged him to the front of the room and paddled him before the entire class. Of course, she couldn't have gotten away with such "cruel and inhuman" punishment today, but she believed Proverbs 29:15 and all the other instructions Solomon gave for discipline. The results were good though! She practically made a saint of this classmate and used him as an example to any of us who might disregard her instructions.

For a few days I was almost afraid to breathe, lest I might offend her. However, she redeemed herself at the end of the month by showing us pictures of various toys and other items children might desire. We made our choices and the following Monday she brought each of us a gift, including one for the battered one! My fear of her had turned into a feeling of awe, a mixed feeling of reverence, fear and wonder! I later thought of God in this same respect. (Psalms 47:2)

Some of the most delightful times of my early childhood were centered around the family meals, the Saturday "go-to-town" trips, and association with my cousins (of which there were plenty). There were not only my relatives around Plant City but those still in Georgia. Each summer we would go to "Grandma Payne's" for usually a two or three week visit. What was a vacation for us probably was the exact opposite for my Grandmother and Grandfather Payne.

My Payne grandparents were first cousins that married each other and had thirteen children. The only physical deformity, which sometimes occurs when close relatives marry, was when one son was born with a finger missing on one of his hands. It didn't seem to affect his life or longevity. He passed away at age 105.

There was usually a July 4th family reunion at the home of my Georgia grandparents and it was around this time of year that all the children, grandchildren and great grandchildren would come, sometimes all at the same time. I remember once that 54 people spent the night at the old home place, on pallets, in the hallway, on the porch, in cars, everywhere!

I was one of the 54, asleep on a pallet among many others in a back bedroom. Imagine awakening in the night with an urgent need to go to the bathroom, which the grandparents didn't have inside the house. There was, of course, a room at the end of a path! Dad was sleeping on the floor beside me when I awakened him and announced my plight. "We can't walk out of here without stepping on everybody," he said, and suggested I wait until daylight, which I couldn't. Somehow we made it, trying to figure where to step, or not to, in the darkness. What blessed relief!

One of my cousins tells of the time when he was visiting the grandparents when he was a small boy. Unexpected company arrived during the night and he, sound asleep, was moved from his bed to the quilt box. This was a rectangular, wooden box, similar to a casket, except deeper. He later awoke, turned over and bumped one side – then the other. He decided he was dead and buried and his screams of alarm aroused everyone in the house. He was relieved to discover he was still alive.

The family reunion gathering in Georgia was an occasion to which I always looked forward. The farm encompassed about 90 acres and there was always a super garden and a smokehouse filled with hams, bacon, etc. The yard was well populated with chickens. In the field and garden there were beans, peas, corn, squash, cabbage, tomatoes, carrots, okra, you name it. There were watermelons, cantaloupes, figs, pears, scuppernongs, apples, peaches and peanuts. The cool, clear, unpolluted creek and Blue Pond were nearby for fishing and swimming. Almost heaven! (Not only in West Virginia, but in South Georgia as well!)

One day an uncle, who lived nearby, brought two of his sons to rebuild the well curbing and shelter for my grandparents. When all the old, rotting wood was removed, it exposed the round hole some three feet wide with water at the bottom some fifteen or so feet down. At this point the boys got into a fight. They were wrestling, throwing punches and crisscrossing the well. I was terrified! What if one or both fell in? A sure drowning I thought.

I pleaded with my uncle, "Please stop the fight! They are going to fall in the well!" My uncle responded, "Let 'em! It'll be good enough for them!" Fortunately, the battle ended with both still on terra firma. Soon the new curbing, shelter and pulley were in place and I was greatly relieved.

Another time a cousin told me the pears were ripe, so we sneaked behind the big barn to grandpa's favorite pear tree. We climbed the tree trying to reach the biggest, prettiest pears. The weight of the pears and the two of us was too much. There came a cracking sound and down came almost half the tree, pears, and both of us. Fortunately, uninjured, we decided for some reason we had better pick the pears and hide them.

If we had left them on the broken limb, perhaps Grandpa Payne would have suspected the abundant pear crop, coupled with a windstorm, had broken the tree nearly in half. But when he saw the pears we tried to hide beneath the garage ramp, then the broken tree, he returned to the house breathing "threatenings and slaughter" against both of us. This was logical since we were the only grandchildren present. We escaped with a severe tongue-lashing!

Attending church on Sundays was a vital part of my early life, both at home and when we visited South Georgia. My maternal grandmother Payne saw to it that everyone possible would be in the worship service at the Liveoak Wesleyan Methodist church. The pastor lived far away and often did not make even the once-a-month appointment. In such times my grandmother conducted the service and did the preaching.

The old pump organ would play and songs like "Rock of Ages" and "Amazing Grace" would sound out through the open church windows and across the country-side. Both she and Granddaddy Holbrook had a very profound impact upon the very young me. I wasn't sure which one scared me most as they demanded repentance, conversion and holy living in order to miss the eternal fires of Hell.

Their religious influence, plus my family upbringing of Bible-reading, prayer and church attendance impacted me so deeply that I began seriously considering being a Christian while still very young. Perhaps I might even become a gospel preacher like my grandparents some day.

Another dynamic event that contributed to my youthful ponderings about living a life for Christ occurred when I was eight years old. Our church conducted a special series of services designed for children. The gospel was presented on our level of understanding. There were peppy and ear-catching choruses with physical participation like clapping our hands, motions with our arms and feet and loud chants.

This was followed by Bible quizzes, prizes and simple gospel stories about Joseph, Moses, David, Peter, Paul, and most of all, Jesus. These narratives presented the simple plan of salvation and invitations were extended each evening. It was the final service that moved me so deeply. Up to then, I figured there would be plenty of time down the road of life to see about spiritual things. But that night, the urgency of "now" was so strongly emphasized, I found myself moving toward the altar, along with several other children.

I prayed as best I knew how, asked God to forgive all my sins and invited Jesus Christ to come into my heart and life. What followed is very difficult to put into words. I sensed an inner feeling of serenity that permeated my entire being. What an incredible religious experience! Even at such a tender age I was mature enough to realize that what was happening within was the most real, powerful and wonderful thing I had ever encountered. I felt Jesus was inside of me like a big bundle of joy, peace and pardon, all in one. I was fully convinced that Heaven itself had flooded my soul.

I went home that night in a "heavenly daze" and an obsession of "joy unspeakable and full of glory". (I Peter 1:8) Even during the night when I awakened, it was right there, an elation beyond measure and an assurance that I was now right with the Lord. It seemed angelic beings were making songs and music in the deepest part of me, and surely they were. (Dr. Luke 15:10)

Early the next morning, I bounded into the kitchen where Mom was frying eggs and bacon and baking biscuits in the oven of our "wood stove". "Mama," I asked, "Do you feel real good and real light on the inside when you get saved?" "Yes," she responded. That was all the evidence I needed. There was no doubt. I was saved! My fears of being eternally lost were gone!

It was Monday and what was usually "blue Monday"! Blue for me because there were five days of school ahead before another Saturday, (go to town day) and Sunday (go to church and see all my cousins day, and get to go home with some of them, or they with me!). But strangely, this Monday didn't seem blue at all. In fact, I was anxious to get out and tell about what had happened to me.

It was about a half mile to the school bus stop but I made it with ease. The eight or ten mile ride to Cork school couldn't pass soon enough. I had great news to share with teachers and fellow students.

The bus driver always stopped to let us off at the Knights Station School while he proceeded north on Highway 39 to the Hillsborough-Pasco county line to pick up more students. Some of us would pass the time on the school swings. It seemed my swing went higher that morning than ever before.

As usual, some students from the other schools called us "Corkstoppers" because of our school name, which we considered an insult, but even that stigma didn't seem to apply this particular day. Upon arriving at Cork school, the walk across the soft, sandy schoolyard to the classroom was the least difficult I had ever remembered. I guess it was the spring in my step, emanating from the overflowing joy in my heart that made the difference.

When I began telling everyone I could about my newfound joy, the response wasn't exactly what I had anticipated. A few persons did say they were happy for me but some looked puzzled. Others seemed either shocked or uninterested and I think I detected a couple of teachers and peers whose reaction suggested I had become some sort of religious nut. If I thought everyone would be as excited as me, I had another thought coming! They weren't!

But why wouldn't everyone be ready to rejoice with me? What I had found was so real to me I had difficulty trying to understand why anyone wouldn't be thrilled with me. I was about to embark on the road to reality. The reality that many other people did not have beliefs and views that were synonymous with mine. But I knew deep within that I had found a peace and hope like never before.

For me, it would be nine years from such a unique conversion to Christ to the time of a complete rededication and renewed commitment to Him at age 17. It would cover those years of adolescence and times of my life when I longed for the prodigal son's world, (Luke 15:11-13) to search out what the world system would offer me. During this period of time I allowed God to be moved from the front to the back seat of my life. Instead of pursuing Christian faith and conduct, I was primarily interested in seeking things that were enticing to my carnal nature. Like pleasure, fame and fortune.

During those teen and World War II years, my mind went from one fantasy to another. One day I was an airplane fighter pilot shooting down Japanese Zeros and German Messerschmitts. The next, I might be trucking an 18-wheeler down the highways of life. Then my thoughts would turn to being a star of the Grand Ole Opry or a big cattle baron. But the unique religious experience I had at age eight remained with me. Thank God, it never left me!

But, my fears of eternal damnation, based on the sizzling preaching of my Grandfather Holbrook and Grandmother Payne haunted me! Any sort of crises would move my heart to repentance – until the scare subsided. One special incident that made headlines was some religious somebody's prediction that the world would end. The date I recall was September 17, 1945.

As an eleventh grader in high school, I thought how sad this could be if it were possibly true. I was just getting ready to take on life in the world as an adult – and now this! Despite the fact our church leaders discounted the prophecy as unscriptural, I still was relieved when the dreaded day passed and nothing happened! I knew enough about Bible teachings to realize no one is to set dates for the rapture of the church, the return of the Lord to the earth, or the end of the world. (Matthew 24:36, 42 & 50)

Yet I knew all these things would someday come to pass, including the coming of the Antichrist and the Great Tribulation. (II Thess. 2:3-4 and Daniel 12:1, Matthew 24:21 and Rev. 6:16-17) And knowing this, along with the fact of God's love for me and everyone, (John 3:16 and Romans 5:8) it helped me to never forget a very awesome spiritual encounter I had experienced at such a young, tender age.

My religious experience at age eight was marvelous, but certainly not a panacea for life's difficulties. The fact that I was disappointed at the lack of wholehearted community approval was only one thing. There were many more to come.

First, my "big" brother left home to attend Mount Berry boarding school at Rome, Georgia. It was a school founded by Martha Berry, a dedicated Christian and Educator, and provided the ways and means for the underprivileged to obtain a quality education. The school and college have a history par-excellent.

I am not aware of the details of why and how Ralph got enrolled there, but he paid his tuition by working in a hospital and achieved academically sufficient to earn a scholarship for another year. When the time came for his return, both Mom and Dad got real sick so he had to stay home, tend the farm and make the living for the family for a time. He never returned to take advantage of his achievement.

Another incident happened on a cold, wintry day. While mine and my uncle's families were working in the strawberry fields, I was left at home to see after my little sister and play with three young cousins. As a result of our inventive genius, we filled empty one gallon syrup buckets with dirt, put on the lids, ran wires through the tops and bottoms and thus created ideal roller pull-toys.

The road out front was being paved. The asphalt process back then was much slower than it is today. The mixture of tar, petroleum, sand and gravel had to go through several days of drying time before the final application. Into this unfinished mess, we pulled our "semi-trailer" buckets. Dressed in new school clothes and shoes, I tripped and fell headlong into the sticky goo.

Upon the expert advice, and with the assistance of my one-year-older-than-me cousin, we poured a five gallon can of kerosene into a number 3 washtub. This, he said, "will dissolve the tar from the new streaked overalls, red sweater, shoes and you." So, I plunged into the tub, fully clothed.

Fortunately for me, my mom and brother arrived just in time to pull me out and keep me from blistering from the petro. The clothes and shoes were ruined. I felt I was ruined also, especially after receiving the correction that Solomon recommended for such behavior. (Proverbs 22:15)

Once, while on an outing at a lake near Winter Haven, I stayed in swimming too long and encountered severe sunburn. Huge blisters broke out on my back and shoulders and I had to lie on my stomach for three weeks. What a miserable time for me. I felt like I was on fire.

Another time, I was walking barefoot to a garage to get my bicycle. I stubbed my foot on the wooden edging of the paved road and wound up with a big wooden splinter in my foot. It buried beneath the skin so deep that all Mom's and Dad's efforts to remove it failed.

In about two weeks, the skin on the bottom of my foot turned very white and it looked as if it was becoming infected. My parents showed it to our next-door neighbor, who was a registered nurse. She had my mom apply a piece of white bacon and wrap it securely to the infected spot. All that night, I would awaken feeling a "drawing" sensation. The next morning, a splinter larger than, and as long as a match, was lying between the bottom of my foot and the bandage. The wound soon healed completely.

Not long after this, we moved once more, this time just inside the Polk-Hillsborough county line. Here, early on, my earth-shattering adventures continued. I actually got involved in a "shootout." For a short period of time, it seemed to be a life and death situation. It happened in our strawberry field some three or four hundred yards behind our house.

The pretty robin "red breasts" were not so pretty to strawberry farmers. These northern feathered creatures winged south for the warm winter weather and for them, a berry patch was an ideal spot for a gourmet meal. Left unattended, a crop could be decimated in short order by the hungry intruders. Thus, the southern response to the trespassers was scarecrows, shotguns and rifles.

This cold winter day, it fell my lot to guard our precious fruit. Since I was so young and small, I preferred the rifle over the shotgun because the 12 gauge "kick" always left my shoulder black and blue. (My brother had watched one day as a hired helper was knocked flat on his back from the wallop the shotgun had produced when shot.)

With rifle in hand, I headed to our strawberry field. Some one hundred yards or so away, a neighbor's field cornered with ours. I noted two of our neighbor's young sons with their gun, out to perform the same security measures as myself. Presently, they were joined by an older brother who was home on furlough from the Navy. He was a standout, all adorned in his white military uniform. I watched as he took their rifle, aimed it in my direction and fired away.

I was startled as I heard the bullet "sing" through the air above me. In a moment, another shot rang out which sounded even closer to me as it sliced the atmosphere overhead. I wondered if the Navy brother had gone crazy or something. I quickly lay down behind the graded dirt road that bisected our field, hopefully to protect myself in this bizarre situation.

I could see the three of them standing in front of the frame building which served as a "packing shed" for their strawberries. I aimed my gun slightly above the building and fired a "warning shot." In the course of the distance, the bullet dropped enough that it hit the wooden siding, just above their heads.

They started screaming, "Stop shooting! You almost hit us." They then began to wave a white handkerchief in surrender. They begged, "Please put down your gun! We have! We want to come and talk to you."

Noting that they had laid down their rifle, I waved for them to come over to where I was. They explained that they shot "way above my head" just for fun and I had almost hit them. I told them if they shot again, I would aim lower next time. They promised there would be no next time. Whew!!

The two younger boys told me later that it was their brother from the Navy that started the whole thing, not them. Reflecting on the incident, I shuttered at the thought of what could have happened and was once again grateful for a watchful, guardian angel, protecting all of us.

Rather than eating at the lunch room at school, I preferred to bring my own lunch from home. The main reason was the fact that spinach was served on a regular basis and I simply could not stomach it. I did not care to be a "Popeye, the Sailor Man," if such required spinach.

The next reason was my mom's "sugar" pies. These were tart-like, half moon shaped crusts fried with cinnamon, butter and sugar. Of course, there were sandwiches to be eaten first. Made with either loaf bread or biscuits, the variety included egg, baloney, ham, white bacon, cheese or peanut butter and jelly. But the sugar pies were for "dessert" and were my favorites!

And not mine only! I soon learned I could swap half a sugar pie for most anything my school chums had: marbles, tops, knives, comic books, pictures, pencils, other toys and even nickels and dimes.

One boy had a picture of the Lone Ranger and Tonto, standing back to back with guns drawn. I wanted it but he refused to part with it. One day after he had traded everything he had, he gave in and offered it to me for one-half of my sugar pie. A very sweet deal indeed.

Through these early childhood experiences, I think I was learning that life serves up both bitter and sweet, good and bad and everything in between. I was elated at the things that were favorable and was grateful I had faith in God and His Christ for the unpleasant things that came my way, seemingly much too often.

The John Paton Holbrook Family (My great-grandfather's family)
First row second from left (As best we know): Aunt Pearl, Uncle Arthur,
Virgil (My dad), Uncle Curt Second row: Aunt Mary, John Paton
Holbrook, Jane Elizabeth (Elliott) Holbrook Third row: My grandparents
Jessup and Nora Holbrook holding Aunt Elsie
(Children of Jessup and Nora not yet born: Janelle, Audey and J.T.)

Doctor Martin Truman Bramblett (In the carriage) His sons - Left to right: Dr. Rader Hugh Bramblett, Dr. Joel Thaddeus Bramblett and William Corbett Bramblett (My great-grandfather and great-uncles)

Jessup and Nora Bramblett Holbrook
(My grandparents)

James Thomas and Mary Jane Spurlock Payne (My grandparents)

Virgil Ernest Holbrook (My father)

Minnie Julia Payne
(My mother)

TWO

THE GENESIS YEARS – PART TWO

Train a child in the way he should go,
and when he is old he will not turn from it. Proverbs 22:6

The joys and pleasures of the years of my youth were centered in a number of situations and activities. Music, singing, going to church, fishing, hunting, horseback riding, swimming, softball, baseball, football, the Georgia family reunions, playing with cousins and neighbors, you name it! These were preferred above going to school, hoeing and picking strawberries, tending the cows or mowing the yard.

But my dad and mom always saw to it that there were rewards for faithful laborers. I was paid to work by the hour or job, or quart of strawberries, hamper of beans, peas, peppers, etc. By the time I was ten years old I was the "champion" strawberry picker. It was a very humiliating time when a family moved from Arkansas to work on our farm. A girl among them "out-picked" me. A girl! Was I glad when they moved elsewhere? Guess!

In the strawberry fields back then, children were used to do much of the harvesting. We were younger, had a lower center of gravity and not nearly as much back to hurt from the "on the ground" picking. A number of the Hillsborough and Polk County, Florida, schools were referred to as "Strawberry Schools," commencing the first of April and running until just before Christmas each year. This was to accommodate the strawberry season – January through March – so school children could pick berries.

What a shocking day when these school terms were eliminated. Surely dictatorship had arrived and Antichrist would soon be revealed! I cannot recall any injuries to my mind or body from these "child cruelty" years. But anti-strawberry school officials prevailed and our school schedules changed to coincide with all the others. It happened the year after I graduated from high school.

I worked very diligently those years, as did my siblings and parents but we looked forward to payday, time off between crops, plus camping and fishing trips, sometimes overnight. My older brother Ralph was my "big brother" hero. When I felt threatened at school or elsewhere, I let it be known I had a big brother at home who would "take care" of anyone who messed with me.

My closest playmates were my cousins and my oldest sister's son, who was only a few years younger than me. While playing softball one day he became angry at something I did and put a cursing on me. He called me "an old crazy damn." Not bad for a seven year old. This still brings laughter to our family members, though it was not funny when I told his mother back then.

There was a time when I thought I always had to be at some of my cousins' houses or they had to be at mine. This pleased us well but did not always set well with our parents. An occasion of my grandfather J. J.'s illness allowed us to be together many days and nights. Granddad was at the point of death, but to us it was a time for fun and games.

J. J. was a "teetotaler" when it came to alcohol and it was a shocker when the doctor prescribed straight bourbon whiskey for his ailment. He rebelled at first but finally gave in. A son who didn't profess being a Christian was sent to the liquor store. Granddad then had the bottle wrapped in foil for disguise and referred to it as his "tonic." I later heard him asking, "Is it time for my tonic?" The family attributed his recovery to prayer, but the Doctor said, "Isn't it amazing what a little booze can do?" Perhaps it took some of both.

During the several weeks that my Granddad was absent from the pulpit, another minister had filled in for him. When my granddad was ready to resume pastoral duties, some of the congregants wanted the other minister instead. A vote was called and it was split 50-50, ballot after ballot.

After the impasse, it was decided that half of the congregants would move to the old Foursquare church, downtown, with the other minister. The building had been vacant and was available, thus First Assembly of Plant City was formed, so named because Mt. Zion was outside the city limits. Little did I dream that someday I would pastor Mt. Zion for 12 years, plus preach numerous times at First Assembly, as well as conduct many business meetings for them.

My grandfather Jessup was always figuring out ways to try to make some money. I'll never forget a visit my dad and I made to his house along the Cork Road one day.

Grandma Nora heard us drive up, came out the front door and invited us in saying, "If you can get through Grandpa's cotton." "Cotton?" I thought. Yes! Would you believe a living room full of it? I mean all the way up to the rafters of the unceiled room, with only a small walk-through trail to the dining room.

In amazement, we followed a fussing Lou Nora along the narrow passageway as I learned about the cotton-growing episode of Granddad, right here in central Florida. He had grown an abundant crop on 220 acres near Brandon, Florida, another 100 acres or so just north of Dade City, as well as several acres along the Stafford Road near Plant City.

Too late, at picking time, he realized he had no place to store the cotton and that the nearest cotton gin was at Lake City, Florida. Besides this, he had no way to transport the hairy-like white stuff. So, he borrowed my dad's huge, slat-bodied ton and a half truck, loaded it with cotton and burned up the motor enroute to Lake City.

This brought about a fiery father-son confrontation and needless to say, an end to his cotton-raising adventure. One of my cousins told me his family grew cotton at their place on the Miley Road for two years, stored it in an old abandoned house beside their field and found a market for it in Ocala, Florida. He said he was grateful when they too quit the business of growing cotton.

An incident that triggered several accidents happened when my dad came home from town one day and announced that our family was way too "sluggish" and needed a "good working out." "Little Liver Pills" were the answer. Louise was spared the medical cure-all experiment since she was already married and gone. Linda, my youngest sister, hadn't yet been born. The directions on the pill bottle called for two pills for adults, and one for children ages six to twelve.

That evening before bedtime, Dad gave four year old Joann and eight year old me the adult dose of two pills each. He gave Mom and Ralph three apiece. And he took four! "After all, if a dose is good for you, a double-dose will be twice as good," he reasoned. It is fortunate the logic stopped there. The pills were very tiny and who could know their potency? We soon learned!

29

Our bathroom was still a room and a path, located some fifty or sixty feet behind the house. Dad was up and out first the next morning. From the kitchen door, Mom observed him washing his trousers and under-clothes at the water pump on the back porch. Her laughter at him backfired. She never made it out of the kitchen!

I woke up feeling an extreme urgency and headed for you know where at top speed. Too late! Joann went out the door, stopped halfway and returned walking awkwardly and crying.

Around the breakfast table we pondered the happenings and decided that only my older brother, Ralph had escaped. He had left at daybreak to hoe strawberries. As we approached the field to work, we spotted Ralph's underwear hanging across a rafter at the packing shed. Needless to say, that ended forever our overuse, or use, period, of those pills. We dared not take even a normal dose after all that!

Strawberry setting time was rather hectic. One group would be taking up plants while another would be setting them in the freshly bedded rows. Once, the action was taking place about a mile apart and Dad needed a driver to bring the plants to our field. Since most of the route was off the county line road through the woods and the fields, I was chosen to be the transporter, even though I was only eight years old at the time.

With a few brief driving instructions, and by sitting forward and looking through the steering wheel, I became an accomplished driver in a matter of a couple of trips. My brother said he looked up and here came a car loaded with strawberry plants with no driver. There were ooo's and aah's as the workers in each field observed the young driver zooming around the curves and across the country-side.

Overconfidence and pride preceded destruction. The corner fence posts at the entrance to our rented property were old, huge wooden poles formerly used for electric wires, cut to gatepost size. When I failed to turn soon enough, the one on the right side never gave one inch. The car fender of the 1935 Pontiac took the full impact. The crash was heard at both fields.

Dad made his way to where I stood in a state of disbelief. He asked me if I was OK. I said "Yes," even though I was anything but! He backed the car from the post, pried the fender off the tire, drove it through the gate, stopped and got out. "Well, don't just stand there! Get back in the car. We've got work to do." He never mentioned it again. A few days later he came home with the fender all straightened and repainted.

This place, where we lived for four years, had a big porch across the front and around one side. It was some four feet high from the ground. One rainy day, Joann, Ralph's wife and I were playing on the porch. I was wheeling around on my huge tricycle and they were playing traffic cops, instructing me when to turn, how far to back up, etc.

I would back up to the porch's edge and they would shout "Stop!" I looked back and I was two feet from the edge. Next time when Joann yelled, "Stop," I was still a ways from the edge. The third time when "Stop" was announced, I decided to see how close I could come to the edge. A four-foot fall into a wet flowerbed backwards is quite a plunge, especially with a big tricycle on top. And to think they laughed!

But even that fall wasn't of the magnitude of the tumble I took at the Plant City Park. There, on a picnic with the family, I was running, following a squirrel making its way through the tree tops. Looking up all the way, suddenly the whole world gave way from beneath. I landed flat on my back in about 3 or 4 inches of muddy water in the city septic tank drainage ditch that runs through the park. I think I discovered the meaning of "great was the fall of it." (Matt. 7:27) I mean me!

The previous two falls were accidental. The next one was premeditated, but not entirely my fault. Blame it on Superman! The Thomas place had a one-room second story about 15 feet wide and 20 feet long. It had 14 windows, 5 on each side and 2 on each end. When we moved in, we found this room had stacks of books of all sorts, including scores of Superman and Captain Marvel comic books. At every opportunity, Ralph would read one book or another and I indulged in the comics. I rationalized that if these guys could fly – why can't I?

From atop a small utility shed located behind the house, I soon was prepared for the trial launch. With a towel for a cape and an umbrella (as a backup), I wasn't sure how high or far out I might go, but with a pounding heart and excited emotions – I ran and jumped. In record-setting time the feat was accomplished. The cape did not work, the umbrella inverted but nothing hurt until the sudden stop at ground-level.

I landed on my feet and shockwaves reverberated from ground zero up both legs, through my torso and up to brain-level, or to the place where if there were any brains they certainly had not been functioning properly. Some understanding was now taking place in the gray matter, namely, that what worked for Superman had not worked for me. After healing in body and mind, I thought I might try again, this time flapping my arms and hands like wings. But somehow I never got around to episode number two.

I attended Winston Elementary School near Lakeland, Florida, from 1936 to 1940. The first day I rode the bus to school on Swindell Road I was amazed at all the turns and curves. The next day I counted ten of them.

Our wait for the bus in the afternoons was about 30 minutes. One day a couple of fellas who lived near me rationalized that if we took a straight line home, we could beat the bus. But the straight line led across fences, through thick grass, weeds and woods, and about halfway home, we saw the bus roll on by. We never challenged the bus again!

I became a celebrity of sorts at school when it was discovered I could play a guitar. Two of my classmates played harmonicas and we would sing and play quite often at school. One morning, when we were scheduled to perform, I went to the store across the street with one of them before classes began. This store was strictly "off limits" on school days.

On the way back, the teacher on duty caught us and grounded us on the steps at the east end of the building. We were not to move from there until the first bell rang. When she left, my fellow rules-breaker asked where my guitar was. "Right inside the door," I responded. "Get it, and we'll make some music." When the teacher patrol returned, we had a crowd of some 50 students gathered around listening to us play and sing. She was furious! "I'll take care of you later," she threatened. We were grateful that she never mentioned it again.

We had one outstanding brat in our class. He was known as a rabble-rouser, was the school bully, and constantly stayed in trouble with the teachers, principal and everyone. "Fight" could have been his middle name, but one by one the guys got enough and took him on. By the eighth grade about every guy in the upper classes had "whipped" him.

I was always fearful of him. But my time came one afternoon while we were waiting for the bus. He grabbed and kissed my little sister, Joann. This was the limit. Reckoning day had arrived. I plowed into him, beating him mercilessly to the ground. It would have been even worse for him had not other students pulled me off him. He never bullied me again and he never tried kissing Joann again, either.

One day during recess, a group of us were discussing religion. Different ones told what church group they attended. Then, they zeroed in on me. I braced for what I knew was coming. "What are you and where do you go to church?" they quizzed. "The other side of Plant City," I answered, hoping that would suffice. It didn't. "What religion are you?" they continued. "Assembly of God," I said. "Never heard of it."

"Our church is Pentecostal," I finally admitted. "What is that?" one asked. "I know," said another, "It's them "Holy Rollers" and "tongue-talkers," as if that were the sum and substance of our church activities. It wasn't the first or last time I was belittled because of the church I attended. One student rushed to my defense by saying, "You should go to one of them sometimes! They sure sing good." But another said, "We go once in a while just to see what they'll do next." I was relieved when the bell rang. Some of the criticism and jokes were probably justified, I'm sure. Even I had problems with some of the "carryings on" in my church circles back then. Perhaps now also! I believe things should be done decently and in order. (I Corinthians 14:40)

During those years I became a competitor. One other student and I were the school's fastest runners. I played shortstop and pitched in softball. We played several other schools, winning some and losing some. I was pitching at Griffin Elementary and an eighth grader who had failed several times was on the opposing ball team. He looked like he was 20 years old and was about six feet two inches tall.

At his first bat, his whole school was screaming and hollering, "Home run! Home run!" I got him out! What a relief! The next time up he hit one of my pitches undoubtedly the farthest I had ever seen. Up, up and away it went! Out of the playing field and over some big oak trees behind. He could have run the bases twice while our guy was retrieving the ball! We lost the game. Big!

I tested my skill as a salesman during this time. The traveling salesman left me 12 boxes of Cloverine salve. At 25 cents each, I quickly sold them and eagerly awaited the salesman's return with more. The next time I took 24 boxes. But I had to ride my bike further seeking new customers and encountered the "dog-patrols." They ran at me, barked furiously, nipped at my feet and legs and otherwise tormented me. The return trip was no different! Dogs galore! Frayed nerves!

On the third trip, my dog "Tippie," started out with me. I tried to run him back, to no avail. When I approached the first house, as usual, out came the big, black angry dog. But instead of going after me, he headed for Tippie.

A few growls and smells later, we proceeded. The same thing happened at each house we visited. Dog problem solved! All the salve sold!

The candy sales weren't as successful. A neighbor boy, who "helped" me, ate all of his and my profit! Plus I had to go to my dad for money to pay the big salesman. My merchandising soon ended after that.

At school, marbles, root-the-peg, spinning tops and "taking land" by flipping a knife, filled our recesses and lunch periods. And we began noticing the girls. I had several favorites among them but we moved during the middle of the year to the Trapnell area in Hillsborough County. Goodbye girls! And goodbye to the brat, too! Thank Goodness!

Being four years my junior, I had always lorded it over my younger sister, Joann. But not long after we had moved, she knocked me out, cold! I always declared she used a stick of stovewood, which was nearby, but she insists it was her fist. Either way, my lights went out for a few moments. And to think she would do this, after I had saved her from the school brat. However, I never tried to put her nose in a "cow pie" again.

I finished the seventh and eighth grades at Trapnell Elementary School. My schoolmates there included my Raburn cousins. Hitler's onslaught had begun and the Japanese bombed Pearl Harbor December 7, 1941. The United States was at war, World War II.

We had scrap iron drives to help the war effort and someone had donated an old, bodiless car frame with motor, transmission and rear axle intact. The front end weighed about 400 pounds and one boy could pick up the front end all by himself. We were amazed! No one else could!

I immediately established myself as the pitcher of the softball team, and when we played the Hopewell Elementary team we sustained the worst whipping I have ever witnessed. If I recall correctly, the score was like 54 to 9. My pitching ability suffered its worst humiliation and I never reached hero status in softball at Trapnell.

The ninth grade brought me to Turkey Creek High School, a very large, rural school numbering almost 1,000 students with the combined elementary school. Four years there would bring many new acquaintances with students, faculty, the school principal and new girl-friends.

It would also see me involved in the Glee Club, FFA band and quartet, three big school dramas and the "Florida Strawberry Pickers" country and western band. It would also be a major decision time as I faced adulthood, the choosing of a profession and the beginning of the search for a future spouse. It was a wonderful, marvelous and frightful future, but I moved into it with excitement and high hopes!

One afternoon we were riding the bus home. I asked my buddy and next-door neighbor how close the bus came to town. "It goes right to the city limits," he said. I asked what he was supposed to do when he got home. "Hoe strawberries," he answered. "Me too," I returned. "Why don't we stay on the bus, ride to town and go see a movie?" I asked. "We can hoe strawberries tomorrow."

He reluctantly agreed. When we failed to exit the bus at our stop, the bus driver asked why. "We are going to town," we told him. "You boys are going to get into trouble and your parents are going to blame me," he grumbled. But he let us ride to where he turned around.

What's far better than working in the strawberry field? A movie, popcorn and coke, any day! At least we so reasoned at the time. We thumbed a ride nearly home and walked the rest of the way. My neighbor's house was right before mine and it was almost dark as he entered his front door. Immediately, I heard a "whap, whap, whap," with him begging, "Please don't hit me Mama! Please, I'll never do this again, I promise!"

Fear gripped my heart. My house was next stop, just across the road. Dad wasn't home and Mama threatened to tell him. I escaped a flogging by promising to do double- duty in the field next day.

Our fields joined and Sunday morning was mine and my buddy's day to stay home from church to keep the robins out of our strawberry fields. After our families left for church, my friend said he had something for us. He pulled a paper sack out of his pocket and from it took a plug of chewing tobacco and two cigars. I indulged in both and was soon seeing double. I found it difficult to walk to the house when Mom called, "Dinner is ready!" I didn't want any dinner and was as sick as I had ever been. Of course, Mom and Dad could see right through me without looking, and Dad guessed what had happened. He said, "Son, I hope you have learned your lesson!" I had!

Once, my cousin Robert Raburn and I bought cigars and gave them to all the agriculture class at Turkey Creek High School. We only faked smoking the stogies and thought it was hilarious when almost all of the fellas got sick. When the agriculture teacher discovered what we had done he had some choice words for us. We had ruined his evening program for the whole class! We had regurgitating instead!

Robert was a bad influence on me, as were others. Of course, if you asked them, they would tell you the very opposite. Once we were on a school class picnic at Madeira Beach near Bradenton, Florida. Robert and I had been asked to drive and help assist with a class that was one year ahead of mine and two ahead of his. This being the case, we did not have dates. We spotted two boys leaving their girlfriends out in the water about shoulder deep. The rest of the class had come in to prepare the picnic lunch.

Upon seeing the two girls left alone so far out, we went to see about them. Soon, their two boyfriends spotted us with them and came angrily splashing toward us. When they reached us they grabbed Robert and me and tried to hold us under water. They would not reason with us. They were going to teach us a lesson. Both guys were older and bigger than we were.

As I was pulled beneath the water I carried my attacker with me. I decided if we were going to drown, we would drown together. At the point of total exhaustion I felt his grip loosen as he struggled for air. The identical thing happened to Robert. Both the assailants broke loose from us and headed for shore, leaving us with their dates. I'm not sure just how close we came to drowning, but it wasn't far.

Another time I had driven to school and had obtained permission to go to Pinecrest High School to schedule a country-western concert for the Florida Strawberry Pickers. This band we had started had become quite popular at the area schools. Robert had not gotten permission to go with me, but did anyway. After we met with the school principal and made the arrangements, we decided to take off the rest of the day. Some would have called it "playing hooky." We did not particularly view it that way.

It was summertime so we drove to Boiling Springs, located just north of Highway 60 a few miles east of Hopewell, Florida. The crystal clear springs flowed into the Alafia River and were in a wooded and secluded area. While we were swimming we looked up to see a man standing on the bank. He was dressed in prison clothing and was between us and the car where all our clothing and billfolds were and the key was in the ignition.

He talked and sounded very friendly for a few minutes then hurriedly made his way into the woods. Moments later a sheriff's deputy drove up beside our car. We thought we had had it, either for skipping school or for bathing in the nude. But the deputy was hunting for an escaped convict! And we had just conversed with him! Another very close call as we later pondered the situation.

This was Friday and back at school the following Monday I was handed a note by my homeroom teacher. It stated I was to go immediately to the office. I arrived at about the same time as did Robert. The school secretary wanted to know what kind of trouble we were in now. The school principal asked why we didn't return to school the previous Friday. When we told him the story, almost like it was, he wrote us an excuse for all the classes we missed but warned us to be sure we got a written excuse ahead of time, next time.

Apparently, some students had seen us leaving school that Friday morning and had turned us in at roll-call. The teachers in turn had reported us to the office. We were being taught the lesson of Numbers 32:23, "Be sure your sin will find you out." We played hooky with four other classmates later, and had to cut the grass during recess when "all" the schoolmates came by to watch and tease. Such can greatly reduce your standing in your own eyes, and probably everyone else's. Call it "eating humble pie!"

One Sunday afternoon I had gone with a couple of Plant City High School football players to swim in one of the phosphate pits near Hopewell. It had rained overnight and a small wooden boat anchored at the spot was about one-fourth full of water. It made an excellent diving board. We would run from the bank, land on the boat seats and dive into the water. The boat took in a little more water as we kept diving, and finally was full.

As I made my way up the bank to prepare for another dive, an old dilapidated pickup truck drove up. Out came one of the ugliest little men I thought I'd ever seen. He was filthy, unshaven, wreaked with odors of alcohol and who knows what, and was shorter than me. I stand five feet five inches with my shoes on! When he ordered us to empty the boat of the water and "stay the _ _ _ _ off it," I asked, "And who's going to make us?" After all, there were three of us and two of us were almost six feet tall and had football player muscles.

Surprisingly, neither football player made an effort to give me back-up support. They humbly and quietly stayed in the water. The next thing I knew a rifle was jammed into my stomach with an order, "I said, get the _ _ _ _ water out of the _ _ _ _ boat!"

As the cold steel intruded into my abdomen area, my bravado evaporated – immediately and completely.

I don't know if records are kept for how quick a boat can be emptied, dried, and replaced in the water, but we certainly would have come close to setting a world record. I said we. Three of us cooperated fully and then inquired of the little stinker if there was anything else we could do! He left peaceably and we were grateful. We did not use his boat for further diving.

One day in algebra class the teacher had presented a multiple part problem to the class with the challenge to see how she arrived at the correct answer. It was a case where the book would give the nature of the problem, then the answer. The method by which the answer was reached was the issue, in several steps. A toughie, indeed!

I discovered she had skipped a couple of steps but somehow had managed to come up with the right numbers. As she kept calling for someone to show how she did it, I came forward, worked in all the proper steps and came to the right answer. Several students agreed that I had worked through the problem properly and they were amazed at how she "lucked up" with the right answer.

After a few moments of this, she walked over to my seat which was on the front row, and slapped me into stardom. Believe me, I saw plenty of little white lights and was momentarily addled. I collected my senses, left the class and went straight to the principal's office. When I told him what had happened, he hit the ceiling. It turned out that this was not the first time this teacher had slapped a student.

He immediately called the teacher to the front office. In my presence he asked her if what I had told was the truth. She began crying, admitted it was, and started begging him, and me, for mercy. But because this had happened previously, she was told to find employment elsewhere by the end of the semester.

I felt bad for her and saw her later downtown where she once again begged forgiveness. I think I was learning how God feels towards us and will "abundantly pardon," when we truly repent and make whatever amends we can. (Isaiah 55:7)

Life for me was a constant challenge during those teen years, and almost every day brought experiences that would later turn into memories; some good, some bad, when I would quit "seeing visions and only dream dreams." (Joel 2:28)

There was the time Dad bought this "homemade" tractor from a man who was six feet and seven inches tall. When he would walk down the streets of old Plant City he would have to duck his head in order to miss some of the overhead signs hanging in front of the stores. I came with Dad to drive the tractor home. By sitting on the extreme front of the seat I still could not reach the gas pedal, clutch or brakes. We had to tear the seat off the platform and move it forward about fifteen inches.

Dad once got a "bargain" in an old truck. It would save us from carrying our farm products to market in our car. The shift patterns in those days were as an H. Lower left was low, upper right was second and lower right was high. Upper left was reverse. We loaded the truck with several crates of strawberries and I was assigned to drive them to market. When I got in and took hold of the gear there was no H pattern. It moved every which way. I asked, "How am I ever going to know how and where to shift gears?" Dad responded, "Go ahead! It'll work fine!" He said that he had driven it and had gotten here OK.

I kept on until I finally found a forward gear. It turned out to be "high" and I went jumping forward in jerks and uncertainty. I tried to shift, and when I found what I thought was "second," the truck came to an abrupt halt, then without choking down it began going backwards until I arrived at exactly the place from where I had started. The whole packing-shed crew got a good laugh out of that.

I later thought how much our life is like that old truck. How many times we are searching for the proper gear. And how many times when we think we are on the verge of making progress we wind up where we were, or even further back. I refused more and more to try to drive that truck. Our mechanic said it wasn't worth fixing. The man who bought it from us was sure he could fix it. It took him several minutes to ever get it to move and he stalled out several times before he got out of sight. Sometimes a 'bargain" isn't really a bargain at all.

Another very humiliating experience was my first date. My very first date! She was a very beautiful girl and I had just gotten my "unrestricted" driver's license. All we had then was a truck we used for hauling cattle and farm products and necessities. It was very odorous to say the least. My brother, Ralph, had gone into the Air Force and his wife was staying with us. She offered to loan me their beautiful, black four-door '36, V8 Ford. With bad brakes!

I drove up into the yard of my date's house proudly, and off we went to a movie. The church forbade movies, but I was a "backslider" and didn't feel too bad about going. When I think back to the movies we saw then at the local theatre, many of them would have been rated G. Anyway, we went

39

and afterwards stopped for ice cream sodas. The juke organ was playing, "It Had to be You," and "Don't Sit Under the Apple Tree With Anyone Else but Me."

On the way home there was a steady rain falling and I saw my next-door neighbor walking down Highway 39 South in the rain. I had been warned about the "trickiness" of the brakes. When I applied them to stop and pick him up, the car skidded and came to rest in a ditch that was so deep I could hardly see the road when I looked out. He started running across the field thinking someone was trying to "run him down."

A kindly gentleman we had known for years took the three of us home after we failed to get the car out of the ditch with his tractor. Next morning, Dad and I hired a wrecker and the car was easily pulled from the ditch.

The driver told me that if I had been "driving" instead of "necking," this wouldn't have happened. I let him know very quickly that it was bad brakes and a slick road that caused the accident. Fortunately, there wasn't a scratch on the car. I was so embarrassed I stayed home from school a week. My girlfriend thought I must have been injured. I was! My pride! Again?

Because of my upbringing, I'm sure, I never desired to go to places that sold booze or where there was dancing. One night there were three couples of us in our car and the girls dared us to stop at a "juke joint" in east Plant City. World War II was in full swing and the place was filled with soldiers from near-by Drane Field.

I was driving, so I parked among the many cars with a very uneasy feeling. We decided we'd better not go in. Except me! I went to the men's room. When I returned to the car, an inebriated solder had opened the driver's side door and was trying to kiss my date.

Before I realized it, I had pulled him out and knocked him flat on the ground. In a moment I was surrounded by soldiers and found myself in a five to one fight. I expected my two buddies to help me out. They stayed in the car. Seems I knew how to pick friends who are friends as long as I stayed out of trouble.

A truck driven by my girlfriend's suitor had been following us around town. He and two buddies jumped out of their vehicle, joined the melee and he said to me, "Get in your car and get out of here. We'll take care of these guys!" I gladly obliged. Later, I thought he surely didn't do this for me, but for my date. What a benefit, in my favor!

A few days later I saw him and asked how the fight came out. He said, "We won, and the five soldiers were arrested for drunkenness and disturbing the peace!" That was my last trip to a bar, except later in my ministry when I was asked to go and witness to someone about Christ.

Looking back, I realize how difficult the adolescent state can be as one emerges from childhood to the adult stage. What to do and not to; who to be with or not be with; where to go and not go. How fortunate is the young person who is privileged to grow up with both a mother and father, and siblings, in a home of love, discipline and security; a home where parents care for and take a devoted interest in their offspring and lead by setting good and Godly examples for living. And especially, a home where God, Christ and the Bible have a prominent place and the family goes to church regularly together. A child who does not have these blessings has two strikes against him before he ever comes to bat in the game of life.

An awareness of all this is why for many years in my daily radio ministry I designated each Friday program to young people. I used upbeat music, news, statistics and sermonettes slanted toward youth. How often I would say, "Young people, you've been influenced in some way by your home-life, your culture and by a religion of some sort. But now, your life's steering wheel is in your hands. You are on your own! Drive well! Remember, you can choose God and good, or Satan and evil. You can associate with virtuous companions or hoodlums. If you are rebellious, you can get yourself into more trouble than Mom, Dad, friends or even God can get you out of!"

Many times I have gone to court with troubled young people from good homes and homes not so good. I have pleaded for mercy and promised the judge my sincere assistance to try to guide them toward the straight and narrow way. In order to avoid repeated trips to the courts, foremost in my efforts was the attempt to lead young people to a personal relationship with Christ, a true born-again experience. (John. 3:5-7) Mere promises to do good and avoid lawbreaking (both God's and man's) is not enough. Human efforts are weak at their best. Genuine conversion to Christ brings a power within that one doesn't have by himself. (John 1:12)

So many persons and groups, even religious ones, never seem to arrive at this truth. How many strive diligently to be moral and even gain salvation by trying to observe a set of rules, without experiencing a spiritual rebirth from above. Self-righteousness is unacceptable with God. (Isaiah 64:6)

Christ's righteousness, the only kind God accepts comes by grace through faith (Eph. 2:8 -9), and not by a person's achievements.

I learned much of this by my own experiences as a teenager. I repented every time I got caught in wrong-doing. I made promises to God, parents and others. I tried New Year's resolutions, turning over new leaves and anything else I could think of. But the big difference came when I finally, fully recommitted my life to Jesus Christ, allowing Him to become the Lord of my life. My carnal nature resisted my every thought about complete surrender to God. But victory came to me when I did, and only then.

First row left to right: Nora, Jessup and Curtis Holbrook Second row: Elsie Holbrook Raburn, Janelle Holbrook Walden, Bessie Holbrook Sullins, Virgil Holbrook
Back row: Autrell (Audey) Holbrook, Pearl Holbrook Benner, Arthur Holbrook

The James Thomas Payne Family
Sitting left to right: Crawford, Mary Jane, James Thomas and Clyde Payne
Second row: Leonard and Paul Payne Third row: Virlin, Pearl and Julia
Payne (My mother)
Fourth row: Homer, Howard, Lester, Canty and Luther Payne

Virgil Holbrook with an award-winning large mouth bass caught at Lake
Reedy, Frostproof, Florida, about 1928 (12 lbs. 3 oz.)

THREE

THE DECISION YEARS

Choose you this day whom you will serve... Joshua 24:15

From early childhood I realized how very distinct people are. They have different looks, habits, likes and dislikes, as well as different talents, occupations and goals. Their views are diverse about what is right or wrong. They hold different religious beliefs or none at all. Respect for moral and social values is not the same for everyone. The list seems endless.

Religious ties, when ardently pursued, can be among the most binding in the world. Consequently, unless one is very humble and other-directed, religious pride (I'm right and you are wrong) can lead to extreme self-righteousness, hypocrisy, human hero worship and many other radical beliefs and behavior. Like hosts of other people, I perceived that my way of viewing things was right, especially things pertaining to Christian beliefs, even though I wasn't faithful to most of those beliefs in the adolescent and teen years.

What I believed and what I did, as shown in Judges 17:6, 21:25, and Proverbs 21:2, was "right in my own eyes." No one should try to convince me otherwise. Like Simon Peter, I was always ready in my early teen years to defend my faith with the "sword" (verbally and even with my fists, if necessary). Once on the schoolyard at Turkey Creek High School, I took a boxer's stance during a religious argument, telling my foe I would fight to prove what was true religious faith (mine, of course)! And yet we both espoused Jesus Christ as the center of our beliefs.

My concepts of Christian religion were based on my ancestors' views, specifically my mother's mother, Mary Jane Spurlock Payne (lay-preacher of the Wesleyan Methodist group), and my father's father, the Rev. J. J. Holbrook. Granddad Holbrook, who was convinced there was a deeper walk of faith and spiritual power, attended a Pentecostal camp meeting at Durant, Florida, during the late 1920's.

After experiencing the Baptism of the Holy Spirit with the initial evidence of speaking in other tongues (Acts 2:4, 10:46, 19:1-6, etc.), my grandfather founded a Pentecostal church, Mount Zion Assembly of God, near Plant City, in 1931. He was a vital influence on many people and most of his own children and grandchildren followed him in his new-found religious belief. I was among the group.

In my earliest recollections of attending church meetings, we were in the frame building that he and his supporters had erected on property he owned on Sam Allen Road. It had open trusses and a tin roof. I recall amidst the sounds of happy songs of excited worshipers the additional noise of rocks pounding the roof and eggs and tomatoes hitting the outside walls.

With the doors and windows open, except in cold weather, the sounds of the long and emotional services and preaching angered some neighbors. They and their friends and relatives took it upon themselves to try to disrupt and even bring to an end such noisy intrusions in their neighborhood.

One Sunday morning my grandfather was in the middle of his sermon when in walked a very angry resident from across the road. He went right to the pulpit, grabbed Granddad by the arm and led him to his front porch where his sister was experiencing an epileptic seizure. Blaming the church noise for her condition, he knocked my grandfather off the porch, breaking his jaw. Granddad got up, dusted himself off, went back to the church and finished his sermon.

A few nights later the church building burned to the ground. A five-gallon gas can was found in the debris. A sheriff's office investigation determined the fire was deliberately set but no one was ever charged. Most of the church-folk were pretty certain the folks across the road and some of their relatives were involved. Some of the church adherents carried pistols, expecting more trouble, but thankfully no more came from either side.

A "brush arbor" was hastily erected on the burn site, but it was determined that a new church building would be located on other property owned by my grandfather on Thonotosassa Road, where the church remains to this day. Efforts by the church people to bring the church-burners to justice were largely ignored by the authorities. Not many people were sympathetic toward Pentecostals back then, including lawmen and prosecutors.

With $500.00 insurance money and Granddad furnishing property and some of the materials, he and the congregants began constructing a new 40' X 60' frame building. It was raining one day and the men were hurrying to get the roof finished. I was four years old at this time. Mom was pregnant with my soon-to-be sister, Joann. I was out in the rain, Dad was on top of the church and Mom couldn't get me back into the car. One of the men had come down to get more nails and Dad told him to make me get into our car. He tried and I ran from him. He finally caught me, gathered my overalls in front and nailed me to a big pine tree.

Try as I may, I couldn't get loose. The only way I finally decided I could, was to climb out of my overalls. I couldn't even manage that, so I promised if he would set me free, I'd get in and stay in the car. He did, and I did. Later, when pastoring Mr. Zion myself, I told the members I was destined to be the pastor there because I was once nailed to the premises.

After my rededication to Christ and a call to the ministry, my attitude toward Christian believers of other denominations and persuasions changed considerably. I grew to realize that the same Jesus Christ is our redeemer and Savior and that saving grace and faith in Him is paramount, superceding all else. I began to understand we were on the same side, believing the same Lord, serving the same purpose and headed for the same heaven, which apparently is not sub-divided for religious denominations.

Not that I changed my religious convictions or that the stigma was removed. I ran into a former high school classmate who, when he found out I was what he called a "Holiness" evangelist exclaimed, "What? One of them? Why, you can't even go out and 'raise hell' anymore!" Not that I had once "raised hell," but detecting he was partly joking and mostly serious, I told him I was working to help people and the community from doing such things.

Today it seems amazing that some of the practices once espoused mostly by Pentecostals have crossed many denominational lines, like lively music and singing, uplifted hands in worship, and glossalalia (speaking in other tongues).

As for the Assemblies of God, we now rank in the top ten in numbers in the U.S.A. with two and one-half million adherents, and more than fifty million worldwide, making it one of the largest protestant denominations in the world. It isn't as unpopular to be a Pentecostal as it once was. I'm not sure if this is good or bad for us. God grant that we remain "little in our own eyes" (I Samuel 15:17), so that the Lord can continue to add His blessings to our efforts to help other Evangelicals evangelize the world for Christ.

Reflecting, I am grateful for the stand our particular denomination took on several issues: preaching the Gospel of Jesus Christ at home and abroad, repentance and faith, genuine conversion, Godly attitudes, church attendance and worship, Bible reading and study and on the Baptism of the Holy Spirit to empower us for witnessing. (Acts 1:8 and 2:4) The stance my church has taken against the use of alcoholic beverages and tobacco strongly influenced me to avoid both.

A battle loomed within me, however, even as it did for Paul in Romans 7:14-24. The allure of the world-system surrounding me was often in direct conflict with what I understood God and the church required of me. This caused me a most miserable existence at times during my teenage years as a "backslider." (Proverbs 14:14a)

Before my rededication to Christ, my reason for church-going was mostly for the fun and fellowship with relatives and friends. I always looked forward to one particular cousin whose stories fascinated us. His all-encompassing mind would take us vicariously on his African safaris, or through the jungles of South America and most anywhere else in the world. Tarzan never had it better or worse than he did as he narrowly escaped ferocious lions, tigers, crocodiles and headhunters.

Whether it was fleeing wild elephants, discovering gold, or bringing fugitives to justice, he kept us fascinated. I often wondered where he got his stories since he always came up with something new each time.

I said to him one day, "From now on, when you are in the middle of one of your mind-boggling thrillers, please tell the kids that I was right there with you, going through everything you did!" But he never did. I've often wondered what might have happened if Hollywood had discovered him.

Having cousins, by the dozens (literally), we thought Sundays weren't Sundays unless we could go home with one another and spend the afternoons playing together until church time again. As we grew older, most of us would have stayed outside during the church service had our parents allowed us. Thank the Lord for wise and caring moms and dads who helped and guided us through all those "know it all" adolescent times. The pastor also assisted in dispelling the darkness by installing a bright light outside at the water pump.

As the years continued, the critical time of dating began. I liked lots of girls and fantasized not only about them but of many other things as well. I liked country music and singing, and being somewhat talented, I dreamed of being a star myself someday. A good friend of mine from Nashville later told me he was glad I never made it "big time." "That life is not what it's cracked up to be," he said. "Look at the stars, their drinking problems, and the divorce rate among them. They are addicted to pills - uppers and downers, they are owned and pushed by a manager and they are traveling continuously. You are very fortunate you never made it to Nashville except as a gospel preacher," he concluded.

The four years at Turkey Creek High School were filled with many enjoyable activities. I particularly liked the Glee Club, the Future Farmers of America (FFA - where our quartet and string band won the local and state contests two consecutive years), and most of all, "The Florida Strawberry Pickers" country and western band which I helped form and manage.

These were the years before television so we were soon entertaining large audiences in several area school auditoriums. Such popularity won the favor of school principals, teachers and fellow-students.

Robert Raburn and I built typing tables, installed a dishwasher (which never did work properly) in the school cafeteria and I ran several errands for the school. Some of these activities, including the band playing away from school, resulted in some missed classes. I had received the American Legion Award for my scholastic achievements in the ninth grade and somehow managed to achieve membership in the National Honor Society in grades eleven and twelve. I also had an honor roll average for all twelve school years. To my knowledge, I was never favored by any teacher in the grading process.

The Turkey Creek High School athletic director invited interested boys to meet during lunch break for a new sports program for the school. Boxing! In addition to softball, baseball, football, and basketball, this new sport would help determine who the really tough guys were. The response was overwhelming. Tuesday night came with a boxing ring set up on the school auditorium stage and several three round bouts of one minute each scheduled.

I was second on the list. The first two guys slugged the three rounds and the judges ruled one round to each, and one round a tie, thus a draw. I entered the ring with a fellow much taller and consequently with much longer arms than myself. I playfully danced around exchanging jabs, when all of a sudden I saw stars. Several lights, like lightning bugs were spinning around inside my head.

I thought to myself, "This guy means business. He wants to play rough." I plowed into him, beating him all around the ring. The ref pulled me off. After separation, I pounced on him again, beating him mercilessly into the ropes. The referee stopped the fight before the end of the first round declaring me, "the winner." Amidst applause, I returned to my seat to watch the next bout. A boy sitting next to me said, "Hey, you didn't have to try to kill him. We are supposed to be boxing for fun."

Fun? It wasn't very funny to me. Someone else nearby told me we weren't supposed to get angry, which he said I had done. On the way home, I began to notice a pain and soreness starting in my chin and jaw. It awakened me several times during the night. The next morning my lower face was so sore and swollen I couldn't eat breakfast. When I got to school I observed other bruised faces and black eyes. Guess what soon went by the wayside? Boxing! Since there were no volunteers, it became history!

One day the principal chose me to run the projector for a movie he had obtained to show the students. The several hundred seat auditorium was filled to capacity, the film was running perfectly, and for no particular reason I got up and proceeded to walk around the projector to check out things, that did not need to be checked out. In the dark, I stumbled over the stand, which resulted in the film breaking. With some assistance from a qualified someone, we managed in about 15 minutes to get it going again. Afterwards, the principal said something must have gone wrong with the projector for it to break a film in two. Or perhaps it was a bad film, he mused. I dared not tell him what really happened.

We often played tricks on each other at school, and two such tricks were very embarrassing to me. First, I ripped my trousers from the belt loop to the crotch while working at the Agriculture barn. I waited, half dressed, while Robert took them to the girls' Home Economics class for re-stitching. Several girls afterwards would look at the seat of my pants and giggle when I went past them.

The other was when a group of girls pushed me into the girls' bathroom. As I walked down the hall between classes, one girl flung open the door while four others rushed me and pushed me right inside. The room was full of what now became screaming and squealing young ladies. Although he never admitted it, I'm sure Robert Raburn helped plan the event. He just "happened" to be standing there at the time.

But amid the fun and games, studies and all else that goes with high school, it was also a crisis time decision-wise. At that time, college was not deemed nearly as important as it is now. Besides, how could poor truck farmers afford the tuition? I put in an early application with the railroad as I pondered a possible future occupation. I was also looking for a girl I could love, marry and with whom I could spend the rest of my life.

I loved the spotlight and it's a wonder I didn't get into much deeper and hotter water than I did. I am grateful I was also surrounded by people who loved and prayed for me. I can truly say I'm indebted to them, along with the Good Lord, for helping save me from a whole lot of potential trouble. God does hear and answer sincere prayers and helps us in so many ways, in spite of our very strong self-centered wills.

I had a very scary experience at this point in my life that could have resulted in disastrous consequences. My brother had first joined the National Guard, serving in the 116th Field Artillery. Once, the unit was on maneuvers in a vast wooded area just southwest of Lakeland, Florida. This acreage later became Drain Field during World War II. Today, it encompasses an industrial complex, corporate offices, the Lakeland airport, an auto auction, subdivisions, and is intersected by the Polk Parkway.

From where we lived at the time, along the Hillsborough-Polk County line, we could hear cannons blasting away and the resulting explosions. A friend and I rode our bikes down a trail in order to get a closer look at the "war games."

We came to a several-stranded barbed wire fence with a very large warning sign to would-be trespassers. We wanted to cross the fence anyway, but a new burst of cannonfire unnerved us and we stayed outside the restricted area. What an eerie and uneasy feeling as the ear-splitting blasts and ground shaking booms resounded again and again.

The woods obscured a visual observation of the events and a later revelation to my brother about our whereabouts during these military exercises brought about the "boom" being lowered on us. By him! We could have been in danger of a misfire.

After the war began, this unit was sent for further training and then to Europe. Ralph left the unit and joined the United States Air Force and became an airplane mechanic. He was stationed at two different places in California, then in Naples, Florida, and finally in Hawaii, where he remained until the end of the war.

During my final year of high school, I visited he and his wife, Lauredo, for one week while he was at the Air Force base at Naples. Knowing that I was intrigued with airplanes, he took me for a tour of the base one day. On the flight line we watched the P-39's taking off for target practice over the Gulf of Mexico. Then, one by one, they would return to the base.

A few weeks before, a plane returning from such a mission had a malfunction in the landing gear. Only one wheel had lowered for the approach, then would not retract. The manual backup also failed. The base commander got into another airplane and flew beneath this plane as it circled the base. Upon observing the situation, it was decided that a "belly-landing" was out of the question.

The pilot was instructed to keep flying until the fuel was almost gone, then set the automatic pilot toward the Gulf, out of harm's way. He was then to bail out over the field. The pilot parachuted to safety, but the pilot-less plane did not stay the Gulf-bound course. It did a 90-degree turn-around and headed right back toward the airfield, even tilting downward as if coming in for a landing.

This sent the air base personnel – including my brother – scurrying for a hoped-for, safe place from this uncontrolled phantom-like, "ghost-piloted" aircraft. A sigh of relief swept over the concerned observers as they watched the plane climb and then circle back towards the Gulf. It took another turn and crashed along the beach, not hurting anyone.

With this story fresh on our minds this tour day, the crew chief accompanied my brother and me to where the incoming planes were being parked. Upon request, the crew chief told me I could climb into a particular airplane cockpit. Elated, I sat there imagining I was engaged in an aerial "dogfight" with enemy aircraft.

I gripped and squeezed the trigger-button. The airplane started shaking violently as the machine guns went into motion. The exiting pilot had forgotten to turn off the trigger mechanism, and the crew chief, my brother and I, all three, almost had three heart attacks simultaneously!

Fortunately, I really should say <u>very</u> fortunately, the ammunition had all been used up, which was not always the case. Besides, the plane's guns were aimed directly at the base headquarters building. Had there been some remaining ammunition, who knows what might have happened: possible deaths, injuries, building damages, three arrests, two military court-martials, a 17-year old tried as an adult, and who knows what else. Thank the Lord for a pilot who used up all his bullets! And thank the Good Lord for a guardian angel watching over a foolish teenager. Me!

Perhaps my greatest enticement was "The Florida Strawberry Pickers" band. Besides singing the most popular songs of the day, we also wrote songs and comedy acts that "brought the house down." We did well enough to attract promoters, got an audition with radio station WLAK in Lakeland and had a good contact that looked promising for an audition with the Grand Ole Opry in Nashville, Tennessee. At one high school concert, during a comedy act, one of my uncles laughed so that he slid out of his seat into the aisle, which resulted in even more laughter from those seated near him. He later said, "Ernest, one of these days you're going to make it to the top." But I'm grateful now that I didn't make it to that top!

About this time a man who owned some night clubs approached me about entertaining for him. His offer was pretty big money for then, and he said he would dress our young group to look much older so we could perform where alcoholic beverages were sold and dancing took place. Can you imagine a seventeen year old lying awake at night when he should have been sleeping, thinking about big time, fancy cars, clothes and hundred dollar bills? And at the same time battling his conscience as well as the prayers and advice of loved ones?

The audition with WLAK was accepted. By the time the day came for the big radio show I was on cloud nine, wherever that is. The radio station had secured sponsors from among Plant City businesses and allotted a full hour in prime time from twelve noon to one p.m. on a Saturday. Despite our nervousness, the program went well enough that the station manager told me he would pursue signing us for a regular weekly program. The station was one of only about four that could be heard in our area at that time, and was the one most listened to.

When we returned to our Plant City headquarters, quite a group of our supporters were waiting for us. Some had come there to listen to the program – not everyone even had radios back then – and others came to pour on the accolades. We were eating them up like a hungry puppy at his dinner dish.

Everyone was excited, except for one person! My grandfather! He was in tears as he approached me and I could tell they weren't tears of joy. I greeted him, smiled and was stunned as he said, "I didn't know I'd have grandchildren who would be advertising for a liquor store." At this he walked out. We knew he was referring to Robert, my sister Joann and myself, all part of the "Florida Strawberry Pickers" Band.

In the studio, we had not heard all the sponsors and did not even know one was a bar and lounge. When I realized it, I talked with someone nearby and they had heard it, but said, "Well, next time you can tell the radio station personnel that you absolutely refuse to have such a sponsor as this."

My mind was becoming clouded. Thinking about this, along with the nightclub offer, and my granddad's reaction, was taking me from a very high, high, to a really low, low. Again! And I hadn't told my grandfather about the nightclub proposition. Nor would I ever!

Meanwhile, a young evangelist was conducting revival services at Mt. Zion. I took to him immediately since he played a Spanish and steel guitar as did I. For quite a time now, playing my instruments at church was a prime motive for my attendance. Robert was also playing his bass fiddle, thus we had quite a musical group.

The preaching in this meeting was very appealing. He seemed to be so joyful as he related his conversion and call to the ministry. I tried to play it cool, pretending I was OK with the Lord, while all the while conviction was mounting up within. During the invitation one evening, I was strumming my guitar when I was cornered by an uncle and a cousin.

I was embarrassed as they knelt on each side of me and started praying for me. What is this, I thought? I don't need prayer. I attend church regularly, play my musical instruments and participate in Sunday School, even though our teacher always had to separate Robert and me for disrupting the class with our talking.

I angrily laid down my guitar, and since others had come and knelt in front of me, had to stand on the pew and climb over their bowed heads to take my leave of them. A big mistake! Once outside in the dark, an even darker feeling was gripping my inward being. Besides, there wasn't anyone else outside that night but me. I felt alone!

To make bad matters even worse, I went back inside to discover Robert was surrounded by a praying group. And, of all things, he was praying too, crying his heart out to God. He had made his surrender to the Lord and informed me he was quitting the band. The next night, after battling my thoughts all day, I went forward. What an awkward and awesome feeling.

In only a matter of minutes of thorough repentance and a total resurrender to Christ, I felt as if a ton of weight was lifted from me. The joy of forgiveness flooded my innermost being and I felt a spiritual renewing I hadn't experienced since my deep religious encounter at age eight. What a relief! The ecstasy Peter described as "joy unspeakable and full of glory" (I Peter 1:8-9) had returned. Once again I had the inward assurance of my salvation. What a cumbersome load was removed from my shoulders and my heart!

With this major spiritual roadblock removed, my rejoicing suddenly faced many other obstacles I hadn't anticipated. The first was the reality concerning the "Florida Strawberry Pickers" Band. Because of the direction it seemed to be going, I felt that I, like Robert, would also drop out.

It wasn't easy to tell the remaining band members about my decision. I urged them to carry on, but each said there was no way with both Robert and I gone. So I cancelled all our future shows, and refused to pursue the radio programs or the Nashville audition.

Many of our fans were deeply hurt at our decision to disband. Several people, including schoolteachers and two high school principals, said we were throwing promising careers down the drain. Others said we had gone off "the deep end" over religion.

It was reassuring that a couple of teachers agreed with my decision about the matter. "You have to follow your heart and live your convictions," they said. "It is for you alone to decide." It was, and I was certain that I was on the right track in doing this. In some ways I could tell my popularity was slipping at school. It is strange how friendships can turn cold overnight.

The next big step was the proposition of equally dividing what equipment we had purchased for the group. There was no cash on hand and no easy way to settle things. We did the best we could under the circumstances, although everyone wasn't satisfied.

I tried to make peace with everyone, because if you knew my heart, I wanted not only to be right with God, but also with my peers. I was learning that you can't be one without the other. After all, the Ten Commandments include both. The first four Commandments are vertical (our obligation to and relationship with the Lord), and the last six are horizontal (our obligation to and relationship with our fellow man).

Robert and I, along with my sister Joann, plunged headlong into church activities. We were seeking to be baptized in the Holy Spirit and were soon leading the church youth group and teaching Sunday School. We played and sang and gave our testimonies of rededication to God at our home church and others in the area.

Then, up pops the issue called "restitution." In my devotions, I began to recall two incidents where I had stolen money. While working after school and on Saturdays (stores were closed on Sundays), I had made a sale of $4.85 one night and decided since no one was looking, to put it in my pocket instead of in the cash register. Of course, someone was looking. (Proverbs 15:3)

This was at Wright's Furniture and Hardware Store in Plant City, the location where the "Florida Strawberry Pickers" Band called its headquarters. Since this was the smaller amount of money I had taken, I decided I would deal with this first.

I approached the owner and confessed the theft and handed her the $4.85. She refused the money, began to weep and said my honesty was worth far more than what I had taken. I walked away with the money and peace with God about the matter.

The next was a much larger amount which I had taken. From my dad! It happened when I was driving our strawberries to market, cashing the check and bringing the money back to Daddy. I was beginning to date regularly and my outgo was exceeding my income. So I began to first keep $5.00, then $10.00, and once or twice, about $15.00.

I wasn't sure of the exact amount I had kept over a period of several weeks, but I estimated it to be about $75.00, more or less. I finally got the nerve to tell Dad and offered to repay him as soon as possible.

To my utter amazement, he began to weep and also commended me for my honesty. He, too, refused the money and even said he should have been paying me more for my labors. Wow! Now, both of these money matters had been settled and I wasn't out a penny. (And no, I did not wish I had taken more for which to be forgiven!) I was greatly relieved and my conscience cleared and cleansed!

I realized that my misdeeds had cost somebody. The storeowner and my dad. Later, upon reflection, it was a reminder of my great sin debt which Jesus Christ had paid for me when He died on the Cross of Calvary. Salvation had cost me nothing. It cost Christ His all, His life!

As Robert and I continued to seek God, another item appeared in the restitution column. Would you believe a bass fiddle string? It had happened during our band days. We needed a new set of four strings and only had enough money for three. The strings come one to a pack and we discovered after we had purchased the three strings that one pack contained two strings, both alike.

We returned to the Lakeland music store and swapped the duplicate string for the one extra that we needed. Now we had the proper four for the price of the three.

Together, we returned to the music store, confessed our misdeed to the owner and paid for the extra string. He accepted the money, but he too, began to weep and commend us for our honesty and restitution. Thus, three different efforts to make things right had brought positive results both to the stealers and those from whom they were stolen.

A dedicated lady minister took a special interest in us and invited us to sing and play at revival meetings which she was conducting. It was at Pleasant Grove Assembly that I received the Holy Spirit baptism and was amazed at unknown words I heard myself speaking. But the overflowing joy was mine and I was experiencing some profound blessings from above. A new spiritual power seemed to engulf me. (Acts 1:8)

Before the same Sunday School class, in the same area of the church where I was once spanked on the hand by a teacher for talking in class, I was now standing and teaching. (I remembered it was her son doing the talking and me getting the spanking!) But now as I stood before the four and five year-olds, an overflow of words from my heart and lips seemed to keep their attention. In recent years, one day after I had conducted a funeral, a relative of the deceased came to me and told me how much he was inspired by my teaching back then, which later resulted in him becoming a Christian as an adult.

It was along about then that our church pastor scheduled me to speak in a Wednesday evening service, which was mostly youth oriented, but strongly supported by the adults. The purpose of this weekly youth program was to encourage and train the church young people for future participation in church activities or even possibly the ministry. Our pastor always thrust the youth of the church into the spotlight.

Along with the anxiety of trying to chose a topic and prepare my thoughts, I arrived at church only to discover that our District Superintendent was present. Immediately, I went to the pastor and requested that I be excused in favor of him. The answer was, "No, he wants to hear you!" Horror of horrors!

I had chosen a scripture text from James, Chapter three, verses one through ten, which is all about the pride of the carnal nature exhibited through the tiny, but evil, boasting tongue of a person. But as I stood to give a tongue-lashing to everyone, my own seemed to be tied, and my mind sat down almost completely.

I managed to rattle on for about five minutes, and having exhausted the entire content of the ten verses, I nervously and embarrassingly relinquished the pulpit back to the pastor. The service was opened for testimonies. Mercifully, various adults stood and confessed the sins of their tongues, which helped my feelings a little. Even my preacher granddad came to me afterwards and muttered something like, "Yes, all of our tongues need a good whipping." There had been no secret that granddad had wanted one or more of his five sons to follow him in the ministry. Since this did not happen, he next looked to the grandsons. After my abbreviated performance that night, I think he thought he would have to look to grandsons other than me.

In another few months a spontaneous revival had broken out at our church services. Attendance was growing, conversions were happening and an overall spiritual excitement prevailed. Out of seemingly nowhere, the pastor announced that my cousin Robert would be the speaker each night for the coming week. The opening Sunday night service was jam-packed with people and I was utterly amazed at the dynamic sermon that proceeded forth from my bass-fiddle playing cousin. It continued all week. For a young man seventeen years old, everyone was shocked as well as overjoyed at the powerful ministry of Robert. No Bible school or seminary training, yet profound scriptural expositions!

On the following Sunday evening, I was on the podium area to play my guitar when I overheard the pastor say to Robert, "We've got to continue these meetings. Things are going too well to stop now." His response was, "There is no way! I have preached the whole Bible this week and this is all I can do." The pastor turned to me and said, "Ernest, you will be preaching in the service tomorrow night." Just like that! I couldn't believe that I heard myself come back with, "O.K!" On the way home, and on and off all night I wondered why I said I would. After the humiliation of the previous try, I had settled it in my mind that "preaching" sure wasn't for me. As I prepared the next day for a message I also prayed very earnestly to the Lord. "Now

Lord, you know the mess I made before. And if this happens again, I'm sunk! Never again will I attempt to speak!"

When I arrived with my family that Monday night at church in the latter part of May, 1947, the crowd was overflowing the building. The old wooden church, which incidentally was later moved and made into a home by a church family, seated about 250 or more. I could not believe what I was seeing. It was like "The Strawberry Pickers" concerts, the house filled to capacity, and then some. The song service was lively but I don't recall a song that was sung. There were some testimonies and I remember someone saying something about Joel's prophecy about God's Spirit being poured out upon the young people. (Joel 2:28-29)

I thought, "Lord, if you are ever going to do it, let it be now." And it happened! Although I don't recall my topic, as I began to speak, the words poured forth like a gusher. The people responded with "Amens" of approval. I looked at Robert and he was as carried away over me, as I had been of him a week earlier. I happened to glance at my dad. He was freely weeping with joy. I carried on for about 30 minutes and when I gave the invitation, several adults and young people came forward to receive Christ as their Savior. Afterwards, several of the church elders said I had preached like an experienced, seasoned minister. I was overwhelmed. The meetings continued for two more weeks on a nightly basis. Robert and I rotated preaching after the second week.

It was now completely settled in my mind. I would be a gospel preacher and use my musical talent in church services in the name of my Lord and Savior, Jesus Christ.

After the truck-farming business, my dad, brother and I had leased a dairy and purchased a herd of cattle on credit. The business looked and did well from the very start. I was working day and night in the dairy at this time but the ministry decision was completely overshadowing any secular business considerations. I hope I was doing justice to "the call to milk" with my mind overwhelmingly absorbed with "the call to preach the Gospel of Jesus Christ." Invitations to conduct revival services were already coming in from other places.

One night I went outside the milking area to inhale a breath of fresh air and looked up into the wonders of the Milky Way. All of a sudden I heard the loud sound of fire burning in the sky above me. A gigantic ball of fire came rolling across the horizon apparently not far above the tree tops. A vapor-like trail extended behind it for what looked like several hundred feet. It "rolled" on toward Tampa and left me so unnerved I had fallen to my knees.

I mentioned it to my co-workers but neither had seen it. I listened to the radio the next morning and again, nothing. During the next several days I asked several people but no one had seen it. The fact that it came by at about 2:00 a.m. would certainly explain why most people were not aware of it. But I thought surely somebody would have had to see such a phenomenon as this. It lit up the whole night sky and sounded very loud. But I never found anyone who had observed it but me. A mystery indeed!

One morning at about 2:00 a.m., I was running milk over the cooler in the milk room located in the front of the dairy barn. The front door facing Highway 92 was a screen door which we kept hooked shut. I heard a knock at this door and walked there to behold a well-dressed, very attractive young lady.

"I'm stranded," she said. "Could I please get you to take me home?" "Where do you live?" I asked. "In South Lakeland," was the reply. I opened the door, invited her in and told her I would take her, but had to awaken my dad to work in my place while I would be away.

I went next door, aroused him and told him what as up. "It might be dangerous for you to go alone," he said. "I'll go with you." We told the co-workers to cover for us and away we headed for Lakeland. I'll never forget the conversation my dad had with her on the way.

"Where is your car? Why are you stranded? What are you doing out at this time of night?" She said she had been dancing at a nearby tavern with a date. After they had a few drinks, he had driven and parked with her over on the old Tampa-Lakeland road just across the railroad tracks from our dairy. "When I wouldn't play his game, he threw me out of his car and left me stranded. I saw the lights from your dairy and walked over for help," she concluded.

Then the sermon started. Dad lectured her about the many pitfalls of drinking alcohol, dating and dancing with a stranger and being out this late at night. She admitted she was raised to go to church but had dropped out, much to her mother's displeasure. She lived at home with her mother and her dad had passed away.

"I hope this has taught you a lesson," Dad continued. You need to get back in church, renew your relationship with the Lord and stop going out to places like a tavern or staying out late at night." Upon arriving at her house, we walked her to the door with her expressing gratitude to us for the ride and the good advice. She promised everything Dad had admonished. Dad could hardly speak a word in Church without weeping but he had shocked me no end with his powerful admonition of right and wrong to this young lady.

The incident reminded me of a time when we had once lived even nearer to this tavern. It was located just inside the Hillsborough County Line. Hillsborough County was "wet" (allowed to sell liquor) and Polk County was "dry." One night we heard gunshots from the tavern. We later learned that a man had gone there to discover his wife drinking and dancing with another man. He drew his gun, dropped down on his knees to shoot the man and wound up shooting himself in the leg and then being arrested. Needless to say, this place was "off limits" to us.

When I announced that I planned to be a full-time evangelist and would probably be away much of the time, it seemed best for me to relinquish my interest in the business. Dad and Ralph told me I could work for them anytime I might need to.

So with the decision made, I "cast my bread upon the waters" (Ecclesiastes 11:1), and dedicated myself to the ministry of God's Word. I realized my inabilities, lack of proper education and experience, but determined I would give it my best shot as invitations for meetings began to pour in. Like Abraham of old, Robert and I launched out by faith, even though we didn't really know where we were going. (Genesis 12:1-4 and Hebrews 11:8-10) We would go as an evangelistic team of two.

The Virgil Holbrook Family
Front: Joann and Ernest Back: Ralph, Julia, Virgil and Louise

Mt. Zion Assembly of God, Plant City, Florida – Young Boys Sunday
School Class
Robert Raburn and Ernest Holbrook standing in left door (About 1943)

Strawberry picking in Plant City, Florida (About 1930's)

A view of downtown Plant City
Intersection of Haines and Collins Streets about 1940's

Congregation at Mt. Zion Assembly of God, Plant City, Florida, about
1946 or '47
7th from right: Ernest Holbrook, Robert Raburn, J.J. Holbrook, Virgil
Holbrook and Joe Walden

Some of my senior classmates
Front row left to right: Muriel Welch, Ruby Griffin, Elizabeth "Sally"
Stanley, Delores Wetherington, Delores Mercer, Jewel Brown Back row:
Hoyt Wynn, Gerald Herring, Ernest Holbrook, Bill Thomas, Lowell
Jaudon, Mack Stokes

The Florida Strawberry Pickers Band
Left to right: Ernest Holbrook, Stanley Jaudon, Ennis Porter, Ruby
Harrelson, Robert Raburn

Left to right: Joann Holbrook, Ruby Harrelson, Ennis Porter, Robert
Raburn, Ernest Holbrook, Stanley Jaudon, Jenette Hutto

Band Rehearsal – left to right: Robert and Charles Raburn, Joann Holbrook, Stanley Jaudon, Jenette Hutto, Ernest Holbrook

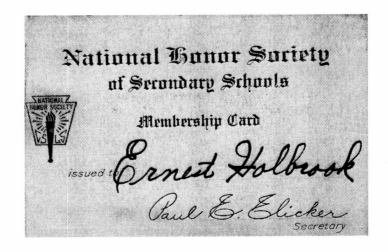

FOUR

EARLY MINISTRY

...repentance and remission of sins should be preached in His Name...
Luke 24:47

What a turn-around! What a feeling! And much more than just a feeling. It was a genuine sense that, first of all, all was well between my soul and my Savior. And next, an overwhelming, enraptured and enamored awareness that I had arrived at my proper niche for life. All of my fantasies about doing other things as a vocation had vanished.

To me, it was unquestionably an obsession of divine purpose. A glorious assurance that I was finally centered in God's will for my life. I was certain that I had been called of the Lord to minister His Word and love to whomever and wherever I could. I thought about two very special persons in my family, preachers that preceded me, Granddad Holbrook and Grandmother Payne.

My Grandmother Payne had raised 13 children, ten of them boys, almost as many as Jacob. The boys were not saints by any measure and Grandma wasn't about to let them get away with their devilish deportment without stern warnings at home and from the pulpit. Much of her sermon content had to do with the riotous living of her sons, grandsons, visiting relatives and neighbors. Booze, tobacco, chasing women (white trash), and the frequenting of bars (juke joints) and movies, were often mentioned in her sermons.

Despite having little or no education she fervently preached grace and forgiveness for those who would repent and be born again. She had previously used tobacco (snuff) herself, and when she became convicted of it she tried to quit and found she couldn't. She said she tried a swap-off with God: she would fast a meal a day in exchange for a dip of snuff a day. But she said God wasn't interested. With prayers and determination she finally quit.

Her sermons, zeal for God, and holy living stuck in my mind. She died before I entered the ministry but I would draw inspiration from her all my life. Granddad Holbrook said he never knew a more Godly woman than she!

But I still had Granddad Holbrook. He continued preaching, giving his testimony and remaining strong in spirit into his seventies. Although having only a third-grade education, he was well versed in the scriptures. The respect he gained in the community as a dynamic Christian tended to remove some of the Pentecostal stigma. Robert and I determined to continue his convictions and ministry. We had too much Godly influence by him and family members to let them down. Our desire, like them, was to serve God and people.

First off, Robert and I began an intensive study of the scriptures. Within the first few weeks I had read through the entire Bible. With the help of a Thompson Chain Reference Bible I learned to keep scriptures in context, cover all the related teachings on various subjects, and get a better grip on basic Old and New Testament teachings.

The focal point of our sermons was to preach Christ Jesus crucified and resurrected for our salvation and justification. We used Bible stories, illustrations and personal experiences to encourage people to come to repentance, the new birth (a spiritual one) and the Baptism of the Holy Spirit. Using our musical instruments and sacred songs, and being ages 18 and 17 served as a drawing card (some out of curiosity I imagine) and resulted in many conversions and baptisms.

After an early morning prayer meeting at our home church one morning, I returned through Plant City doing 25 miles per hour with a "busted" muffler in a 15 miles per hour school zone. A city policeman hauled me in to the city courthouse and fined me $15.00, which was all I had.

I was told I could appear in court later and plead my case. Fifteen dollars was big money for a country boy back then so I decided to take my chance by appearing before the city judge. I was fourth in line. The first man's fine of $15.00 and time served in jail for vagrancy stuck, and he was released.

The second man had been in jail one week and was fined an additional $25.00 for something he did. The third man was charged with drunkenness, reckless driving and resisting arrest. His fine: $50.00, plus an additional 30 days in jail.

By now I was wondering if I might have been better off not to appear here at all. The officer told the judge what I had done. I felt so small and guilty before the big judge chair and a judge who spoke with authority. He looked at the paperwork, and then exclaimed, "Ernest Holbrook! You any kin to the Reverend?" "Yes, he is my grandfather!" He said further, "He's a good man! I used to sit on the front seat at church with him every Sunday morning, until he went and started his own church.

"If you turn out to be half as good as him you'll be alright!" I responded, "Your honor, I am endeavoring to follow his footsteps. I have dedicated my life to the ministry. I just hope I can live up to his good name!" "Great," he said! "How much did we fine this boy? If he is a preacher he needs this money. Give it back to him! I'm sure he didn't realize he was speeding. It's easy to get heavy-footed at that spot! Case dismissed! Go over to that window and tell them I said to get a refund and good luck in your ministry!" I could hardly believe my ears! I immediately grew in spirit from three inches tall to the stature of a giant!

Word soon spread about the several weeks' meetings Robert and I had conducted at Mt. Zion, our home church. My dad's oldest sister lived at Clermont, Florida, where her husband was chief of police and constable. At her request, the pastor of their recently formed church invited us to conduct revival services there.

Off Robert and I went to discover one of the prettiest little towns I had ever seen. It consisted of steep hills with a lake at the bottom of many of them and was surrounded with huge lakes: Minneola, Minnehaha and Lake Louisa. We would stay with our relatives who had two daughters that were about our ages.

Right off I asked if anyone had ever run into one of the lakes in their car. I discovered that one of my relatives had. His Dad worked for a furniture store and loaned him a pickup truck belonging to the owner, for a date. Afterwards, he was walking his date to her door. She lived on a steep hill just above a lake. Having left the truck in high gear, gravity overcame the gear and the truck rolled into the lake. He ran down the hill and all he could see was the top back of the cab and the tailgate.

After his dad's wrath subsided, they took the truck, got it dried out and repaired, and returned it to the business without the owner ever finding out. Some things in life we can hide from others, but not all. I recall as a youngster how I tried to conceal things from Mom or Dad by telling little white lies, if there is such a thing, but they could usually read me like a book. I read once where a lady said her husband could look at her and never see her – like when she had on a new dress or hairdo. But a husband said his wife could see right through him, without even looking. I think we should ever be reminded of God's all-seeing eyes from which nothing is hidden. (II Chron. 16:9)

When we used to sing "There's An All-Seeing Eye Watching You" at church, I was fearful God was looking for every shortcoming of mine so He could clobber me real good, either now or later! As a great theologian once said, we picture God as a big policeman in the sky ready to pounce on us with His huge bully stick each slip we make. I like what I heard another minister say, "God loves us all so much, He just can't take His eyes off of us." How very gracious and merciful is He!

By now, I was dating Junell on a regular basis and she and her family attended and sang at many of our revival services. She had accompanied me when we had gone to Clermont previously to play our instruments and sing at the meetings under the tent. By now the church had been built at the same location on a hill right above a lake near downtown.

The building was made of cement block with a concrete floor. The very first night when I connected my electric guitar into the amplifier, I received a terrific shock. The pastor said that it was a short in my equipment. I insisted it was the concrete floor. I reversed the electrical plug which helped a little. Finally, I put a throw-rug on the floor. As long as I stood on it, all was OK. If I happened to step off it while playing the guitar, I felt the "power!"

Once while playing my guitar at camp meeting at Pleasant Grove, another young man came in and set up his guitar and amp. Later in the service, which was being conducted by a "healing" evangelist, this young man asked for prayer while still holding his guitar. The evangelist, holding a microphone, laid his hand on the young man's head and the fire flew (literally)! "I really felt the 'power,'" the young man said. The preacher looked at me and said, "So did I! Electric power!"

A very noteworthy situation happened at the Clermont meeting. The elderly pastor stated emphatically in the preliminaries each evening that ever since his conversion, Christ had been his healer. "I have not gone to a doctor, taken any medicine or rubbed any on, nor will I ever," he proclaimed night after night. Robert and I considered this in our daily Bible studies and discussions and even though it didn't coincide completely with our previous beliefs, the pastor was a seasoned veteran and surely must be taken seriously.

Even though prayer for the sick was a regular part of our church services, such total rejection of medical help had never been so strongly emphasized. We had always combined prayer with our need for therapeutic assistance and went to the doctor, or sent for him (remember when doctors made house calls?) when we felt we needed him. But a complete rejection of doctors and medicine, period, was a big order!

I recalled what Grandmother Holbrook had said when J. J. first mentioned the "divine healing only" idea in his early religious considerations. Having come from a family of doctors (her dad and three brothers), she would reserve the right to "doctor" her children when they needed it! Even Jesus said those who are sick need a physician (Matt. 9:12), and Paul mentions Luke, the beloved physician, in Col. 4:14.

Regardless, Robert and I viewed this pastor's testimony as a valid "faith" challenge and were determining that this would be our future practice as well as proclamation in our coming meetings! So you can imagine what an utter shock it was when we received word that the pastor had fallen unconscious with a massive heart attack on a sidewalk in Groveland, Florida, during our revival meeting.

When the ambulance came, his wife refused to allow him to be taken to a hospital, so they brought him home. He lived in a small mobile home behind the church and in the life-death situation she finally sent for a doctor. Thus came the diagnosis, the shots and three different prescriptions to be taken every two, four and six hours apart.

He regained consciousness just before service time, and the church-folk held very serious prayers in his behalf. I could not help thinking about his previous statements about doctors and medicine. Since his wife was also very elderly, Robert and I took turns sitting up every night after church to give him his medications.

He was battling two crisis situations: one, his physical condition, and perhaps even greater, his testimonies about healing. "Will God forgive me?" he asked me. "Yes!" I said. "God loves us all dearly and will never leave us nor forsake us." "But I feel I have failed God by having a doctor and taking medicine," he continued. I tried to assure him the Lord would not hold this against him.

But who learned the greatest lesson? Robert and I thought it was us! We were experiencing something very unusual. Never would we state what we would do or not do about medicine. Or perhaps other things as well! It is easy when you are healthy to boast in your health. But when you are very sick, it's comforting to pray, and to doctor!

Despite the pastor's illness and a street fight of sorts downtown, the Clermont three-week long revival meeting went excitingly well for two young preachers. There were numerous decisions for Christ and baptisms in the Holy Spirit. We baptized several persons in water in Lake Minnehaha (the lake of many laughs, Indian interpretation).

With the blessing of the chief of police (my uncle), we held a street meeting downtown on a Saturday afternoon to advertise the church services. We took our musical instruments, played and sang, and soon a large crowd of people had gathered.

My uncle, in addition to being the chief of police, was also a clothing salesman on the side to supplement his income. In the middle of my street-sermon he spied a man who owed him some money for clothing. When the man made excuses about not paying, my uncle, in full uniform, cap, badge and gun, let loose a "haymaker" and knocked the man down on the street and under a car. The attention turned from me to them and I soon closed with a prayer and invitation to our meetings.

My aunt did the preaching on the way home. She said to him, "You have not only disgraced my preacher nephews, the church, the city of Clermont and yourself, but also God Almighty and you are in danger of going straight to hell if you don't repent!" He halfway apologized to us, but justified his actions on the basis that the man should pay his honest debts or else face the consequences.

Our cousins were pranksters. They short-sheeted our bed once, another time filled it with marbles and still another time put a fake snake under our covers.

We talked them into short-sheeting the chief's bed. (Another of our many mistakes!) As usual, he came home from policing about midnight. We stayed awake upstairs, waiting. All of a sudden, loud, strong language reverberated throughout both down and upstairs. Auntie and the girls went flying into his bedroom when he angrily demanded to know what was wrong with his bed.

78

The chief had taken off his shirt and tie, hung his trousers on the bedpost, lifted the top sheet and attempted to climb in bed. One foot went right through the folded sheet and the other stopped abruptly at mid-bed. When he crawled back out of bed, off came the covers with one sheet wrapped around his foot.

They soon had things back to normal amidst more choice words and stern warnings that such had better never happen again. He suspected that Robert and I had put the three of them up to the mischief but fortunately they never divulged our secret. He later became a dedicated Christian and took a special liking to me. He called on me for counseling and fellowship on several occasions. When he turned 90 years old, I helped him plan his funeral and later assisted in conducting it.

One other thrilling event at Clermont was a ride on the "roller-coaster" road. It was the old road from Clermont to Winter Garden and had been built on the natural, hilly terrain which had very steep up and down slopes. There was little or no traffic on it since the new Highway 50 had been built. At a speed of 55 miles per hour or more, the automobile would leave the road momentarily and go airborne. Ideal entertainment for teenagers! Bad treatment for an auto's tires, coil springs and shock absorbers!

What memories linger even years after that special time at Clermont, Florida. I suppose it was because it was only our second revival meeting, such a beautiful and unique place, and the sheer joy of being instrumental in proclaiming the Word of God and seeing many souls turn to Christ. Our Clermont relatives housed, fed and otherwise wonderfully entertained us those special three weeks. Plus, the young church was uplifted and strengthened.

Our next meeting was at Pleasant Grove where I had previously sought the Lord diligently about my future life. The pastor and his congregants gave us much support and encouragement along the way. I was able to establish friendships that have lasted to this day.

One of my dear minister friends, our former superintendent, resided there on the campground until he passed to his eternal reward. I loved him dearly and revered him as one of our top Greek scholars and preachers. I never held it against him that he gave Robert many sermon outlines and me, none! Who knows, after hearing Robert and me preach, perhaps he knew Robert needed them most! (Just kidding!) Or perhaps he thought I was past help!

From there, it was back to Mt. Zion again for another two week meeting. Robert and I returned now as "seasoned" ministers, with at least three months preaching experience and numerous converts to our count. We were scheduled next at a country church east of Meigs, Georgia, named Zion's Grove after Mt. Zion and Pleasant Grove.

Some area ministers had helped start the church many years before. In the meantime, the church had closed its doors and now Robert's uncle and aunt, and some family members, had gone up to hold several weeks of meetings and re-established the church.

So, we packed up and headed toward South Georgia in my 1938 Pontiac. Upon arriving, we found ourselves about eight or ten miles east of Meigs in a farming community. Our accommodations were very modest since Robert's relatives had left their large singlewide mobile home parked in the yard of the pastor's house. His wife promised us three square meals a day. These meals, along with those provided us by the church congregants, resulted in my going from 138 to 152 pounds in five weeks.

Almost every night after the evening church services, someone would have us out to their home for a full-fledged meal. As you can imagine, they were heavy on sweets: cakes, pies and homemade ice cream, not to mention steak, ham, fried chicken and pork chops. If I'd had a heart specialist back then, I might have saved myself many blocked arteries later.

While our sermons emphasized temperance in all things and total abstinence in others, somehow it was hard to practice self-control when it came to all that food. After all, the Bible does say, "Eat whatsoever is set before you," (I Cor. 10:27) but it doesn't say, "Eat as much as you possibly can!" To the contrary, Solomon warns the glutton in Prov. 23:2. Also, I Cor. 9:25 insists on moderation in all things, while I Cor. 10:31 declares that we are to eat and drink to the glory of God.

A preacher friend of mine, now deceased, said he announced his sermon title one Sunday morning: "Temperance". He said he looked down to read his text and could hardly see his Bible because of his protruding stomach. He then told the congregation that his sermon was as much for himself as it was for them.

One day during the Zion's Grove meeting Robert and I were invited to eat with a family who lived about three miles away over some hilly, South Georgia clay roads. It came a "frog-strangler" rain just before noon and I drove cautiously, slipping and sliding the entire way.

When we approached the car for the return trip after the meal, Robert insisted that he could do a better job driving than I had done. Before we had gone a hundred yards, he got turned crossways in the road. I had a very difficult time trying to remain quiet as he, facing an approaching car labored to get our car straightened out. When he finally got the car to jump the deep clay ruts, it went too far and criss-crossed the other way. The other car's driver waited as we slid past him, trying to avoid his car and the ditches on either side. After my fears somewhat subsided, I laughed heartily. Robert did not think it was funny at all.

The meeting drew huge crowds with many decisions for Christ. With such an influx of new converts, the pastor said we should hold a water baptismal service and start urging the new believers to receive the Baptism of the Holy Spirit. Our church holds the Holy Spirit Baptism as a separate, subsequent work of Grace from salvation. It is a deeply emotional, but spiritual experience initially accompanied by "speaking with other tongues as the Spirit gives utterance." (Acts 2:4) The Baptism of the Spirit is an enduement of Holy Spirit power providing boldness for Christian believers to be special witnesses for Christ Jesus. (Acts 1:8)

Upon the pastor's request, we baptized numerous people in the creek nearby and urged them to come forward each night at the invitation and seek to become Spirit-filled. I boldly announced that my sermon the next night would deal exclusively with the Baptism of the Holy Spirit.

After the service that evening, a man confronted me with a threat. I could smell alcohol on his breath as he pulled a narrow metal plow from his hip pocket. He insisted he could knock a squirrel out of a tree 40 feet high with this steel missile. Furthermore, if I even mentioned them "unknown tongues" in my message next evening, he would throw the four inch wide, ten inch long, sharp pointed plow and split my skull! He said his church had taught him that speaking with unknown tongues was of the devil and he was determined to put a stop to such nonsense.

I had become aware that different religious denominations have diverse views about the "unknown tongues" issue. Many did not practice it and others downright forbade it. But to attribute it to the devil was something else. I certainly did not perceive my own experience of the Pentecostal Holy Spirit as a work of Satan. To the contrary, it had brought me a confidence and boldness as I labored for the Kingdom of God.

And, in accord with the beliefs and teachings of my church, I surely wanted every new convert to also be baptized in the Holy Spirit. But I had not anticipated such opposition right in this church amidst a flourishing revival meeting. I thought about dialogue to hopefully present my view of the matter. But considering the sight of the plow and the odor of the man's state of inebriation, I quickly decided against such action. The man abruptly turned and worked his way through the crowd and out the door.

Taken aback, I was at a loss to know what to do. Should I share this information with some of the men of the church, or the pastor, or with Robert? Surely this man wouldn't carry through such an act of violence right in the church service! Or would he? I told no one except the Lord, and all that night and the next day as I was preparing my message, I couldn't get what had happened off my mind. Prayer hadn't brought me an answer and I found myself imagining tomorrow's newspaper headlines: CONGREGANT KILLS YOUNG EVANGELIST WITH A SMALL PLOW. And underneath: A DIFFERENCE OF OPINION REGARDING PENTECOSTAL THEOLOGY BRINGS DOWN A YOUNG MINISTER WHO FLOUTED HIS DOCTRINAL VIEWS DESPITE WARNINGS!

All of a sudden the solution hit me like a ton of bricks: I would ask Robert to preach tonight. "Why?" he asked. "Because I'm not feeling too well." (I wasn't!) "You look fine to me!" No amount of persuasion could sway my first cousin. "I preached last night. Tonight is your night! I'm not prepared!"

Service time arrived. The singing began. From where I sat up front, I scanned the packed house and there he was, seated near the back, looking right at me. The singing ended. Then a few testimonies. They ended. Pastor began introducing me as the speaker of the evening and even announced my topic: "The Baptism of the Holy Ghost."

As I began preaching, I forgot the man, and the threat. I ended the sermon, gave the invitation and several people came forward to kneel at the altar to seek salvation or the Holy Spirit Baptism. As I walked back and forth encouraging the seekers, a hand from behind was laid on my shoulder. I turned and it was him. I thought, "O Lord, I'm dead." Instead, with tears in his eyes he tremblingly said, "You have convinced me the Baptism in the Holy Ghost with speaking with other tongues is Biblical and real." Whew!!! He lived across the street from where we were staying and became very friendly and even played marbles with us after that.

South Georgia's water wells back then fascinated me. The pastor's well was just like the one at my Payne Grandparents at Ashburn. I enjoyed looking down at the water below and drawing up a bucket-full. It was always so cool and refreshing to drink, especially at night after a long, hot, no air-conditioning, people-packed church service. "Wow, this water has to be as good as that at Clermont or Zephyrhills, Florida," I thought.

That is, until one night I brought up a 10 inch long catfish in the bucket-full of water. I ran in and showed the fish to the pastor. "Put my catfish back in the well," he said. "Why?" I foolishly asked. "He keeps the water clean." So I put him back, and somehow the water never tasted quite as good after that.

One of the Sunday dinner invitations was at a small house with lots of people, including Robert and myself. A daughter of the host family had a crush on me, I was told later. With some 14 people crowded around a small table in a small dining room, Robert was seated with his back to the wall with no way to keep his tiny tea glass filled, except around me. This young lady was serving and kept asking, "Brother Raburn, do you want some more tea?" Of course, he did, since it was on a very hot day and he had a teaspoon sized glass. One time she would reach in front of me, next time behind me and next time just about all around me.

In a few moments, she would renew her request and go through the procedure once more. She managed to wrap herself around me several times. Robert will never let me live it down. Every time he gets the opportunity, he asks, "Brother Raburn, do you want some more tea?" Then he has to enlighten whoever we are with about the scenario once again.

One day during our five-week stay at Zion's Grove, Robert and I went fishing with the pastor. After we got back home, we played marbles and loafed the rest of the day. It was my night to preach. A few days before, I had struggled all day to come up with a fresh sermon. Even when I arrived at church I still didn't have an inkling of an idea what subject I would use.

I did not have a repertoire of sermons since we had not been preaching that long and were now in the fourth week of meetings. I had exhausted my outlines. But on this night when I entered the pulpit I read a simple gospel text and preached about 30 minutes from it. The response to the invitation was tremendous. It seemed my very best sermon to date. It was totally "out of the blue", no preparation whatever! Wow!

So today, I said to myself, "Why bother? I am not going to study, I am going to play and goof off. And when I get to church the Lord will 'give me what to say.'" (Matt. 10:19, taken totally out of context) Ever heard of a dud? A super colossal one? This was it! I had opened my bible at random, read something, I forget what, and struggled to come up with hardly anything.

While I was agonizing myself and the congregation I was also praying and promising God if He would help me through this mess I would never pull such a stunt again. He mercifully helped me; I caught onto something and finally came through with some redeeming value and a good response. Never again did I go up without properly preparing. Certainly I have shot several more "blanks," but at least I had given time, effort and prayer to the presentation. Sometimes when I felt I had done the very worst, the results seemed the best. What a shocker, when after what you feel is a total failure in a sermon, someone comes up and says, "What a wonderful message! God used you to bring it to me!" How wonderfully confusing!

Ever had your comfortable house moved right out from under you? This happened to us at Zion's Grove. One day while we were gone, the owners came and got the singlewide mobile home. We had not been immediately forewarned and so we discovered the empty spot, plus our stuff that had been stuffed in a very tiny "junk" room of the pastor's country frame home.

The room was about 8' X 8', not ceiled and a crosscut saw and other items lay across the rafters overhead. There was no closet space and hardly room to turn around much less study or dress. And yes, there was a bed. Of sorts! The sleepless first night was more of a nightmare. To avoid exaggeration when we would someday share with our grandchildren the hardships, hazards and pitfalls of the Gospel road, we actually measured the sag in the mattress between the head and foot of the bed.

Can you believe nearly nine inches? We tried to shift the slats to improve the chasm but the bedsprings were squashed and our adjustment efforts failed. Another cousin came up with Granddad Holbrook and some others from Mt. Zion for a visit to our meetings. When "Pap" found it out – "Pap" was the pastor's dad who lived in a very nice, modern home next door – he asked me to come with him.

He showed me an available bedroom where he said some of us could stay. It was beautiful, ceiled, wallpapered, had a closet and the bed was level. I mean a perfect bed. Granddad and I stayed there for a couple of nights and my cousin took my place on the sag-bed. When they left for home, Robert told me to move my things back in with him.

I said, "Nothing doing. Why should I leave luxury and an inside bathroom for a backbreaker bed and no facilities?" When I say no facilities I mean exactly that. The pastor did not even have a room and a path. When we first arrived and I asked pastor's wife where the facility was, she said they didn't have one.

I asked where she went and she said, "the chicken house." I then inquired, "Where do the men go?" She said, "Out behind the barn, out in the field, the woods, wherever." So when I told Robert I was staying at the invitation of "Pap" for the duration, the next thing I knew Robert came bringing his suitcase and clothes hangers.

One night after service we were eating a "snack" with pastor and Mrs. and their three children. Milk and cake was the menu! About the time Robert started to take a drink, a big moth-like creature fell from the ceiling right into his glass. The milk turned purple and as Robert was preparing to pour it out, Mrs. reached with a big spoon and dipped the whatever-it-was out and said, "Drink it, it won't hurt you. The county sprays our ceilings with poison and when bugs light there, they die and fall down. It happens all the time." For some strange reason, Robert suddenly lost his appetite and left the table.

One day someone told us that a tornado had touched down near Meigs so we went to view the damage. I had gone through tropical storms in central Florida but had never encountered a tornado. I recalled how our frame house had shook from 100 miles per hour winds and on two occasions we had sought shelter in sturdier buildings, once at Turkey Creek High School and at the Simmons grocery store at the corner of Highway 39 and Trapnell Road. But I had never seen anything like this.

A swath about 100 yards wide had been made right through a pecan grove. It looked as if it had been cleared for an airplane runway or a golf fairway. Fortunately no houses were in its path and there were no physical injuries, but what a scary sight. And this was labeled a small tornado. I shuddered at the thought of a large one.

Mail time was another thing. This being the first time I had ever been this far away from my immediate family so long, I found myself looking forward each day to see if I had any mail. My mom was the most faithful one to write and by now I had been corresponding with Junell. Before leaving home she had promised to write but the lack of letters from her wasn't too encouraging.

A letter from her a few days later, helped cheer me somewhat, but it did not contain even one hint that there was a spark there. So I reminded myself that I "must be up and about my Father's business," and trust Him to help me in the super-colossal proposition of choosing a mate for life. But I hoped and prayed it would be her.

In the meantime, there were several very nice Christian girls at Zion's Grove and at later meetings that were free with their glances and admiration. In fact, some, with the help of their mothers, made very emphatic offers of availability. But one girl and one girl alone would be my heartbeat from now on. You know her name!

Several smaller children came forward for salvation in those meetings, and in those days it wasn't unusual for converts and believers who were very emotionally excited about their experience with the Lord to dance and shout. They told me when I was very small, perhaps age three, during a singing part of the service, I had jumped down off the pew by my mother and danced a bit, then sat back down. Afterwards, an uncle who had observed this came over and told Mom that I was going to make a preacher.

One night during a dancing episode at our church when I was asleep on the floor under the pew, I unknowingly moved my arm and hand from under the pew. Ever had your hand danced on by a high-heeled shoe heel? I later wondered what part the Lord might or might not have played in such an incident.

At Zion's Grove, some of the children, with the encouragement of their parents, got into the dancing mode. One night in the middle of my sermon, two little brothers about eight or ten years old, jumped out on the wooden floor and with their farm brogans began to go cloppity-clop-clop! This continued to happen. We complained to the pastor and his only reply was, "Don't quench the Spirit!" (I Thess. 5:19) "After all," he said, "a little child shall lead them." (Isa. 11:6b)

Robert and I decided these scriptures did not apply to this situation. Next evening he said to me, "If those little guys jump up during my sermon tonight, you grab one and I'll grab the other. Let's set them down and tell them not to move until the sermon is over." After he started preaching, up they came and so did we. The parents were offended, but that ended the sermon-disturbing performances. We had rationalized: "There is a time for all things," (Ecclesiastes 3:1-8) and this wasn't the time to disturb the sermon; and that "God is not the author of confusion," (I Cor. 14:33) and what these boys were doing was confusing our messages. I'm sure the little fellas didn't know better but we hoped that what we did got across to someone who did.

During the meetings visitors were coming from all around and we were told that a group, along with their pastor, had come from First Assembly of God in Moultrie, some sixteen miles away. After the second visit, the pastor wanted to know when these meetings would end. I told him next Sunday night. "Then I want you to begin with me on Monday night," he said.

We were tired and homesick and wanted to go home for at least a week, but the Moultrie pastor insisted and we finally agreed. "I'll have it advertised and ready. You come on Monday. We'll house you and feed you and take good care of you," he concluded. Some of the Zion's Grove folks said we were in "big time" now since the Moultrie church was much larger than theirs.

We were hoping that perhaps the offerings would be better also since they had been very meager here. We had actually conducted services for over two weeks and not a single word had been mentioned about an offering. Even on the Sundays no collection was taken, not for the church and certainly not for us. What little money we had brought was gone and the gas tank in the car was near empty. At the beginning of the third week, the pastor's sister told us her brother did not believe in tithing or taking offerings. But she said, "I do, and here is my tithes. Take them and split them between you." We divided about thirty dollars and she gave us that much again later.

'Twas then a neighbor minister named Paul Golden, returned home and began attending the meetings. He took it upon himself to receive offerings for us a couple of times each week for the last three weeks. Thank the Lord for providing!

When an offering had first been taken for me at Mount Zion I had refused it. But my grandfather pulled me aside and said, "You take it! I have always worked for the church and preached for nothing and even paid many of the church bills myself, and the people let me. But it is scriptural for people to bring ten percent of their income, plus offerings, and the pastor is entitled to a portion of it." So I changed my attitude and adopted the one that says, "They which preach the Gospel shall live of the Gospel." (I Cor. 9:14)

We closed the meetings on Sunday night amidst tears and a promise to return in one year. We told the most anxious ones to visit us in Moultrie. On Monday, we arrived at our next appointment with high hopes for a great revival in the "big" church. "Big, for us!"

Ernest Holbrook – Graduation from
Turkey Creek High School
Plant City, Florida December, 1946

Robert Raburn and Ernest Holbrook
As young Evangelists

Pastor Olin Lloyd, Robert Raburn, Joe Walden,
Ernest Holbrook, Paul Golden

Water Baptismal Service, Zion's Grove, 1947

Some of the converts at Zion's Grove in 1947

FIVE

NICE BREAKS FOR YOUNG MINISTERS

As we therefore have opportunity, let us do good to all men...Galatians 6:10

First Assembly of God in Moultrie, Georgia, helped significantly to put Robert and me on the map as bona fide evangelists. It had only been about six months since we began preaching but this was the break that got us some recognition. Four weeks of well-attended services, along with many converts and baptisms resulted in our getting requests from several more places for meetings.

I've thought about it since, quite a bit. It was the days before television. Most families had only one auto, and when that auto was driven to church, usually all the family went. Families were larger. And I'm sure our type services served as entertainment to many. Plus, we were young, single, simple and honest. And we had the musical instruments, including the big upright bass fiddle. Our services on most occasions had overflow crowds.

One of many rude awakenings I would be in for throughout the years came one evening during the altar service after I had finished my sermon. A church deacon accused me of collaborating with the pastor to use my sermon to condemn the deacon. I was shocked and told him the pastor had not said one word to me about him. I don't think he believed me but when I later mentioned it to the pastor, he laughingly said, "Don't worry. It's just his conscience bothering him." I was completely innocent and neither the pastor nor deacon ever told me what the issue was about.

The pastor did relate problems he had encountered in two previous meetings. One meeting had flopped, and in the other, there was an uproar in the church. This young, single, well recommended evangelist had come for a series of services. The Moultrie church had several, perhaps 25, young ladies in their middle to late teens. He went downtown, had pictures made of himself, gave them to all the young girls and announced he was available.

Some of the girls, with assistance from their mothers, decided he would be a desirable catch. Jealousy ensued and it almost split the church. Pastor closed the meeting and ordered the young evangelist to leave town! "How can I? I've spent all my offerings on pictures and other things. I'm broke!" Pastor said, "I took him to the bus station, bought him a ticket and told him never to return!"

Robert and I had numerous requests for pictures. In the light of what had just happened, we carefully approached the pastor about it. He agreed if we offered our pictures for a price and did not give any to the girls, it would be OK. We were very careful to abide by both of his suggestions. Things went well and though we sold many pictures, we were careful not to give away any or to become socially involved with any of the young ladies.

We lived in with the pastor. They had a parsonage situated next door to the church and the front bedroom was ours. Pastor had informed us that they only ate two meals a day, at 9:00 a.m. and at 3:00 or 4:00 p.m. But they were good meals, cooked by pastor's wife and it gave us an opportunity, especially me, to lose a few pounds from the gluttony at Zion's Grove. It was also a time of extensive Bible study and prayer, with the church so handy next door.

One evening after we had all gone to bed, I was praying silently on my way to slumber. In my prayer, I asked the Lord to show me my guardian angel. (Hebrews 1:14) To my utter amazement, I suddenly saw a glowing form like a person, standing in the darkness beside my bed. I realized it wasn't Robert because I could hear him breathing beside me.

My heart began to pound as I observed this phenomenon. Was this my imagination? No, it was much too real for that. Although I prayed for this, I was shocked at the sight. It was like when the early church prayed for Peter to be released from prison and doubted it when he was. (Acts 12:5-17)

After some time, the form and glow disappeared and I have never seen anything like it since. I was fully awake and I was afraid and I'll always wonder about it. I told pastor and his wife about it and they both assured me it was neither of them.

I had a pleasant surprise at Moultrie. One day I heard a knock on the door and lo, and behold, I opened the door to see Junell and her parents standing on the porch. They had come to visit some relatives not too far away and decided to stop by. I was really excited about the whole thing and my heart did summersaults. I reasoned in my mind that had Junell not been interested in me she would not have come. But she did! Or was it her parents' idea? She later told me it was hers! Glory!

Mom's letters were always welcome and I did something in response to her letters that has embarrassed me ever since. She addressed my letters to Ernest Holbrook, while other letters I was receiving were to: Rev. Ernest Holbrook, even Junell's. So I wrote my mother about the "proper" title to use in addressing future letters. I later repented my pride and I wrote to her and asked her forgiveness. However, I never got another letter from her addressed to Ernest. It was a lesson in humility which I can never seem to adequately learn.

Webster's collegiate dictionary says *reverend* means: worthy of reverence or deserving to be revered. I know that "Holy and Reverend is His (God's) Name," (Psalms 111:9) but such certainly never could apply to me. Only Christ's righteousness in any of us could ever command reverence, and that belongs only to Him. If a crown should ever be forthcoming, it surely must be cast at Christ's feet. (Rev. 4:10) Some people honor ministers with this title out of respect for their calling and office. (Lev. 21:7-8 NIV) Perhaps Romans 13:7b could also apply to clergymen, but it would be out of this context. Reverend should never be something we ministers attribute to our own selves. (Matt. 23:7-11)

What an exciting four weeks at Moultrie. There were huge crowds of people, many converts and many Holy Spirit baptisms resulting in a return invitation the next fall. That was something to look forward to but by now we were homesick, and could hardly wait to head the '38 Pontiac toward Plant City, Florida. We couldn't even wait until Monday morning. We left on Sunday night after the final service.

Being home again after nine long weeks, and especially for the Christmas and New Year's holidays, was thrilling. In the eyes of our families and around our church circles life would never be the same again. We were invited to preach at our home church and several others, at area youth rallies and even at a gazebo-like building the owner of a big grocery store had built behind the store at Maxey's corner just west of Plant City. We helped conduct several Friday and Saturday night services there. We took our musical instruments, sang several songs, preached and gave invitations for salvation. We welcomed every possible opportunity!

The time at home also afforded me the privilege of dating Junell. One night after service when we had dropped Robert off at his house, she, having been seated in the front between us, stayed put. This brought another shakeup of the heart and as I recall was the night of the first goodnight kiss. A 20 mile drive home doesn't seem as long when you are head-over-heels in love.

Add to this the fact we were scheduled to preach revival services at her home church at Lithia in early January. This allowed me to see her every night and to sing a duet with her as well. We've been singing and making music together ever since! Her family always entertained friends and acquaintances royally and it seemed there was always plenty of food on hand at the parsonage.

Junell's dad was a jokester, and I enjoyed his funny stories. At my first meal with the Players, I watched him load his plate with several food items including collard greens. He then took the syrup bottle and doused the entire plateful. I used to come home from school and take fried white bacon and a biscuit and cover them with syrup. But syrup on collard greens?

Later, I was invited for oysters on the half-shell. One look and I said, "No way!" Brother Player had once operated an oyster bar in Marianna, Florida, so he said to me, "You can't ever be in my family if you don't eat raw oysters on the half-shell." What was I to do but try - and gag – and give up in despair? Finally, with the help of a saltine cracker and some sauce, I finally put one down. Then another, and another. I made the grade.

Fifty years later, when Robert and I celebrated 50 years of ministry at Mount Zion, June 23, 1997, a lady gave testimony that she was converted in that Lithia revival. Immediately following, another lady stood and stated that she was converted 50 years earlier in our Mt. Zion revival. What an added thrill for this celebration!

Not everyone, however, was singing our praises back then. A young lady, who had attended Turkey Creek High School with us, when told about the Raburn – Holbrook preacher duo thought that was about the biggest joke she had ever heard! And not only her! Even some of our relatives made slight, even insulting remarks about our "supposed" calling and ministry. This hurt, but only strengthened us in our resolve to steadfastly pursue the work of the Lord. It also provided a further humbling process for young egos!

Along about this time some of our minister friends told us we needed minister's credentials. This would give us recognition with our church organization and separate us from "independent" churches who were on their own and accountable to no overseeing organization. Too, it would help us establish sound Biblical teaching and save us from the pitfalls of "every wind of doctrine." (Ephesians 4:14)

Robert and I went to the Peninsular Florida Assemblies of God office in Lakeland, which was affiliated with the General Council of the Assemblies of God headquartered in Springfield, Missouri. We picked up credential forms and soon met the Presbytery Board for interrogation. We were nervous but found the elders of our district very warm and encouraging. They had heard of our meetings and welcomed us aboard.

We were told of the three-step credentialing process. Step one was "Exhorters papers." We were to enroll either in Bible College or in the required correspondence courses provided by the denomination. Robert and I felt Bible school was out of the question because of finances. My dad later offered to put me through Bible College but since we had several meetings scheduled, Robert and I ordered the materials for the first year of the correspondence course and continued our revival meetings.

By this time younger brother Charles Raburn had joined our evangelistic team. We borrowed the money from Granddad Holbrook and bought a "house trailer" (mobile home) from the pastor at Clermont. I'm sure there was an ulterior motive when Jessup forked over $1,400.00 for the trailer because he then began to travel with us to give his *testimony.*

I'll never forget his exuberance and enthusiasm for the Lord. He now had three grandsons in the ministry and he loved to urge us on. He would say, "Keep your sermons short. Fifteen minutes is long enough. Don't bore your congregation! Keep them wanting for more and they'll come back the next night!"

Of course, he always asked for a place to give his testimony each evening before one of us preached. It wasn't unusual for him to carry on for 30 minutes while wanting us to hold down to 15. Once, when Charles challenged him on this issue, he simply replied, "Ah, I didn't take that long, did I?" The answer, though unstated was, "Yes, you did!"

I've often wished we had kept accurate records of the many conversions, baptisms, etc., since it wasn't unusual to have perhaps a hundred or more in a single revival meeting. Those were not the days of mega-churches in our circles but we often had two to five hundred or more in attendance at some of our meetings.

But in those days we were not accustomed to the importance of record-keeping. All we knew was that when a person became a born-again Christian believer there was rejoicing in the presence of the angels of God, (Luke 15:10) and their names were written in the Lamb's Book of Life. (Luke 10:20 and Rev. 21:27b) Surely heaven's records were adequate and most important. Plus, it was the churches' responsibility to follow-up and disciple the new converts.

The days, weeks and months ahead would bring a time of fervent evangelical efforts, intense Bible studies and spiritual growth. A fuller and deeper understanding of God's Word would help broaden our appreciation of all Christ-preaching churches and believers.

Our personal libraries would grow to include books written by great preachers from other denominations as well as our own. Our scope of the Kingdom of God would enlarge considerably and we would ever be grateful to be just a very small part of Christ's Kingdom on earth.

My grades on my study courses were all A's, and at the end of the second year our district secretary wrote A++ on one course. He said it was the best he had ever graded (brag-brag). But I remained determined to strive for high marks in my ministry, not just good test scores.

I praise God that even in this sophisticated, technologically advanced age in which we now live we still have a Holy book, the Bible, and a Savior, Jesus Christ, and the power of the Holy Spirit to guide and keep us.

For me, there is only one Lord, one faith, and one baptism. (Eph. 4:5) There is only one God, the Lord God Almighty and only one true Son of God, Jesus of Nazareth. I believe the Bible is divinely inspired and that there is only one name given among men by which we must be saved, Jesus Christ. (Acts 4:12) And I believe the only Gospel that is genuine and will stand the test of time and eternity is the Gospel of the Lord Jesus Christ. (Gal. 1:6-8)

This has worked for me for all my years on this earth! And I believe it will remain for all eternity.

Ernest Holbrook

Junell Player Holbrook

December 25, 1948

Rev. and Mrs. J. M. Player
with daughter Junell and son J. Frank Player (About 1946)

SIX

CONTINUING EVANGELISTIC TRAVELS

. . . If ye continue in my word, then are ye my disciples indeed. John 8:31

One of our next meetings was close by so that we could commute nightly. The pastor and his wife were wonderful hosts, and we discovered a family there that had moved from east of Ashburn, Georgia, near where the Paynes and Holbrooks lived back in the 1920's.

The building was jam-packed with people every night and I was surprised to hear the pastor mention that he hoped the good spirit of the revival would help solve an internal church problem. We learned about the problem one evening after service. We were eating a snack at the parsonage next door when a frustrated lady church member came to the door. "Please Pastor, come over to the church and help us deal with this situation." At that, Pastor replied, "I'm not gettin' into none of your fussin'!"

Her further pleadings got her nowhere and she left. We learned that there were too many musicians and a satisfactory solution for using all of them had not been found. Even a rotation basis was not working. I thought it was sad that some churches had no pianists or organists while others had the problem of too many. I'm not sure if or how everything worked out about this, but it did not deter the revival spirit or attendance.

The gentleman from Georgia could keep you in stitches as he told stories about his early childhood in South Georgia. On another evening after church during the nightly snack-time at the parsonage, he told one of his "spine-tinglers."

A neighboring farmer had a very sick horse. The horse was so ill that it had lain down on the concrete barn floor and couldn't get up. After efforts to get the animal back on its feet failed, the neighbor offered to give it to him and his brother if they could get it up and take it to their place. They reasoned that a little feed, water and tender care would net them a horse, practically free.

When their attempts at getting the creature up also fell short, an alternate plan was devised. No big deal! All that was needed was a hefty lifting contraption. A stout rope was attached to a hammock-like sling made of burlap bags that was inserted beneath the horse's belly. The rope was first run through a pulley attached to a rafter ten feet above the horse and then through another pulley attached outside on the eave of the barn. From there it was run to the ground and attached to the single tree (a wooden bar) that was hitched to the traces of their unwary mule.

All things being ready, from inside came the go-ahead signal. His brother outside said, "Giddap." The mule moved forward, but balked when it felt the rope tighten. "Whack him," was the instruction from inside. After a couple of harsh whaps, the mule lunged forward, picking the frail horse up, clear to the rafter above! Having reached its limit, the mule let up, only to be pulled abruptly backwards at breakneck speed. His rear end crashed into the side of the barn as the horse came down with a resounding thud to the cement floor inside which killed it dead on the spot! I could not help creating a vivid mental picture of the scenario as it was ingeniously painted for the listeners. So much for the horse!

The pastor also was a teller of cute tales and anecdotes. He, like the other gentleman, would usually laugh louder than those to whom he told the stories. Robert and I later preached for him at Auburndale, and Junell and I conducted services for him at Niceville, Florida, next to Eglin Air Force Base. Incidentally, a lady who attended the 50th anniversary of ministry meeting for Robert and me brought a picture of us she said she bought during that meeting, 49 years before, when we ministered there as teenagers.

The revival was going so well after three weeks that the pastor wanted it to continue. We were scheduled to go to another state the following week so we decided Charles and I would go there and leave Robert here.

My old '38 Pontiac had been acting up so Robert's dad volunteered to grind the valves. On our way, we stopped to gas up at Stark, Florida, and couldn't find any oil on the stick. It took three quarts to fill it and five more the rest of the trip. A mechanic there told us that when you grind the valves, you also have to replace the rings, which he did, for $30.00.

The two week meeting hardly paid our gas and laundry bills, so with the car problems, I had to write home for money. Dad wired it to me both then and at other times when expenses exceeded income. And he never let me repay any of it. He said, "This is my donation to your ministry." What a dad!

The church situation here was quite unique. The young pastor and his wife lived in the back rooms of the church. The rooms had been built for Sunday School classes but had been converted to an apartment. Pastor worked as a secretary downtown to supplement their income. The church folk had put a bed in another Sunday School room for Charles and me.

One day the Pastor's wife told us that she had married just to get away from home. If that didn't set well with us, another young, beautiful, non-working wife, would come and spend time most everyday with pastor's wife. "I feel uncomfortable with us here with two women," Charles said to me. So did I. Because of this, we figured a way to be gone most of the days.

We went fishing twice, to a near-by city twice, recorded some songs and music at a downtown studio, went to a "Haunted House," did some other sightseeing and ate at downtown restaurants during the day.

The meeting, however, went well. The church seated about 150 and was near full on weekends. We were thrilled to have several people come forward to our invitations for salvation. Another plus was well-attended altar services each evening with quite a number of people seeking salvation, some rededicating their lives to Christ and others seeking the Holy Spirit Baptism or a closer walk with the Lord.

One Sunday morning we were eating breakfast in the small dining area just behind the wall behind the pulpit. An altercation ensued between the pastor and his wife. She had set a pot of grits on the table and dipped them with a big spoon. As the conversation became more heated, she grabbed a spoon-full of hot grits and intended them for her husband, but her baseball-batter-like swing resulted in most of the grits splattering on Charles and me. He had a cute mustache-like cake of grits across his upper lip and mine was on my white shirt and tie. We were shocked!

She immediately ran to their bedroom and slammed the door. Her husband apologized for her behavior and assisted us in the clean-up process. Back in our room, Charles wondered aloud, "Do you suppose she will come to church this morning?" She did, all dressed up in a beautiful dress and hat, led the children's church and taught a Sunday School class. The incident was never mentioned again.

A gentleman came forward to kneel at the altar each evening seeking to be baptized with the Holy Spirit. He seemingly prayed earnestly and anxiously but with no positive results. One evening after the church service he asked Charles and me if we would like to go fishing. We both answered "Yes," simultaneously. But I told him we didn't have any fishing equipment; no reel and rod, no poles, no tackle, not anything. "That's OK," he responded, "I've got everything we need." He gave us directions to his house and told us to be there at seven o'clock in the morning.

The next morning we were right there on time. He came out of the house and asked if he might ride with us. "Sure," I said. He got in the car as I asked where the fishing paraphernalia was. "Oh, we'll get it later," he muttered. We drove a mile or so down to a beautiful river.

He directed us to park beside a small frame building sitting on the river bank. He got out, unlocked the door, went in and presently came out with a small outboard motor and an oar. "Come on," he said, as he went down the slope to a boat on the water, chained to a tree. He unlocked the chain, mounted the motor and told us to get in the boat. My curiosity prompted me to ask once again, "But where is the fishing equipment?" And one more time he said, "We'll get it later."

After a few pulls, the motor responded favorably. Down the river we went, right through a lovely city park bordering the river. The azaleas were in full bloom in a gorgeous array of colors: white, pink, red and purple. It was enchantingly radiant as the sun cast its early morning beams throughout. I told Charles we would have to visit here later, which we did, and the splendor was breathtaking.

About 30 minutes downriver, I guess I was expecting another "boathouse" where we would find fishing equipment, but I was beginning to suspect that something "fishy" was going on. Our friend cut the motor as we headed into a backwater eddy, picked up the oar, showed us a crooked nail on one end, and calmly stated, "This is our fishing tackle!" We watched in amazement as he took hold of the flat part on the oar and reached and probed in the water until he snagged something.

Up came a wire basket with several fish trapped inside, one bass and some brightly colored brim. He unloaded the basket and dropped it back into the water. We moved on down the river to similar places and repeated the procedure twice more. I asked, "Is this legal here? It isn't in Florida!"

"No, it isn't legal here either," he replied. "Say, preachers, do you suppose my illegal fishing is why the Lord won't baptize me with His Spirit?" I said, "I don't know, but I sure hope the game warden doesn't catch us and the headlines tomorrow read: YOUNG EVANGELISTS CAUGHT ILLEGALLY TRAPPING FISH. How do you suppose that would affect our meeting?"

He then proceeded to pull the baskets out again, throwing each one onto the riverbank. On the way back I sure hoped we'd not be caught with fish and no tackle. Fortunately, we didn't.

The old '38 black Pontiac didn't use any oil on the way back home. We still had to drive very slowly for some miles until the new rings were "seated." Our next project was the outfitting of the car in preparation of pulling our recently purchased house trailer, a 23 X 8 foot Trotwood. We installed a sturdy trailer hitch, wired for lights and brakes and obtained a couple of coil springs to handle the extra weight of the trailer. It was a whirlwind week getting prepared for a Pelham, Georgia, tent revival. I managed to date a couple of times, but soon we were off to Georgia again.

The Assembly of God, situated about six miles west, southwest of town, was down to six members and the new pastor had secured a 40 X 60 foot district tent in an attempt to revive the church and relocate it in town. Everything was set when we arrived, with 200 folding chairs, plus an elevated platform to accommodate a lectern, plus all of our musical instruments. The pastor's daughters also conducted a "children's church" each evening, 30 minutes before the regular service, drawing numbers of children.

By the third night the tent was full of people. And by the weekend more people were standing outside all around the tent than were seated inside. Someone counted around 600 people on Saturday and Sunday nights. And night after night responses to the invitation for repentance and salvation were absolutely marvelous. It was a sight to behold. I only wish we had taken movies or pictures of some sort to reminisce all this.

Because of the overwhelming success of the meetings the church was reorganized and a sanctuary erected inside the city limits later. One evening, I sang in a quartet with the pastor's daughters and it angered a young man who had a crush on one of them. Because of his jealousy of me, he waited until I started preaching and then threw a rotten tomato at me from outside the tent. It missed me, but guess who it hit? She was sitting right behind me and it splattered all over the front of her dress.

Because of the large crowds, and many cars parked up and down the street, which was a main road in and out of town, the police were out each evening to keep the traffic situation in order. It so happened that the tomato thrower was caught in action by one of the policeman, he was immediately arrested and spent the night in jail. He later apologized. And he didn't get the girl, either.

We were asked to hold special prayer for the sick in the services and I couldn't believe that some evenings up to a hundred people would come through the line for prayer. There were also some testimonies of miraculous healings. One very crippled man from Griffin, Georgia, through relatives, heard of the meeting. He rode a bus to Pelham, came through the healing line and testified that he was marvelously healed.

Incidentally, the same bus driver who had helped him on and off the bus previously, was amazed that the man without help from anyone, or even two walking sticks, stepped right on the bus with a word of praise to the good Lord as he headed back home. Never before, or since, did we put such special emphasis on "divine healing" because we felt our calling was to win souls. Certainly we did pray for the sick upon request, but the Pelham meeting stands out as a very unusual one for testimonies of miraculous healings, as well as numerous converts. But during the meeting we also found anew that the devil is alive and well and most assuredly still goes about seeking whom he may devour. (I Peter 5:8)

Our house trailer was parked beside a house where the pastor's family lived, several miles out in the country. It was situated on a huge farm owned by a prominent farmer who had given a prime lot in a residential area of Pelham for a new church building for the Assembly of God.

One day when we were clearing the lot, trimming trees, mowing the grass and digging for the building footer, two policemen drove up. They announced that the City Council had revoked the building permit because of hostile reaction from the neighbors. Pastor was informed that he would be arrested if he even set foot on the property again.

I often think of the plagues upon the Egyptians, just before Israel's exodus when I recall the history of the Pelham Assembly of God. After the four weeks tent meeting was over, the opposition intensified. Six men, who were so bitterly opposed to the church locating in their community soon died. Heart attacks, cancer and other illnesses felled them on a regular basis. After his buddies had passed away, one other man, a barber, suddenly went blind, though only middle-aged.

Relentlessly, even after being blind, he fought the church all the way to the Georgia Supreme Court and lost. He even tried to go to the U.S. Supreme Court but they denied even hearing his lawsuit. The church was finally built and I later preached there after I married. It was a beautiful block building and fit well into the community after all was said and done.

One evening after service, while still under the tent, a couple who had been converted to Christ in our meetings, asked us to come for a meal with them the next day. He ran the Pelham Golf and Country Club and lived in a house located beside the clubhouse, right near the ninth green. Until then, we didn't know anything about golf. We had a splendid meal and visit and after we had eaten, he asked if we had ever played golf. Of course, our answer was, "No!" "Would you like to?" "Yes," Robert, Charles and I replied in unison.

This was back when playing golf was considered a "worldly pleasure," and thus a sin, amongst some of those in our religious circles. But we decided that if the Lord would save a man and his wife who ran a golf course, then surely it would be alright to play. (Perhaps this logic wouldn't always work.) He had sets of clubs in bags that he rented, but to us they would be free. I had always picked strawberries, hoed, cut wood and batted left handed, despite writing right handed. I felt awkward trying to swing right-handed clubs so he said, "No problem." Out he came with a left handed set.

We watched as a group of men "teed off" on the number one hole in front of us. I was hooked immediately! I watched as a man hit that little golf ball and it gained altitude right out over the center of the smoothly mown grass they called the fairway, over the hill and out of sight. Wow! The other men did likewise!

We were next! We made a few practice swings and Robert went first and Charles followed. Both made contact and Robert's ball scooted across the grass to the left about a hundred yards. Charles didn't do any better. I thought, "Wow! This is going to be easy, and it's going to be fun." In high school when we got into baseball, the balls flew further than the softballs. And by what I had seen, I realized these pretty little white golf balls would go even further than a baseball.

I swung with all my might! I looked down the fairway to see where it went and Robert pointed to the tee. The ball was still there, untouched. I vigorously swung seven more times. Same result! The ninth swing I caught the ball. Up and away it went, higher and higher, bending more and more to the right, so far right that it went right out of the golf course and across Highway 19 into an old cotton field that was grown up with grass and weeds. I was told I could go try to find the ball.

I ran across the road, climbed the fence and found eleven golf balls. Back I came, and on down toward the flag stick we thrashed our poor balls. When we all three finally got on the green, our host told us to get our putter. After we all putted back and forth past the hole several times, when we got as close as the length of the putter, he said, "That's a *gimme!*" "A what?" we asked. "A *gimme*. You don't have to finish putting. It's a free shot." I have since taken all the *gimmes* I can get!

We misinterpreted exactly what a *gimme* was. We played a few more times during the meetings and when we got within a putter length, we not only gave ourselves the putt, we didn't even count the "give me" a stroke. Needless to say, we had a long way to go, not only in trying to learn how to hit a golf ball, what club to use, and so forth, but also in understanding the very strict and demanding rules of golf.

I have continued to play golf for recreation through the years. This, along with fishing for fresh-water bass, has been my main source of relaxation and recreation. My youngest daughter, Phyllis, learned to hit golf balls in our back yard when I was practicing. She had a "hole-in-one" her very first outing at the Par 3 Publix course in Lakeland, Florida.

She won her high school competition three years and was in the top five of the Western Conference twice. She has won the "longest drive" four times playing in some of our minister's and laymen's golf scrambles. She weighs at least 95 pounds and stands about five feet two inches.

Back in Pelham, the Raburn Brothers and I were scheduled to preach in Andalusia, Alabama, next. But with the tent meeting going so well in Pelham, pleas were made for it to continue at least another week. We discussed splitting up as we had done previously, but decided against it. It wasn't the same without all of us.

We tried to call the pastor of First Assembly in Andalusia but failed to reach him. So the next day, we drove over and met him personally where he lived beside the church. When we told him we needed to delay the services by a week or more, he blew a fuse. Up he jumped from his chair and stormed back and forth across the room, ranting and raving. We were shocked!

"I have the meeting advertised in the paper, on the radio and with flyers. There's no way we can delay it. We must start on schedule." We tried to reason with him, but it only got more heated. Finally he said, "OK! If that's the way you feel about it, we'll cancel the meeting! We'll forget the whole thing! I'm sorry I scheduled you in the first place."

With that, he was joined by his wife. She had been listening from an adjacent room. She chimed in and let us know just how irresponsible and unstable we were. Such deportment would soon result in our being unable to get a meeting with anyone, anywhere. To add insult to injury, she also agreed that calling it quits was best. They would announce Sunday on the radio, and at church that we had failed to live up to our promised commitment.

We departed with strange and mixed feelings. We had more invitations than we could possibly fill, but this event hurt us deeply. We had never faced such reprimands as these and they had come from two, well-established ordained ministers. We worried about the outcome. As we drove back to Pelham, we committed the situation to the Lord. After all, we preached and sang that He was a "problem-solver," so now we were invoking His ability to help us solve this one.

Nothing that had happened at the Andalusia parsonage bothered the Pelham tent revival. The crowds continued to grow in number, souls were saved and the "foundation" (people) of the future church there was being secured. During the middle of the next week we received a shocking and pleasant surprise. We had a personal visit from the church pastor in Andalusia, Alabama.

"Please forgive us for the way we reacted to your visit and your request for postponing the meeting," he said. "After thinking it over, we realized we were wrong. We want to give you an invitation to come hold services for us whenever you can, next week, or the week after, just promise us you will forgive us and come when you can."

In those days we always tried to schedule as loosely as possible, to allow for extended meetings such as this. We would usually leave open a month for each revival and hope it would last only three weeks so we could have a week at home as often as possible. We didn't want to be gone too long. I had a girlfriend to see and I was hearing that other fellas were trying to cut in, and I didn't like it. I had heard that "absence makes the heart grow fonder," but with rivals vying for the girl of my dreams, I didn't want to take any chances. And sure, I missed Mom and Dad, my siblings, cousins and friends at home as well.

The Andalusia meeting started with a bang! No, no one was shot, but expectancy had preceded us. The announcements about the meeting starting date being delayed because of the overwhelming success at Pelham had apparently whetted the spiritual anticipation of both the pastors and the congregants.

Before the first week was over, the building was overflowing with people. We sang and preached over the local radio station and by the start of the second week, the building would not accommodate the crowds. A neighbor pastor brought a huge school bus load of his congregants.

To make access, the front double doors and all the windows were opened and pews and chairs from the Sunday School annex and another church were placed on one side and in the front yard of the church. The altar invitation responses were amazing. I don't know how many professed to be saved and Spirit-baptized, but a prominent evangelist and later very successful pastor, who resided in Andalusia at the time, visited the meetings. After church one evening, he asked if he might visit us in our mobile home an hour before service the next night. We said, "Yes!"

He came right on time and brought with him two large bags of groceries. We graciously thanked him, even though we only snacked in the trailer. Invitations were abundant for us to eat out with the pastor, and congregants, both at their homes and in restaurants. We even had invitations for breakfast some mornings.

On one occasion, the wife of a very successful businessman had told us to be at her house at eight a.m. the next morning. The house was one of the prettiest and nicest in which I had ever been. She seated us at a bar (not a wet one) and gave us several breakfast options. Her husband was away on business and she had nothing else to do all morning but cook for us. If she didn't have what we wanted, she'd go to the grocery store and get it. "So, just name it and you've got it," she continued, "bacon, eggs, grits, biscuits, pancakes, sausage, ham, coffee, orange juice, milk, toast, cereal, etc., etc!" Wow! We couldn't forget the warning of Proverbs 23:21, "...for drunkards and gluttons become poor..." This was difficult, but one can easily see it was the congregant's fault, not ours!

112

But back to the visiting evangelist. He first told us who he was, his extensive educational background, a graduate from two different colleges and a Seminary, and all the larger churches at which he'd preached. He said, "It has taken me to my mid-thirties to get where I am in the ministry, and here you three boys are, 16, 18 and 19 years old, no Bible school or college training, no degrees, and yet I have never been close to having the crowds you are drawing. I preached a meeting right here a few weeks ago and the very largest crowd we had on Sunday morning or evening would not have been more than forty or fifty at most. You are drawing several hundred. What do you boys have that I don't have?"

I responded that all we had was a sincere desire to serve the Lord, preach the Gospel and win souls to Christ. I told him we were involved in Bible study courses and were simply using musical talents we once used on the stages of school auditoriums. I added that any success we had had, or were having, was strictly by the mercies and blessings of God.

We told him we knew of no magic formulas or anything else that would make us attract more people than him. And we also told him that the largest churches we had preached in averaged about 200 in attendance. He had heard that the Pelham tent revival attendance reached 600 some nights.

He asked if we would mind letting him sit on the platform so he could "learn from us." I really wasn't sure if he meant it, or if it was sort of a put-down since we were so unprepared compared to him. After a few nights, I decided he was very sincere. He joined in the singing, gave hearty "Amens" to our simple preaching, and worked diligently at the altars with the people who had come forward to seek for God to come into their lives.

Some years later I visited a church where he was preaching. He greeted me and told me his whole approach to the ministry had changed as a result of our Andalusia revival meeting. He said, "I became willing to unlearn, to simplify my sermons, and I started just being me instead of trying to be a big-time, high-brow, preacher."

We were still young boys and naturally attracted young people, both boys and girls. Several young people lived close to the church and they would gather after school and on Saturday and Sunday afternoons at the church where our mobile home was parked. One day a couple of boys came up on motor scooters. They offered us a ride. After we had ridden with them a few times, Robert asked if he might see how he could do operating one.

I remembered how he had driven on a wet clay road at Zion's Grove, but I got on the little vehicle with him anyway.

Off we sped down the road and then onto a side, unpaved road. The dirt was fairly smooth so Robert gave it full throttle. We cruised up and over a railroad crossing and as we headed down, the dirt ruts became more pronounced, perhaps eight or ten inches deep.

From a house along side of the road, out came the dog patrol. It was a medium-sized black and white pooch clearly ready to tear limb from limb violators of its territory. With both the dog and us breaking the dog and motor scooter speed limits, too late, the furious dog apparently realized we were bigger and louder. It applied its anti-lock brakes that did not hold in the soft soil. It landed smack ka-dab in the rut right in front of us. Our brakes did no better than the dog's.

End over end, over dog, over Ernest, over scooter, over Robert, went us all. And "Great was the fall thereof," once more. We scrambled to gather ourselves together as we watched the defeated and wounded pup retreat to its patrol station under the house. We checked our bruises, brushed off what dirt we could, and picked up the scooter, which wouldn't start. We pushed it all the way back to the church, wondering if we had just bought ourselves one. Fortunately, the scratches weren't too bad, and the young owner was able to get it cranked, so we were forgiven and thus concluded our scooter-riding, at least for the duration of that meeting.

To this day, I have not forgotten how angry that little dog was at first, or how pitiful and desperate he looked when he realized he had taken on much more than he bargained for. I haven't forgotten either, how close we came to serious injury in such a freak accident. The Lord is good! He is merciful and very protective of us even when we may not be aware of it. I will not comment further, on Robert's driving!

Only a day or so after the little dog incident, we were in downtown Andalusia and saw a huge dog try to take on a truck with very large tires. The truck was moving slowly down the main street and the ribbed, grooved treads attracted the dog with a challenge.

He ran alongside the turning rear tire and kept nipping at it until he got a good grip on one of the protruding treads. He was hurled over and over until he finally was disengaged. Completely disoriented, he finally made his way back to the sidewalk where his owner was anxiously calling him. Charles remarked, "Isn't that dog so much like humans? Trying to take on things with which we have no business and could get hurt bad while trying?" "Amen," we agreed.

Meanwhile, we saw a huge crowd of people gathered at the corner of the main thoroughfares and went to see what was happening. The people were all looking skyward. We joined the upward gaze and saw nothing but a few clouds and blue sky. I asked a man standing beside me, "What are we looking for?" "Beats me," he answered. We saw this soldier staring toward the sky and we were trying to see what he is looking at.

I asked someone else. His answer was, "I don't know. I haven't seen anything in particular." I made my way to the soldier and asked him, "What are you looking at?" "The sky," he answered. "I just wanted to see how many people I could cause to do the same." We had been "taken!" It is so easy for this to happen. At least it didn't involve any money – just a few minutes of our time.

But it made some of the lookers angry with the soldier, so we moved out of the crowd lest there be some trouble. Most of the people did the same, after a few of them had some choice words for the soldier. "Is there a law against me looking skyward?" we heard him ask as the crowd dispersed. Robert said, "I guess human curiosity can get us all in a mess. And this also should help teach us how easy it is to be misled by someone else."

Charles laughed and said something about how gullible we all can be at times. I thought, "Wow, if a simple act by one man can attract so many, what power a person can have to influence for good – or for evil." In my heart, I knew I wanted to persuade as many people as I could to the Lord and Christian living, and a different kind of "sky watching." (Matt. 24:27 and I Thess. 4:16-17)

As mentioned, the Andalusia church had an early Sunday morning radio program. It was followed by a large group of black singers and we all had to use the same and only studio. There were only a couple of minutes for one group to exit while the others entered. We ended our program, grabbed guitars, amplifiers, the big bass fiddle, Bibles and music books, and tried desperately to go out the single door confronted by the incoming group.

Realizing they weren't going to make it on time, one singer grasped a microphone and hit a note with a humming –oooo- sound. Another got around us, ran and joined in with a harmonizing –oooo- sound, then a third and so on. Then they started singing. We whispered to a late comer to inform the group to come on in while we were concluding and we would move out as quietly as possible. This worked well.

The last Sunday morning we were there, after we had loaded our instruments and were driving out, one of the singers came running up the driveway toward the radio station. As he passed us, struggling for breath he said, "I just can't got here on time." We've often laughed about this statement and used it at times. We had the radio on and heard them announce that Brother so and so had finally arrived, and as soon as he could catch his breath from running two miles to the station, they would start the singing.

One afternoon a violent thunderstorm rolled across the Andalusia area. I was next door at the parsonage taking a bath. As the lightning flashed, the thunder boomed and the winds began to howl, right into the bathroom with me came the pastor's wife. The door did not have a lock and as she burst through, she began apologizing. "Forgive me! My husband is gone and I am terrified of stormy weather." In shock, I hurriedly departed, wet and half-dressed, back to our trailer-home, leaving the poor woman and her fears.

Robert, Charles and I watched from the mobile home windows as rain came down in torrents. Then we started hearing clunkedy, clunk sounds atop and against the sides of our little twenty three by eight feet abode. "Hail!" Robert said.

Robert grabbed two pans and out into the deluge he went, picking up pieces of ice all across the church yard. Several pieces hit him, but he made it back in with a couple of containers of ice, some almost as large as golf balls. We had seen hail before, but never to this extent. It actually covered the ground. It wasn't long, however, that it all melted, both outside as well as our ice "souvenirs" Robert brought inside. The rain continued until dark so we never made any effort to get ready for church.

Back home, back then, it would have been considered a "washout" and the services would have been canceled. Charles happened to venture outside about dark and discovered the church lights on. He went around to the side of the building and saw the church parking lot full of cars and the building full of people.

He ran back in, made the announcement, clothes went flying and we heard the song service resounding from inside. Upon making our belated entrance we observed a full house, except there were no people sitting on the outside. Like the faithful postman who is never deterred from making his rounds, no matter what, these Andalusia people made it to church on a very stormy evening.

Three weeks passed and we finally closed on Sunday night. By the time the last prayer was prayed and closing goodbyes said we were hooked up, plugged in and on our way into the night. We would leave our mobile home at my uncle's house in Thomasville, Georgia; go home for a few days, then on to Mobile, Alabama. After that, we were scheduled to begin a tent crusade in Albany, Georgia, to establish a new church, which would become First Assembly of God there.

My uncle, one of my mother's brothers, always welcomed our visits and seemed to look forward to us coming by and leaving our traveling home. On some occasions we would spend the night, but most times we were too anxious to either get home or back on the road. On the way from Andalusia this particular night, while we were approaching Elba, Alabama, Robert was driving. Charles was asleep in the back seat and I was asleep in the right front seat.

I awakened just in time to see by the headlights the road making a sharp turn to the right. Ahead lay a dark ravine and Robert was headed right into it. I yelled, "Stop, stop, we're going right into it!" Charles awoke screaming from the back seat, "What's the matter?" By the time Robert stopped, the car was well over the chasm and we hadn't fallen in. We were sitting flat, high and dry on a new blacktop highway that had been built across the gorge. Its purpose we later learned was to straighten the road to keep cars out of its depths!

Robert said, "What's wrong with you Ernest? You scared me nearly half to death." I said, "Well, what do you think you did to me?" Charles, now sitting up in the back seat, said, "Both of you are making me a nervous wreck." We continued on and a few miles after we had passed through Hartford, suddenly we saw fire flying from the car dash, smoke coming out from the engine compartment and just as quickly the lights went out and the car went dead. Charles said, "I even saw fire coming from the house trailer."

We got out the flashlight, looked under the hood, then the dashboard and finally at the trailer brakes and lights connections. Everything seemed normal. The smoke had cleared and we attempted to crank the car but the starter wouldn't even budge. We were in the middle of the night, in the middle of a country road covered by fog. We tried to push the car and trailer off the road but couldn't budge them. Fortunately, no traffic came, but we were at a total loss as to what to do.

Robert said, "Let's pray!" So we three got down on our knees on the pavement and asked the Lord for help. Robert got up and said, "Let's get back in the car." "Why?" I asked. "Because I believe it will crank now." It did, and the lights worked perfectly – until daybreak. As we approached Thomasville, Georgia, they went out again, but by then we could see and the car kept running OK. We went to a relative's service station where we often stopped and traded when we went through Thomasville.

The owner was my uncle's son-in-law. He was married to one of my favorite cousins. She told me at a recent Payne Family Reunion that she was a go-between for my future dad and mom, and delivered the first letter from him to her. My mom-to-be was so young, 12 or 13 years old, that the relationship had to begin in secrecy.

While we were chatting with our relative, his mechanic came over, said he replaced a couple of burned wires and fuses and everything now seemed to be working properly. That was good news. When we went to pay-up, the news was even better! "No charge!" With thanks for the free repairs, we made our way to our free trailer parking spot at my uncle and aunt's house.

With little fanfare, we set our course south on Highway 19 and 98 for dear old Plant City, where we had until Friday to enjoy dating, fishing, and home cooking. After all, it had been almost two months since we had seen girlfriends, parents, siblings or the Hillsborough River. But in a whirlwind, the few days had vanished and goodbyes were being said once again to home and loved ones. By now, we were beginning to feel like veterans in the gospel ministry, even though it had only been about a year since we began.

Our next scheduled meeting was in Mobile, Alabama, at the Union Avenue Pentecostal Church. Charles would stay home to help with family farm chores and the pastor in Mobile told us we wouldn't need the house trailer. They too, lived in the rear quarters of the church and had a bedroom there for us. We would also eat with them.

Robert and I headed westward on Highway 90 and finally came to the tunnel under the Mobile River as we approached the city. I had never been inside a tunnel and it was somewhat scary. As we went down and under, I kept thinking, "What if the tunnel collapses?" That's not a particularly good thought to dwell on while you are in a tunnel, especially if you have even a wee bit of claustrophobia. Fortunately, it was safe when we passed through and when we returned.

Even though the church was "independent" we had no qualms about preaching there. Our burning desire was to win souls for Christ anywhere we could. Besides, the pastor, often referred to as "Cowboy," had been an Assemblies of God evangelist for many years previously. He wore his cowboy boots when he preached at Mt. Zion when I was a little boy and he had on cowboy boots as he came out and greeted us upon our arrival in Mobile.

He and the Mrs. were congenial hosts. They reminded me of Mutt and Jeff as they stood side by side. He was about six feet two inches tall, weighed about 250 pounds and the boots made him look taller still. She was every bit of four feet ten inches, about the size and height of my grandmother Payne. He also had a huge "bay window" (stomach).

Pastor told us of a time he was preaching in a small country church behind a homemade pulpit. As he leaned over to read his text, the top trouser button got caught on a nail that was protruding. As he leaned back to straighten up he realized he was caught. He pulled, with no results. He pulled much harder and stripped off several buttons. This was before zippers were used for the pant's fly. His trousers came loose and he had to preach his sermon with one hand holding them up and the other pounding the pulpit to try to drive home his points. I noticed that now he always wore suspenders.

The attendance grew every night as the word spread about the meetings. Several new converts were recorded early on. Then one evening extra chairs had to be brought out to seat all the people. We soon discovered that a church group of a different persuasion had invaded. Once the altar invitation was given and people came forward to kneel, this group infiltrated the area and began telling them they were from the "true" church and we were the "false" one. This continued the next service also, deeply concerning us as to how to deal with the situation.

We had planned a water baptismal service for Sunday afternoon at a nearby creek. Pastor and I baptized about 20 or so people. The creek bottom was steeply slanted and the tall pastor put short me, five feet five inches, on the deep side. He stood waist deep and I was up to my chin. When he lost hold of a very heavy lady, I had to go under to retrieve her. Robert said he watched as I disappeared beneath the surface. But I managed to come back up with the lady.

Near the conclusion of the baptismal service, several other autos began arriving. Out came members of the "true" church and with them this time, their pastor. At our last "Amen," he moved forward, opened his Bible, invited us to stay and stated he wasn't going to throw mud on anyone. Then he immediately began to declare how totally wrong we were, even in our process of water baptism.

As Robert and I and our congregants stood there in a state of shock, a big man moved between Robert and me, with a firm grip on each of our shoulders. It startled us! The "enemy?" No, a "friend!" of sorts! With quivering lips and tears in his eyes, he said, "Boys, you don't know me, but I feel like I know you. I'm not a Christian but my wife is. I carry her to church and sit in the car outside and listen to you both preach. I like you, and this so-called preacher is slinging mud on you and all of us. I'm going to 'baptize' him. I'm going to throw him into the creek."

Pastor told all of us to get into our cars and get out of there. Robert and I hurried to ours. I looked back to see the big man grab the other minister with his right hand. He ran his finger down his collar and twisted it until the preaching (mud slinging) stopped. The preacher couldn't speak. His breath was cut off.

After we arrived back at the church, up drove this big man and his wife. We were out in the church yard as he got out of his car and came to us. "My wife says I owe you boys an apology for what I did at the creek," he said. "So I apologize. But I'm not sorry for what I did. I stopped his service and sent him and his congregants home, and if I had to, I would do it again. But I apologize! I'm not going to let anyone pick on you!" I guess as a result of all this, none of the congregants from that church showed up at our meetings anymore, which was a relief to say the least.

A few more interesting things happened at Mobile while we were preaching there. One was a picnic to which Robert and I were invited. Pastor had reluctantly given us a so, so, OK to go. A couple of mothers came by to pick up Robert and me. Accompanying them were their two upper teenaged daughters. We went to Fairhope, where there were steep banks that slanted down to a beautiful white beach on the east side of Mobile Bay. After an excellent lunch, the two mothers suggested Robert and I go with the two girls and let them show us the scenery along the beach – cliff area. It seemed that the mothers and daughters may have had fair hopes that something might develop from this Fairhope picnic.

We romped and played along the slopes, sliding down to the sandy beach area and then walked in the water with our shoes off. Finally the picnic came to an end, we were delivered home and did not realize these "dates" would continue next day, which was Sunday.

There was a tent meeting in progress just across the Mississippi line. We had been asked to come and eat at their "dinner on the grounds," then to play, sing and me to preach at the 2 pm service.

After our morning service, I went to load the instruments in my car and discovered I had a passenger that wasn't Robert. At that moment he drove up in a sporty black coupe, stating he had been asked to drive a mother and daughter to the tent meeting.

Yes, it was the same two girls from yesterday's picnic, and yes they were very nice and very pretty. But I could not allow my thoughts to shift to Mobile because my heart had already been captured by a girl back home. Plus, it wouldn't be too long that Robert would be all wrapped up by a Georgia maiden named Merle.

Reflecting on this and similar situations during my single years, I really can't blame young ladies, or their mothers, for looking into possible liaisons with Christian young men. Marriage is a very serious matter and should be approached with reverence and discretion. It is a biblically instituted proposition and Christians should carefully and prayerfully seek to be united with a Christian spouse. Marriage between a Christian man and woman makes for the best success for a lasting relationship.

Another girl at the church had had a misfortune. She had been involved in an automobile accident which had left her face all scarred and deformed. She wanted to take Robert and me out to get a "spinning wheel," a milkshake type of drink then popular at Mobile drive-in restaurants. Some of the girls at church told her we would not take her out because of her looks.

When I found out about it, I went to her and told her we would be honored to go out with her. She gladly obliged and treated each of us to a very large spinning wheel. This was back when we knew little of cholesterol, good or bad, triglycerides and blocked arteries. Heart attacks and strokes were for *old* people and we were forever young, or so we thought. Anyway, we had a delightful evening and the young lady certainly seemed elated. We drove! She paid! A nice three-some!

Once, a young man, who had been deeply impressed by my preaching, asked if I'd meet him for lunch downtown where he worked. I met him at the appointed time and picked him up at the corner of his office workplace. He directed me to Morrison's, the first cafeteria to which I had ever been. He said, "Get anything you want! I'm paying!" He had also pre-advised me to either go light or skip breakfast so I'd have a good appetite at noon.

I entered the line, grabbed a tray, utensils and napkin and proceeded to "load up." I looked back to see his tray about one-third as full as mine, and he was looking sort of funny at me and mine. I soon realized that I could only eat about a third of what I had, and had to gorge myself in order to do that. Another lesson for Ernest.

Our visit was cordial and he expressed to me how my ministry had touched his heart and won him back to the Lord. I apologized for the gluttony, justifying myself on the first time cafeteria experience. In the checkout line his bill was $1.10, mine was $3.87. (This was 1948. Those same two meals today would cost much more.) He kept fumbling for money and I offered to help him pay. He finally came up with the $4.97 by digging for all the change he had.

One night at the conclusion of my sermon, I had walked out in front of the pulpit and was standing behind and between the two altar kneeling rails. As I gave the altar invitation I saw a very, very big lady arise from the back pew and start toward the front. She apparently was physically handicapped and consequently hobbled slowly forward. I did not remember seeing her before and as she came I noted tears flowing down her cheeks.

I thought surely that here was a genuine convert in the making. But instead of turning to the left or right to kneel at one of the altar benches, she proceeded straight to where I stood. Before I could figure what was up, I was! She grabbed me around the waist and lifted me off the floor. She held me firmly in her vice-like grip and began to say loudly, "Bless his little heart, bless his little heart." Apparently she did not know she was smothering me. As I struggled to be set free, I could hear Pastor and Robert Raburn on the platform behind me, laughing.

For me, this was no laughing matter, rather, more a matter of life and breath. Finally, she put me down. She turned to the congregation and announced to them that we had another (she named a then famous evangelist) in our midst. I accepted it as a compliment. But most of all, I was glad to be breathing again!

One afternoon Pastor knocked on our door and asked us to go with him. We went to the home of a lady congregant to discover a screaming, hysterical mother, whose son had just died in an automobile accident. The young man had recently returned from military service and had forsaken mother, God and church and was running with a rowdy crowd.

Earlier that day, he had asked his mother for money to finance a trip to New Orleans for a "night out on the city" in the French quarters. She said, "Son, I've already given you all the money I have. Please stay home and go with me to church tonight to hear two young men sing and preach." He cursed his mother, berated God and church and in a rage ran out to an awaiting auto, slamming the door behind him as he went.

It was only three blocks away that the speeding car in which he was riding skidded out of control, collided with a utility pole then rolled upside down. His drunken driver friend had succeeded in ending this young man's life. He was pronounced dead at the scene of the accident.

By this time, the living room and other rooms were filling up with sympathizers. One after another tried to comfort the mother but her grief was inconsolable. Finally, a would be prophetess entered the room and announced a vision from God in which she said God revealed to her the boy had repented and trusted Christ as his savior, seconds before he died. One can only hope this was true. This did not seem likely since the attending police officer had told her that her son died instantly, not knowing what happened. But we certainly hoped it was true that this young man had made peace with God.

We went to the funeral home the next evening to view the body with the family and friends. The young man's face was cut, bruised and bloated and a piece of cork filled the place his right arm and hand were supposed to be. It was a sad situation indeed. Our meeting closed and we left Mobile before the funeral was held.

We were thankful for the meeting at Union Avenue Pentecostal Church, with all the souls won to Christ and the variety of experiences that will forever be etched in our minds.

Left to right: Charles and Robert Raburn, Ernest Holbrook
(The Raburn-Holbrook Evangelistic Party)

SEVEN

EVANGELISTIC TRAVELS – PART TWO

...continue thou in the things which thou hast learned and hast been assured of... II Timothy 3:14

When an evangelist looks forward to being home more than being off in a revival meeting somewhere, there must be a good reason. How about being in love? I was, with Junell! That's why I became more and more anxious to leave a meeting as soon as it closed on a Sunday night. Drive all night, sleep a little the next day at home, and then head for Lithia, her home.

I hadn't even unpacked the musical instruments or sound system in my anxiousness to see my girlfriend. That Monday evening we rode to Lakeland, played carpet golf, indulged in ice cream sundaes, and parked by Lake Mirror. We walked around the lake to the seats at the promenade behind the New Florida Hotel, later known as The Regency, and even something else now.

After sitting for a time looking at the sparkling city lights reflecting off the gentle waters, holding hands and whispering sweet nothings, we returned to find a policeman rummaging through the back seat of the car. I startled him when I asked what he was doing. He quickly backed out and asked if the equipment was mine. "Yes," I said.

"Well, where is your car tag? And what proof do you have that this is your stuff?" We looked and saw where the tag holder had broken off the car. I told him I had just come home from out of town and it must have fallen off somewhere along the way.

After looking at my driver's license, he apologized for opening the music cases. With the tag missing he said he thought the car and all the stuff might have been stolen. He told me to apply for a lost tag and said we could go.

About a month later, I received the lost tag in the mail from a construction company. They sent it from a stretch of road they were rebuilding between Floral City and Bushnell, Florida. This was the very rough road route we had driven coming home from our last meeting in Mobile. The vibration had broken the tag holder.

After a few days home to recuperate, date, and otherwise reflect on the very strenuous and extensive meeting we had held at Pelham, Georgia, Andalusia, and Mobile, Alabama, we were on the road again to pick up our traveling home in Thomasville, Georgia. We, as always, were welcomed with warm greetings and smiles.

We talked and laughed while we were getting the trailer hooked to the 1938 Pontiac. My aunt made us aware that my uncle would put on his shorts and work in the part of the garden that was beside the road where the high school girls walked to and from school. I was amused at her jealousy of a sixty-year old husband with scrawny legs (revealed by the shorts) and sixteen and seventeen year old girls.

I later learned that most married people are jealous of their spouses at any age, young, old, or anywhere in between. I also learned that some young girls "cash in" on older men who become foolish over the girl's youthful attractiveness. My uncle would listen to my aunt's jealous remarks and laughingly discount her concerns. I thought of Job and the covenant he made with his eyes. (Job 31:1)

Proper jealousy is natural. Even God is a jealous God when it comes to His love for his people. (Exodus 20:5, 34:14, etc.) Moses gave laws from God about jealousy between a man and his wife in Numbers 5:11-31. Paul had a "godly" jealousy for the Corinthians and explained it to them in II Corinthians 11:2-3. But a jealousy that is cruel and uncontrolled (Proverbs 6:34 and Song of Solomon 8:6) can result in violence, murder, and even wars. How much better is forgiveness and reconciliation? (Ephesians 4:32)

We pulled out of their yard and made our way up Highway 19 to Albany where property had been secured and the tent pitched for the establishment of the new church. We were directed to a nearby trailer park on the east side of Albany and the Flint River, just a couple of blocks from the tent.

A space had just opened right beside the Park office, which also contained rest rooms, shower stalls, laundry facilities and a meeting room. Everything was very convenient and we were ready for the meetings.

The pastors had advertised the scheduled meetings well and about fifty people attended the first service. Then, as the days and weeks passed, the crowds grew to the tent capacity of about two hundred or more, and there were a number of people converted and baptized in the Holy Spirit.

We went to a creek east of town several miles for the water baptisms. The water was very clear and I remember how clean I felt inside and out as Robert, Charles, and I baptized several people.

I recall a brother who was converted, and had us over to his house for a meal and fellowship. He later became an ordained Assembly of God minister and pastored a number of years. While at his home, Robert and I played with small airplanes on the adjacent tennis court. They were made of light wood with propellers driven by rubber bands. We would wind up the props and the planes would take off and fly and then usually crash land. (We were still little boys at heart occasionally.)

Charles wasn't present with us that day. He had become "employed" by a man we called "Peanut Butter," who had contracted to build a house for a man. When we took Charles to his house that morning we discovered "Peanut Butter" didn't have a vehicle. We had to take them both to the proposed home site. We were soon to discover that "Peanut Butter" didn't have any money, any knowledge of building, or in fact all of his "marbles," period. Charles got no pay for his work of several days and quit just before "Peanut Butter" got sued by the client.

During the meal that day the host told us a fascinating story. A friend of his was a well digger. He and a helper were digging a well not far from the Flint River for a new home site. The man was digging and sending the clay up in a bucket pulled by his assistant. When the hole had gotten about fifteen feet down, the helper leaned over to return the bucket. He heard a gushing sound and saw water pouring into the hole and the digger missing. Divers were called in but could not find the man's body in the underground stream. All hope seemed gone and family and friends were in mourning at the loss.

Three days later, the missing man, all disheveled and with torn clothes, stumbled to a house near the river about a mile or so downstream. After a tearful and happy reunion with family and friends, he told this story:

"When I realized the ground had caved in and I found myself frantically trying to swim and catch my breath, my feet touched solid ground and my head was above water. I tried to collect my wits as it dawned on me that I had fallen into an underground stream. As reality set in, and I was enclosed by utter darkness, I tried to look up for the opening through which I had fallen. I moved about but could see no light above me. I wandered about for what seemed an eternity groping in darkness, water and underground caves.

Sometimes I was in areas without water. At other times I wandered into deeper water. I often felt fish or something bump into my feet or legs.

"In my desperation, I sought God. I repented of all my sins and promised God if He would help me find the opening I fell in, I would dedicate the rest of my life to Him. I soon lost sense of time, day and night, and almost my sanity. At my wits end, I would sit down in a dry area, doze off to sleep and awake in torment of mind and body. I kept wandering and finally got caught up in a briskly flowing, swirling stream of water. I was pulled under and knew for certain that was it. I was drowning. Suddenly I realized that I was being pushed what seemed upward and I could see daylight. I came up in the Flint River and swam to shore. Lying breathlessly on the bank, I could hardly believe what had happened. I found that I was near Radium Springs and made my way to a house. When I told the people there my 'fantastic' story, they phoned my wife to come and get me."

Our host heard this friend tell his story. It resulted in him turning to Christ, as did many others. The well digger had now passed on and our host had drifted away from God and church, but had rededicated himself in our tent meeting before later becoming an ordained minister and pastor.

After hearing this story, I realized how many incidents or crises provide a challenge for surrender to the Lord. Jonah's surrender happened after (or during) a 3 day ordeal inside a huge fish's stomach; Peter's at a very unlikely net full of fish; Paul's on the road to Damascus; and mine when I was totally frustrated on the road to who knows where. All these years I've been so grateful that Christ was my light at the end of a very dark and miserable tunnel, and continues to be until this day.

When I later told the story of the well digger to my mom she told me about many caves near Ashburn, Georgia, where she grew up. Once, a neighbor's dog had chased a rabbit down a hole under the house. Only after three days did he re-appear, with almost all his hair gone. He probably was lost in underground caves.

A phenomenon that fascinated me was Ross Lake. I always wanted to go see it when we visited our Payne relatives. Not far from my grandparents' home, Deep Creek runs into this long, broad lake. It has an outlet in the bottom that slowly allows the water to go into a subterranean passage.

In very dry weather, all the water will run out of the lake leaving it dry. When rainy season comes, it fills up again. Efforts have been made to dam up the hole, but when the water returned it always broke loose, leaving an even larger hole. I recall seeing timbers and other debris from these attempts, made in hopes of turning the lake into farmland. Nothing doing! It didn't work.

One of my first cousins, William Payne, wrote a book on the Payne family history and Turner County, Georgia. In it he mentions Ross Lake and two other "freaks of nature." One of the two is the Sink of the Creek near Dakota. A small creek begins to sink into a deep ravine for more than a quarter of a mile above the sink. It finally empties underground about 40 feet deep where the gully is about 100 feet wide.

The other is the "Rock House" just southeast of Ashburn. It is a hole some 500 feet in circumference and about 70 feet deep. It too has an outlet in the bottom where the water escapes. The story is told of a Mr. Hamilton riding a horse during a rainstorm in the night. This was in 1830. Not being able to see, he was letting his horse instinctively follow the trail. Suddenly the horse stopped and wouldn't proceed. No prodding could make it go forward. Mr. Hamilton sat out the night by a tree, awaiting daybreak. At first light he saw why his horse had abruptly halted; the hole with very steep walls was directly in front of them. The horse had saved both of their lives at the "Rock House."

One noon during the Albany tent revival, we observed P-51 airplanes from a nearby air force base diving down over a wooded area northeast of town. We were returning from lunch and began meeting military jeeps and ambulances headed in the direction of where the planes were circling. We followed them and soon saw a huge column of smoke rising from the wooded area. The vehicles continued east down a lane but we cut left behind a civilian jeep straight toward the column of smoke where a P-51 had just crashed. As we got out of the car, we saw debris scattered everywhere. Robert lifted the edge of a parachute to a sickening sight. I picked up a cushion with a name and number written on one side. I threw it into some bushes near our car as we continued looking.

Other men were there picking up plane parts. Just then the military arrived, ordered all civilians out and cordoned off the area. They also told everyone to throw down what they had picked up. The cushion was out of the roped area and I was afraid to put it back with military police and Air Force personnel everywhere.

We took the cushion and drove away. We later learned that one plane had left the formation and collided with another, causing it to crash. The other plane was able to land safely back at the base. A couple of days later, a newspaper article listed the name of the dead pilot. Robert and I used the cushion in our car seat for several years. It often brought back eerie thoughts of the man who had sat on it in a U.S. fighter plane.

The Albany pastor had a Cocker Spaniel dog that went in the car everywhere with him. He would perch himself atop the driver's backrest and lay his paws on the car door just behind the pastor. One day we hit a washout on a clay road near Doerun, Georgia. The pastor hit the brakes and out went doggie, head over heels. He rolled down through the road ditch, then up and out and landed in a cotton field. It took much coaxing to get him back into the car. He lay down in the back floorboard by my feet. It was several miles but when almost back to Albany, he regained his nerve and again perched himself back on top of the seat and car windowsill.

Having relatives living at Albany, I renewed acquaintance with them while there. We visited their home sharing fellowship and meals with them. They were very active in their church but visited our tent meetings. For years as a child I had seen them at the summer Payne family reunions at the home of my grandparents, but when my grandparents died, so did the reunions. Years later, another cousin renewed the reunions which continue to this day on the third Sunday of each May, at Camp Kirksey, near Albany, Georgia.

After 48 years, I drove by the First Assembly of God in Albany; a big, beautiful edifice located at 1211 Stuart Avenue, and memories of the beginning days of the church flooded my mind. I thought of a lady who lived near the tent and attended all the services except Sunday and Wednesday. She was a member of another denomination.

When we set the church in order and took in charter members, the pastor asked her if she was going to join our church. Her response was, "Why, if there was one hair of my head that wasn't (name of her denomination), I'd pull it out!" That settled that! But she continued to attend and supported the church, as well as her own.

One day I started from our house trailer to the facilities next door. Out of nowhere, a young woman ran up to me, grabbed me around the neck, and drew up her legs from the ground. I staggered and grabbed under her drawn-up legs to keep her from choking me and both of us from falling to the ground. There we were going round and round, and me holding a woman I had never seen before!

130

Robert and Charles ran out the door to see what was happening. And just as quickly, the woman turned loose and disappeared among the other trailers. We never saw her again. They teased me about this, accusing me of a "secret love affair!" But honest to goodness, I have no idea who she was or what her intentions were. Honest! (They say the truth needs no affirmation!)

Another day I was in conversation with the owner of the trailer park. He previously had shunned us, I think, because we witnessed to him about Christ and had urged him to attend the tent services. But this day he was talkative. Somehow the discussion came up about his wife and he told me she came from a little place in west Florida called "Two Egg." At first, I thought he was joking, but later discovered he wasn't.

The Albany tent revival ended after 4 weeks of good attendance, several converts, Holy Spirit and water baptisms, and the church established. The pastors served for many years. They first bought a small wooden church building and had it moved to the church location. They later constructed a cement block building. It would be years later that the church would move to a different location.

We were tired and homesick, and since our next meeting was a return to Zion's Grove near Meigs, Georgia, we left our mobile home at the home of a congregant, Rev. Paul Golden, who had invited us to park there during the upcoming revival.

This trip home I decided it was time for Junell and me to get down to business about our relationship. We had grown very fond of each other and were pretty well decided about making a life commitment. At least I was.

We dated every night I was home and for once did not go somewhere to church every night, as had been our previous custom. We took time to talk and began to make some plans.

Sometimes we would go to a drive-in and get a coke or ice cream, or both. It didn't matter where we were or what we were doing as long as we were together. One night, I once again told her I was committed to being a full-time gospel minister and needed a wife who would share the same calling. She agreed that her goal in life was to be in God's will and to be fully devoted to and involved in the work of God's Kingdom.

We embraced and I popped the question, "Will you marry me?" My heart was pounding so hard and so loud I knew she could hear it and feel it. She answered, "Yes, I will marry you!" There are really no words to describe it. With tears in our eyes and a scary joy within, we had decided to join our lives as husband and wife. I told her how happy she had made me since I had become acquainted with her.

We began to finalize our plans. I would continue my revival schedules with Robert and Charles and she would finish school, as planned, at Franklin Springs, Georgia. We would marry early the next summer after she finished her school term.

When we talked about telling her folks, she told me I was going to have to ask her daddy for her. I said, "Do I really have to do this?" Nothing sufficed. I would have to face her dad and ask. I put it off for a few nights but time was running out if I was going to do this at this time.

After her folks had gone into their bedroom one night I gathered all the nerve I had as we approached their door and knocked. They invited us in. They were already in bed and her dad, in a gruff voice wanted to know what in the world was going on. My courage vanished. Junell prompted me. She said, "Ernest wants to ask you something." I did, and I didn't!

"What?" was her dad's even rougher response. I thought, "What's gone wrong here?" It seemed he had always liked me before. I had even complied with his requirement that I learn to eat raw oysters. He had even bragged on my preaching. He had joshed with me one night when I had made a theological blunder and otherwise joked with me in what I thought was a general approval of me as a future son-in-law.

So why the sudden change now? I only later remembered that Junell or her mother did not seem to share my alarm. And I'm sure that the anguish on my countenance stood out pronouncedly. Her dad must have observed it too and decided enough was enough. He started laughing and I felt like the calm in the eye of a hurricane. The ice was broken and now I had to muster all my courage for the big question.

"Brother Player," (that's what I called him) "I've come tonight to ask you for your daughter. We want to get married..." Before I could continue with my reasons and promises to take good care of her, he interrupted with, "Son, we are happy to give consent for Junell (he called her Jennell) to marry you. We are not losing a daughter - we are gaining a son. Welcome to our family." After hugs and nervous laughter, he then suggested that we lovebirds leave his room so he could get some sleep.

We happily complied and talked until way after midnight. I told Junell I didn't want to leave her. She said, "Just think! Before too long we can go home together!" Wow! As I drove away I felt as if I had just conquered the world! No longer would I have to worry about those other young ministers who had an eye on her! Their chances were gone. She was committed to me. She would wear my engagement ring until the time I added the wedding band to her finger. Indeed, she would soon be mine for keeps!

But once more we had to go through the agony of parting. I drove her to the bus depot in Lakeland and waved goodbye as she headed for Emanuel College in Franklin Springs, Georgia. And for me - it was going with Robert, Charles and Granddad Holbrook to Meigs, Georgia, and Zion's Grove for a second go-round!

On our way up the year before, Robert and I had had to sharply swerve to avoid a head-on collision in Sulphur Springs, Florida, as we crossed the bridge over the Hillsborough River in North Tampa. It seemed the devil was trying to kill us on our way to our first out-of-state meeting. But all went well this time and we arrived safely at the Golden's huge farmhouse about halfway between Meigs and the Zion's Grove Church.

Our mobile home sat parked right in their front yard where we had left it a few days before. Mama Grace and her beautiful teenage daughter, Merle, would cook for the four of us when we weren't eating out with other congregants. They were such lovely people and most gracious hosts. Merle's father was a jovial soul, most always laughing, and he always had a "sermon" to share with whomever he was with. Simply being in his presence would stir a spiritual spark within and help ignite us for the night sermons. The meeting was again very successful and we enjoyed great fellowship with our friends and the many converts from the year before.

Perhaps the biggest event of the second Zion's Grove meeting was what happened one night after service. We had all returned to the table for meal number four for the day, as usual. We ate, talked, laughed, and near midnight had one by one headed for bed.

Granddad, Charles, and I lay down and waited for Robert. One hour passed, then another, and we were concerned. Charles and I got up, walked around the house where the lights of the dining room were still on. Inside, still at the dining room table were Robert and Merle in deep conversation. Robert did come to bed about 3 a.m., or thereafter. He had fallen head over heels in love. With Merle! And some of you know "the rest of the story."

The meetings went 4 weeks this time, and in addition to many new converts, those from the previous year's meetings were growing in the grace and knowledge of the Lord Jesus Christ. This was very encouraging to us as we shared their exciting testimonies about God's wonderful love and power.

One night after service, Robert, Merle, Charles and I were taking two of Merle's girlfriends home. When we arrived at the home of one of the girls, Charles decided to walk with her to her front door. They got out of the car, opened the gate and walked toward the house in the darkness. In a few seconds Charles came running at breakneck speed, cleared the fence in one giant leap and was in the car telling us to "move it," as fast as we could. When they had stepped up on the dark front porch, her daddy was sitting in a rocking chair. With a shotgun! We did move it, pronto!

I expected to experience buckshot or birdshot to the rear of the car as we sped away. Fortunately it didn't happen. When we realized the young lady was only 13 years old and was not supposed to come home with guys, we sort of understood the concern of her father despite the fact we were preachers and in a group of six persons. I guess this incident reflects the protective instincts of most every father for his young daughters.

Granddad Holbrook got in his "testimony" each evening and folks there responded to him as well as they did to us. Sunday evening, at the close of the meetings, as usual, we headed home. We left our mobile home there since we'd be returning in a week to nearby Moultrie. We hit a pothole coming through Gulf Hammock and lost a bushing in the left front wheel. We had to drive slowly, arriving at a Tampa garage for repairs, which took several hours. We were totally exhausted upon arriving home. It was a pleasant few days, but I missed Junell who was away at school.

We arrived in Moultrie for our second meeting at First Assembly. Before we could hardly get unhooked and set up, Robert asked for the car to go see Merle, about 16 miles away. As he zoomed off I heard a strange crunching sound and ran around the trailer to see the front of the car suspended in the air with one front wheel spinning. He had run over the top of the propane gas tank controls that supplied the church and parsonage. Fortunately there was no damage to the car or the gas controls. We managed to get the car backed off and Pastor told Robert he could understand his anxiousness to see Merle. But he also laughingly reminded him that sometimes "haste makes waste." (What a person in love won't do or will do!)

The meeting went well once again and Granddad continued with his advice about the necessity of preaching fifteen-minute sermons. "This gets the best results," he would say, and people wouldn't stay away since they knew we didn't drag out the service with long sermons. He continued his "testimonies," as usual, of which most usually went much longer than fifteen minutes. But they were exciting, well accepted and added much to each service.

Problems with some of the single young ladies began to re-surface. One evening we were invited by a young lady to eat an early meal before church the next evening with her and her mother. We inquired of Pastor, who gave his OK, since the four of us would go. Upon arrival, we discovered it was a narrow very long "shotgun" type of house. We were ushered through several rooms and past the kitchen to a closed-in back porch area where a table and eight chairs were set up for dining. Eight...? Yes!

Present was the young lady and her mother. Plus her sister! And her grandmother! We four sort of gave each other looks of "what's going on here?" They seated us in every other chair and they sat between, putting each of us between two of them. Granddad was matched with grandmother. I got the mother on one side and a sister on the other, followed by Robert, the other sister, then Charles. After Granddad was asked and had graced the table, the young mother remarked, "Isn't this cozy?" We have laughed many times about this, but at the time it was more uncomfortable than cozy with their cunning plan. Nothing happened but dinner!

Charles' dad came the next day to take him home. He said he needed some help on the farm and that Charles needed to be back in school. It saved Charles from another young lady who first had a crush on me, and upon learning I was engaged, turned to Robert, who was also engaged, and then to Charles. She wanted to get married to any of us so she could "travel with us in the house trailer." She said she just loved to travel and she promised she would cook for all of us.

Charles was relieved (I think) to be taken home because of her persistence. She was such a pretty girl but so miserable at home she couldn't wait to get away. At church that night I watched her come in. She kept scanning the front platform of the church where Charles should have been sitting beside Robert and me, playing his guitar. Then she began to look everywhere in search of him.

During the altar service, she came to me inquiring the where-a-bouts of Charles. She was visibly shaken when I told her he had gone home to Plant City, Florida. Charles saw her a few years later walking down a street in

135

Moultrie. She had two small children with her. Perhaps her dream to travel did not come to pass.

The repeat revival meeting at Moultrie went 4 weeks once more with great attendance, good results, and another invitation to return the following year. The pastor and his family were splendid hosts and wonderful to work with. The church's young ladies gave us nicknames this time around: Robert was "Sissy;" I was "Prissy;" and Charles was "just plain Charles." The dry cleaners also gave us nicknames of a sort. These I'd rather not divulge.

Since Thomasville was so accessible for our coming and going, it saved us 300 miles each way when we didn't need to pull the trailer home. On occasions, my relatives invited us to spend the night. Robert and I did a few times. We would be awakened to the smell of breakfast on the stove and come to a bountiful table filled with ham or bacon, sausage, grits, eggs, butter, biscuits, coffee, milk, and orange juice—Wow!

Can you imagine my uncle's diet had consisted of all this all his years? The milk he drank was hand milked from his cow and was neither pasteurized nor homogenized. I was advised to quit most all these things when angina changed my lifestyle beginning at age 49, or before.

But my uncle did well on this sort of diet. He was a prime source of Payne family genealogy information in his nineties. He was the center of attention at the Payne family reunions. When I called on him to pray he would ask, "Can I recite a poem I learned when I was nine years old?" Of course he could, along with other sayings and interesting items.

One evening at home in Plant City, Florida, I was watching Channel 10 TV news. All of a sudden there he was along with another elderly gentleman. They gave the age of my uncle at 100 years. I called the station seeking information and discovered it was a clip on a nursing home from a Tallahassee TV station and was filmed in Thomasville, Georgia. I told Channel 10 personnel about this being my mother's oldest brother. He later told us he could name every person and nurse at the nursing facility where he spent his last 6 years or so.

At one reunion, I asked him how he had retained such a remarkable memory. He said he woke up every morning at 4 a.m. Breakfast was at 6 and he said during those two hours, in his mind, he would recite scripture, poems, and the people's names at the nursing home. He became blind in his mid-nineties and depended on his memories, and by repeatedly rehearsing these things, stayed mentally alert right up until his passing on at age 105.

At each annual Payne Family Reunion he was the star. Family members would gather around his daughter and son-in-law's auto when they drove up. Then, with all the greetings and hugs it was difficult to get everyone inside the building for a worship service we held at 11 a.m. I would ask him, "Uncle, are you ready to come in and open with prayer?" He'd say, "Yes, if all the kissin' is done." Perhaps my aunt did have a reason to be jealous of him after all!

Charles, Ernest and Robert
Albany, Georgia (1948)

Ernest and Robert with friends of Merle Golden

Merle Golden – Soon to become a Raburn
(My '38 Pontiac in background)

Ernest, Mama Grace Golden and Robert ('38 Pontiac)

Geneva, Vivian and Merle

Ernest and Junell
at Lithia Assembly of God where they were married

141

EIGHT

THE EVANGELISTIC PARTY SPLITS

And the land was not able to bear them, that they might dwell together...
Genesis 13:6

Since Robert and I were both planning our weddings, we were beginning to realize that the size of our evangelistic party was going to be larger than we could accommodate. One thing that enlightened us about this was the young lady's offer to marry one of us and travel with all of us.

We joked about the seven of us living and traveling in an 8 X 23 feet masonite Trotwood trailer; Robert and Merle Raburn, Ernest and Junell Holbrook, Mr. and Mrs. Charles Raburn and Granddaddy Holbrook. The trailer only had sleeping facilities for four with little or no privacy for anyone or anything.

After several days of discussions, it was decided I would go on my own until I was to marry the following June. I would take part of the scheduled meetings and Robert and Charles would stay together and take the rest.

We pulled the trailer to Marianna, Florida, where I would begin a meeting out in the country south of town. Robert and Charles would head for a meeting at First Assembly of God in Mobile, Alabama. They needed a car so they swapped their two-thirds of the trailer for my '38 Pontiac. I would purchase another automobile.

The pastor here worked as the service manager for the Plymouth-Desoto dealership in Marianna. I told him I needed a car. He said a new 1948 four-door Plymouth with radio and heater was due in any day. I could buy it for $1,400.00. Cars were still hard to get even three years after World War II ended. The scarcity had caused long waiting lists and black market prices.

An acquaintance of mine had been first on the list in another city and purchased a new 1946, four-door Ford, for $600.00. Before long a man stopped by and offered him $1,200.00. He sold it, then went to the dealer to order another new car, only to find he was number 100 on the waiting list with cars arriving at three or four per month.

He went to a nearby city to try to buy another new Ford. No luck! Same story. But the salesman told him he had a like-new '46 Ford on the showroom floor he could buy for $2,200.00. Upon close examination he discovered this was the car he had just sold for $1,200.00. The dealer had paid $1,800.00 and now it was available for $2,200.00. He had to wait several months before he could get another new car and at a much bigger price.

In the meantime, the government stepped in and put price controls on new vehicles to try to stop the black-marketing. So the dealers turned to the used car market for their profiteering. With used autos also in great demand, some began to require a trade-in on each new car they sold, and offered very, very low prices on the trade-ins.

Soon, I was notified that my new Plymouth had arrived. I went down to the dealership and there it sat, shining on the showroom floor. I went into the sales office and told them I was ready to make the down payment and arrange the financing on the balance. I was told the owner would have to OK the deal. While I waited, I looked through the glass partition at this medium blue beauty and could hardly wait to drive it out.

I had been riding with the Pastor and his family to the nightly meetings but it wouldn't be long until I would be driving my own brand new car there, and everywhere! The top man finally came in, looked at the papers, and asked about my trade-in. When I told him I didn't have one, since I had sold my car to my cousins, he said that a trade-in was required with every new car sold and he would make no exceptions.

My world seemed to collapse from beneath me. However, my hopes and dreams that seemed to be shattered in a matter of seconds were revived again as he said, "Wait a minute! Perhaps we can work out something after all!" Up came my spirits as I thought, "Wow, he's going to sell me this car after all." But down things went again as he said, "Tell you what. You go buy a good used automobile and bring it to me and we'll see what we can do."

I left with a small bit of hope until I began to look for a car to trade in. Most that were available were pre-war models with sky-high prices. And if a postwar '46 or '47 model could be found, they were priced higher than the new ones since there was no price-freeze on them. Where I was staying was only about a mile from downtown so I walked there most everyday

144

but had no luck finding a car I could afford. I found myself in a valley of despondency, and I'm sure it was reflected in my ministry there.

Whatever the cause, the attendance at the nightly meetings was very poor and the offerings were even poorer until a certain man began to attend. Then they picked up considerably. The Pastor asked me if I had a problem accepting offerings from a "bootlegger." I said, "No, why?" "Because this is now where the major part of your income is coming from."

For some reason the "bootlegger" took a liking to me. He had once been in the ministry but had returned to his former lifestyle. I learned he later rededicated himself to Christ and returned to the ministry. I hope I had a small part in this.

The lack of attendance at this meeting caused me to miss my Raburn cousins all the more. Reports of their overwhelming success at the big church in Mobile didn't help any either. Besides this, they now had "my" car. I couldn't help but size up my situation: I had a house trailer with no automobile to pull it; I had a revival meeting with very few people and even fewer converts; I had small offerings except when they were supplemented by income from illegal whiskey; I had a "one man band" when I had been used to three; I had to preach every night when before it was every third night; and on top of all of this, Junell was far away in northeast Georgia writing to me about all the activities of the college girls and boys there. Boys? I didn't even want to hear about it!

Another letter from the Raburn brothers listed overflow crowds at their Mobile revival. It was by far the largest church to which they (or I) had ever been. And they were staying with a very wealthy parishioner and spending their leisure time in his speed boat cruising up and down the Mobile River with his two beautiful teenage daughters! Of course, their dad was chaperoning every boat ride; ha, ha, ha!

Thank the Lord there was a handful of new converts at my meeting. We baptized them in the lake adjacent to the church and almost had to break the ice. I almost froze.

I rode with the pastor to Panama City to pick up a new Desoto for his boss. I tried to buy it. Same results! No trade-in, no deal! Finally, after three weeks, it was time to close the meeting and move on to the next one, some 25 miles northeast of Marianna.

The pastor arranged for me to stay with a very nice young couple from the church. He was a brother of a young minister who later became one of my very good friends. On the way to their house, I suddenly spied a sign that said "Two Egg." I recalled that the Albany trailer-park owner's wife came from there. If I had blinked my eyes twice in a row I probably would have missed it. A sign and a small country store, and that was it.

The family I stayed with lived a mile or so from the church, which was way out in the country. They were very friendly and she proved to be a great cook and hostess. Her brother also played a guitar and sang, so we became buddies. We would get together to practice and then play and sing at the nightly meetings. It seemed good to have a backup again.

What a meeting! From the very first service our crowds were overflowing. We had to place additional chairs in the sanctuary aisles, the choir area, and along the side and back walls. There must have been about 50 boys and girls near my age. I wondered where in the world they all came from. And they all got saved. Someone later told me they got converted in every meeting that was held. Oh well! Anyway, they were excellent for numbers, evangelistically speaking, and my ego soared. Once again I was a world-renowned evangelist on my way to several hundred more converts right here!

At the end of the service one evening, two very attractive young ladies came up to me as I was putting my guitar in the case. One said to me, "We have something to tell you. She (the other young lady) is in love with you." I was taken aback and looked at my new admirer. Why I did, I don't know, but I heard myself asking how old she was. She answered "twelve." She looked 15 or 16. "I'm sorry," I said. "I am already spoken for. I plan to be married next June." A look of dejection swept over her countenance. But I knew at her age she would recover quickly, about the time the next single evangelist came along.

The meeting progressed, the crowds increased and my enthusiasm soared, until one night during the second week. I preached on the second coming of Christ and emphasized that it could happen soon. Pastor's husband cornered me after the service. "I've been hearing this second coming stuff preached all my life and He hasn't come back yet. If you want me to listen to you, you'd better come up with something better to talk about." I was shocked!

At least it made me think. I knew that "No one knows the day nor hour, only God." (Matthew 24:36) And though I never even considered trying to set a time for it to happen (many have, only to be proven wrong), still, I believed it could happen at anytime, thus behooving us to always be ready.

(Matthew 24:44 and many other scriptures) But I never took issue with the Pastor's husband. He had said enough himself.

Whether or not he shared his views with others in the church I do not know. But no one else mentioned anything about it to me. Different ones did tell me he didn't attend church with his wife very much and that he was a "thorn" in her side as well as the church. I thought, "Well, I'm not the only one he has confronted," and I must say it was a relief for me the many nights he did not show up at the revival.

About midway through the four weeks of meetings, another friend, who lived at Marianna and pastored a church nearby, came to the revival. "I'm going to Dothan, Alabama, tomorrow to trade cars and I'd like for you to ride with me." I agreed. Next morning about nine o'clock he picked me up. He was driving a very old Plymouth and I wondered if we'd make it to Dothan. We did, and by noontime he had found a nice looking off white, 1946 Ford. The trade was completed by mid-afternoon and we were on our way back.

I had looked at some cars also while at Dothan, but a salesman and part-time deputy sheriff that attended First Assembly of God in Marianna, had also heard I was looking. He sent me word that he'd have a very nice '46 Ford available in a few days that I could purchase for about $1,500.00 with no trade-in. So I was waiting to hear from him. Thinking about this, I was comparing and enjoying the ride home from Dothan in this '46 Ford. About that time, the car started skipping and came to a dead halt right in the middle of nowhere.

We got out, looked under the hood, checked the spark plug wires and kept trying to restart the car. All of a sudden it cranked. We were on our merry way once again. And once again it died. Dead! A kind gentleman stopped and offered assistance. He said the car was getting gas to the plugs and every spark plug was firing. So we cranked and it started once again. Before the man was out of sight it stopped again.

By now it was about six p.m. and my service was to start at seven. At seven, we were still stranded in the dark on some country road in the boonies. I knew two hundred or more people would be waiting for my appearance, which didn't take place. Finally, about nine p.m., the start, stop, start, stop, on again, off again, on again '46 Ford, delivered me home. As we passed the church, all but a few cars had left.

My hosts explained how much they missed me, asked what happened, and soon I was eating a warmed over, but delicious meal. The pastor had preached, the service was good and she had assured them that I would be back the next night. I was! But she wasn't there! I wondered what had happened to her. I later learned that her husband had forbidden her to go because he objected to the continuation of the meetings.

It was during this service that things got out of hand. During the singing, a young lady burst out of a side room with a broom. She began sweeping around the pulpit and altar areas, then down the center aisle and out the front door. Everyone was looking at her with disbelief and shock. When she came back up the aisle, a deacon stood, called her by name and asked her what she was doing. "This is not the time to be sweeping the church," he said.

"Oh, yes it is," she responded. "I'm sweeping out the devil." Things calmed down until after I had finished preaching and began with the invitation. Another young lady then joined with the first young lady and using "unknown tongues and interpretation" began to try to coerce people to surrender to the Lord. This continued until they actually began to threaten people with immediate destruction if they did not respond to the invitation.

In the absence of the pastor, I consulted with a deacon and we decided the best way to stop all this was to dismiss the service. I told the congregation that the pastor would be back the next night, so I closed with prayer. I left with my hosts and while eating an after service snack, they told me I should have dealt with the overzealous young people while at church. I told them I had rather let the pastor handle it.

Before we had finished eating, some young people from the church, in two car loads, had driven up in the front yard. Two of them came in and told me that God wanted me to return to the church because I had resisted His power by trying to dismiss the service. They asked me to return with them, so I did.

When we returned to the parking area, which was still full of cars, I noticed that the church lights were off. When I asked about the lights, I was told that "God" had instructed them to turn them off. I requested that the lights be turned back on, only to be told that anyone who touched the light switches would be struck dead.

I recognized a deacon by the car lights and asked him to lead me to the switches. I turned on the lights, did not fall dead, but was amazed to discover about 75 or more people still there. Some were kneeling in prayer while others were lying around the altar in close proximity to each other – men, women, and teenagers.

When the lights came on, most of the people got up and returned to their seats. A deacon asked me my opinion of the night's events. He said he was apprehensive about what was going on, but was afraid to say anything for fear he might "quench the Spirit of God." He said, "You set us straight about all this. I believe our pastor would expect you to."

In a matter of seconds I was confronted with the prospects of a totally unprepared, "impromptu" sermon, in hopes of imparting some profound scriptural guidelines for the "straightening out" process. I thought of the excesses and abuses of the Gifts of the Spirit by the Church at Corinth. Paul dealt with those errors specifically in Corinthians, chapters 12, 13 and 14.

I asked the congregants to turn there in their Bibles and I pointed out that the Gifts of the Spirit are for profit. (Cor. 12:7) That is: spiritual benefit, blessing, good! Since unknown tongues and the interpretation was a main issue, I mentioned that these were on the very bottom of the gift list and that wisdom and knowledge was at the very top. "Every gift then must be used in wisdom and with Spiritual knowledge," I admonished.

I emphasized the regulation concerning tongues and interpretations in Chapter 14, verse 27: two, and at the most, three! "Surely not more than this," I said. I read verse 19, which says that five words in understanding (English) are better for proper teaching than 10,000 in unknown tongues, and verse 20 which urges maturity in these matters and not childishness. I also mentioned that in Scriptures, "darkness" was related to Satan and evil while "light" was related to God, Christ and Christianity. "Let's keep the lights on!" I said!

Next, I read 14:40, "Let all things be done decently and in order." "This has not been that way this evening," I added. Then I read of "the more excellent way," (12:31) which is discussed in Chapter 13, the 'love' chapter! I insisted that "God's love at work in us" is the greatest gift. "Better than speaking with tongues; better than prophecy; better than understanding mysteries, better than faith, better than giving all you have to the poor, or offering one's body as a burnt offering."

"All of the above are totally worthless and useless unless they are permeated with God's love – and consequently, His grace. 'Love is patient, kind, never envious or proud. Love is not self-seeking, is not easily angered, does not behave itself unseemly, does not seek her own, is not easily provoked, thinketh no evil and rejoices not in iniquity but in truth. (God's truth) Love never fails.'

"Paul insists that speaking with tongues should not be forbidden, (I Corinthians 14:39) but certainly must be regulated. Now, I love all of you," I concluded, "but things have gotten out of hand tonight. Let's study our Bibles and properly interpret scripture, (II Timothy 2:15) seek the true leading of the Holy Spirit, and give way to Godly wisdom and the experience of the church elders. We have a great revival going. Let's keep it that way."

When I ended my nervous admonition, I once again dismissed in prayer. Several of the people, mostly adults, gathered around me and expressed their support and thanked me for sermon number two. And they pleaded with me to not let what happened discourage me. They hoped I would stay on and continue the meetings. I told them I would discuss the situation with the Pastor the next evening, and decide from there.

By then I was wondering if some of the same group that brought me back to church would take me back home. They didn't! But someone else offered me a ride. The folks were still up awaiting my return. I briefly told them what had happened and then we went to bed. It took quite some time for me to drop off to sleep.

The pastor returned for the rest of the meeting and things calmed down somewhat. A few of the young people dropped out, but the pastor promised me they would continue to love and try to teach them.

A day or so later, I caught a ride into town to see about "my" car. It was there, at the Ford place. It was actually the salesman's car. It had 35,000 miles, was a beautiful off-white, had radio and heater, bumper guards front and rear, a spot light and fog lights. I had a few hundred dollars saved up and Dad had arranged a loan for the balance of the $1,500.00. I was only 19, and learned that an adult, twenty-one years of age or older, had to sign the papers.

We decided that airmail was the fastest way to do the transactions, since Marianna to Lakeland mail normally would take three or four days, one way. I called Dad. We sent the papers and Dad would sign them, airmail them back and wire the money. It should be signed, sealed and delivered in two or three days. Wow! What a beautiful car. But for now, it was parked and locked in the Ford warehouse out back.

I called the pastor and asked for a ride with her from Marianna back to the church that night. It had turned very cold again and the salesman drove me to her house where I had supper with her, her daughter, and her husband. Her husband was nice enough, but he belittled her, and again wanted to know if we were going to "run the meeting until eternity!" He said he would not attend that night.

We loaded up in their 1935 Chevrolet. "We don't have a car heater, so you'd better sit in the front with us," Mrs. Pastor stated. She got in, her 15 year-old daughter sat in the middle and I sat on the outside (inside the car, of course). Mrs. Pastor was very talkative and dominated the conversation all twenty-five miles. We were very tightly confined in the front seat and I had to hold on to the door handle to not crowd her pretty daughter. At least we kept each other somewhat warm!

As we approached "Two Egg," it was getting dark, and by the lights of the car I suddenly saw that the road ahead was full of huge hogs. I interrupted, "Sister Pastor, stop, look, hogs!" She talked the louder. I tried again! Again she raised her voice to stress her point! The third time I yelled, "Stop! Hogs in the road!" Too late! It felt like an earthquake accompanied by the sounds of squealing hogs.

When we finally got stopped she asked, "What in the world happened? What did we hit? Why didn't somebody warn me?" Her daughter replied, "Mother, Brother Holbrook tried to tell you three times! You just wouldn't stop talking long enough to listen." I got out and by the car lights could see two or three hogs lying around. The rest had run away. The lower front of the car was bashed in, the bumper broken off at one end and wedged under the car.

I worked and twisted and pulled for dear life, but the bumper wouldn't budge. Finally, her daughter helped me and we got it out from under the right front tire while her mom backed up. I got a rope from the trunk and tied it so it wouldn't fall back under again. Mrs. Pastor sighed and said, "My husband is absolutely going to kill me." He didn't, but I imagine he made her wish she was dead. It was great news later, to know her husband surrendered to the Lord and served God until he passed away.

Now what? What else could possibly happen that hadn't happened? Well, let me tell you! A weather front moved in with heavy clouds, dense fog, and endless rainfall that absolutely grounded all Florida airplane flights for about five days. No airplanes could take off or land at Tallahassee or Tampa. Apparently, my car papers were also grounded. I called Dad day after day. On the fifth day, he finally got the papers. "I airmailed them back to you," he said. "Airmailed?"

In the meantime, I had gone to Marianna every day waiting! I asked for the keys to "my" Ford and I would go back in the backside of the warehouse and look at it, sit in it, crank it, then lock it, and leave it, once again! But on this particular afternoon just after the eventful meeting had closed, an envelope had arrived at the Ford place with the money and signatures. I could hardly believe I was actually cranking it and driving out.

And now I thought of nothing but home, sweet home. It was almost dark as I left Marianna. Junell was coming from Franklin Springs to Marianna for Thanksgiving. Her folks would drive up and meet her there as would I. But that was a week away, so I hit the road. I stopped under a street light in Quincy, Florida, got out and looked around my "new" Ford. Wow, Again!

At about 10 p.m., I was so exhausted from all the rigors of the past several weeks, I found myself falling asleep. I picked up a soldier in Chiefland who was headed home to Dade City. He offered to drive so I obliged. He awakened me when he arrived at his home.

I later considered what I had done. Fortunately, there was nothing amiss. Had it been today, it would have seemed even more foolish. He could have robbed and killed me and taken my car. Instead, he graciously thanked me and offered to help with the gas. I politely refused and thanked him for his help. It was nice to be at home again with my family. They didn't seem to mind me awakening them at about one a.m. for the homecoming. It had been almost two months.

Ernest and Junell on a picnic in 1948

My auto and traveling home

Ernest, house trailer, guitar and 1946 Ford
(Musician, singer, dairyman, evangelist)

NINE

MT. ZION – MY FIRST PASTORATE

...feed my lambs, feed my sheep... John 21:15-16

After a few days at home, I went back to Marianna, Florida, which was Junell's home town before she moved to Plant City. She would come by bus from Franklin Springs and spend the Thanksgiving holidays there. Imagine the excitement of meeting her at the bus station. I had not seen her since late August and letters aren't nearly as real as the real person. There she was and soon, about seven months, she would be my wife. If only I could wait that long.

We were elated to be together again, even if it meant being in the company of several family members. One evening, seeking privacy, we went out to dinner, drove around town a while, and then parked by the courthouse. No sooner had we stopped, when up drove a policeman who parked beside us.

The officer got out, shined his flashlight on us, and said we had been parking there for long periods of time for several nights. My insistence otherwise went unheeded. We were ordered to "move it!" I thought, "These pesky policemen! Why can't they leave us be?"

The restaurant where we had gone had been my favorite eating spot during the two months I was in and around Marianna. My favorite song on the juke box was, "My Happiness." Junell and I adopted it as our love song and it has been to this day. We often play and sing it and when it was re-released on a CD, we obtained it. Believe me; it sure was better to be hearing it in that Marianna restaurant and her with me – than me having to listen to it all by myself. She has truly been my happiness throughout these many years.

As we drove back to her granddaddy Waller's, where we would spend the night, I couldn't help but recall an incident that had happened a couple of blocks from there several months earlier. A close friend had passed away. Junell and her parents had invited my sister Joann and me to travel with them from Plant City to Marianna for the funeral. We went with them in their pre-war 1942 Plymouth. We split up in Marianna to spend the night with various friends and relatives of theirs. It was determined that Junell and Joann would stay with a certain lady. Brother Player handed me his car keys and told me to carry the girls there. It was raining and some of the roads were not paved and were clay! Upon delivering the girls, I proceeded back to Granddaddy Waller's where I would stay.

As I approached a stop sign on the wet clay I applied the brakes. I had been cautioned that they were not the best. Where had I heard that before? (Oh yes, my brother's 1936 Ford, on my very first date.) Instead of the car coming to a stop, it actually seemed to speed up. It slid sideways across the intersection and out of control down the hill on the other side. I frantically tried to steer it. I barely missed two gasoline pumps and the car lights revealed the store building into which I was about to crash.

Being a farm-type supply store, it had a huge concrete loading platform across the front. In a split second I visualized how much damage the old car might sustain. I didn't have time to think of my own fate except how would I face Junell's dad, if I did survive. Dying, or facing him weren't two preferable options.

I braced for the crash, felt the car swing around and when it finally stopped I realized it had missed the building and was sitting in the next intersection. Don't ask me how! An angel? I don't know! Pure luck? Is there really such a thing? Anyway, I thanked the Lord for a "miracle."

Just imagine trying to get to sleep after all that! My pounding heart had one consolation: somehow I had escaped crashing Reverend J. M. Player's 1942 Plymouth. Next morning, when I took the car to go get the girls, I drove the route again to try to see where all I had slid the night before. There were skid-marks in the clay that curled across the road, around two gasoline pumps, right alongside the loading platform and then in a loop back into the clay road. Whew!

After getting the girls we went back by the "nightmare site" but I never said a word to them. I later told Junell, after we were safely married, but a nervous encounter occurred when her dad saw his clay-spattered car. "Where in the world did you drive with my daughter last night to get all that red clay?" I reminded him that it was raining and that the clay roads were very muddy and slippery. He seemed to accept that explanation. I dared not elaborate further!

156

The Thanksgiving holidays came to an end all too soon. I kissed my darling goodbye and watched the bus pull out of the station. My '46 Ford was pointed back toward Tallahassee and then south to Lakeland. What an automobile! It seemed such an improvement over my 1938 Pontiac. Besides, Dad had bought a new 1948, four-door black Ford and I had driven it once between meetings on a date to see Junell. Now I had my very own, but the payments were a whopping $54.00 a month for 24 months. I would make them somehow, even though I was on my own as an evangelist and would be getting married come next June.

With no meetings scheduled during the holidays purposely, I worked at the dairy and attended Mt. Zion, my home church. It came as a shocker when our pastor announced her resignation from the church. The next surprise was when the deacon board and other members approached me about becoming their new pastor. Wow! But I was only 19 years of age! Still, my granddad assured me I could do the job. I agreed to be voted on and was elected. I found myself surrounded by well-wishers! And plenty of advisors! I would begin the first day of January.

My burden to win lost souls to Jesus Christ could now be centered on relatives, schoolmates and residents of my own home-town, Plant City, Florida. I had to cancel several meetings I had scheduled but that wasn't too difficult since I was on my own. It was lonely and empty without Robert and Charles Raburn.

Although anxious, I prayerfully determined to give pastoring my very best shot. I was willing to learn the ropes as I went. What a brand new world! What a change of events! I would now be pastor of the church pioneered by my grandfather and have the privilege to actually be his pastor. How awesome it all seemed! I only knew I wanted to be in the center of God's will, be it at home, or wherever.

A disparaging remark, made by a district department official, actually became an incentive to me to work all the harder at being a successful pastor. Having heard the church had called me at such a young age, the minister predicted the church would die and have to close its doors in six months. This prognosis was told to a relative of mine, except the teller did not know this person was my aunt, who passed the word along to me. In six months, we not only had not closed down the church, we had broken all previous attendance records.

I had a trailer hitch installed on my car and my dad and I went to Marianna, Florida, to pick up my mobile home. By the time we got it connected and headed for home, it was dark. South from Tallahassee on highway 19 and 98, we encountered some areas with very dense fog. At times, it was so thick we could scarcely see at all. We had to creep along. This continued until we got past Perry, Florida.

All of a sudden the fog disappeared as quickly as it had shown up. By now it was about 10:30 p.m., and I was able to speed up considerably. Then the strangest thing happened. A little voice within spoke to me and said, "Ernest, stop the car!" I gently chuckled to myself and dismissed the thought.

But it returned, this time more emphatically, "Ernest, stop the car!" In a few minutes it was so strong in my mind that I shared it with my dad. He responded, "What do you mean, 'stop the car?' We've just gotten out of all that fog and I need to get home. I've got a lot of work to do tomorrow." So I kept driving and all the while the "silent" voice was pounding in my mind, "Stop the car."

Finally, I said to Dad, "I've just got to stop! I can't get away from this voice." We were approaching Salem and there was a wide place in the pavement so Dad said, "Here's a good place for you to pull over." As we began to slow down the car began to jerk and bounce and I could feel the trailer pulling us sideways. When I managed to get stopped we got out and by flashlight could see the trailer sitting several feet to the side and closer to the car than usual. We then noted the dolly springs and wheels that connected the trailer to the car had come apart on one side and were lying on the pavement. Even though it was in shambles it was still attached to the car and trailer. What a mess!

The obvious question, "What if this had happened at 50 or 60 miles per hour?" Dad and I looked at each other and he said to me, "I'm glad you listened to that mysterious voice. It must have been the Lord speaking to you." We did not have adequate tools to repair the dolly and besides several bolts were missing, probably scattered somewhere between Marianna, and where we were now.

A school or something was located beside the road where we were stopped and lights were on. A few cars were still there and as one came out, the driver stopped to see if he could assist. He had no tools or bolts either, but he told us where we could get help. We disconnected and headed back north until we saw the light by the road he said we would see. The man had already gone to bed but very obligingly arose and went with us. He observed the situation, jacked up the trailer, got out a tool box, then another little wooden box with an assortment of bolts.

Within about a half hour, he had realigned the springs, replaced and tightened all the lost bolts and had us hooked up and ready to go. When we asked how much we owed, he said, "Nothing! I'm glad I could help." After insisting, he finally accepted a ten dollar bill, which, of course, was a lot more then than it is now. But it was still a bargain, as well as a real time-saver for us. And having stopped when we did may have even been a life-saver! Thank the Lord for the "still, small voice" that became profound enough to get my undivided attention, I Kings 19:12. We got home safely about 2:30 a.m.

The Christmas and New Year's Holidays were nice, but hectic. With no meetings scheduled and consequently no income, I worked in the dairy to keep a few dollars coming in. Expenses didn't stop simply because payday did and now there would be a car payment coming due just before Christmas and every month thereafter. The church salary wouldn't start until a week or so into January.

It did not take long in the dairy to be reawakened to the fact of the rigors thereof. I suppose atop the list of unpleasant realities, is that it seems you work 14 days each week. Two shifts of five to six hours each, seven days a week equals the 14 days I mentioned. Add it up for yourself. You begin at one o'clock (that is a.m., like one hour after midnight) and you work until all 150 cows are brought into the barn, stanchions closed, cows fed, bags washed and milked, turned back out and everything cleaned and sterilized. The process is repeated at one p.m.

I recalled that part of the time I also hauled the milk to the processing plants. First, it had been to Borden's on Lake Wire in Lakeland. Then to Sealtest, down past the harbor and near Seddon Island in Tampa. Now, it was to Pipkins Dairy on Pipkin Road in Lakeland.

I remembered one morning as I arrived at the Borden plant, milk was running down the driveway into Lake Wire. A dairyman had added two gallons of water to every ten gallon milk can. The plant manager discovered it and poured it all out. The same dairyman had previously set some empty milk cans on his truck hoping they would count as full. This was the last straw. He was closed down for good and had to sell his dairy business.

If hauling milk at daybreak after working all of the wee hours wasn't enough, going to Mulberry, Florida, to try to cash a dairy check was; especially when you were sixth in line and the bank honored only the first five. Then you had to wait two more weeks and arrive way ahead of time in order to get paid. An entire morning could be ruined by the pay delay when a dairyman needed to be sleeping because 1:00 p.m. was hurriedly approaching when the same 150 cows would be lined up at the gate for the afternoon shift.

No wonder I told my folks jokingly (but I meant it), that I had quit the dairy in order to go out preaching and now I needed to do the same again! I didn't mind the work as much as I did the time – or lack of it. Junell had come home for two weeks for the holidays and I had to squeeze in time to be with her. This, to me, was far more important than milking cows, hauling milk at daylight or trying to get milk checks cashed. It was even more important than making money except, oh yes, there now were car payments in addition to everything else.

After the afternoon shift, it was a race to get showered, shaved, dressed and off to Lithia just in time to go to church somewhere, then back to the usual full-fledged meal at the Lithia parsonage. Time seemed to fly and I had to leave at 12:20 in order to make it to work at 1:00 a.m. Now you know why I said things were hectic. Perhaps I should say almost sleepless also.

One weary night when I made it back from Lithia just in time to go to work, I filled the feed-cart and put out the feed for the first line of cows. Upon returning to the feed-room, I noticed how inviting the half-full cart looked. Since I had a few minutes, I lay down for a supposed quick nap and went sound asleep. My two co-workers looked in vain for me, carried on without me and only found me when one of them came into the feed room to distribute feed for the next line of cows. They were getting ready to send out a search-party to look for me when they discovered me.

During this time I was also negotiating with the church about my duties as the new pastor. I was to be in charge of all the services, the Sunday School hour, the morning worship and the evening evangelistic rally. I was also to conduct the Wednesday evening prayer and Bible-study meetings. I was to head up and promote Sunday School outreach and teacher training, the children's and youth programs, the choir and music programs and visitation and follow-up of new prospects. I was to see about the ill, needy and elderly and make periodical visits to all the members. Also, I was to cooperate with and implement the district and national home and foreign missions programs.

I was expected to preach Sunday mornings, Sunday nights and Wednesday nights, except when we had an evangelist holding protracted meetings or visiting district or national officials or missionaries. And now the big news, my remuneration: Fifty dollars per week. This was 1949. Since there was no church parsonage, I would be allowed to live in my trailer, parked at my parents' house, and even engage in moonlighting at the dairy to supplement my salary, as time permitted. I consulted with my dad and brother and they said they could always use me for as much time as I could spare. I would fill in but never be expected to work Saturdays, Sundays, Wednesdays or any other time church duties called.

I was soon to learn that there were many other aspects to pastoring. It hadn't been unusual to have people seek my advice on whatever issues that may have troubled them, even from the beginning of my evangelistic ministry. Despite my youthfulness, inexperience and a total lack of training in the area of counseling, the fact that I was a minister of the gospel apparently led many people to consult me for their frustrations, unanswered questions and decision making.

This intensified when I became a bona fide church pastor. It was to become a time consuming task listening to people in every age group from young to old who expected me to produce God-given answers to a quagmire of bafflement. I became a good listener, which I learned was very important. I was very careful about specific advice, and always admonished earnest prayer concerning most situations. I always referred to the guidance offered in the Holy Scriptures and thus was able to get by most of the time. But not always! For who can tell a love-stricken teenager which suitor will make the best husband or wife?

How can one explain the Book of Revelation in 15 minutes, as one hurried young man requested? Indeed, who can explain the Book of Revelation, period, what with its mysterious beasts, horses and horsemen, plagues, holocausts, antichrist, Mystery Babylon, etc.? Suffice it to say it is a book that, as one minister I heard describe it, "scares one spitless!" But, thank God, for the faithful Christian believers, it ends up with great victory for those who accept Christ, the King of Kings and Lord of Lords," Revelation 19:16.

And who can answer whether or not a person should go to the big city tomorrow, or which route to take to avoid an accident? How about if a certain business deal will be lucrative or not? Should I go, or should I stay? Why does God allow the devil to exist? Why do good people suffer and bad people prosper? How can you really know you are saved? Can you prove there is a God? Why doesn't He make Himself visible to the human eye and remove all doubts? Which came first, the chicken or the egg? Can God make a rock big enough that He can't lift it?

Who is the anti-Christ? When will He come? When will Jesus Christ return? How soon before the world comes to an end and burns up? These are merely a few of the many things sought out from me, not all in my first year of pastoring, but in subsequent years. Thank God that today there are trained, anointed, Christian counselors. Even they don't have all the answers, especially to foolish questions, but they can certainly provide direction and comfort to many troubled minds.

I took Junell to the bus station in Lakeland, Florida. It would be Easter before I would see her again. I was wondering how I could survive that long. Time has a way that seems to pass so very slowly when you are anticipating some great, longed-for event. To counteract such, busyness is the order of every day. Which I was! But there was time for letter-writing in those days. Complete mush! Maudlin sentimentality! Mine, much more than hers! She has kept all my letters and occasionally shows me one to remind me of all those promises I made in those days and months before our marriage. Talk about "blackmail!"

At the dairy lease-renewal time my dad and brother were served notice that their lease would not be renewed. The alternative was to purchase land and build a new barn as well as feed and milk rooms. They looked at land as far away as 15 miles north of Polk City, but settled on 607 acres about two and one-half or three miles north of our leased location adjacent to Highway 92. The new acreage was adjoining the Knights-Griffin Road.

With the rushed construction job completed, next came the "cattle-drive!" Reminiscent somewhat of the olden days' cattle drives in the west, they had arranged after the morning milking shift to drive the cows by foot to the new location. With horses and riders and cooperation from neighboring pasture-land owners the fences were lowered and the drive accomplished in several hours. But the next biggest problem was geographical.

The old milking barn on Highway 92 was at the south end of the dairy pasture-land. The new one was on the north. At milking-time, for a few days, the cows went to the south fence, which was one mile from the barn and across a canal. I sure was glad I was heavily involved in the "ministry" and thus mostly spared the ordeal of the "reorientation." But living so close to the situation and being somewhat involved, I made an observation. I know the Bible refers to believers as "sheep of His pasture," however, I also noticed a similarity between cows and church members, when it comes to habits.

The case in point: One Sunday morning I told the church congregants we were in a "rut" and needed to be free from it. I said, "One thing is the place you sit in church. You come to the same pew and get disturbed if someone has gotten it before you arrive. Today, we are going to change places. Not only are we going to change sides but I want those who sit up front to move to the back and vice-versa. Most cooperated, though reluctantly.

I even changed the order of the service. I preached first, gave the invitation and then concluded the service with singing. And about three-fourths of the members "backslid!" (Not really, but almost.) One lady declared she would hunt another church to attend if I ever did such an idiotic thing again. Another one said, "You ruined the service! I simply cannot worship from this side of the building!"

By then, I had arrived at the front entrance of the church where I usually stood and bade farewell to the exiting congregants. The critiques continued! "I have never seen anything as messed up as this service was," another lady said. Then one of the deacons lingered, and after most of the people had departed, came up to me and said, "Brother Ernest, I don't believe what you did was a good idea. Maybe you'd better not try this again." I agreed with him and assured him I wouldn't! At least cows can't speak, but they can kick. And have you ever had a cold, wet cow tail in your half-asleep face? And have you ever tried in your novitiate state to pastor a mature, well "rooted and grounded" group of church people? (Who wish to stay with the status quo totally and completely?) I have!

But pastoring is fun! Most of the time! The biggest chore is trying to please God and people all at the same time. It isn't easy trying. In spite of everything, the church began to grow. From time to time attendance records were broken. On occasions there were new converts, which is priority number one, the winning of lost souls to Jesus Christ. New members were added and there were Holy Spirit baptisms and periodic water baptismal services. At first, we baptized at a phosphate pit just southeast of Plant City. One Sunday afternoon we were headed for the pit for such a service. Several people who had no autos were riding with those of us who did. I had a car load. One of the baptismal candidates inquired of me whether or not I could swim. I answered, "Yes, why?" "Because I can't," she responded.

Again, when we arrived, she told me I might have to save her from drowning if she got "happy" and started "shouting" while being baptized. I said, "Remember that 'there is a time for all things,' and besides, the pit is some 30 to 40 feet deep just off the ledge where we will be standing." Sure enough, as I brought her up, she started slinging her arms, screaming for joy (I guess) and started falling toward the deeper water. My heart was in my throat, but I managed with the help of another man standing by, to get her out of the water safely.

I could imagine the newspaper headlines, "PASTOR DROWNS CONGREGANT WHILE TRYING TO BAPTIZE HER IN DEEP PHOSPHATE PIT." Thank the Lord it didn't happen, but since, I have read of some who have drowned at water baptismal services. I was glad when we were allowed to baptize in Moore's Lake, near Dover, Florida. The bottom of the lake gently slanted downward and was a much nicer and safer place to hold such services. I thank God today for church baptistries.

My interest in radio returned and I soon had a one hour Saturday program on WPLA, 1570 on the a.m. dial. It was a 250 watt station, the only one in the local area. There were plenty of listeners and this brought several visitors to our church, some just to see what I looked like. I have been amazed throughout the years that I've been on radio how people react when they meet me in person, having first heard me on the air. "You sure don't look like you sound," several have told me. "You are supposed to be real tall," one lady said.

In later years, a lady visited our church. After service she said, "I sure had you pictured differently in my mind. You are supposed to be very young, and six feet, six inches tall, with lots of black hair." Unfortunately, my hairline has steadily receded. I tell my grandchildren and other small children that my wife pulled it out. I'm sure there have been many times she would have liked to so do. "At least," this lady continued, "your voice is six feet, six inches tall." I said, "Thank you very much."

I can only recall just one occasion where a lady told me that I looked exactly like what she had pictured. "You fit your radio voice precisely," she said. Several people were converted to Christ, resultant from those early broadcasts and have led their families and their children's families after them to the Lord. One lady that I recall who was converted, later won her sister to Christ, then her brothers and other sisters. Today, scores of them serve the Lord in various churches and two of them are now church pastors.

Not long ago, after some 45 years of almost continuous broadcasting of the gospel, two men came to me within several days of each other. They had worked for the radio station and brought me on the air from time to time. Both of them had been converted to Christ as a result of my preaching on the air, but neither had ever told me. After 30 years, they made their way to personally tell me of this. And neither knew the other had come to me with his Christian testimony. Certainly, only eternity will reveal all the results of this gospel radio ministry the Lord allowed me to conduct over the many years.

One great lesson I learned in that "beginner" state of pastoring was that it was difficult to fulfill all the expectations of every congregant. For the most part, however, they supported me, prayed for and with me, enthusiastically joined my programs for the church, and overlooked many times my adolescent blunders. There were slip-ups, some that I have made over and over, even though I am now much older. Suffice it to say that those who so strongly stood by me probably could have found more fault with me and my ministry than those who "let me know for sure."

God was and is very merciful. Otherwise, I never could have been a pastor to some two or three hundred people at such an early age. But I feel the Lord gave me a pastor's heart, which has served me well and helped me survive as a minister and pastor for more than 50 years.

The Saturday radio broadcasts attracted a group of listeners from a nearby town. They visited our church during revival meetings and invited me to speak at their church. I conducted several nights' meetings, the attendance overflowed the building and another visiting group invited me to speak at their church. I told them I'd have to get an invitation from the pastor before I could do this, one that I never got.

But I did receive an invitation from a new church of another denomination near there. I went, preached under their tent, and helped them establish a church. With people from my own church affiliation! My innocent childlikeness was severely shaken when the District Superintendent called me. I was facing charges of unethical conduct by a pastor whose church I had helped to nearly empty, unawares!

The superintendent sent the District Youth Director to deal with me. It was under his ministry I had rededicated my life to Christ and surrendered to a call to the ministry. Junell and I had also asked him to officiate at our upcoming June wedding. He informed me that he would come to see me as opposed to me coming to the District Office.

We met at the appointed time at my mom and dad's home where I had my mobile home parked. I was uptight but he soon set me at ease. He reiterated the charges filed against me: "stealing church members and putting them in another church of a different denomination."

"The situation is this, Brother Ernest. For twenty years this husband-wife pastor team has refused to have an evangelist come, despite numerous requests to the District Office for such. It is these members who have left their church after threatening to do so for many years. You just opened the door of opportunity for them.

"There are ethics involved, however. You must refrain from speaking at the other church and you probably won't hear anymore about this matter." I thanked him, apologized for my ignorance of proper denominational ethics, and I never heard from the District about it again. Perhaps both these ministers and I had learned a lesson!

At this time though, I made many friends of other church members through our Saturday night youth rallies. One of the young men who was converted in that tent meeting later became a minister. On several occasions, I have had people tell me they were converted to Christ as a result of our radio ministry and became members of other denominations. I thank God for any part I've ever had in winning anyone to Christ, regardless their denomination or church.

Linda Holbrook and Gail Green
January 2, 1949

Ernest and Junell (1948)

TEN

OUR WEDDING

...a man shall leave his father and mother, and shall cleave unto his wife...
Genesis 2:24

Easter came and went. Junell's whirlwind trip home soon ended and now there was only a little over two months until the wedding. But even sooner would be the time I would go to Franklin Springs, Georgia, for her graduation, and bring her home again, for keeps.

In the meantime, I was becoming a "seasoned" pastor. Or, so I thought! Having long ago exhausted all my evangelistic sermon outlines, I was ever praying, studying and searching for new topics and thoughts. I had two major sources from which I drew. One was the Word of God, coupled with my studies in the Assemblies of God ministerial Bible courses. The other was prayer.

Long before we had moved the dairy, I had established a place of prayer down in the pasture some several hundred yards behind the dairy barn. On nights while Junell was away at school and when I was not in church services, I would resort to my favorite prayer spot. The area was a little south of where Interstate 4 was later constructed.

Apparently, I assumed God was near deaf, so I often cried aloud during my prayer-time. I was totally unaware that anyone was listening to me, except the Lord. One day a handsome young man drove up to where I had my house trailer parked beside the dairy barn and my parents' house. He introduced himself as a neighbor that lived down a graded road along side our property and the dairy pastureland (which incidentally, wasn't very far from my prayer place).

He said to me, "I am a Christian and an aspiring minister. Are you a Christian?" I responded, "Yes, and I, too, am a minister." He then asked, "Do you pray at night back in your pasture?" I said, "Yes, why?" He said, "I've been sneaking across the fence and listening to you for several weeks now. You have got me all fired up and I want to pray with you and study the Bible with you."

We became bosom pals and were able to spend some time together in fellowship, prayer and in the Word. He later pastored in Plant City and then in Zephyrhills. Afterwards, he contracted a brain tumor, from which he subsequently died. It seemed so strange to me that such a fine, young, spirit-filled minister would be called home so suddenly and so early in life. His funeral service brought back such warm memories of our association.

One Sunday night I was preaching away in the Mt. Zion pulpit area where I had once fallen over the railing in embarrassment. In those days we had a room and a path. In fact, we had two rooms and two paths, one for the ladies, and one for the men. A unisex privy was unheard of in those days in our area. The rooms were situated directly behind the church some fifty feet from each other and the back of the church. A back door alongside the pulpit area provided a shortcut to either place.

Unawares to me, an eight year-old young lady proceeded to cross behind me on her way to you know where. I backed up in order to lunge forward to stress a profound point in my dynamic theological exposition. She saw me coming, tried to dodge, but the collision was unavoidable. I backed over her, knocked her down on the floor and did some fancy footwork trying not to step on her or fall to the floor myself. I still don't remember which way she went when she got up. Nor could I remember the point I had planned to lay on the congregation.

Somehow that pulpit area wasn't always kind to me. It was, after all, the same place from which I had once run being pressed to surrender my life to God and which, at that point, I wasn't willing to do. But despite these things, I suppose the anointing I received in that "sacred" area far outweighed the troubles I had encountered there.

Hey, it was finally time to go! To get Junell! My uncle and his wife asked if they might go with me as far as Bainbridge, Georgia, to visit her parents. Then two sisters, who were church members, asked if they might hitch a ride to Moultrie. The five of us headed out and I remembered thinking, "Wow, this will be great on the way back from Bainbridge. Junell will have to sit in the front middle, real close to me all the way home.

Having dropped off my passengers, I was alone, headed to northeast Georgia. Passing through Athens, I realized I was getting into some beautiful, hilly country. Atop the terrain, my emotions soared and my spirits were even higher as I anticipated what lay ahead.

The layout of Emanuel College just outside Royston, Georgia, at Franklin Springs, was rather small, but beautiful. And even more beautiful was my darling Junell. It was a very famous preacher who said: "God sure knew what man needed when He provided a Savior, Jesus Christ, and a woman for a wife!" I totally agree!

Junell's parents had also arrived for her graduation as well as her brother, who was stationed at an Air Force base not far away. His fiancée had come also and they abruptly announced they had decided to get married, now! We went with them to Anderson, South Carolina, where they obtained the license and tied the knot. Junell's mother said, "I'm losing both of my children at the same time!"

We had a couple of days until the graduation ceremonies so Junell took her parents and me up near Toccoa, Georgia, to a rather small mountain she and some of her school peers had climbed. Her parents didn't get very far up, but she and I climbed to the very top and enjoyed the view for miles around.

The climb left us pretty winded and I figured going back down would be a laugh. It wasn't! I didn't realize how many muscles one would have to use "putting on brakes" to keep from falling headlong down the mountain. I awakened very sore the next morning.

We went down to one of the springs where the school had constructed a gazebo. We marveled at the water gushing up out of the ground and took several pictures of it and ourselves. Then graduation ceremonies came and went, along with the pomp and circumstance, and a powerful sermon on "The Seven Foundation Pillars of Wisdom," by one of the denomination's ministers.

Although Junell's graduation was from high school she had also picked up several college credits which would later count toward her college graduation from the University of South Florida in Tampa. Goodbyes all said, suitcases packed and a last look at the campus, the 1946 Ford and us were headed back towards central Florida, Mount Zion and our wedding at Lithia. Glory!

We were soon rehearsing with the several attendants in the Assembly of God Church in Lithia. I had a "honeymoon suite" reserved far, far away;

in Lakeland, Florida: It was a simple motel room but adequate for a young couple deeply in love.

The wedding itself was not without several incidents. First, there was no air-conditioning in the church. An overflow crowd on a very humid, June 24th night, added up to a "sweat-box" situation. Next, the time had arrived when I was to sing the first verse of "I Love You Truly" from the altar area to Junell as she entered the front door. Could I make it?

I had sung all my life in every sort of circumstance, as a child, in quartets, on the radio, in the Florida Strawberry Picker's Band and even at a political rally that included a top Florida official. I had sung in numerous revivals before hundreds of people but now as I stood perspiring profusely amid my several male attendants, I had never encountered such nervousness as I heard my voice tremblingly singing: "I love you truly, truly dear; life with its sorrow, life with its tear; fades into dreams when I feel you are near; for I love you truly, truly dear."

With that hurdle behind, I heard a sweet voice from the front doors echo back, "Ah, love, 'tis something, to feel your kind hand; ah love, 'tis something, by your side to stand; gone are my sorrows, gone doubts and fears; for you love me truly, truly dear." I thought, "Praise God, gone are my doubts and fears, also!" They were! Now, if I could just hold out for the rest of this!

I looked and up the aisle she came, adorned in her beautiful wedding gown. I had not seen it, nor had I seen her that day. But in a few moments she was standing beside me and the minister was reading the "wherefores" and "do you's?" We both managed our way through this and then it was time to kneel down for the wedding prayer.

We had asked an elder of the church to pray over us. As I prepared to kneel, I realized a much smaller satin-covered kneeling bench had been placed in front of the bigger altar. It was not there during the rehearsal. It was only about eight inches high but I promptly knelt on the carpet and put my elbows on it. I thought it seemed too low and by then Junell was nudging me to put my knees on it and my elbows up on the big rail.

It was too late! Already, the elder had placed his hands on each of our heads and began praying with "gusto!" - as one of my late friends used to say. I began the effort to lift my knees and arms to the proper places. By then, I was sweating even more and my efforts to raise myself were met with resistance by the intensified pressure from the elder's hand on my head. I managed to get one hand across the big altar but couldn't get my knees but about half-way on the little one.

My brother Ralph, who was my best man, told me later that he looked down to see me crawling all over the floor. Perched in such an awkward position, my sweaty right hand, which was holding me in limbo, began to slip. As the prayer and push of the hand increased, so did my desperation. I also began to pray, silently of course, that this boisterous prayer would end. "Please God, help him to stop praying! Now!"

He did, and not one second too soon! In another, my hand would have slipped and I would have fallen backwards, probably flat on my back in the floor. Horror of horrors! As I tried to stand, my back was in pain and it seemed that gallons of sweat were pouring and every nerve on end as I was being instructed to kiss the bride. I can hardly remember it but the pictures show that I did.

The pictures of the wedding also showed something else! Situated above the platform area on the back wall was a very large sign that had been placed there perhaps long, long ago. It read in very big, bold letters, "PAY THE PRICE AND RECEIVE THE BLESSING!" I have often joked that I received the blessing first, and had been paying the price ever since. I said, "joked." Anyway, we were married and after the pictures we were set to go to a nearby home for the reception.

In order to keep my car from being "decorated," I had hidden it behind the dairy barn at home, went to the wedding in another car, to the reception in another, and finally would leave in still another. It took some doing, but we had it all arranged. At the reception someone told me that some of Junell's cousins were going to "kidnap" me and throw me in the Alafia River, which was close by. After the cutting of the cake, we headed out. They doused us with rice – and one person ground salt into my hair.

But by leaving there in the other car, we outsmarted the would be kidnappers. Then, as we went back to the house for Junell to change clothes and get her suitcase, they cornered me in the yard. As she came out, I said, "Let's make a run for the car." (It was my sister's '48 Ford coupe.)

By the time I had cranked the car they had picked up the back end (rear wheel drive). I accelerated, but only to the sound of spinning wheels. We went nowhere, fast. I rationalized that soon they would tire and have to put the car back down on the ground. So, I put the gear in reverse. I told Junell what I had done and she begged me not to. "You might run over some of them." "Good," I said. (Although I didn't really mean it.)

"Please don't," Junell pleaded. There were about five of them and soon I felt the car being lowered. As soon as it hit the ground we moved backwards and I heard them scrambling to get out of the way. Can't you see the headlines next day? "YOUNG MINISTER BACKS OVER FIVE MEN ON HIS WEDDING NIGHT. SPENDS NIGHT IN JAIL" Fortunately for all concerned only about three of them got bumped slightly. They did learn that I should not be bothered on my wedding night.

I recall one of my uncles telling me about a shivaree he and his buddies planned for a country Georgia couple that had just gotten married. That night, they waited in the woods by the newlywed's house, until the lights were turned off. Out they came with pots, pans, and horns and singing. After a few rounds of this, the front door opened and off went both barrels of a double-barreled shotgun into the night sky above them. They were warned that the next shots would be horizontal. He said, "We started fleeing through the woods into the night. In the darkness, we ran into trees and bushes, but we left off serenading!"

Finally, with the "well-wishers" blessings over, and the would-be pranksters left behind, we proceeded to our "new world." We went by our trailer-home, exchanged automobiles and soon arrived at the hallowed threshold across which I carried my bride. Our honeymoon was all we had expected and looked forward to. We had entered what a late, great writer referred to as, "The halls of highest human happiness." We were now partakers of the sacred union of husband and wife which the creator planned from the beginning.

We would both be on cloud nine for days, weeks, months and hopefully for years, till death do us part. We went to church and I preached both services on Sunday. We ate with my parents, then hers. On Monday, we drove to Thomasville, Georgia, where we spent the night.

We then drove to the beach at Gulfport, Mississippi, where we spent the next several days. One afternoon, we went for a swim in the Gulf of Mexico with the son and daughter of the motel owner. The boy was about 8 and the girl 12. We had been in the water only a short time when I felt a streak of "fire" across my back. I let out a scream, not knowing what had happened. We came to shore and Junell and the children observed a very red streak on my back. The little boy screamed: "Stingray! You'll be dead in 30 minutes!" Tragedy of tragedies! And me on my honeymoon!

I had been to the beach at Clearwater, Bradenton and Naples, Florida, but had never heard of a stingray. We all ran to the motel office to get help. You can imagine some of the thoughts that went through my mind. Here I was, just married five days, and now I would die. I had always wanted to go to Heaven, but certainly not at this particular time. I recall an incident when an evangelist came to Plant City with his big gospel tent. One night with several hundred people present, he asked how many were ready to go to Heaven if they should die, or Jesus return for the rapture. Many hands were raised all across the seating area. The preacher then proceeded to pull a pistol from the pulpit and then asked, "Who wants to go right now?" No hands went up. As for me, I felt Heaven could wait, if at all possible.

The motel office was empty and the children went to find either their mother or father while Junell and I waited and prayed. Presently, the owner came from down among the many rooms and observed my back. "Sea nettle," he said. "Rub some lotion on it and it will stop stinging after a few minutes!" It did! And were we ever relieved! I don't recall now, but I'm sure we gave God the glory! Anyway, a ton of anxiety was lifted and the honeymoon resumed.

We had heard of a famous religious family who traveled the country with a big tent. The principal speaker was a son, to whom I had been compared by the lady in Mobile several months earlier. They had a nightly radio broadcast on XERF, Del Rio, Texas. The station was a 50,000 watt a.m. clear channel station with the transmitter across the border in Dia Conya, Mexico. The family was also very musical. The program had hosts of listeners and supporters and was heard across much of the nation as well as parts of Mexico.

We listened to them and heard them mention their tent meeting in nearby Biloxi. We also saw posters advertising the services and decided we would attend. The tent was massive, with an announced 1,000 seats. We were there the very first service but I counted only about 200 present. They expressed their disappointment with the crowd but predicted better attendance for the nights to come. We soon had to return home and did not see whether things picked up for them.

We later read articles in the paper concerning some bad accusations regarding some members of the family but hoped they were only that –

accusations. We were learning that the news media seemed to go out of the way to magnify and misconstrue any negative thing they could about men of the cloth. The very sad part is the fact that some preachers, who are just as human as anyone, often fail to hold up the very high moral standards that are rightly expected of them. The good news is that they can be forgiven. The bad news is that their influence for God and good is greatly diminished.

Perhaps though, even back then, we were learning the lesson of putting too much trust in man. Christ is our example, the Altogether Lovely One. He alone is the Rose of Sharon and Lily of the Valley; (Song of Solomon 2:1) the Way, the Truth and the Life; (John 14:6) the Chief Corner Stone; (I Peter 2:6) the Bright and Morning Star; (Revelation 22:16) the Word of Life; (I John 1:1) and the King of Kings and Lord of Lords. (Revelation 19:16) One cannot experience a failure of any degree when their eyes are fixed continually on the One and Only begotten Son of the One and Only Almighty God. (John 3:16) The failures come when the carnal nature is allowed to dominate.

I called home to see if Mt. Zion had survived without me over the weekend. It had! My Sunday School Superintendent informed me that all Sunday School records had been broken with 229 persons present. In one way I was delighted. In another, how could this have happened and me away? It did, and I was probably being taught some more vital lessons. Apparently God and the church could fare very well without me.

After a trip to New Orleans and across the Huey P. Long Bridge above and over the mighty Mississippi river, we set our sights for home. There had been no arrangements for a full year of honeymooning, as set forth in Deuteronomy 24:5, so we determined as a result of running out of money, and duty calling in Plant City, Florida, that we'd better finish our year of honeymooning in our trailer, at Mt. Zion, and at the dairy barn! Junell had visited Mt. Zion several times during our courtship, so she was well-received and fit right in the church and radio ministry.

We had engaged the minister who performed our wedding to hold a series of revival services for us. While still serving as the District Christ's Ambassadors president he also continued to hold evangelistic meetings. During this time we worked up several musical numbers together. The meeting was well attended and recorded quite a number of converts and Holy Spirit baptisms.

Shortly after the meeting I received a call from our District Secretary. "We are pitching one of the district tents in Frostproof, Florida, in order, hopefully, to establish an Assemblies of God Church there. I have asked the District Youth Director to go and we both would like you and your wife to help. You are a good musical team together and you can alternate preaching."

We had visited the Youth Director and his wife and had sung with them when they conducted services at Southside Assembly of God in Jacksonville, Florida, after the Mt. Zion meeting. At that time they had approached us about the possibility of forming an evangelistic party. We had promised to consider it and pray about it. So now, I was telling the District Secretary we would consult the Mr. Zion folk to get an OK for the Frostproof meeting. I had quite a few relatives there, on my mother's side of the family, and I wanted to go.

With an agreement from Mt. Zion that we would return home for the Sunday services, we pulled our house trailer to a park beside Clinch Lake in Frostproof, where our co-workers had also set up. Clinch Lake was the center of rumors about a "sea-monster" that had appeared there from time to time in years past. My parents, along with several of my mother's brother's families, who had moved to Frostproof from South Georgia in the late 1920's, were aware of the spooky tales about this lake. Some had suggested that an underground stream from the Gulf of Mexico had provided a route for this supposed "Loch Ness" type monster.

Nothing of course had ever been proven about this, so it was kind of exciting to be parked there. I was born in Plant City, so I had never lived at Frostproof. But now here I was. We joined the new pastor of the promised new church, in downtown Frostproof where a lot had been secured for the tent meeting. We mowed the lot and pitched the tent. We advertised with posters around town and opened on Thursday night with 60 persons in attendance.

I had invited most of my relatives and some attended the very first service. We played and sang and our Youth Director preached the opening service. I preached the next night and the number had increased to 120. On Saturday night 600 persons were present. To assist, the pastor of Lakeland First Assembly had brought a bus-load of some 40 people from his church. The altar call response was overwhelming from the start. An uncle's family, along with many others, became charter members of the church.

From then on for four weeks, the tent was packed to capacity night after night. A family who had moved to Frostproof from Winter Haven gave three lots of choice property across the road from Lake Reedy for the new church. I don't recall the number of converts and Spirit baptisms but it was quite a lot. The church was organized with "flying colors" in a very short time. The Raburn brothers, Robert and Charles, followed us and kept the meeting going several more weeks.

I now recall several incidents of interest that transpired while we were at Frostproof the entire month of November, 1949. One was on a Sunday morning when we were heading back to Mt. Zion in Plant City for the services. Running late, we made our way on old Highway 27 through Babson Park to Highway 60 in Lake Wales. As I looked up the street (Old 60) it was wide open. And so was I! There was no one in sight! Until I heard the siren.

As I pulled over, the officer wanted to know where the fire was. I said, "Officer, I don't know about any fire. I'm on my way to church at Plant City and being late, I was trying to make up time on this wide open street. I am a minister. I am conducting a tent revival in Frostproof. I am scheduled to preach in Plant City at 11:00 a.m. This is why I was in a hurry." Having looked at my driver's license, he handed it back to me and said, "Get on your way! Drive careful!" I thanked him, but once out of his sight, I cheated on the speed limit again.

When a dear friend of mine was superintendent of Georgia, he was stopped for speeding. When the patrolman asked how fast he was going, he answered, "All it would do! I've got the prettiest wife in Georgia, I've been away from her several days and I can't wait to get back to her." This broke the highway patrolman up. He started laughing and told him he could go. I guess it pays to be honest even when you get caught speeding. Excuses like "speeding to blow-dry your car" just after you've washed it won't suffice.

One morning my co-worker came by my trailer and said, "There's a fishing demonstration going on down by the lake." We headed there to find some twelve or fifteen men watching a salesman cast a reel, "guaranteed not to backlash." After he demonstrated, even with his thumb off the spool, several of the men tried it. None was able to get the reel to backlash (which is a tangled line). But guess who did? I took the rod in my hand threw the bait very hard, wasn't even trying to make it tangle, but it did! It was such a mess it took several minutes to get the line straitened.

All the men who were getting out their billfolds to purchase this jewel, started putting them away and walking off. The sales man said to me, "You have just cost me hundreds of dollars." I apologized and offered to try it again, but was refused. We later rented a boat and motor and went bass fishing on the lake. We didn't see the sea-monster and we did catch a few bass.

We also made an observation of human logic (fishing logic). We watched boats from our landing take off across the lake to fish on the other side. We also saw boats from the other side come to our side to fish. If the grass is greener on the other side of the fence, I suppose the fish bite better on the other side of the lake. By experience, I know that there are many times they won't bite on any side of the lake. But hope of catching that big one drives the fisherman, just as hope keeps one looking for ships, most of which never come in, or of winning the lottery at odds of 14 million to one.

When my parents and my older sister and brother lived in Frostproof, Dad had a job cutting meat in a downtown grocery store. He entered a fishing contest and each morning on the way to work, would cast a top-water plug along the edge of Lake Reedy. One morning he caught a large mouth bass that weighed 12 lbs. 3 oz. He won the contest, $25.00 cash, and a year's subscription to a sports magazine. The sponsors mounted the fish and put it in the American Legion hut located on Lake Reedy.

One Saturday afternoon we were walking along a downtown street a short distance from the tent. We were dressed for church which would begin in about an hour. A lady walked up behind me and said, "Brother Holbrook, you left your dry-cleaning tag on the back of your trousers." I wondered why I had drawn some giggles as I walked along.

We noticed the theatre was closed as we passed by. Someone said it was because of the tent revival. I later learned the theatre manager had gone to the mayor and asked him to shut down the tent meeting, which he refused to do. I was told he told her that the tent revival was one the best things that had happened in Frostproof in a long time.

I visited one of my uncles, who worked in a downtown bar. He had for years been a foreman for a man who owned large groves, was a fruit processor as well as a cattleman, and who owned most of Frostproof, as well as the surrounding countryside. Upon retiring, my uncle had taken the bartending job. He had not been to the meeting but when I walked in, he greeted me heartily and told some seven or eight patrons who I was. He said, "This is my preacher nephew, my sister's son, and he is one of the ministers conducting the tent crusade. Now you stay quiet and stop drinking while he invites all of you to the meetings."

Everyone gave me their undivided attention while I made the announcement. Afterwards, with tears in his eyes, Uncle told me he had strongly felt the call to preach at an early age. "But now I'm so sorry that I failed. You see where I am at the end of my life." I told him the Lord still loved him and would forgive him. I didn't realize that the next time I saw him, he would be lying in a coffin in Ashburn, Georgia.

By the time our part of the Frostproof meeting ended, we had decided to join up with the District Youth Director and form an Evangelistic Party. He had several meetings scheduled and since this one at Frostproof had gone so well, perhaps the others would also. We submitted our resignation to Mt. Zion, giving them 30 days notice. We would join the other couple in Flint, Michigan in January, 1950. We were going to be on the road again!

Junell in front of the administration building at Emanuel College

Junell Player – Graduation Emanuel College
Franklin Springs, Georgia (May 1949)

The Bride and Groom
Junell and Ernest (June 24, 1949)

The Wedding Party – Left to Right: Joann Holbrook, Linda Vickers, Iris Blount, Linda Holbrook (Flower Girl), Louise Holbrook Green, Junell, Ernest, Ralph Holbrook, W.L. Porter, Joe Walden, Donald Waller and Rev. Tommy Waldron, Officiator

How sweet it is!

185

My beautiful bride
Junell Player Holbrook

Junell's "New House"
Linda looking on and a '49 Mercury and '46 Ford in the background

ELEVEN

THE EVANGELISTIC FIELD AGAIN

Go. . .and preach the good news to every creature. Mark 16:15

The decision to resign Mt. Zion did not go as smoothly as expected. After all, we had only been there for one year, the church was doing very well and several members did not want us to leave. This would be the first of five resignations, including the final one when we retired from pastoring. Each was very difficult, not only for us, but also for the many faithful supporters who begged us to stay.

Despite all of this, we planned to head to Michigan for a January meeting with our new co-workers. The farthest I had ever been in this direction was Franklin Springs, Georgia, and Columbia, South Carolina. I had never seen snow nor driven on icy roads.

I had traded my '46 Ford for a new '49. Junell had driven it to Mt. Enon School to play the piano for a school Christmas program. I had pulled a night shift at the dairy and had gone back to bed. She awakened me to tell me she had wrecked our new car. And here we were ready to head out to Michigan!

I said, "Well, where is it?" "It's outside," she answered. "I drove it home." I got up, grabbed my clothes, ran out, inspected it all around and saw nothing out of the ordinary. "Where?" I asked. "You were just kidding me!" She then showed me a very small dent right beside the front bumper on the left side. She had bumped another car while backing out of her parking place at the school.

I took the new Ford to where I had purchased it. They repaired it for $2.00. I'm not joking! Can you imagine today what it might cost? Probably four or five hundred dollars - after a police report, an insurance appraisal, perhaps even a court case, a fine and possibly a suspended license. I'm exaggerating some, but not much, to make a point. It's called a hyperbole, "exaggeration for effect," not meant to be taken literally. Christ used this method at different times, such as in Matthew 5:29-30 and 23:15.

Back to the car dent. Junell reminded me that I had not even asked whether or not she had been injured. It seemed, she said, that I was more concerned about the car than I was her, which seemed to be true, but wasn't really. I had not observed any "dents" in her.

To begin our trip to Flint, Michigan to join our party, we left in the wee hours and got to Dillsboro, North Carolina, the first night. That was quite a haul for one day with no interstate highways. We lodged at the Jarrett House. We never did get warm even with the radiator heat at its best and a stack of quilts. The next morning, we sat down to breakfast at a long, wide table loaded with eggs, grits, ham, bacon, sausage, butter, biscuits, jelly, orange juice and coffee. About a dozen other people were eating with us or us with them. Again, I was enjoying all those good things, many of which have long since been eliminated from my diet.

Next up, the Great Smoky Mountains! The Moultrie, Georgia pastor had told us how beautiful they were. We stopped a few times to take pictures and see the views, including the ones from Newfound Gap which sits atop the North Carolina - Tennessee line. We stopped for a coke in Gatlinburg. There was a governor's conference being held at the huge hotel and the Ford motor company had provided brand new "pink" Ford automobiles for each governor. I fell in love with the then small town of Gatlinburg and have spent many vacations there since, as well as at nearby Pigeon Forge.

After Knoxville, we continued north on Highway 441 and 25 into Kentucky. It began to be stormy and dark and the narrow, crooked roads through the Jellico Mountains became scary. Rounding a steep curve loaded with traffic including a big semi, I saw a sign which said, "Prepare to meet God!" I thought for a while just how true this might be.

We found a motel in Corbin and again had difficulty keeping warm. As Junell said, it was a good time for "scrooching" up. The next morning I ordered grits along with eggs and bacon for breakfast. The waitress said, "We don't serve grits! How about hash-browns?" I learned that grits was mostly a southern tradition.

By now the cold was really setting in. My new "49 Ford did not have a heater. "Why put a heater in a car that's going to be used only in Florida?" the salesman asked me when I had asked, as if it never got cold in Florida.

At the time of the purchase, I didn't know I would be headed for Michigan in January.

I found a Ford dealership in Berea and in about three hours, the '49 was heater-equipped for $28.00, plus $7.00 for installation. Between Lexington and Cincinnati the radio announcer repeated warnings about icy road conditions. Creeping along at 30 and 40 miles per hour I realized I was in everyone's way as they zipped past and around me. Soon, a Greyhound bus zoomed around us at breakneck speed.

In about 30 minutes, the radio gave a bulletin stating that a Greyhound bus had slid off a curve into a ravine. We looked as we progressed but never saw the accident. Perhaps it was another bus elsewhere. In heavy Cincinnati traffic a truck and a car ahead of us sideswiped. I saw what I thought was an entire fender falling off the car. It turned out to be a sheet of ice. The fender remained.

We made Toledo, Ohio, where we turned in for the night. I wasn't prepared for what greeted me when I looked out the motel window the next morning!

Snow! I don't know how much, eight or ten inches, perhaps. Everything was covered, all the cars, as well as the road into the motel. I dressed and stepped outside. I returned and told Junell we were snowbound, "I don't know for how long!" Soon I saw another man clearing the snow off his windshield and rear window. I went outside and tried to follow suit. I asked him how we would get back to the highway. I could see cars passing by out there. He said, "Just follow the clear place between the trees, and hope you don't get stuck in a hole or the ditch."

I followed his tracks out and apparently snowplows had cleared the main road. We finally reached Flint and found the address where we would stay. The folks at Riverside Assembly of God had arranged for a church family to keep us for the duration of the meeting. The wife was our co-worker's wife's sister. They were also staying there. They showed us to our bedroom and I noticed two windows were slightly open. I was freezing, so I promptly lowered them.

After dinner, when we started to bed, I noticed the windows were raised slightly again. I closed them again. The next morning I came in after breakfast and they were opened to the previous position. I lowered them and went in the living room where everyone was and asked, "Who keeps opening our bedroom windows?" "I did," our hostess stated. And I would be obliged if you would stop closing them. We keep them opened a little to help circulate the heat from the furnace. If you get cold, cover up."

Her husband laughed and took me down and showed me the basement and furnace and explained how the heat system worked best. I took a liking to him immediately. He worked at the Chevrolet body factory (Fisher, I believe) and drove a Ford. He said Ford bodies were better because he saw everyday how his plant "stretched" the metal too thin. He was glad I was driving a Ford.

He took us to the Buick assembly plant. We started where the bare frames were and walked the entire route watching workers add shock absorbers, springs, engines, transmissions, drive shafts, rear axles, bodies, steering wheels, wheels, the whole show. At the end of the line a huge barrel-type roller was situated in the floor. Each car's back wheels were put on the roller and the speed set, I recall, at 35 m.p.h. They told us it was to check for vibrations, and so forth.

Outside, we saw where cars were driven through water troughs and overhead sprinklers to check for leaks. The guide told us that they occasionally, purposely, turn a car over, and also crash them into cement barriers to check the body structure. I asked if such tests ruined the auto. "Yes," he stated. I then asked, "How about not wrecking one that you would have, and give it to me." "Yes, for me too," our tour guide chuckled.

We went through the engine manufacturing plant, watched them forge crankshafts and engine blocks, and toured another area where they were "stamping" hoods and fenders. I was amazed to see a piece of flat metal move under a huge contraption, and after it fell on the metal, a perfect hood or fender resulted. We also went through the primer and paint factory. Our host later brought me a small can of white touch up paint for my Ford.

While walking downtown one day with him, I saw my first television set. It was in a store window and looked like a 13 inch screen. The picture was very snowy, just about like this Michigan winter I was in.

Driving was something else. It had snowed, then iced over. As I slipped and slid, I wondered how people and their cars survived in such conditions. On Sunday afternoon, we went across town to hold a church service at the jail. I cautiously crept along, put on brakes to stop at a traffic light, and slid sideways right through the intersection. A car driver approaching from the right saw my dilemma, and managed to barely miss me. He slid the other way.

Another driver attempted to pass me and as he pulled by and tried to get back on our side of the street, his car completely did a 90 degree spin-around. He proceeded back toward us just as if he had planned it that way. When we arrived at the jail, the pastor's new 1950 Buick had the front bashed in. "I slid into another car," he said.

One noon, going home from the morning prayer meeting at church, I had stopped for a traffic light by a school. It was snowing, the windows were fogged up and I proceeded to go through the intersection when the light turned green. I was spinning and barely moving when I began to hear a knocking on my driver's side window. I stopped, opened the window and there stood, I know, one of the homeliest little school traffic officers I had ever seen. He was even shorter than me and had snaggled teeth.

He was raging! "Why didn't you stay stopped when I yelled at you?" he railed. "I didn't hear you," I said. "If you weren't from out of state I'd run you in," he fumed, "but since you are, I think I'll let you go." My carnal nature wanted me to get out of the car and roll him over and over in the snow. But I decided to let well enough alone, and move on.

On a Saturday, being a night we didn't have service, we went to Dearborn, near Detroit, and went through the Ford museum. What a delightful experience to see and read the history of Henry Ford, the birth of the gasoline engine and the automobile assembly lines. There were some of the earliest autos, many "Model T's," right up to the first 1949 Ford that had rolled off his assembly line.

On another day we went to Windsor, Canada, a few miles across the river from Detroit. It was like turning back the years many times over. On the way back we stopped on the elevated Ambassador Bridge over the Detroit River. Junell wanted a picture of the Detroit skyline. It was near zero, temperature wise. I had bought a scarf and felt hat, and borrowed a heavy overcoat to ward off the cold. When I stood on the running board to get the picture, the wind took my hat.

I watched it go over the railing. I ran to see it flying down, down, toward the water. The bridge was very high, and I thought I could see the hat clear the water and land in a railroad yard along the river. Everyone in the car laughed and told me to forget the hat. "There is no way it could have blown from Canada to the United States," they joked.

I crossed the bridge, turned right and worked my way back to the railroad yard. There was a gated entrance with several tracks parallel to the river.

"Your hat flew from where?" the gatekeeper asked. I motioned, "From way up there on top of the bridge." "Well go ahead and look. But watch out for the trains. You could get run over." We made our way across lines of parked railroad cars, and waited for a passing train. Up and down between cars we looked.

Finally, I crossed the last line of boxcars situated beside the river. Down the way, I saw a man taking off his cap and putting on a hat. Mine! I ran to where he was, out of breath and freezing. He had handed the hat to another worker who had now put it on his head and placed his cap in his hip pocket. Breathlessly I said, "Hey, that is my hat." One man said, "No, I found it and it didn't fit. I gave it to him. What do you mean 'it's your hat'?"

I motioned to the high bridge. "It came from there! It blew off my head while I was stopped taking a picture." With some curse words, the other man took off the hat and gave it to me. I lost the hat again on the way home from Michigan. I must have left it in a restaurant or somewhere. I did not find it the second time.

I was surprised at how well the revival services were attended. I had figured the snowy, icy weather would put a damper on the crowds, but not so. I whispered to Junell that they must have come out to see the snow. I was also delighted at how well we had been received. These "northerners" seemed to like our music, singing and preaching. One day the pastor asked me to drop by his office after the morning prayer meeting. He paid me a most uplifting compliment. "Your sincerity, your talent and your anointed messages will take you a long way. Keep up the good work." I thanked him.

In summation, the services were sort of a healing for the church which had recently had a split and lost about 100 members. For me, it was a learning process. The worship was more reserved, and instead of praying around the altar area, they went into an adjacent "prayer room." But I also observed a depth of reverence and worship which was very inspiring. The pastor told me his church folk just loved southern evangelists. All in all, it was a very pleasant experience!

Our co-evangelists had flown up for the meeting, so they rode back with us. We got 21 miles per gallon in my 1949 Ford on the return trip and he immediately traded his '48 Plymouth for a new 1950 Ford, when he returned to his home in Clewiston, Florida. He also had purchased a 25 foot

Spartan Manor Mobile home. We would travel in both cars and live in their mobile home to cut expenses.

The meetings at Norwood in Jacksonville, and in St. Pete went well, even as they had at Mt. Zion, Frostproof, Flint and Jacksonville Southside. But two very negative factors were apparent. One, the living arrangement was unsatisfactory – for all of us, and the remuneration, even at the largest churches wasn't adequate to support two families and mobile homes. So after much prayer and consideration, we decided splitting the party was our only alternative. I thought, "Oh no, I have to go through this again." So after the St. Petersburg meeting, at what is now Suncoast Cathedral, we agreed to go our separate ways. He would keep his schedule of meetings and I would arrange mine.

I found a Spartan Manor in St. Petersburg just like theirs, purchased it, and sold mine to my wife's brother. I made a few phone calls while I was working again at the dairy and soon the meetings began to materialize. I was riding our big tractor chopping palmetto and other bushes in the pasture the day before we were to leave to begin a meeting in Elba, Alabama. The palmetto patch had recently been burned, and as I crisscrossed it, a huge bunch of burned palmettos flew up in my face.

My right eye sustained quite a serious cut. It kept me awake most of the night and became very irritated the next day as we drove to Elba. We parked our Spartan behind the parsonage and beside the church. By midnight, I was in such pain Junell awakened the pastor to take me to a doctor. He got up fussing. He said, "We don't go to doctors, we trust God for healing." I said, "Listen, I trust God, too, but 'the sick need a physician' and I am sick. Just tell me where I can find a doctor and you can go back to bed."

I realized this probably wasn't a very good way to get off on the right foot for the meeting, but at the moment my right eye needed immediate attention. He finally agreed to take me across town to the doctor, griping all the way, and again reminding me of the worth of believing in prayer for healing. (During the meeting, his little six year old daughter got sick and we noticed he took her to the doctor, pronto.)

After a few bangs on the door, an old, sleepy doctor opened up. He took me into his office, which was a room in his home, and examined my eye. "Mmm," he muttered. "a pretty nasty cut on your eyeball." He cleaned it and gave me a bottle of eye drops which he said should help ease the pain. He also recommended I take aspirin, which I had already been doing. "If it is not better by tomorrow, come back and see me," he said. He charged me two dollars. I soon was asleep and the soreness left my eye in a couple of days but a big scar remained.

The meeting went well. The attendance was very good and there were numerous converts and Holy Spirit Baptisms. It was here we met the future wife of Charles Raburn, Sally Ann Wise. She and her mother were already Christians. Her dad was converted in our meeting and became a pillar in the church for many years until he passed away.

Word came to us that the Raburn Brothers were preaching at another church not too far away. Their converts numbered 600, they said. Wow! It was another of those meetings that drew hundreds of people night after night and resulted in numerous professions of faith in Christ. It is the kind of revival every evangelist longs and prays for. My Raburn cousins were experiencing another "Pelham like" attendance overflow. This was another reminder of the times I had spent with Robert and Charles on the evangelistic field. I still missed being with them.

From Elba, we went to Enterprise. What a revival meeting! Big crowds, many seekers and converts and a daily radio program each morning before daylight, broadcast from the parsonage living room, next door to the church. One morning, still half asleep, Junell and I proceeded to sing the song titled, "Heaven Bound Train." She would jerk the accordion and I would plunk the guitar to sound like a "choo-choo" train taking off. Then, at the end, we would chug to a stop and she would squeal the brake sound on the high notes of the accordion. A good drawing card, before television came along.

On one particular morning, for some reason, I could not find the proper pitch. As far as I know, this was the first and last time this ever happened to me. We stopped and tried to start again. Same results. Finally, the third time we made it. I told the early morning radio audience that I was very sorry about the "train-wreck."

Among our newfound friends at Enterprise was a man who played his violin (fiddle) nightly in the song service. But he was not a Christian. He had played at length with a country music singer and songwriter who later became very famous! He took a liking to us, but would make no move toward the Lord. We began praying he would be converted.

One night as I was giving the invitation, I noticed his head bowed. I had never seen him do this before, even when we asked people to bow their heads for prayer. So I said to myself, "This is the night for him to come forward." I gently pleaded and waited. He did not respond. I felt impressed to go back and whisper an invitation personally. As I laid my hand on his shoulder, he almost jumped out of his seat. He had been asleep. Needless to say, he wasn't in any mood to come forward. You can imagine how I felt.

We preached three meetings at Enterprise, all within a period of about two years, but to my knowledge, he never did respond. The pastor told me later that he had passed away, at an early age. One handsome young photographer who had married a girl from the church, and had also made it well financially, came forward one night. He surrendered to Christ and became so overjoyed that he jumped up from the altar and exclaimed, "Let's all shout!" He, all of us, and the angels of heaven certainly did have something to shout about. (Luke 15:10)

I went with the pastor to the hospital to see a man who was an alcoholic. Not being able to afford to buy liquor, he drank a whole bottle of rubbing alcohol. He died. Another time we went to Kilby prison in Montgomery, Alabama, to death row, where a man who used to attend the Enterprise church was waiting to die. He had gotten into an argument with a small grocery store owner over a small amount of money, hurried home, came back with a shotgun and killed the grocer in cold-blooded murder.

At Kilby, I was shocked at how many sets of steel bar doors we went through to get to where the man was. I counted eleven. I remember thinking how difficult it would be to try to get out of there without the cooperation of the prison guards or the help of an angel of the Lord. (Acts 5:19 and 12:5-12) We finally reached death row. Every man in every cell on each side was condemned to die. I tried to study the looks on their faces as I passed by. Their countenances were such as gave me a very deep, scary, hurting feeling within.

When we arrived at the intended cell, we confronted the man who was scheduled to die in a few days. Pastor dealt with him about his soul. He was "as good as anyone," he said. Was he remorseful over the killing? "Not one bit. If I had it to do over, I would kill him again." I couldn't believe what I was hearing. Here is a man who killed a man over less than three dollars, is scheduled to be electrocuted in a short time and isn't repentant, not in the least. He insisted that the Governor of Alabama would commute his death sentence. He was right. We read in the newspaper that the day before he was scheduled to die, the governor spared his life.

The pastor was an avid fisherman, as was I. One day we fished up the Choctawhatchee River and then turned up a slough. After a while we heard something that kept splashing the water ahead of us. We rounded a corner to discover a big bass jumping out of the water, again and again. It had been hooked on a trotline and was furiously battling to get free. We fished on up the slough to a dead end and turned to go back to the river.

When we passed the trotline, the bass was still jumping. Pastor said, "There is no telling when whoever set this trotline will return. It was probably set for catfish anyway, so before the fish gets free, why don't we take it with us?" We? He took it. It weighed about six pounds. When we got home, his wife cleaned it and put it in the freezer.

About two years later, when we were conducting a meeting at First Assembly of God in Plant City, where this pastor had become their pastor, they invited us to dinner one evening before the service. Yes, we had fish. Bass! And, yes, it was the one he brought from that slough in Alabama. It was delicious!

The first time I had ever gone through Enterprise, I noticed a statue of something in the center of the street downtown. While riding with the pastor to the hospital, we passed it again. I asked what it was. A "boll weevil" he answered. "The boll weevil infestation destroyed the cotton crops, causing the farmers to turn to the highly lucrative peanut crops. Therefore, a tribute to the boll weevil!" I thought, "Well, good can come out of the bad." (Romans 8:28)

One day the pastor's son asked if I'd like to go hunting with him and a couple of other fellas. "Sure," I responded. With borrowed shotguns we headed for the "happy hunting-grounds." "We'll hunt for doves," one of the men said. There were no doves in the first location, so we headed through a very thick area of trees, bushes and underbrush toward another place. We had to walk single-file most of the way through. I brought up the rear and found myself facing the pastor's son's shotgun barrels several times.

Three times I asked him to point the gun upwards, not horizontally. "No problem," he said. "I've got the safety on." After several hours of no dove or anything else, we spotted a crow sitting atop a big tree. "Let me shoot it," he exclaimed. "OK," said one of the guys, "shoot away." He clicked the safety and we braced for the blast. He pulled the trigger – and nothing happened. Then, he clicked the safety back to the position it was while pointed at me numerous times in the thicket, and "blam!" I nearly fainted. When I regained my composure I was once again grateful for a guardian angel!

Ernest and Junell and their musical instruments
(Traveling evangelists)

199

REVIVAL
NOW IN PROGRESS

·DON'T FAIL TO HEAR

Waldron-Holbrook Evangelistic Party

at the

ASSEMBLY OF GOD TENT

In the Heart of Frostproof

SOME OF THE FEATURES OF THE SERVICES:

- Rev. and Mrs. Waldron playing the Accordion, electrical Hawaiian and Spanish Guitars.

- Rev. and Mrs. Holbrook playing the Accordion. Spanish and Hawaiian Guitars, also Bass Fiddle.

- Solos, Duets and Trios will comprise the Special Singing.

- Hear the Old Time Gospel in the New Time Way!

SERVICE TIME 7:30 P. M.

FIRST SERVICE. WEDNESDAY, OCTOBER 19th

A Cordial Welcome is Extended To All

ASSEMBLY OF GOD

WALDRON-HOLBROOK
Evangelistic Party

DYNAMIC
PREACHING
☆
SOLOS
DUETS
TRIOS
QUARTETTES
☆
Combinations
of
Seven
Musical
Instruments

SERVICES NIGHTLY 7:30 Except Saturday

RIVERSIDE TABERNACLE

2215 LEWIS STREET AT MABEL AVENUE

Over the Air Daily 10:30 A. M. WBBC Tuesday Through Friday

M. A. JOLLAY, Pastor

TWELVE

HIGHLIGHTS OF EVANGELISTIC TRAVELS AND JACKSONVILLE, FLORIDA

I must preach the kingdom of God to other cities also... Luke 4:43

As word spread concerning our good meetings at Elba and Enterprise, Alabama, invitations began to come from numerous places. From April, 1950, until the spring of 1952, after Elba and Enterprise, we preached revival meetings in the Georgia cities of Columbus, Albany, Thomasville, Moultrie, Pelham and Bainbridge.

In Alabama, we returned twice more to Enterprise, and to Newton, Dothan and Ashford. In Florida we co-pastored at Jacksonville, Kings Highway Tabernacle, conducted meetings at Vero Beach, Arcadia, Clearwater, Niceville, Plant City First Assembly, Milligan, Marianna, Panama City, Bonifay, Dunnellon, Long Beach, Frostproof and Pace.

We also conducted services in Stamping Ground, Kentucky. We went with some special friends to Oneonta, Alabama, to explore the possibilities of establishing an Assemblies of God Church there.

We tried to schedule our meetings with sufficient time off at least every few weeks. During such times we always looked forward to spending days at home where we could supplement our income by working at the dairy. It also afforded us the opportunity to preach locally at our home church, fellowship meetings and youth rallies.

Too, it presented many occasions to go fishing with my dad, brother, sisters, the Raburn brothers and others. Our favorite spots were: the Hillsborough River, Camp Mack on the Kissimmee River (where we had access to Lakes Hatchineha and Kissimmee), and Lakes Rosalie and Tiger and the connecting creeks and canals.

203

"R & R" (rest and relaxation) were at their best as was the fellowship with loved ones. Fishing, as we did it, was long hours and hard work! We liked to engage in it from daybreak until dark. Solomon said in Ecclesiastes 9:10, "Whatever your hand finds to do, do it with all your might," which we did, whether it was preaching the Gospel, milking cows or fishing. We even fished some at night in the phosphate pits at Hopewell.

Our first love, of course, was our work for the Lord. The basic goals were: (1) to preach the Gospel of Christ whenever, wherever and to whomever possible; (2) to win every person possible to Christ Jesus; (3) to re-establish those who had drifted from Christ and the Church; (4) to urge all believers to seek to be baptized with the Holy Spirit in order to be better witnesses for Christ, (Acts 1:8); (5) to baptize new believers in water as an outward witness of their conversion to Christ; (6) to get converts established in a church home for the benefit of Christian fellowship, spiritual and moral growth, and the development of their talents to be used for Christ; and (7) to encourage pastors and laity to intense dedication and faithfulness to God's work, both at home and abroad.

We preached and taught that a life of "holiness unto the Lord" could be achieved by a person being born again on the inside (from above) and that Holy Spirit power was available to those who sought it. We stressed regular Bible study, daily prayer and obedience to God's word. We encouraged a life full of good, Godly works adorned by the fruit of the Spirit. (Galatians 5:22-23) We also taught that the acts of the sinful human nature were to be crucified and avoided. (Galatians 5:19-21) We emphasized that all these things were possible by living and walking daily in the Spirit of God. (Romans 8:9 and Galatians 5:16)

Once, as we journeyed from Enterprise, Alabama, to Albany, Georgia, we encountered a very rough and bumpy road somewhere between Blakely and Albany. Upon our arrival, I opened the door to our mobile home to discover several pieces of what were once dishes, glasses, etc. The cabinet doors were all opened; pots, pans, furniture and about everything was scattered, and whatever could be damaged, was!

While we were holding services at Albany, now in a beautiful cement block building, the startling news came about the war in Korea and the U.S. involvement there. It was also between services, prayer and sermon preparation that I secured our mobile home cabinet doors and made arrangements to otherwise protect against future bouncy roads. Junell and

I also sang and I preached on the radio while at Albany. We also were able to fellowship with our relatives there once again. Plus we always enjoyed the pastors.

The Pelham meeting followed. The cement block building was now completed. The services went well, but there was nowhere near the attendance of the earlier tent revival. During this meeting, the pastor's wife and Junell spent many hours crocheting. The pastor and I would find crochet needles everywhere around the house; especially on the couch and other living room chairs. We kept "warning" them, "One of these days somebody is going to sit down on a needle." It happened! It was to their then 14 year-old son.

He came running into the living room, plopped down on the couch and came up yelling in pain and grasping his backside. We tried to remove the needle but couldn't. The small hook on the end was firmly embedded in the flesh.

Off to the doctor's office we went. Upon failing to extricate the needle, the doctor administered a shot for pain, cut the trousers around the needle and then removed them. After a few minutes, he then pulled the crochet needle out and we were homeward bound. It was really funny, later. To everyone but the young victim!

Pelham had a thread mill. One of the congregants told me he would get permission for me to fish in a small lake that was enclosed by a high fence which surrounded the mill and the lake. He said there were supposed to be fish in the lake but he knew of no one who had ever caught any. One afternoon, I caught three bass, one weighing about three to four pounds. I became known as "the fishing preacher," at Pelham after that.

One day word came in a letter from home that Mt. Zion was open again for a new pastor. This Pelham pastor quickly told his wife, "Pray, while I pack." We all laughed. I was surprised the pastorate would come open so soon after we had left. Truth is, it wouldn't be all that long until it would be open even again.

On a later visit to Pelham, Robert and Merle Raburn with young Terry stopped by. When I had first seen Terry as a very small baby, Robert had said, I wouldn't take a million dollars for him, and wouldn't give two cents for another just like him." On that occasion, Terry grinned his little "sideways" grin at me. I was later told that at his baby stage, it was probably gas that produced the smile, rather than my face, but he still has that cute "sideways" grin.

Terry was walking now and had picked up some small object and was beating it against the front screen door. A middle-aged bachelor evangelist was preaching a revival meeting for the Pelham church and was staying with the pastor. Observing little Terry hitting the screen, he ran over, grabbed the object and said loud enough for Robert and me to hear, "It looks like some people could control their destructive children."

Robert's response was quick and to the point: "Yes, and it takes someone who has never had any children to tell you how!" I laughed as the evangelist sulked to his room. There was little or no conversation from him as we ate the noontime meal. But Robert and Merle, Junell and I, and these dear ones had plenty to share with each other.

For one of our next meetings, we went to Panama City, Florida, to the Dirego Park Assembly. The meeting boomed from the outset. A man who had long been an alcoholic had recently been converted and he set out to win other men, from among his drinking buddies, to Christ. The timing was perfect and as a result, some 16 men professed Christ as their Savior during the three week meeting.

The former alcoholic told us that just before his conversion he had gotten so drunk he passed out. When he came to, he was out in the woods in a swampy area and his automobile was no where in sight. After a long walk, he found a road, caught a ride and then hired an airplane to fly over the area until he found his car. He said that incident so shook him up he realized it was time to turn his life around. Efforts before had failed, but this time he turned to Christ and had a genuine change of heart and lifestyle.

One man, of those who were converted in the meeting, told us he had been a bootlegger for many years. The revenuers had pulled several raids and searches on his some 40 acres. "But," he said, "They never once looked in my chicken coop!" After his conversion he, himself, destroyed the still and invited his former customers to come to the revival meeting with him.

Continuously, there was a steady stream of men converts, each giving testimony of sins forgiven and a new life in Christ Jesus. As a result of so many men converts, there were also many ladies and young people who made professions of faith in Christ. We could hardly wait from night to night to see what the response to the invitations might be. As word got out about the unusualness of the meetings, visitors came from all around, filling the big sanctuary time and again. The intensity of the altar services was conducive to many being baptized in the Holy Spirit. The meetings stand out as some of the most successful we ever conducted.

It was also in this meeting that we met a family who would become long-time close friends. He was a great fresh-water bass fisherman and gave me several new pointers on bass fishing. When they later visited our meeting at Milligan, their then four year-old son asked, "Daddy, are we going to spend the night in this school bus?" He was referring to our Spartan Manor mobile home.

He worked in the paper mill and on his days off, he would set up a trip somewhere on a river or creek. We fished and picnicked with them and some of our relatives on a clear creek near Panama City. We "loaded" the boat with shell crackers and bluegill, and just as we headed back to the picnic area where the girls were, three monumental things happened. First, it started raining! More like a day of Noah's flood. Next, the outboard motor wouldn't start. Third, our relative said, "Hand me the oar and I'll 'skull' us in". About the third "skull" we heard a loud crack. The oar had broken in half. And yes, you can come in on a half oar. It just takes longer! Much longer! But there was no way we could have been "wetter!"

That wasn't the first or last time I had my "parade" rained on! But I don't recall ever being more miserable. Other fishing trips were at Holmes Creek near Vernon, and the Choctawhatchee River. My new friend was one of only a few fishermen I couldn't equal or "out fish." I was with him when he caught a seven pound bass in Crestview, and a ten pounder in the Hillsborough River.

Once I was driving back from Marianna to Panama City when all of a sudden I felt I was being bombarded by bricks. A covey of quail had hit me head on. One broke my spotlight. I loved that 1949 white Ford until I saw the pastor's brother in his 1950 Mercury. He came to our meeting and I thought that was one of the most beautiful automobiles I had ever seen. I confess I coveted that car. I felt I had to have one just like it. The carnal nature was alive and well!

When we arrived home for a few days rest, we discovered that Dad, Mom and my younger sisters Joann and Linda had been involved in an automobile accident. They had turned off the highway into the driveway of their home, and a drunken man driving behind them hit them. When they turned, he thought the road curved and he crashed into them some forty to fifty feet into their yard. Fortunately, none of them were seriously injured, but their 1948 Ford was totaled. Dad had a new car sitting in the driveway. Yes, it was a new Mercury, just like the one I had already coveted.

Being home a short time and having the privilege of driving the new Mercury made things worse. I was making car and trailer payments, and those, along with the expenses of traveling, were consuming everything we were taking in financially. Trading cars should have been on the very bottom of my "want" list and totally off my "needs" list.

But why does it drive and ride so much better? Why is the design more beautiful? It does have more horse power and that would help in the pulling of my Spartan. Ah yes! Now I have a legitimate excuse, I mean reason, to trade for one. Dad wasn't very excited about it. After all, if I ran into financial difficulty, which I frequently did, he knew he would be the one that would have to bail me out. So I would keep my '49 Ford. For now! Surely I would figure a way soon.

Robert and Merle Raburn had decided to settle down in Thomasville, Georgia, to start a new church there. With Georgia District approval, plus the loan of a District-owned tent, Robert had contacted me to help hold his opening services. We had everything ready and started pursuing a location for the tent meeting. First of all, the city frowned on tent meetings and had passed an ordinance banning any inside the city limits.

Next, our efforts to find a suitable place as close to the city limits as possible proved vain. We searched for several days with no results. It seemed our prayers were going no higher than the ceiling or treetops. One morning while we were eating breakfast Robert said, "Let's back off today and go fishing. I know where there is a beautiful lake called Miccosukee, just across the Florida State line about 20 miles or so south of here." So, we went.

The lake normally is very big, covering several hundred acres. It stretched several miles from one end to the other and was fairly wide. Shock of shocks! When we arrived, the lake was dry, all except about three or four acres or so at one end. The boat landing was high and dry, several feet above the very low water level. The owner of the boat rentals and docking area came out and explained to us what had happened.

"Every few years, all the water runs out of the lake through a huge hole at this deepest end of the lake," he said. "It'll come back, soon, I hope. Until then, we are closed." We could see fish swarming and churning all across what was left of the lake, so we asked him for a boat. The owner agreed, provided we pull it to the water. "No charge," he said. Before we launched, I threw an artificial lure (Paw-Paw), and caught about a two pound bass with the first cast.

From that, we figured we might catch a haul similar to the one Peter, Andrew, James and John did when Jesus told them, "Put out into deep water, and let down the nets for a catch." (Luke 5:4-7, NIV) That never happened, but we did catch about twenty bass, some weighing up to four pounds. We went home, cleaned them and had a sumptuous fish fry with all the trimmings, including "hush puppies." We went to sleep on probably a "too-full" stomach, got up the next day and found a beautiful lot adjacent to the Thomasville city limits upon which to pitch the tent.

For several nights we sang and preached, the crowds increased, and as a result of the converts to Christ, Robert was able to establish the First Assembly of God of Thomasville, Georgia. It was a most satisfying and rewarding experience.

One of our next meetings was in Jacksonville, Florida, at Kings Highway Tabernacle. It was a new work located on Kings Highway (Highway #1) on the west/northwest side of the city. The pastor had pastored First Assembly there some years earlier. He then went to Pleasant Grove at Durant, Florida, and now had returned to pioneer a new church. The effort had the support of some folks from Lakeland, Florida, with whom we would become acquainted a short time later.

The church took to our music, singing, and preaching readily, and a revival spirit became prevalent. Night after night the crowds grew and the invitation responses were very good. After three weeks we were scheduled to be elsewhere, but the Pastor insisted we continue on. Soon, he implored us to cancel our entire future schedule and remain indefinitely with him. We decided we would, after much mind-searching and prayer.

He officially named me as youth minister and associate pastor. I would be involved in all the church ministries including the building program and radio ministry, in which I was becoming more and more interested. He would receive an offering once each week for my support, as well as furnish parking for our trailer, all utilities and even groceries. It seemed like a wonderful opportunity to learn and grow under a successful pastor that had also previously served as a District Youth Director and Assistant Superintendent.

The church seemed to have great potential. Several things were happening that were very encouraging. In addition to new converts being added almost every service, a city-wide, Tulsa-based tent crusade resulted in quite a few more coming.

The Tabernacle was in its early stage of construction. The Lakeland support was a jump-start sufficient to purchase the property and "hull in" the building. The walls were up, the roof completed, the windows installed, the huge, high platform roughed in, restrooms completed and other plumbing and electrical items in place. The floor consisted of white sand, seated with numerous old pews adequate to accommodate several hundred people. The overall layout would eventually include church offices, a youth auditorium, several Sunday School rooms and a large foyer.

One night during the church service, a lady had put her small child down to play in the sand. A new family that was visiting was seated right in front of them. From what they had heard about Pentecostals, the new family was somewhat uptight about what might happen in such a service. When the baby crawled forward under the pew and grabbed the visiting lady's ankle, she jumped up, screaming at the top of her voice, drawing the attention of everyone else present. She was doubly embarrassed, having made more noise than anyone else, as well as making a spectacle of herself.

One night in the altar service I knelt beside a new friend, a young man who had come from another Pentecostal church. He had been seeking to be baptized with the Holy Spirit and as I prayed thusly, he stopped me. He informed me that he had to backtrack and re-seek sanctification. "Why?" I asked. "You told me you had already been 'sanctified'." He answered, "Yes, I had, but today I lost it. I drive a city bus. I got into a fight with a passenger and had to throw him off the bus."

The pastor's family was one, big, exciting group. There were ten children, and nothing would satisfy them but for me to park the mobile home right next door to their house and eat every meal with them. They bought groceries every day for that day only, reminding me of Israel and the daily manna. A congregant owned a grocery store and dairy nearby so either Pastor or his wife went daily to bring home the vitals. To say the very least, there was never a dull moment with children ranging in age from under a year to 18.

The Pastor and his wife went to Key West to visit her folks, leaving us to 'baby-sit." We slept in their master bedroom with their youngest son in the baby crib. I was abruptly awakened at daybreak by a loud crashing sound. He had awakened and had thrown his glass suck-bottle across the room against the wall. Apparently it was his signal for: "Time to rise and shine! Feed me!"

One frosty morning we were eating breakfast after the children had gone to school. Junell sent me to our trailer to get something. I hurried to beat the chill and turned too abruptly on the icy back porch. I landed flat on my back out in the yard, breathless. Upon recovery, I sat up and looked about to see if anyone saw me. Then I slowly arose to see what might be broken. Thankfully, nothing except my pride, once again.

One day we were working at church and sent Pastor's brother and another man to pick up a piano someone had donated to the church. They took a flat-bed semi-trailer and soon returned. As they drove up, I saw the truck-bed empty and asked, "Where is the piano?" "On the trailer – can't you see?" was the answer. I asked, "Where?" He looked and said to the driver, "Oh my goodness. I told you not to take that corner too fast." Sure enough we went and found the big old upright at the corner where they said, lying flat in a mud-puddle! We reloaded, cleaned it up, and amazingly it was still playable and in tune.

I had quite a bit in common with this pastor. He had once lived where we now had the dairy. He later lived in a small shack behind my grandfather's house and worked in strawberries. He could make your "skin crawl" and your hair almost "stand on end" as he told stories of his upbringing. Once when his father and grandfather were fighting at the Hillsborough-Polk County line, he stepped in, grabbed the knife blade and broke it off, apparently saving his father's life. His grandfather kept stabbing his father with the broken blade, but fortunately, it wasn't long enough to penetrate deep enough for serious injuries.

Pastor's stepmother despised him. One morning, he was sent to work for my granddad Holbrook, some ten miles away, without any breakfast or lunch. After work and running home the ten miles, he asked for some supper. When she refused, he grabbed a metal flashlight and almost beat her to death. When his dad came home, he tried to attack him, but he ran away into the night. This is when he began to stay in the shack at my grandfather's.

Earlier, because his father was a fugitive from justice, they had lived in the Everglades west of Lake Okeechobee. They survived among snakes, alligators, mosquitoes, panthers and wild hogs. Walking out to get supplies or to go to school, they often had to wade in waste deep water.

His other grandfather also lived quite some time in the Glades near Arcadia. He had fled from the law after having killed a man in a gunfight. He would, on occasions, ride his horse into Arcadia for supplies and no lawman would confront him. He would ride his horse right into the bar and order whiskey. Once, when they refused to serve him on horseback, he shot up the ceiling. Another time his horse balked at crossing the Peace River just west of town. He ordered a young man from a family camping nearby to lead his horse across the river. The boy tried – with no success – and he shot the boy dead on the spot. He stuck his spurs deep into the horse's flanks and the horse lunged into the river and across. He was never brought to justice.

From such a background and upbringing, this pastor, as a teenage boy, was invited and taken to revival services at old Mt. Zion by my grandfather. He was gloriously saved and baptized in the Holy Spirit. They sang the chorus at church, "I'm grazing." He thought they were saying, "I'm crazy." So for several days he worked in the fields and sang, "I'm crazy." He said, "I was, really! Crazy to love and serve the Lord Jesus Christ."

He soon surrendered to the call to preach the Gospel. With a haphazard eighth grade education, he would read and study the Bible for hours by lamplight. His preaching became powerful, anointed and effective. He and his brother hitchhiked to Key West to preach. This is where he met his future wife. On the return trip, hitchhiking back through the keys, they spent the night at Marathon with several hundred Civilian Conservation Corps workers. They held a church service, sang and preached and nearly all the men made a confession of faith in Jesus Christ.

A few days later, an unpredicted major hurricane, hit Marathon and hundreds of men drowned. What a consolation to these young men that they had had the opportunity to share Christ Jesus with them. And it was this pastor who suggested that I someday build a church at the Hillsborough-Polk County line between Lakeland and Plant City, Florida.

During the six months we were at Jacksonville, we would slip off to visit our folks at Lakeland and Lithia. About once a month, we would leave after the Sunday evening services. I still enjoyed driving at night. It took about four hours for the trip and almost every time we would be passed up by a train headed south around Hawthorne. The railroad tracks paralleled Highway 301.

One Sunday night, while Junell was asleep, I decided to see just how fast that train was going. I kept up with it until I reached 95 miles per hour! That was all the '49 would do, but the train moved away. I guess they don't have railroad patrols like they do for the Highway. Someone later told me, when referring to my 95 miles per hour speed, that the little '49 Ford's road weight was about 15 pounds at that speed. They added, "You could be lying flat in the road and be run over at that speed, and it wouldn't hurt you." I wondered who would be foolish enough to try. Just about as senseless as driving 95 miles per hour, I suppose.

While returning from a preaching engagement, Pastor was seated on the airplane with the president of the Gibson-National Music Company. The president granted him an "at-home" agency allowing a 40% discount for instruments for friends and church-folk. I purchased a new National guitar, amplifier and a new Scandalli accordion for Junell. I also helped several others purchase the discounted instruments. However, after a short time, this all stopped. Somehow the Gibson dealers learned of it, complained, and that ended that.

The instruments were shipped by freight. We would pick them up at the Jacksonville train depot and pay cash for the shipping costs. Some weeks later, we were summoned to the depot and asked if we had paid cash for the freight fees. We confirmed we had and produced our receipts. This money, plus other payments by cash, had come up missing. The signatures on the receipts were fake. We were asked if the same person had waited on us each time. Again, we said yes! We were taken on a tour of the depot to try to spot the agent. After viewing eleven men, we could not identify the one that had waited on us. "One of them had to be the one," they told us.

Others who had paid cash had also failed to recognize him. He kept changing his appearance and thus fooled us. But the company set a trap for him, caught him pocketing money, arrested him and fired him. A judge ordered him to repay all the money, plus he was given some jail time.

As the months passed in Jacksonville, I began to get an itchy feeling for the road again. Things were leveling off somewhat at church and the daily routine was becoming sort of boring. Besides, Pastor's philosophy of pastoring wasn't the same as mine. When I suggested various programs I wanted to pursue, he wasn't too excited about them. When I told him I wanted to evangelize again, he didn't take to that either. But soon I insisted and started making contacts for future revival meetings.

In the meantime, on one of my trips home, I finally traded for the car of my dreams, a new Mercury. No, it wasn't a 1949 or 1950, but a 1951. I didn't care for the 1951 design as much as I had the two previous year models but it was a beautiful, medium blue, four-door sedan. I even had a heavy-duty trailer hitch installed with overload springs for Spartan-Manor towing, just in case. And the payments were only a little more than those on my '49 Ford.

It took more dialogue with the Pastor, but observing my unrest, he finally reluctantly agreed to let us go. Meanwhile, I had been contacting pastors with whom I had cancelled previously scheduled meetings and one of the first I rescheduled was at Bonifay First Assembly of God. We arrived as planned and when we drove up he came out admiring our new Mercury and shiny Spartan Manor Mobile home. Pastor exclaimed: "My, I'm being honored by wealthy evangelists. This is one the nicest rigs I've ever seen. If I had an outfit like this, I would go back on the evangelistic field myself."

In self-defense, I let him know the liabilities: car and trailer payments, plus everything else involved in traveling. The meetings were well-attended and the congregants responsive to our music, singing and preaching. It seemed good to be back "in the old swing of things," the evangelistic ministry. And how wonderful it was to see the altars filled with "seekers."

We were invited to an early morning breakfast at the Pastor's house next door to where we had parked and hooked up our mobile home. While we were eating, I noticed the pastor's wife's face turn sideways and down, her eyes were moving extremely to one side and she began foaming at the mouth. I thought she was dying. Pastor jumped up, started talking to her, grabbed a washcloth and began washing her face. He led her to the bedroom and soon returned, explaining that she had had an epileptic seizure. "She had neglected her medicine again and this is what always happens," he said. I was pretty unnerved.

One evening just before service, the pastor's daughter, who lived at Pace, Florida, (near Pensacola) called, begging her dad to come get her. She had had an altercation with her husband and wanted her dad to drive over and get her and her baby and bring them back with him to Bonifay. His car was very old and questionable for the trip, some 100 miles one way, so I offered to take him as soon as the night meeting was over. He agreed and soon he, Junell and I were on our way. We made the trip in about two and one-half hours, picked up the daughter and grandchild and started back, when it happened!

The new 1951 Mercury died. Dead! It refused to crank. It was now about midnight and I went to a house nearby where an outside light was burning. After several knocks on the door, a light came on inside and a sleepy man opened up. "May I use your phone?" I inquired. "I am stranded and need a wrecker to pull us into town." "Well," he said, "I am sort of a mechanic. Let me get dressed and I'll see if I can get you started." He closed the door while I stood waiting and freezing!

Finally, he came out with a toolbox and flashlight and we raised the hood. He asked me to try starting it again. No luck. He checked a spark plug wire. "It's getting no fire," he said. I insisted that since it was so cold, we try to get a wrecker so we could go into town and get a room for the night. "Let me try some more," he said. I determined that the reason why he seemed so warm when I was so cold was the fact that he kept nipping at the bottle in his back pocket. The next nip was accompanied by his generous offer to let me nip also. I was so cold I could have accepted his offer but my "teetotaler" commitment prevailed.

His efforts continued about an hour. "The carburetor is putting gas to the plugs, but there is no spark," he said. "Listen," I said. "I am so cold I can't keep this up. Please let me call somebody." Pastor said, "The girls are very cold, so I am going to walk back to the Pace pastor's house for help. It's only a few hundred yards." Away he went while my now inebriated, would-be mechanic said, "Let me try one more thing." Oh no! Yes!

What a blessed relief when Pastor and the Pace Pastor drove up and took us back to his warm house. He gave Junell and me the "guest" bedroom. I eventually dozed off as the chill and trembling subsided in my body. We were awakened to a hot breakfast, soon got towed to the Ford place in Milton, Florida, and waited for them to open. We offered to pay the kind pastor, who refused, said he was glad he could help out and invited us to hold evangelistic services for him a little later.

The Ford place took us right in, immediately replaced a $2.25 condenser in the distributor, and presented me with a bill for $7.25 which included $5.00 for labor. I presented my warranty from the Ford Motor Company, which they refused. The car had less than 1,000 miles on it but they said the amount was too trivial to fool with. I paid, got the receipt and before noon we were back in Bonifay.

The Enterprise, Alabama pastor had contacted me and asked me to drive up to Enterprise to schedule another meeting with him. It was only about 40 miles from Bonifay, so one day we went. I began to notice a vibration in my new car and thought I could detect a faint knocking in the motor. On the way back, my concerns were reaffirmed and once back in Bonifay, I discovered I was two quarts low on oil. On the way to our next meeting a skip developed in the engine so I stopped at the Ford place in Madison, Florida. They did some sort of repairs and the bill was about $17.00. They too, refused to accept my warranty.

The next trip home I went to the Lincoln-Mercury place for service and complaints about the excessive use of oil, plus the vibration and strange sounds in the engine. While they were dealing with this, I asked why the Ford dealerships in Milton and Madison wouldn't accept my warranty. The sales manager "blew his top." "Give me those two receipts and I'll see you get refunded," he said. The next time I was in for service (and more complaints); he presented me with two checks, one from Milton and the other from Madison. "They just didn't want to fool with the paperwork for such a small amount," he said, "but I reported it to the Ford Motor Company." $24.25 was worth a lot more back then especially to a young, struggling evangelist with too many expenses.

The service manager insisted that the "break-in" period was longer for some vehicles, so "be patient and soon things will smooth out for you and the oil consumption will stop," he said. But it didn't and they didn't. As the days passed and the miles mounted up, my displeasure mounted up with them.

Once when I brought the "lemon" in for service and hopefully for repairs, the Mercury place asked me to leave it for two or three days so they could give it the "once-over." I was delighted but I insisted I would have to have a car to drive. The service manager went inside and conferred with the general manager. I guess they knew I was near total exasperation with the car. Anyway, out came the service manager with a set of car keys and pointed to a new Lincoln. Wow!

I was shocked but drove away in a brand new black four-door luxury automobile. That evening we were involved in a wedding at Lithia where Junell and I had been married several months earlier. After the reception we were preparing to go back to the church. My wife's father asked if he might drive the Lincoln. Just as we pulled into the parsonage yard, over came the

216

newlyweds, asking us to drive them away from the usual "go overboard" wedding pranksters. I told them to hop in, expecting to take the steering wheel myself. Instead, Rev. Player roared away as they got in and took us on a whirlwind ride down the back roads around Lithia, Balm, Picnic and Fort Lonesome, with three or four cars in hot pursuit.

I was sitting up front with Brother Player. Junell, her mother and the newly-weds were in the back seat. "Go faster!" the new groom said. "They are gaining on us." I had never seen Rev. Player drive over 50 miles per hour at most and usually around 35 or 40. I glanced at the speedometer of the borrowed Lincoln and we were sitting flat on 100 miles per hour. I could see the newspaper headlines: "TWO MINISTERS AND THEIR WIVES, ALONG WITH TWO NEWLYWEDS, KILLED IN MAD WEDDING NIGHT CHASE! IN BORROWED NEW LINCOLN!"

All the while, I was begging to drive. Our wives in the back seat were begging for us to slow down! The new husband kept saying, "Speed up!" We finally lost some of the car chasers but one stayed on our back bumper. Later, thankfully, the chase stopped. Whew! What a relief from a wild ride. Back at the parsonage, we discovered the final auto pursuing us was the bride's brother. He was driving the real "get away" car and was trying to stop us so he could carry the bride and groom to "safety."

When I returned the Lincoln a few days later, I wondered if they would have any way of knowing what all it had gone through. I could imagine getting a call from them asking if I had burned up a Lincoln motor, like I had burned up a Mercury motor. The call never came, for which I was grateful.

When I picked up my 1951 Mercury, they informed me that they had overhauled the engine. This involved "no charges" and would solve all my problems, oil consumption, engine knocking, and vibration, whatever. I would have to observe another "break-in" period since the motor was "like-new." But in reality it was "like-old," with all the same problems continuing as before. What I had coveted so strongly had turned into a "nightmare."

One of our next meetings was at Vero Beach, Florida. Vero, located on the central east coast of Florida, is situated on the Indian River, across which lies the sandy-white beach along the Atlantic Ocean. This was our first time to be this close to the Florida Atlantic beaches which we found breathtakingly beautiful!

One thing I was steadily beginning to realize was the fact I was not drawing the crowds I had previously. They were considerably less, most of the time, than when I traveled single, or with the single Raburn brothers, or even in the later Evangelistic Party. I surely felt I was growing in the grace and knowledge of the Lord and thought that the preaching, music and singing with Junell was as good as ever. Still, with fewer people, the meeting went extremely well. We were able to record several solid converts to Christ.

The pastor here worked as a part time carpenter and painter to supplement his income, since the church was unable to give him full support. The sanctuary and Sunday School annex (two stories) were beautiful structures but they also required a considerable monthly payment.

Pastor's recreation was fishing. The speckled trout were biting (sometimes) at the Indian River where the bridge and road led to the beaches. During the day at lunchtime we would go purchase live shrimp (for bait), stake them out in the water in a live well bucket, in an isolated place, and pick them up to fish after church. The bridge was well lighted and we, along with several others, would line the sides and hope for a catch.

One night we went to get our shrimp bucket and someone had stolen it. No bait and no bait house open at 10:00 p.m.; consequently, no fishing, that night. We found a new "hiding place" that worked better. The bait wasn't stolen any more.

One night the fish weren't biting, period. No one was catching anything. I was standing near a gentleman so I decided to engage in conversation, hoping to witness to him about Jesus Christ. We first discussed the beautiful cool weather and a few general "get acquainted" things. Next, I asked if he were a Christian. "(Blankety blank) no," was his quick response. "All the churches want is your money. You are very young and my advice to you is 'stay away from churches and preachers if you want to know what is best for you'."

I told him it was too late. I had already come to know Christ and had surrendered to a calling to the ministry. I told him where I was preaching nightly and invited him to come. "I won't be there," he said. And he kept his word. Finally, when all my efforts seemed in vain I asked if he believed in Hell. "Yes," he said. "This is hell, right here and now, not catching any fish after all this effort and money spent to buy bait." I gave up, saying a prayer silently for him. Who knows but what a seed might have been planted. I hope so!

Pastor kept his fishing tackle in a room off the side of the choir area in the church. The room was across the church from the side door where we entered the building. So were the light switches. Every night we would come in around midnight or one a.m. and he would once again fuss about the location of the light switches. I would stand at the side door holding the fishing rods and tackle boxes while he crossed with his flashlight to the other side.

On this particular night, with no flashlight in hand, he said, "Wait here. I'll walk across and turn on the light." Suddenly I heard a loud commotion, grunting, scuffling, falling – and newspaper crumpling. I stared into the dark, seeing nothing. After what seemed like a couple of minutes, the lights came one. Sitting on the carpet in the floor, between the altar rail and pulpit area was a terrified man with newspaper scattered all around him.

Pastor came back from the other side and exclaimed, "Who are you and what are you doing in the church? I stumbled across you in the dark and you have just taken ten years off my life." "Well, what do you think you've done to me? How would you feel if you were sound asleep and were awakened with someone walking on you?" was the response!

After things had calmed down, the man said his name was Terry; he was stranded, broke and thought that surely a church would be a good place to spend the night while he waited for his daughter to wire money to him. Finding the door unlocked, he had come in, lay down on the carpet, and covered himself with newspapers to keep warm. Pastor ordered him to leave immediately, then abruptly changed his mind and said he could stay. He even brought quilts and a pillow. I wondered whether we might find our musical instruments still there the next morning. When we got up, the man who called himself Terry, was gone, along with all the newspapers. He also had not taken the quilts and pillow, or anything else.

One afternoon, we went down to a clear, fresh water canal that ran into the Indian River. We tried artificial baits and earthworms but had no response of any kind by any kind of fish. Soon we came to a wide place in the canal and could see it swarming with mullet. We took a weighted treble hook and began to throw it among the fish. We caught two big wooden crates full. We would throw the hook and then snatch it and we would hang a mullet in the side almost every throw. We took turns throwing and catching while the other rested.

Church time was approaching so we had to go. After church we gave away all the mullet we could to the church folk and early next morning (Saturday) we sold several more to a local fish market. Pastor had a working engagement so I borrowed his heavy duty reel and rod, got the snatch-hook and away I went. We had thinned the mullet crop somewhat, but I still was able to fill another big crate.

Once, after taking a mullet from the hook I looked back at the very clear water to spy a very large fish. I think it might have been a snook or barracuda. It looked about 36 inches long or longer, and I threw across it and set the hook in its opposite side.

It didn't take long for me to realize I had latched on to something bigger than a two or three pound mullet. It jumped from the shock, took off upstream and was giving me a battle royal.

With the hook pulling across its back, I suppose it sensed it was losing, so it turned and headed back toward the Indian River. It was clearly breaking the fish speed limit as it passed and I began to tighten the tension on the reel. But it was "stripping the gears." I couldn't stop it. Ere long, all the 60 pound test line was out and the big, stiff rod was bending to the limit. What would I do? What could I do? There was no stopping this "sea-monster." I hoped the line would break. It didn't!

I could hear the line "sing" as it tightened to an impasse. Should I turn loose and lose the reel and rod? I couldn't do that! It wasn't mine and I certainly couldn't afford to buy a new one for the Pastor. But what else was there to do? The answer came swiftly! The hook pulled out of the fish's side and flew back past me like a missile. The zinging noise was very close to my head and I shuddered to think of it hitting me. I could have been seriously injured or even killed! I was shaking all over as I looked backwards into the trees where the heavy snatch-hook had lodged.

It took 30 minutes or more to untangle the line and retrieve the hook from the tree limbs. I was still trembling while trying to collect my wits and the fishing paraphernalia. I soon determined enough was enough and decided to call it quits. Besides, I had to prepare for two sermons, plus the music and special songs for the two final Sunday services. And I silently thanked the Lord for seeing me through another very close call.

On the way back to the church I encountered several of the small sports cars that had been in and around town for the last few days. Someone said they had gathered for a race or something. They came in all makes, models and colors, and day and night you could hear their owners revving the engines. Pastor called them "speed demons" and said he wished they would hurry and leave.

I also had observed a light green 1950 Buick being driven around town with lemons painted all over it and a big sign on top with the dealership name on each side. I thought "Well, there apparently are "lemons" other than Mercurys. Pastor told me later at District Council that the Buick dealer had repurchased the "lemon" at full price but refused to sell the complainer another car. He was told to do business elsewhere.

I suppose automobiles, since they are made by human beings, are a lot like their makers: lots of "lemons." In fact, the Scriptures point out that we are all lemons of sorts and need a "makeover." David, Isaiah and Paul make this very plain in Psalms 14:1-3, Isaiah 59:6-8, and Romans 3:10 and 23. And this is precisely why God sent His Only Begotten Son, Jesus Christ. Only He can make "lemonade" out of us lemons!

With Sunday services completed, we expressed our gratitude to Mr. and Mrs. Pastor and the congregants. I was even grateful for the multitude of fish we caught and snagged (that is, all except one). As at every other place we labored and interacted, we packed up and made ready to depart with many fond memories. Tomorrow, we would be on the road again!

Jimmy and Jean Cain cut their wedding cake

Ernest and Junell as Best Man and Matron of Honor at Jimmy and Jean
Cain's wedding in Jacksonville, Florida

Rev. and Mrs. James Cain – Jacksonville, Florida

Terry Raburn
Son of Robert and Merle Raburn

THIRTEEN

HIGHLIGHTS OF EVANGELISTIC TRAVELS – PART TWO

I must preach the kingdom of God to other cities also... Luke 4:43

With goodbyes said to our friends in Vero Beach, we headed to a scheduled meeting in Arcadia, Florida. On the way, traveling west on Florida highway 70, we approached a very narrow bridge at the same time a big semi-tractor-trailer was meeting us. It appeared the driver was slowing down to let us cross first. When it was too late to stop, or even slow down, we met on the bridge. I felt the car shudder and was expecting to find my Spartan Manor to be shattered on both sides.

I stopped as soon as I could find a wide place alongside the road. I looked back and the truck kept on going. I looked down both sides of our mobile home and the only damage I could find was a slight dented streak all the way down a flange that was mounted on each side about three feet from the ground and protruded about three inches. I thought, "Wow! Sideswiped on both sides with no appreciable damage!" Our quartet used to sing a song: "I don't know what I would do if the Lord wasn't walking by my side!" Amen!

Another time we were going into Tallahassee, Florida, on Highway 20 from Blountstown. It was just after dark and I approached a narrow overpass over a railroad. I had to cross the centerline at least two feet to miss the three or four feet high concrete side rail. Seeing no approaching lights I headed up the overpass. From out of nowhere a speeding automobile, also across the center line on my side, approached me at breakneck speed. Junell was asleep and suddenly roused up giving a groaning sound that was very loud.

It so startled me that I looked over at her momentarily and she settled back down into sleep. Returning to looming tragedy, I found myself moving off the narrow bridge back to the open road. No collision, no nothing! Whew!! She never remembered anything that had happened when I related it to her afterwards. I could figure no possible way we could have met the approaching car and passed each other on such narrow lanes with both of us over the middle line. I told her that her groaning was a prayer requiring split-second deliverance which is precisely what we got. Praise the Lord once again! Do I believe in a guardian angel? Of course! (Hebrews 1:14)

The pastor at Arcadia also had to supplement his income and he was a salesman for the Lincoln-Mercury dealer at Clewiston. And to add to temptation, as well as to magnify disgust, he was driving a brand new Mercury demonstrator. I was hoping I might work up a trade and get out of my lemon, but the trade difference was too much.

The church services were being held temporarily in an old army barracks building and being a new work had very few people. Night after night we prayed, sang and preached our hearts and souls out but the desired attendance increase and response never came.

During this meeting, however, our special new friends from Lakeland paid us a visit. They even spent the night in our "school bus." We offered them our good bed but they insisted on sleeping on the couch, which unfolded to make a double-bed of sorts. I was surprised that anyone with their means would do such a thing. But we learned that these folks who were worth lots of this world's goods, were plain, humble folks who loved the Lord and ate bacon, grits, eggs, toast and coffee for breakfast just like we did.

It was Saturday, and with no night service planned, we went to Fort Myers, fished off the bridge and picnicked. After lunch, when Junell was about to dump the left-over food into the water, our guest stopped her and said, "No, that will make a good salad, later!" I whispered to Junell that perhaps it was because of their frugality that they had accumulated such wealth.

These folks had helped and were helping to build churches around the area. Being in the cement business, they had furnished building materials for churches in numerous places. And now, they wanted to begin a new church in Oneonta, Alabama, about 35 miles north, northeast of Birmingham. And they wanted us to pioneer the work.

On our first open week after that, we met them at Oneonta, and then traveled with them in their car all around the area. They had built a beautiful ranch-style home on lovely hilly acreage about four miles south of town. We covered the countryside and town area scouting for an appropriate location for a new church. Their proposition was to let us live in their house there until he could build us a parsonage, along with a church. They would guarantee our salary and adequate finances for the church until it could become self-supporting.

The area was his boyhood home. We visited his brother who was a state legislator and who once ran for Governor of Alabama. His home to us was simply a mansion and the next day I went with both of them to the Warrior River where they had plans to build a couple of dams to provide electricity and water for the city of Birmingham. They had applied for an eight million dollar government loan to finance the project. My friend said, "That amount of money scares me." I thought, "How much is eight million?"

We went to proposed sights on both the Locust and Mulberry Forks. At one location an old farmer lived high on the banks by the river. He came out where we were looking and asked what we were doing. "We're going to dam this river about here," the brother told him. He exclaimed, "There's no way anyone could ever stop that flow of water. It's absolutely impossible. You should see it rage when the water is high!" The "raging" river has been tamed by a series of dams since then, but not by my friends. Their government loan never materialized and they had to abandon the idea.

One day we were driving a country road up a mountain. I was at the controls, he in the right front and the ladies in the back. All at once they started yelling, "The floor board is filling up with water. A heater water-hose had burst under the front seat and doused the back foot. I thought, "Well, even Cadillacs have problems, not just Mercurys!"

All in all, our trip to Oneonta was exciting and enjoyable, and we told our friends we would make the church proposition a matter of prayer. He told us there was no hurry. They later visited our revival meeting at Frostproof. We told them we had decided not to attempt the new work and thanked them for considering us. They accepted our decision kindly and we remained close friends with them the rest of their lives.

A call had come to Junell and me, once again from our Secretary-Treasurer of the District. A tent had been erected in Dunnellon, Florida, a Home-Missions Pastor appointed and an effort to start a new church there was underway. We were asked if we would go there and conduct a series of services to assist the effort. The work was struggling but, "Perhaps we can have a repeat performance of what happened under the tent in Frostproof," he said. A delightful thought, I thought, except it never happened.

The District rented us a nice apartment, paid our salary and we moved in with very high hopes. First off, we got a stern lecture from the lady landlord who said she was very "persnickety" about her apartment. "No drinking, no smoking, no parties (especially 'wild' ones), no messes she would have to clean up when we left. "Tidiness is required," and she named a few more things. Apparently we did OK, since she never complained as we moved out.

The meetings were well advertised and night after night we had attendance of around 15 people with little or no response to the invitations. Saturday night brought a nice surprise when 60 people attended. A neighbor Pastor brought about 45 of his members from the Ocala Assembly. Sunday morning I preached to the usual 15, perhaps 20 in attendance. Sunday night we again had the usual 15 people.

During the second week of the meeting, I received a call from Bagdad, Florida, near Milton. A member had heard us sing and preach at his brother's church in Panama City. His church was without a pastor and he wondered if we would come and preach Sunday and "try out" for the position. By then, I was ready to do most anything to get out of Dunnellon. So I talked with the "tent" pastor and we agreed to call off the Saturday night service so I could drive to Bagdad. "But you will have to be back to close out this meeting on Sunday night," he said.

The trip was over 300 miles one way, there were no interstates or four lane highways, you gained an hour on the way (going from eastern to Central Standard Time at the Chattahoochee River) and lost it coming back. And highway 90 ran right through the center of Tallahassee. There was plenty of time going over and precious little returning. I hate it when I get in these "rushed" situations.

The Bagdad church-folk had the parsonage all set for us to stay Saturday night and gave enthusiastic response to our ministry Sunday morning. They were disappointed we couldn't stay for Sunday dinner and wanted to know if we would accept the pastorate if we were elected. They would vote that night. "We'll have to pray and think it over and let you know, if you decide you want us," I said. (They gave us an overwhelming vote and we declined but thanked them for the offer.)

Now for the "breakneck" trip back to Dunnellon. By breaking the speed limit every mile possible, we rolled up to the tent ten minutes after service started and ministered to about 15 people. "All that whirlwind, nerve racking, law-breaking nightmare trip in the daytime, for this," I thought to myself. But who knows? If only one soul was brought to Christ, shouldn't it be more than worth it?" "Yes," I told myself.

On Monday morning we packed up, went back to our mobile home parked at my parents' house in Lakeland, and then to the District Office to give my dismal report and accept a check I felt I didn't deserve. The Secretary was most congenial, thanked us for our "sacrificial" efforts and bid us God-speed for our future ministry.

A meeting at Milligan, just west of Crestview, helped cheer us up from the big let-down at Dunnellon. The Pastor had married a girl with whom I had gone to high school at Turkey Creek. The meeting was well attended and our congregation was very responsive. In addition to this the Pastor made a four quart freezer of homemade ice cream every day. How much better can it get? Especially when you don't know how bad too much ice cream can be for one's arteries.

It was also with great expectancies that we went to Bainbridge, Georgia, for revival services. Some of our friends had had overflowing crowds and numerous converts a few months previous there. They gave us a top-notch recommendation and little did we realize we were in store for another "Dunnellon." It was November and we went from freeze to freeze (the weather). Even the very first Sunday morning was poorly attended, which was passed off as a weather casualty. Scarcely 30 people showed up Sunday night and Monday and Tuesday nights fell to about 10 people. Wednesday may have brought 20 but it froze again on the weekend. It was a struggle to get through Sunday, and the following week.

My heart's desire was to be on the road out of town at first light Monday morning. I was stunned when someone on what was to be the final service stood up and suggested we needed to continue the services for another week. Next, I was hearing the pastor announcing the third week extension. I reluctantly gave in and agreed to try once more.

Monday night we had another freeze and an attendance of 15. Tuesday night brought a repeat performance with a surprise announcement from the pastor. He was the sectional C. A. Rep and had been asked to participate in a round-table discussion at the Georgia District Thanksgiving C. A. Convention. He would need an offering for expenses. He got $7.00, of which I gave $5.00. I had received only $37.00 for the previous two weeks.

Wednesday night I conducted the service in its entirety with the pastor away. A phone call came from Jacksonville. The Pastor's sister's baby was still-born and she would have no one but me to do the funeral, which would be held Friday morning at 10:00 a.m. We left after service Thanksgiving night after requesting prayer for the trip from the few people present. We arrived in Jacksonville in the wee hours, conducted the service and barely arrived back in Bainbridge Friday night to minister to 10 people.

Thankfully, there was no Saturday night service and with the Pastor back on Sunday our final love offering was $38.00. If there had been another suggestion to further continue the meetings I think I would have rebelled openly and loudly. Thank the Lord it did not come!

I don't know which the greatest relief was: my exit from Dunnellon or my leaving Bainbridge. Realizing that "all things work together for good to them that love God, to them who are the called according to His purpose," and being "foreknown by the Lord, and being predestined to be conformed to the image of His Son," Romans 8:28-29, I now calculate that these two meetings were very rich and rewarding for me, if no one else. They were a genuine test of my spirituality, patience, humility, and carnality, which was alive and well! There is no doubt whatever, that God knows what is best for us, if we can just believe that. I have been told that God is never affected by circumstances of any kind.

God also knows how, when we are on the bottom, to restore our souls once again, Psalms 23:3. In His great mercies, for my human weakness, our next meeting in December was at First Assembly of God in Plant City, Florida. Crowds once again! Converts once again! Excellent offerings once again, as they always were when we ministered for this Pastor. All this and Christmas at home. What more could I desire? Forget Bainbridge and Dunnellon!

A return trip to Frostproof was also very awesome. The church building was finished and many friends from the previous tent revival were there to greet us and rejoice in Christ with us. My relatives were an integral part of the church from the opening tent revival. My Uncle was now a deacon and served and supported the church until he passed away.

The Pastor and others of our converts were there still. And this being the full moon in January meant the speckled perch would be biting. My Uncle owned a supermarket there and was the principal meat-cutter. He would call and say, "Ernest, I'll be through by noon. I'll have the boat, minnows and poles ready. I'll pick you up and have you back in time for church." We "loaded the boat" (caught our limit) every trip, fishing in Lake Reedy.

On the last Friday of the meeting we were about ready to leave the lake. I looked into the minnow bucket only to see two small, dead minnows. I asked Uncle, "Do you suppose a speckled perch might bite one of these?" "Put them both on your hook and give it a try," he said. I flipped them out in an open place in the thick, grassy edge of the lake and "zoom." There was no doubt I had hooked a nice one.

Uncle said, "Hang on. There have been a couple of five pound specs caught in this lake, and I believe you might have another." The battle went on and on! The fish was going back and forth, across, under and through the grass. With a slim, very flexible pole, and eight pound test line, I let it wear itself out until it gave up and turned on its side, atop the grass. I reached out, grabbed it by the mouth and boated it: an eight pound bass! As you can imagine, my message that night was mixed with a fish story. After all, Peter, Andrew, James and John were fishermen, also. And I'm sure they told some fish stories too as they preached and fished for men. Remember the story about catching so many fish that their nets broke, (Luke 5:6) and the one about the tax money from the fish's mouth to pay taxes for Jesus and Peter? (Matt. 17:27)

A meeting that I held in Clearwater was great. I had a sermon I preached about what Jesus said about Jonah, and that "a greater than Jonah is here." (Matt. 12:38-41) It was a delightful story comparing the "risen" Jonah that preached to Nineveh and the risen Christ, who was not only greater than Jonah, but Solomon as well. You could also extend that to Abraham, Moses and many others, including the angels. (Heb. 1:4) The Pastor said that was the best rendition of Jonah and Christ compared that he had ever heard. That sort of compliment from a pastor expands the evangelist's ego. Watch out!

We had been invited to preach at Stamping Ground, Kentucky. You may not find it on every map, but it is situated about 25 miles northwest of Lexington and some 35 miles south of Holbrook, Kentucky. Holbrook? Yes! (Brag, brag!) My Uncle had told me my grandfather Payne had a "brag patch" on his farm in South Georgia. So, I guess I can brag about Holbrook, Kentucky, as well as Holbrook towns in Massachusetts, Arizona, New York, and Florida. (Just kidding about Florida.) Anyway, Granddad's brag patch was right beside the road where he grew his best of everything – corn, peas, cantaloupes, watermelons, etc., in order to be seen by those passing by. But the Holbrook towns in the United States of America aren't much to brag about as far as size goes. Holbrook, New York, is the biggest with about 26,000 in population as of this writing.

In route to Kentucky we once again traveled through the Smoky Mountains, spent the night in Gatlinburg, Tennessee, and renewed our admiration of the beautiful fences and horse farms around Lexington. Stamping Ground was a very small place we would generally call a "wide place in the road." Of course, such a statement would have infuriated the pastor's mother-in-law, who owned hundreds of acres there as well as the general store which was the only store around at the time.

The country-side is very hilly and the roads extremely curvy. Sometimes you might have to drive a few miles in order to find a place just to turn around. Once a man stopped at said general store and asked Mrs. Proprietor for directions to somewhere. She proceeded to suggest one way, then another, and finally said, "Well, perhaps this road here would be best." The gentleman jestingly said, "Lady, I don't believe I can get there from here!" She fumingly said, "Mister, you can go anywhere in the world from here."

A church family invited us to eat with them Friday evening before church, "if the creeks don't rise." It had never dawned on me until we forded a shallow creek near their house that this saying was true. Sometimes they would be stranded for several days during rainy season or some unusual downpour. When the pastor first came there, he was single and stayed with them. He said he often would have to cross the stream in his swimming trunks while carrying his church clothes in a dry container. Once across, he would dress and proceed to church.

We discovered that this was not only tobacco growing country, but also that most of the ladies of the church worked in a cigarette factory in Lexington. The pastor advised and pled with me not to mention tobacco in any way. I didn't. One lady testified that the frost bit everybody's tobacco patches all around her, but that God had placed his hand over her field and protected it from the cold.

Overall, the meeting went quite well. The church folk seemed to like us and the response was fairly good. Pastor had a dentist appointment in Owenton. We went with him. The old dentist finished with Pastor and asked if I'd like my teeth checked. I said, "OK." He did eight fillings for Junell and me and charged us a whopping eight dollars, one dollar per tooth! How outrageous!

We also visited a nearby town of Mulattos. We were told that these people were descendants of white slave owners and their black women slaves. They had congregated and founded their own little town after the Civil War. Most of the people we saw along the streets had light to medium brown skin. I'm not sure about the name of the town – perhaps New Liberty? We also drove up to Warsaw where we viewed the mighty Ohio River and the state of Indiana on the other side.

The area cemetery was located on a very steep hill not far from the country store. During a prolonged downpour of rain, mudslides developed and several caskets came out of the ground, including the one in which the pastor's sister was buried. The community had to wait until the soil completely dried before they could bury the coffins again, this time much deeper.

Our experience in Stamping Ground, Kentucky, will remain in my memory as long as I have one, as will every place we visited and preached. The geography, culture and certain events relative to a particular place make some stand out more than others. Most important are the spiritual and moral benefits that were brought about in individual hearts and lives. Only eternity will reveal the true accomplishments for good and God in each campaign.

One of the special meetings we had was in my wife's home town of Marianna, Florida. Junell was born and resided there until she was 15 years old. It was like a reunion for her to see all the familiar places and changes and to rekindle old friendships.

As a result of having met and married her, I also had accumulated an assortment of memories of the area myself. I remembered the revival meetings I had conducted near there, the week long fog & rain, the time of waiting for auto-purchasing papers, the breath-taking new 1948 Plymouth that slipped right through my fingers and the seven weeks I went without wheels. I could never forget the near disastrous episode of Junell's Dad's car sliding on wet clay, the false police accusations and the time I spent alone and lonely in a downtown corner café listening to "My Happiness" with Junell hundreds of miles away.

But all that was history now. I was happily married, had an evangelistic party again and was enjoying a beautiful, '51 Mercury (even though it was a "lemon") and a 25' Spartan Manor mobile home (along with auto and trailer payments!). In addition to this, I was singing and preaching at "First" Assembly of God, the City church. And with a good meeting going with several people seeking God in their lives each evening around the altar area, pride had replaced humility which according to Proverbs 16:18 precedes a "fall."

It happened one evening at the end of my sermon and while I was giving the invitation. Just before we had bought the dairy, Dad and I had share-cropped a pepper crop in Valrico, Florida. Lifting 100 pound fertilizer bags had left me with a sore, strained area in the lower right side of my stomach. A doctor's examination revealed a rupture and recommendation that I see a surgeon, if it got any worse. It hadn't, up until now.

After I started preaching, I noticed a slightly protruding area that occasionally caused some discomfort. This particular night, a severe pain was accompanied by a tearing sensation that nearly doubled me over as I continued to try to speak. I excused myself, went to my mobile home that was parked next door to the church and upon self-examination, discovered the protrusion now equaled the size of a taw (a large marble). The next morning it had receded, was not even visible, but was very sore. I managed to complete the meeting and even go fishing (for fish) while I continued.

One of the church members invited me to go with him to Merritt's Mill Pond, a very clear lake fed by Blue Springs. We rented a boat and motor and I proceeded to tie on a "paw-paw" fishing lure on my reel line. He looked at it and stated very emphatically that it would not catch a bass or anything else. "These fish will never hit an artificial lure of any kind," he insisted. After only a few casts, I began to "load the boat."

By the time I had caught the limit (ten bass) with my lure, and he none with his live shiners and earthworms, he asked where he might purchase such a plug for himself. He had to leave to go to work soon, so I gave him all the bass and stayed a while longer and caught several more. That evening after church the conversation was more about fishing for fish than "fishing" for lost souls.

The meetings went well, but once back at home a surgeon in Tampa, recommended immediate surgery for a hernia in my lower right abdomen. I went to St. Joseph's hospital in Tampa, spending 12 days there, and two more months to recover. The hospital bill came to $345.00 and the surgeon's fee was $150.00. My dad and brother covered the bills and let me work it out in the dairy…later! Dad also contributed a good portion of it.

After recouping, it was right back to the Evangelistic ministry and how good it felt not to feel as if your lower stomach was falling out while you were preaching.

After a repeat revival that ran for three weeks at Enterprise, Alabama, we headed for Columbus, Georgia, to Beallwood Assembly, where the Flannigans pastored. Thinking I had enough gas to make it to the next station, the car sputtered near the top of a very high hill some remote place between Eufaula and Columbus. It was early morning and very cold. I set out walking northward not knowing where I was going.

After about fifteen minutes a car came along and the nice gentleman gave me a lift to a service station a few miles up the road. The station owner apparently had either had a bad night, or had gotten up on the wrong side of the bed, or had had a fight with his wife or something! Anyway, he wasn't friendly, was very busy, finally did "find" a five gallon gas can I could pay a deposit on, and "no," he could not get away to carry me back to my car.

Another man, however, did. He had "chugged" up to the station in a dilapidated, body-less, some kind of vehicle, heard my dilemma, and offered to take me back. If walking in the cold was cold, try riding on a frame with only a motor, wheels and no windshield. We never went fast, say 35 or 40 miles per hour, but the "wind chill factor" must have been in the teens. And this was long before I had ever heard the weather bureau use the term. Such miserable experiences always seem to last longer than they really do.

Upon finally arriving back at the car and house trailer, through chattering teeth I tried to ask the man what I owed him. He laughed, revved up his engine, sputtered away and hollered back, "Not a thing!" I finally got the car started, proceeded to the service station, filled up, paid up, and received my deposit from the disgruntled attendant for use of the gas can.

Fortunately, the Columbus meeting made up for all the troubles. The congregation was receptive, attendance was excellent, and the next three weeks was tops. The pastor appealed for groceries for us and night after night the people overloaded us with everything we needed and more. The offerings were the best I had ever received by far. I thought once again I had it made.

The Pastor took us to Warm Springs, Georgia, to see former President Roosevelt's retreat. We also visited and sang for what was called, "the poor farm." I had always heard it called "the poor house," and wasn't aware one really existed. I thought it was merely an expression of people anticipating or experiencing economic disaster.

But here was a real "poor house," sponsored by the state of Georgia for people who had no one, nothing, nowhere to go and weren't able on their own to exist. The inhabitants were thrilled to see the Pastor who went there every week to bring food and other items and to "cheer" them up. What a ministry. He also carried us to the "Fish House," a famous restaurant situated along the banks of the Chattahoochee River. What a feast!

Why couldn't every meeting be like this one at Beallwood Assembly in Columbus, Georgia? Or like the ones we had at Zion's Grove, Moultrie, Pelham, Andalusia and the likes? What a foolish question! How could one appreciate the sunshine, if there were only sunshine? Surely life needs the balance of the lowest valley and the highest hill! If the diet were only hand-cranked homemade ice cream alone, what would happen to the health and well-being of the body?

It took the suffering and dying on the cross of Calvary to bring about the Resurrection from the dead and justification for our sins. It takes pain to bring about the joy of painlessness. And even Christ Himself said, "It is written, and thus it behooved Christ to suffer, and to rise from the dead the third day," Luke 24:46. Paul wrote the young Timothy in Book two, 2:11-12, "It is a faithful saying: For if we be dead with Him, we shall also live with Him: If we suffer, we shall also reign with Him…" This thought is also reflected in Romans 8:17b.

So, enjoy the sunshine, the mountain tops, the "cloud nine" experiences, but grow in the valleys and in the fellowship of His sufferings. (Philippians 3:10) Welcome the Beallwood revivals, converts, food and offerings, and then mature in the Dunnellon and Bainbridge situations. I am growing in the grace and knowledge of Jesus Christ if these truths are internalized and practiced in my everyday walk and talk. God grant that they may!

Our next trip home, I had had it with my '51 Mercury. Dad went with me to the Lakeland Lincoln-Mercury place and asked to speak with the dealership owner. He graciously listened as we related the oil, the vibration problems, the knocking engine, and the multiplied times we had brought it in trying to get it fixed and the "overhauled" engine. We also told him our family members had bought seven new automobiles from him over the years.

He called in the dealership secretary and they reviewed the files on the car. He seemed astonished at the troubles I had encountered with a new automobile. He asked Dad and me, "What would you like me to do in light of all this?" "I want a new automobile," I told him. "How many miles are on your car?" "20,000." Back then, a set of tires had to be replaced after 20 to 25,000 miles. We went outside, looked at the car and he said, "Would you give me 100 dollars for the 20,000 miles use of the car and another 100 dollars for a new set of tires, if I gave you a new car?" "Yes," I said very quickly!

"Then go pick out your new car!" I was so excited I could hardly believe what was happening! Dad had just bought a new '51 Mercury and I wanted to find one just like his, a beautiful two-tone, light blue and grey with a spotlight and sun visor! I certainly didn't want a darker blue like I just had!

Dad spied a green Mercury coupe with an off-white vinyl top that he thought was the prettiest car he had ever seen. "How about this one," he asked. "No way," I responded. "I don't want a coupe and I don't care for the color." "I do!" Dad said! Then he said, "Since you like my car so good, why not take it, and I'll take this one!" His car had only a few hundred miles and I said, "OK." The green coupe was a little more expensive, so Dad paid the extra amount and I was one happy young evangelist.

I soon had a heavy-duty trailer hitch, lighting and brake connection installed, and was back on the road with an automobile that served me for many miles and years with little or no problems. Later, when I was in for service, the service manager told about my other '51 Mercury. They had to overhaul the engine again and a factory representative had driven the car for strange sounds and vibrations and discovered the insulation in the headliner had been left out at the factory. I was happy that I no longer had to worry with it. I felt for the person who purchased it. However, of the several Mercurys our families owned, only this one ever gave us serious problems.

Among our next meetings was the very delightful two weeks at First Assembly in Dothan, Alabama. The Pastor and congregants were very friendly, the kind of people that you enjoy being around. We also relished being on their daily radio program on the Dothan station.

This Pastor also served as Assistant Superintendent of the Alabama District of the Assemblies of God. Plus, he was a great prankster. He delighted in playing tricks, especially on his evangelists. Just previous to our meeting, he had opened his fountain pen, spewing ink all over the front of his evangelist's white shirt as they were headed for the church service. Startled, the young evangelist was going to go back to the parsonage and change shirts. Ere long, the disappearing ink had disappeared!

The first time we ate with them, I proceeded to cut my meat. The steak knife folded and my hand plunked right into my mashed potatoes and gravy. Another time I stirred my tea and then laid down the spoon to discover and ugly green fly. It was "plastic."

Most every night after the church service, Pastor took us to Oscar's, a favorite eating place of many of the church people. Every time the "juke box" played a song, an elevated, curtained, miniature stage would open and a "band" of little plastic men would move with the music. All this, plus Oscar's cheeseburgers, french-fries, milkshakes and fellowship with church people made for a delightful "after church" good time. And most probably, this good food and more like it, later contributed to my blocked arteries.

One day I asked Lucille, the Pastor's wife, if he slept in pajamas. He did, so I asked her to stitch one leg at the knee. She did. That evening, after a snack at their house, Junell and I waited outside their bedroom. It was a frame house with wooden floors and soon we heard: "hop – hop – hop – crash!" We laughed and hurried to our trailer parked close by. The next day his wife described the hop-scotch episode wherein the pastor hopped across the floor and into the wall. Pastor wasn't amused, and accused his wife and myself as collaborators against a "decent, upright minister of the Gospel."

Preparing to leave on Monday morning, Junell said to Pastor and Mrs., as they came out to say goodbye, "We sure enjoyed being with you these two weeks!" He returned, "I sure wish I could say the same!" She came back with, "You could, if you would tell as big a lie about it as we did!" This floored him. He told this far and wide because people still come up to us and repeat it, after all these years.

Our revival services at Pace, Florida, soon followed. This Pastor also served as Assistant District Superintendent, of the West Florida District Council. He was well-respected in the community. The church was averaging near 300 at the time, so the nightly meetings were also well-attended. I have never made any financial demands or requests of any pastor or church. I always worked on the basis of faith and hoped the pastor would understand our needs: food, clothing, travel costs, musical equipment, car and trailer payments, auto insurance, etc.

I wasn't aware of this Pastor's "two offerings per week" for his evangelists, one on Sunday night and the other on Thursday night. Usually, an offering was taken in each service for the evangelist's support. We had arrived flat broke on Monday night to open the meeting with probably 250 or more people present. No offering! Nor on Tuesday night. Junell's parents called Wednesday and were visiting some friends in Panama City, Florida, some ninety miles to the east of where we were at the Pace-Pensacola area of the panhandle of Florida. They asked us to drive over Thursday to meet them there. We would visit, stay for lunch and then be on our way back for the evening service.

With the gas gauge indicating "low," and no money, I told Junell we had enough fuel to get to Panama City, but would have to borrow money from her parents to be able to return. She said, "OK I will ask them." We had gotten back to the town of Mary Esther when I observed "empty" on the gauge. I pulled up to the gas pump and asked Junell for the money, she had forgotten to get.

"Fill-er-up?" the attendant asked as he began to gloat over our beautiful new Mercury. I searched my pockets and came up with the three cents I knew was there. Junell searched her pocket-book which yielded two quarters. "Did you say, 'fill-er-up'?" the attendant asked once again. "How about 50 cents worth?" I said. With a puzzled look on his face, he dutifully pumped a slight bit over two gallons, and then watched with that still strange, questioning gaze as we drove away.

The Thursday night service came, along with an offering, of which I got "nary a cent," until the Sunday night offering. The two totaled almost $200.00, which was a good week's pay back then. We did not see very many of those. But, once again, I felt financially secure and had two more weeks to go there at Pace Assembly. Fortunately, we had had enough groceries to get by until this payday, especially since we had been invited to several meals with the Pastor's family.

Our trailer was parked adjacent to the church on the opposite side from the parsonage. About four a.m. the first morning there, I was awakened by the sound of loud prayers coming from inside the church. I later learned it was the Pastor's wife, who years before had vowed to pray early every morning and had been faithful to the vow ever since. She never told us this, but her husband did, when I asked about it. Anytime after that, for the three weeks meeting, when she prayed loud enough for me to wake up, I from my sleepy bed silently joined her, until I fell asleep again.

Across the street from the church and parsonage (the same parsonage where we had spent part of the night with the Pastor back when our first 1951 Mercury had died in the night near by), was a country grocery store and gas station. It was owned by one of the deacons. I went across to gas up after I had finally received some money. I went inside where he was checking out groceries for a customer. When I told him I wanted to gas up, he said, "I forgot to tell you! I always give each of our evangelists a free tank of gas! (Now he tells me!) Wait until you are near empty so you can get a full tank." "I'm empty," I said.

Another customer came to the cash register so He told me to go to the gas pump on the north end and fill up. When I finished, I walked back inside to thank him. He walked back out with me and asked, "Which pump did you use? You are parked by the kerosene pump." I was, and yes, I had filled the gas tank of my new 1951 Mercury with it. It was the northern-most pump but it plainly said in small letters on the side, "Kerosene." I thought, "Of all the dumb tricks I have ever pulled, this one surely ranks high on the list."

He suggested I call the Ford place in Milton, (the same place that had earlier fixed my "lemon") and seek advice: drain the gas tank, or what? The service manager told me to drive it. "It will probably 'skip' and 'buck,' but run the tank down to half, then fill it with high-test." I was beginning to wonder if this "neck-of-the-woods" was "bad luck" for me and my Mercurys, even though I'm not superstitious.

Every day I would drive some with the motor hopping, jumping, leaping, struggling to pull off from a stop, you name it! I sure wanted to make sure this tank was cleared before I tried to pull my Spartan Manor. When the gas tank reached the half full mark, I filled it with Ethyl and she skipped no more. Glory! I shouldn't have, but I went in to pay the deacon, expecting him to say, "No charge. I'm glad you solved the problem." Instead, he said, "That will be two dollars," and whatever cents. So, only the kerosene was free.

The meeting could have gone longer than three weeks but we were scheduled in Ashford, Alabama, and needed to close. What a high note upon which to close: overflowing crowds, excellent altar responses and many asking us to stay longer or please hurry back. A neighbor church, First

242

Assembly of God in Milton, Florida, had recently had the pastor of six years leave to take another church. Several people from there had visited our Pace revival and consequently invited me to candidate for their church.

By this time we were getting weary of the road again and Junell, especially, was ready to settle down in one spot. And start a family! I agreed to beg a Sunday off from the Ashford meeting to go preach at Milton. I did, and was elected. I asked for a couple of weeks to pray about it and think it over.

After a few days, in the midst of a very successful revival in Ashford, I called the chairman of the Milton church and accepted the call to the church. I told them I would come in 30 days, giving me time to cancel all but two immediate crusades which I needed to fill. In the meantime, an evangelist found out we were settling down and offered to purchase our Spartan Manor. We sold it to him and moved into the church parsonage in Milton, Florida.

The breakdown of a "lemon" car and a one a.m. meeting with the Pastor of Pace Assembly resulted in an invitation to preach a revival for him, which resulted in us getting elected to the pastorate of the First Assembly of God of Milton, Florida. So much for "lemons"!

Junell and Ernest 1951 Mercury and Spartan Manor

First Assembly of God – Dothan, Alabama

Assembly of God, Pace Florida

First Assembly of God – Marianna, Florida

Pastor Max McNab and his nephew, Junell and Ernest at Dothan, Alabama

"GO YE THEREFORE, AND MAKE DISCIPLES OF ALL NATIONS, BAPTIZING THEM INTO THE NAME OF THE FATHER, AND OF THE SON, AND OF THE HOLY SPIRIT; TEACHING THEM TO OBSERVE ALL THINGS WHATSOEVER I HAVE COMMANDED YOU: AND LO, I AM WITH YOU ALWAYS, EVEN TO THE END OF THE WORLD." MATTHEW 28:19, 20.

Certificate of Ordination

THE GENERAL COUNCIL OF THE
ASSEMBLIES OF GOD
HEADQUARTERS: SPRINGFIELD, MO.

This is to Certify:

That ERNEST EUGENE HOLBROOK having proved his Divine Gift and Calling to the Ministry of the Gospel of Christ, and having consecrated himself to said calling according to the Word of God, and having met the standards prescribed by the General Council of the Assemblies of God, has on

this Thirteenth day of February 1952, by the imposition of hands and the prayers of the Presbytery of the

SOUTH FLORIDA DISTRICT COUNCIL

been set apart and ordained to the Ministry of the Gospel. The Executive Presbytery of the General Council hereby recognizes his Divine Ordination to the ministry of the Gospel, conferring upon him the right to

PREACH THE WORD

administer the ordinances of the Church, perform the rite of marriage, bury the dead, and feed the flock of God, so long as his spirit and practice are such as become the Gospel of Christ and he continues to hold fast the form of sound words, according to the established doctrines of the Gospel.

IN WITNESS WHEREOF, the Executive Officers of the General Council of the Assemblies of God have set their hands and seal

On this Eleventh day of March 1952 A.D.

Wesley R. Steelberg
GENERAL SUPERINTENDENT

J. Roswell Flower
SECRETARY

THIS CERTIFICATE IS VALID ONLY WHEN ACCOMPANIED BY CERTIFICATE OF FELLOWSHIP UNDER THE SEAL OF THE GENERAL COUNCIL, WHICH CERTIFICATE IS TO BE ISSUED ANNUALLY.

CLERGY CERTIFICATE, SERIES 1941.   THE GOSPEL PUBLISHING HOUSE, SPRINGFIELD, MO.

Finally, a good Mercury (1951)

FOURTEEN

FIRST ASSEMBLY OF GOD, MILTON, FLORIDA

And He gave Apostles, Prophets, Evangelists, Pastors and Teachers for the perfecting of the saints... Ephesians 4:11-12

It seemed comforting to be settling into a pastorate once again. For Junell and me, traveling, pulling a house trailer, scheduling meetings, setting up musical instruments, P.A. system, etc., was becoming very tiresome. We were moving into a big, comfortable parsonage located about a mile or so from downtown Milton, which was situated on Blackwater River which ran into East Bay close by.

Eight miles north was Whiting Field, a Navy base where naval aviators were trained. AT 6's filled the air around us constantly and some of our church-folk worked at the base. Ere long, we were invited there to an air-show featuring the Blue Angels, a crack Navy flying team, and what a show it was. The jet airplanes fascinated us with splendid precision and formation flying that drew oooh's and ah's from our group seated in the bleachers.

The squadron leader had a mechanism that emitted white smoke from the end of one wing and blue from the other. He crossed over our heads at 500 miles per hour and then spiraled straight up, leaving an embroidered effect of white and blue as far as the eye can see. I relived one of my earlier fantasies as I watched this spine-tingling thriller.

Some twenty-five miles southwest of our new town was Pensacola, Florida. One route to there was a beautiful drive that afforded an elevated and very scenic view of the bay. One of our church families lived along this drive. Pensacola was also the home of the Pensacola Naval Air Station, so we were in the midst of a strong military presence. Since Milton was very small, we found ourselves needing to go to the big city of Pensacola quite frequently. The nearest hospital was there but a nice, new one was built just a mile or so from our church shortly after.

There were many wonderful people in our church, resulting in lifelong friendships. A deacon, owned a huge supermarket downtown. His son was the Sunday School superintendent and a rural postman. We helped influence a barber to the Lord and church. He became a fishing buddy and later Secretary-Treasurer of the church. Who can argue with free haircuts? Three related families were won to the church. Two of them were carpenters and later helped me start construction on a new sanctuary.

One member's husband owned the Dodge agency, along with his dad. My effort to trade for a new Dodge never materialized. I wound up with a new '53 Mercury instead. The trade difference was much less. One member was a deputy sheriff that was in charge of the county jail. Two other men were peace officers. They were deputized for special occasions. One member had once run for sheriff. We found the town was very political. Across the street from the church, which was on a 90 degree, steeply-banked curve was a small grocery store owned by a church member. He was a big, completely bald, jovial, part-time preacher. He, unknowingly, almost scared me within one inch of my life, I think.

It was Easter morning. The church had followed the tradition of a "sunrise" service each year, and I had gone in the pre-dawn darkness to turn on the lights for the service. The light switches were across the building, just like those in Vero Beach. Groping in the blackness, I heard a deep groaning, moaning sound when I was about half-way across the building. I looked toward the sound and saw a round, glowing, halo-like something. Chills started up and down my spine. Was it a ghost? An angel? What?

Another guttural sound followed and I was spell-bound. I couldn't move. The glow seemed to be getting bigger and was moving. I was about ready to "pick 'em up and lay 'em down," when I nervously found the light switches. As light flooded the sanctuary, there by an open window, kneeling in the glow of a full moon through the window was this "bald" brother. He had come early to pray and consequently, almost scared me out of my wits.

It did not take me long to discover the Yellow River that flowed from South Alabama down near Crestview and into the Bay just below Milton. It would become my favorite fishing spot away from home. And would you believe that Robert Raburn had accepted the church at Milligan, some four miles west of Crestview, and 25 miles east of Milton, and he, along with

Merle and Terry, were now our almost next door neighbors? Miller Bluff on the river became our weekly meeting spot, every Monday morning possible. We called it our day off and it was our day on the river.

One freezing Monday morning we had been fishing only a few minutes when we hit a log and into the water splashed Cousin Robert. I have never seen anyone go in and come out of the drink so fast; unless it was Charles Raburn when he fell into the Hillsborough River right near where we had just seen two 10 or 12 feet long alligators.

I loaned my jacket to Robert and almost froze as I revved the motor full speed back to the landing. As he went up the bank to his car, I said, "I'll wait here until you go home, change clothes and come back. The last thing I heard him say as he drove away was, "I won't be back today!" He kept his word!

Our fish stories from central Florida's lakes, rivers, canals and creeks whetted the appetites of several of my members at Milton. Some of them had never caught fresh water bass and especially on artificial lures like we used. One trip home, I had a deacon, his brother and my Sunday School superintendent. We drove all night after Sunday evening worship and my dad and brother-in-law were ready with their two boats when we arrived about 8:00 a.m.

We went to Lake Rosalie, some 15 miles east of Lake Wales. Anticipation of a nice bass catch was the prime subject of conversation. With both boats launched, and three of us in each boat, we set out across the lake toward Tiger Creek. The creek zigzagged through the woods to Tiger Lake and was usually a bass haven.

I gunned Dad's 15 foot boat to get into the creek first since I knew the front boat would stand the best chance for the most fish. My brother-in-law's boat was shorter, lighter and faster, and they zoomed by us leaving a big wake. They too wanted to be first down the creek. I managed to stay outside the huge trough of water from their boat for a few moments.

When it reached us, I turned to cross it and in a split second, we were swamped. All three of us were knocked out of the boat and fortunately I had managed to turn off our 40 HP motor. When I gathered my senses, I looked at our boat completely full of water. One of my buddies screamed, "I can't swim." I told him to grab the side of the boat, which was still afloat. As we all three grasped the same side, the boat turned upside down. But it continued to float and by this time the other boaters, seeing our plight, had returned.

I told them to help our friend who couldn't swim. They carried him to shore then assisted us in pulling our capsized boat to the lake's edge. The gas tank was floating, as was my tackle box. The motor was OK, but in Davy Jones locker was our food, our fishing rods and one new shoe that belonged to my deacon.

He had just bought the shoes for the trip and had taken them off when he had gotten into the boat. One had lodged under the overturned boat seat, but the other one was gone. He asked if I knew anyone who had only a right foot, who needed a new, size 7 ½ D, shoe.

Once we got all the water out of the boat and turned it back over, the majority decided enough was enough. We loaded the boats on the trailers and headed back home. Since we had planned to return to Milton the next day, our much anticipated fishing trip never happened. It was a disappointment to all but we were grateful that none of us had been injured or drowned.

During the weary night we were spending at my dad's home, the phone rang just after we had dozed off. It was my wife's brother's wife. He was overseas in the Air Force and their small child, Linda, had become deathly ill. His wife asked me to take them to the base hospital at McDill Field in Tampa. We waited in the emergency room several hours before a doctor came. He treated the little one and we got back home just after daybreak. Just in time for breakfast and the return trip to Milton. Two nights without sleep for me! Plus a boat wreck!

I was glad I had someone to drive back for me and fretfully slept and woke up numerous times on the way back. There weren't very many fish stories discussed and the city limits were a welcome sight when we finally got home. I asked if the fellas wanted to try it again next Sunday night after church. There were no takers!

Thankfully though, the church was beginning to grow. When we first arrived, Sunday School attendance was averaging about 120, but the morning worship only about half of that. I recall how shocked I was that first Sunday when I watched the mass "exodus" after Sunday School. It was hard to believe such could be happening.

I had always been used to the exact opposite. Usually in most every place, the morning worship attendance exceeded the Sunday School numbers. While I was preaching to my greatly reduced congregation that day, I determined this had to change. I asked the Sunday School superintendent about this situation and he said it had been that way as long as he remembered. By the time I left the church some two and one-half years later, the Sunday School average had gone to over two hundred and I was preaching to just over one hundred. So much for my plans to change the numerical ratio! Thank God at least for some progress in growth, anyway.

I'll never forget the time I first visited a very elderly church member who was a shut-in. When I started to leave she said, "Wait, I want to give you my 'tie' (tithe) money for the church." She told me she received $88.00 a month and gave me $8.80. Having observed her apparent meager circumstances and surroundings I said to her, "Sister Carroll, I can't take this money! You need it more than the church does."

Have you ever received a kind, but sound, rebuke? I was attempting to refuse the money when she said, "Why Pastor, would you, of all people, want to rob me of the blessing of giving to the Lord's work? I've always done this, now you take it! And be sure to come back each month when I get my next check." I was embarrassed but took the money and graciously thanked her and never refused to take it again. Talk about the widow's two mites! This reminded me of it. (Luke 21:2-4)

One night Junell and I went to the Milton High School for some sort of program in which some of our church teens were involved. We lived about a mile or so from the school and on the way back I noticed an automobile approaching us at a very high speed. We lived in the city limits and the speed limit was 35 miles per hour along the street to the parsonage and church. The car sped past us at probably 60 or 70 miles per hour. I did notice by the street lights it was the same make car as mine.

As I approached the big curve where the church and parsonage were located, I recognized a Shore Patrol vehicle (Navy) also speeding toward us around the curve. I waited while it passed, then I turned left into the parsonage yard. When I stopped, the sailor police skidded to a halt, turned around and came into our yard right up beside our car. Out jumped the two officers, and one began to rant and rave and curse me for driving like you know what. "You think you're pretty smart, don't you? You've given us a (blankety-blank) chase for ten miles. You've run several cars off the road trying to get away from us! Now you've turned around, pretending you were coming from another direction." Then he cursed some more.

I had gotten out of the car and gone to the other side to open the door for Junell when they had pulled alongside. She was still in the car, hearing the false accusations. I said, "Officer, I am the church pastor here. I just came from the high school, and I think I met the car you were chasing. I think you owe us an apology for your profanity!"

He interrupted and began his rampage again. "You're not getting out of this! We've followed you from Whiting Field and you are under arrest..." At this time, he was interrupted by his counterpart. "Mack, this is not the car we were after. This is a different color and has a Florida tag!" Mack stood stunned! After a few seconds, without apologizing, in fact without saying a word, he got back into his cruiser and drove away.

I immediately went into the house and called the deputy sheriff, our church member, who worked at the sheriff's office and kept the jail. I related to him what had happened.

He began to get excited. I learned there was a continuous feud going on between the sailor police and the sheriff's office. They could arrest Navy personnel, including high ranking officers, for speeding, drunk driving, disorderly conduct, whatever. But the Shore Patrol from Whiting Field couldn't arrest civilians unless they violated the law while on the base or were stationed there.

In addition to this, the Shore Patrol would come to the county jail to try to get Navy personnel out, but the sheriff and county judge made them "face the music," i.e., go to trial, pay the full fine, even serve jail time. But the Navy police had to release civilians from the base brig, to the sheriff's office.

So, with no love lost between these law enforcement agencies, my member was saying to me, "This is great! Will I ever get them for what they did to my pastor and his wife!" I said, "Hey, wait! It was a mistake! All I want is an apology for the profanity of the Navy police officer toward me in the presence of my wife." We got the apology, later, through the sheriff's office. Evidently, the officer was embarrassed to face us personally.

One evening there had been a prison break in Brewton, Alabama, some 33 miles north of Milton. These prisoners labeled as "armed and dangerous," had fled into a swampy area just northeast of Milton and an enormous manhunt was underway. I spent quite a bit of time at the sheriff's office, sang and preached at the jail on Sunday afternoons and at times witnessed to prisoners one on one. At other times I stopped by to visit the jailer and his family. They lived in an apartment in the courthouse above the sheriff's office. When something exciting came up, he would call me to come and monitor the radio calls with him. This night he called and told me to "hurry on down!"

The two-way radio was tuned in to several deputies' cars around the swampy area. The two auxiliary officers from our church had also joined the chase. "They were last seen going into this area," one radio voice said of the fugitives. Another hollered, "Be careful, it's getting dark and they are shooting at us." Before long, one of our guys came into the sheriff's office. I said, "Wow, did you capture those outlaws?" He said, "No! When it got dark and all those gunshots were going on around me, I decided it was time for me to get away from there!" We laughed, but he said it was serious business! The escaped men were captured in the swamp the next morning.

One of our newly elected church deacons lived on a farm some ten miles out in the country. He didn't have a phone, so I set up a visitation date to go to his house at 4:00 p.m. on a certain day. He and his wife warned me that because of his long hours away in the fields, they had gotten a "biting" dog to protect her when she was alone. They gave their word that they would be there to protect me from the dog when I came.

I arrived on time and the Mrs. came out to the gate with "Barko," the dog, raging. He barked, growled and showed his vicious teeth. She ran him back to the house two or three times before he finally stayed. I walked the 20 twenty feet or so from the gate to the front porch with Barko still fuming. She told me her husband had not yet come in from the fields. He owned numerous acres and was nowhere in sight. She said, "There was certain work he wanted to finish before he quit. But he'll be here most any minute."

We sat on the porch and talked for about two hours. Still, no husband. Barko had lain down under the very high steps at the outer edge where he never took an eye off me the entire time. I finally said, "Ma'am, it's getting late and I need to be going." We had a prayer and then I asked her to walk me to the gate. She laughed and said, "Ah, Brother Holbrook, Barko is used to you now. He will be OK." She stood up, shook hands with me and said, "Barko, you stay put."

He did, until I got about half way! Out he came and "vroomm" I went. I beat him to the gate and when I closed it, he hit it so hard it addled him. He fell back on the ground. I wondered if he'd broken his neck. But it was short-lived. By the time I had opened the car door just outside the gate, he had experienced a "resurrection" and proceeded to climb the very high gate. I slammed the car door and started rolling up the window. He got over the gate and kept lunging against the car window until I thought he might break it.

Mrs. came running out, tried to calm him, and finally got him back inside the gate. I lowered the window glass about a couple of inches as she was asking if I was OK. I said, "I guess. I'm pretty nervous!" She said, "Since you are alright, do you care if I laugh? (Ha, ha, ha!) I have never seen anyone move as fast as you did going through that gate!" I faked a faint "Ha, ha," with her, but it certainly wasn't amusing to me.

Brother Deacon apologized to me the following Sunday at church, not for the dog, but for having to work so late he never made it to visit me. He said, "We'll have to set up another time." I never did. I told him he needed to have no fear for his wife while he was away. I said, "You have quite a watchdog!" I had no desire to ever see "Barko" again.

Among the many life time friends we gained at Milton was a young lady, who later married my cousin. Her grandfather was a minister. Her mother had died when she was very young. Her dad was away much of the time and her grandparents had reared her and her older and younger sisters. They also cared for and kept a nephew who was mentally retarded and somewhat physically impaired. Another grandson who had been seriously injured in an auto accident lived in a small house out back. When he passed away, they asked me to conduct a graveside funeral.

In Milton and Santa Rosa County, it was traditional for the city and county dignitaries to serve as honorary pallbearers. The burial site at the cemetery at Bagdad, Florida, was located on a very soft, sandy hill. The coffin was mounted over the burial hole with six pallbearers standing on one side and the High Sheriff, the county judge, the mayor, the clerk of Circuit Court and two county commissioners on the other. The funeral director, came and stood by me at the head of the grave and indicated he was ready for me to begin. As I began reading the scriptures, I heard what I thought was the sound of distant thunder. Then I felt the ground quivering beneath my feet. In an instant, all the ground on the side where the six officials were standing started caving in under the casket into the hole beneath.

The sheriff was standing at the end and he only went down about knee-deep. He began struggling to get out and help the judge who was in about waste deep. On the end next to the funeral director and me, one county

256

commissioner was trying to keep his balance and was pulling on one of the others who was almost all the way down under. The temporary foundations on that side of the casket had dropped about a foot or so making it even more difficult to get out of the hole and from beneath the casket.

The real pallbearers were trying to help hold the coffin and its supports, and I was getting so tickled, I could hardly contain myself. Finally, when everyone got pulled out and was trying to regain their composure and get the soil dusted off, I was laughing so hard and loud I turned backwards to the scene. The funeral director, seeing his assistant taking charge, turned with me and we both were about to "bust our sides." When we were able to calm ourselves, he leaned over and whispered to me, "Reverend, all these guys are crooks. They are on the take from moonshiners! You name it, they do it. While we've got them in the grave, go ahead and preach their funerals too! It will be good riddance!"

I've often wished I had a video of this incident. It was rumored that some of these men were big-time into moonshine whiskey. When the revenuers got hot on the trail of one of their stills, they would move most of it and then have lawmen "find" it and destroy what little was left. I do not know the veracity of this but I do know the town, political as it was, always had "political enemies" telling these and like stories on each other.

In an effort to reach more people, our church had purchased a bus. But even with it running regularly, I would still pick up some of our church folk who had no auto and lived in out-of-the-way places. One beautiful Sunday morning, I went to get a lady and her four children. Out came the children dressed and ready. They announced that their mother was very sick with the flu and couldn't come. "Please have prayer for me at church," they said she said.

The next morning I went downtown to deposit my check. It was very stormy. Rain was coming down in sheets, the wind was blowing furiously and it was very cold. When I got out of my car to go into the bank, I saw the "flu" lady walking out of the dime store. She was soaking wet and was wearing high-topped rubber boots like we wore at the dairy. When she saw me, she smiled and said, "You sure prayed the prayer of faith for me at church yesterday. I feel fine today!" I said facetiously, "Praise the Lord! Isn't God good to us?!" I don't like myself when I do things like this. I have to keep reminding myself that when I judge people, I am setting myself up for the same sort of judgment. (Mathew 7:1-2) Who knows, perhaps the Lord did heal her. Didn't we pray for such? (Acts 12:5, 13-16)

One of our members asked me to help him relocate in town, near the church. He lived about five miles out in the country and wanted to be closer to his doctor's office, the grocery store, bank, and church. I saw a house for sale that looked just like his about a block from the church. The owners said they wanted to move outside of town and would talk trade. Wow, this is a "made to order" proposition, I thought.

When the realtor and I went to my member's house to discuss the trade, he turned on me and asked what gave me the notion he wanted to move. "I wouldn't leave this place for anywhere, and by the way, when did you become a real estate salesman?" I left in shock, tried to apologize to the realtor and wondered what in the world was going on.

The member was at church the following Sunday, greeted me as if nothing had happened and I wondered at the whole issue even more. The family learned of the situation and apologized profusely to me, stating that their dad was doing many "strange" things lately. Not long after we had moved away, he died and they sent for me to preach his funeral. They told me his mind was gone completely by the time he passed away. At least I learned to stay out of my congregants' real estate deals.

I had gotten off on the wrong foot with another lady over chickens. She had called me to pick out three of her 30 fryers (her tithes) before she sold the rest to a local processing plant. Robert Raburn had just raised a bunch of his own and had filled my refrigerator-freezer and deep-freeze. "Eat all of them you want," he told me. I had absolutely no room for one more chicken, much less three. I asked the lady if she could sell all 30. "Why?" She asked. I told her. She said she could and I suggested she just bring the price of the three as tithes to the church.

Thinking all was well, my faithful "informant" let me know just how deeply I had offended the lady. And furthermore, since I received a percentage of the tithes as part of my compensation, she would never put money in the tithes as long as I was the pastor. Instead, she would put it in the building fund. At least the church would still benefit from her contributions, but I wondered if the Lord would honor it. (II Cor. 9:6-7)

Later, she put her 12 foot wooden boat up for sale. I thought since I wanted a boat, I might be able to earn her forgiveness for my transgression against her, by buying it. I pulled out the $45.00 asking price but she refused it. She said, "No, you take it first and try it out. And if you still want it I will take your money."

I called my deacon fishing buddy and we launched the boat on the Blackwater River, nearby. I mounted and cranked my 7 HP outboard motor, put it in forward gear, revved up the speed which resulted in a totally unexpected ripping, cracking sound. We watched in utter amazement as the entire back of the boat came off, motor and all. I rushed to the front with my friend in order to keep the rear of the now sternless boat above water level. While we were tying to collect our senses, he simply said, "dry rot." He was the same deacon who had lost his new left shoe in our previous boating accident.

Being near the edge in shallow water, we were able to wade to shore, pull out the bisected boat, and retrieve the motor and ill-fated stern. The motor had sunk while still running, but now it wasn't. I thought, "Here we go again." On a previous fishing trip further downriver, this same outboard had slipped off the back of a rented boat, went down while running and sank to the bottom in about 12 feet of water.

The water was very clear and we could see the motor lying on the bottom. We paddled in, got a rope and raised the motor. It wasn't running when we brought it up and before it would, it had to be overhauled completely. But this time we dried the spark plug and it later cranked right up as if nothing had ever happened.

And now, the boat. My partner said, "Let's take it back and I'll be a witness to what happened." I said, "No, let me handle this." I went to the owner, pulled out the $45.00, told her the boat was OK, just needed a little woodwork and without further ado she accepted the money. But she never stopped putting her tithes into the building fund offering while I was there. I took the boat to a cabinet shop. The owner sawed off the dry rot area, installed a new stern, painted it and charged me about $18.00. The new eleven foot boat worked fine and I sold it to my deacon-friend when I moved away later.

One day a couple with relatives who were members of our church asked me to perform their marriage ceremony. I didn't notice it too much when we rehearsed, but at the wedding, when the group had gathered in front of me, I said, "Dearly Beloved...." I looked to see all the dearly beloved, only to see no one except the four people in the wedding party. They were all about

6 feet tall or more. The groom said later that he had thought about bringing a box for me to stand on.

One couple I married there wound up divorcing only a short time later. They did not attend our church so I had lost touch. When I encountered the young lady downtown one day, I inquired about her husband only to discover the separation. I was shocked. Somehow, I was expecting all the marriage "knots" I tied, to hold "until death do us part." I recall what an uneasiness I experienced. I wondered aloud if it could be put back together. "No way possible," she stated.

At least there were no children involved. Since, I have tried to mediate situations where children were involved. I've seen the frustration children experience when the two people most dear to them are at odds with each other. This is one reason why I have worked diligently to keep couples together, if at all possible. The truth is, not only does the couple split when separation comes but the children are torn asunder as well. It takes two people working diligently to make marriage and family life successful. God willed such from the beginning. (Matt. 19:8) Many couples need to try a lot harder in the fear of God!

If there are some down-sides that confront one who is a minister of the Gospel and a pastor, there are also many up-sides. One of the main ones is the genuine converts who come to Christ and the privilege of helping and watching them grow in the grace and knowledge of the Lord Jesus Christ. Another thing is the lasting friendships that are made in every pastorate. Friends are the "spice of life" and portray another friend, one that "sticks closer than a brother," Jesus Christ, the Son of God and our Savior and Lord. (Proverbs. 18:24 and Luke 7:34b)

The James Earl Barnes Family

The "Cook" is calling Ernest to dinner – Milton, Florida, 1952

FIFTEEN

MILTON, FLORIDA – PART TWO

This continued the space of two years... Acts 19:10

One morning about daybreak I was awakened by a frantic knocking at my front door. I grabbed my clothes, quickly dressed and opened the door, still about half asleep. There stood a young woman in agony and tears. Her husband had come home drunk, beat her and their four children and finally threw her out of the house. She wanted to come in and said she had no place else to go. Then she wanted to know if I would go to her house and try to calm her husband down. She warned me that he was a tyrant, the meanest man in town, and even worse when drinking. She indicated where she lived, about two blocks away.

I invited her in, got Junell up and headed out all prepared to give her husband a piece of my mind. I arrived, knocked on the door, it opened and there stood a medium height man with a very humble and kind appearing countenance. "I'll bet you are the preacher and my wife sent you," he said, and invited me in. I agreed to both his accounts as we sat down in the living room. All four children came and sat near him, with the smallest on his lap, as he related his side of the story, after precisely telling hers. The difference in stories left me totally disarmed.

This was to be another lesson for me in my early ministry. The two sides convincingly told, left me needing the wisdom of Solomon (I Kings 3:16-26) and the gift of discernment (I Cor. 12:10) to deal with the situation. After getting them back together, I learned this had happened over and over, and it continued, all through my sojourn at Milton. The family began coming to church occasionally. Then he would get drunk, she would have him arrested, then she would come straight to me to help her bail him out a day or so later.

One day one of our church ladies asked me to visit a home to pray for a lady who was very ill. The sick lady's several children attended our Sunday

School. They either rode the church bus or someone went by and picked them up. When I arrived, I was appalled at the sight. All these people were living in a one-room shack, perhaps 18' by 24'. There was only one bed and the entire house was very dirty. I tried to lead the lady to the Lord. She died soon after I left. Word was that she actually died from disease derived from the filth. Perhaps her illness prevented her from proper house-keeping.

I was surprised at how clean, and even well dressed the children were at church. I wondered how this could be possible out of such a dirty and unsanitary environment called a home. When the event of the lady's death brought the horrible truth of the pitiful condition to the public, the community rose up and acted swiftly. They bulldozed the house to the ground and burned it. Within a few days a nice, new, frame house replaced the old one. The husband and dad was a hard worker in the pulp wood industry and he and his children were overwhelmed by the generosity heaped upon them by the townsfolk. Every bit of the material and labor was donated.

I was reminded of something even much worse, spiritual filth and depravity and thought of the time to come when some people would forever be that way, Rev. 22:11. But I also rejoiced in the fact that others would be righteous eternally because they had availed themselves of Christ's saving and cleansing power from their sins and dirtiness by His precious blood.

Some scriptures stand out over others. One of my favorites; the words of Jesus to his apostles in Mark 6:31: "Come ye yourselves apart into a desert place and rest awhile." The Holbrook version (mine) reads: "Come apart – or you'll soon come apart!" All my life I had purposely taken time off from the vicissitudes of life on a regular basis.

In keeping with this, Robert's family and Junell and I were going to take advantage of a "between – Sundays break." To cut expenses we decided to travel home together. It took a day's drive each way so we would have Tuesday through Friday to visit our relatives and get in a couple of days fishing at our super-favorite locations. Everything was going as planned, until Robert's reel and rod turned up missing.

It happened like this: Charles was holding revival services at nearby Holt Assembly of God and Saturday afternoon, he, Robert and I went fishing on Yellow river. We rented a boat at a fish-camp owned by a member where Charles was preaching. After a good catch of bass and with darkness pressing us, we were hurrying back to the landing. The wide-open motor suddenly sputtered and quit, leaving us to crash into a log-jam in mid-river.

We put gas in the tank, backed out and finally landed in the blackness of night. By flashlight, we discovered one missing fishing outfit: Robert's! "It must have fallen out of the boat when we hit the log-jam," he said. "I can't go home without it next week. And I can't afford to purchase a new one. I'll come back Sunday after church and see if I can find it."

Since fishing on the Lord's Day was strictly taboo in our religious circles, the fish-camp there would be closed Sunday. But since the "ox was in the ditch," Luke 14:5, the owner agreed that Robert and Charles could use a boat to do the searching Sunday afternoon.

We had used our heavier fishing plugs to lift objects we had dropped by accident in the water before, so Charles proceeded to tie one on his line as they motored up-river Sunday afternoon. To make sure his line wasn't tangled, Charles cast his plug into a slough while Robert ran the motor.

The bass lying in the slough apparently did not know it was Sunday. A beautiful greenish-yellowish Paw Paw minnow with spinners afore and aft was too much to resist. Even on Sunday! Robert, in shock, saw Charles set the hooks and start reeling in a splashing, jumping bass frantically trying to undo what it had just done! "Charles, you crazy outfit, let that fish get off," Robert shouted. Charles let it run and jump but it couldn't get loose. So he boated it. "Throw it back in," Robert insisted. "Why?" Charles asked. It's already caught. What did you do with the fish we caught yesterday?"

"Since it was freezing cold, I put them in a number three washtub behind the church. One of our members will get them after church tonight." "Well, add this one to them," Charles said. Arriving at the log-jam, in six or seven feet deep water, they saw Robert's reel and rod on the bottom. Charles brought it up and back to the landing they went.

After Robert made several more efforts to get the Sunday-caught bass back in the river, Charles again refused and put it in his tackle-box so it would not be observed at the fish-camp by the church members. Another church family was visiting this family as the Raburn brothers docked. Out came everyone with explanations being offered by the camp owner that the preachers weren't really fishing. It just looked that way!

The hidden bass began jumping inside Charles's tackle box. Charles started shaking the box to offset the noise and hurried to the car. Back at church, Robert threw the still-flopping bass into the tub of water with the near-frozen dead bass. After church, the man said to Robert, "Can you believe one of the fish you caught yesterday afternoon is still alive and swimming around in that tub? I've never known a bass living that long in a tub!" "Strange things do happen!" Robert responded. We made the trip home, Robert's reel and rod and all!

One day a business man stopped by the church and asked had we ever considered selling it and moving to another location, since it was situated on a steep, dangerous curve. He needed more apartments to rent to military personnel and our sanctuary and educational annex would be excellent to convert to such. He made a tentative offer and even suggested some beautiful property for sale on the main highway, not far away. The price of the new lots was very reasonable.

I presented the idea to the church board and they were excited and 100% for it. "I've always wanted to move to a better location the board chairman stated. This is our chance. We agreed to have the issue announced Sunday for the members to consider it. It went over like a lead balloon. For fear such might happen, those who opposed the idea quickly suggested we build a new sanctuary on the big adjacent lot the church owned on the south side of our property.

The lot had become a shortcut for several houses down a dirt street on the southwest side of the church. Instead of using the proper street when they came from the south, they drove right through our lot. I was almost hit a couple of times while I was mowing the property. Requests had been made by some of our members that they stop crossing this way, but they ignored them and even threatened a law suit to keep it open should we try to close it.

We announced a properly called business meeting for the purpose of the new sanctuary proposal. We needed additional educational space and the old church building would be ideal for conversion to such. The vote to start building immediately, passed unanimously. We would buy building materials as the money came in and do most of the work ourselves.

Within a few days the plans were completed, the building permit secured and under the leadership of our two member carpenters, the actual construction began. On a Saturday morning several volunteers set about shooting the grade, anchoring the batter-boards and stakes and stretching the strings.

Soon, we were digging the ditch for the footer. Near dark the project was completed. The next Saturday we would install the steel rods and pour the cement footer. Early Sunday morning before the Sunday School hour I walked out to review our previous day's labors. To my chagrin I discovered all the batter-boards, stakes and lines had been driven over and knocked down. That morning we had some members ready to draw "Peter's sword," (Matt. 26: 51-52) and slice some tires and perhaps some ears as well.

Early the next Saturday our workers returned and redid what had been damaged by angry local drivers. We set the steel, had an inspector on hand for an OK, and poured the cement. The next morning, I walked out to discover the same disturbing sight once again. Every stake and batter-board had been flattened. A man who held a county office lived along the graded street adjacent to our church on the west side. A couple of our men contacted him to see if he could help us stop this effort to thwart our proposed building.

Rather than assisting us, our men were rebuffed instead. He said the lot we were trying to close had been used for a thoroughfare so long we could not legally close it. We would be doing away with a short-cut several families had been using for many years. He did not mention that he, himself, used it many times, also.

We went to the city fathers and they said we most certainly could close the lot and build a new church structure there. Why else would they have issued us a building permit? A spokesman from the "short-cut" users sent us word that they would "see us in court." In the meantime, we continued with the building process.

Early the next Saturday morning, we had block-layers ready, and by dark, they had the walls up about six feet high all around. Sunday morning I went out again and the blocks had not been disturbed. But we received a warning that all the walls would be knocked down during that week. The county official and his group ordered a survey of all the church property lines. He then claimed we were parking cars for our church services on his property and he intended to put a stop to it.

One of our church ladies went to his house and challenged him. She said, "You once were friendly to our church and we voted for you. But now you are fighting us. Actually, it is God you are opposing and God has your number! If you as much as cause us one bit more trouble for the church, I would hate to be in your shoes!"

In addition to his county office, he was also a foreman of a pulpwood crew and the next day was taking a nap in the backseat of his 1952 Ford sedan, miles away in the pulp woods. The hot sun was beating down and the back car window literally exploded. Some of his men said it sounded like a shotgun shot. He was so shaken he had a heart attack. After a few days stay in the hospital he came home and sent for me.

We had a cordial visit and I offered a prayer for him. He apologized for his hostility toward the church and offered assistance in our building efforts, county trucks, fill dirt, graders, whatever. I thought, "What a change!" What I did not know at the time, and discovered a few days later, was that the survey he ordered showed our church parking area was not only all ours, but so was the entire graded road, and besides, his entire front porch was also on our church property. The surveyor who had done the work had passed the word to one of our men. I relayed the information to our church board and members and we agreed to give him the strip of property if he would pay the legal fees to have it transferred. He agreed, saved his front porch and to my knowledge was never unfriendly toward the church again. With the church building hulled in, no one attempted to use the "short-cut" again.

By the middle of the third year at Milton, Junell and I decided we would make a change. We had a new superintendent of the West Florida District, who stayed at our house when he had to be overnight in our neck of the woods. One day he drove up and told me that the District Youth Minister had accepted Oak City Assembly in Tallahassee, leaving open the position of District C. A. President. He said he and the presbyters wanted me. They would appoint me; since I was already vice-president, and assured me I would have no problem being elected later at District Council.

Add to this a group of people from Mobile, Alabama, who came to hear us minister, then invited us to candidate for their church. We went and preached and were elected with a 100% vote, something we'd never experienced at Mt. Zion or Milton. I told them I would give them an answer in two weeks. In one week, the Milton annual business meeting would be held and I had planned not to allow myself to be voted on anymore. But word had gotten out that we might leave, so a big majority of the church folk began to implore us to stay.

In the middle of this quandary, my telephone rang. It was a deacon from my home church, Mt. Zion, in Plant City. He was a truck-driver and was passing through Milton and asked me to meet him at a certain gas station where he was filling up. I went, we exchanged greetings and he told me Mt. Zion was without a pastor and the deacon board wanted me to allow my name to be considered. By now, my head was really spinning. The District Superintendent called and asked if I had made a decision to be West Florida's next Christ's Ambassador's president. When I told him I hadn't, he stressed what an advantage it would be for our future ministry. The church secretary in Mobile called and said they were anxiously awaiting my reply.

To add to the frustration, I entered my name at Mt. Zion and was elected. During the same week, the Milton church voted overwhelmingly to extend our pastorate there another year. A couple of carloads drove over from Mobile to encourage us to go there. Our superintendent called again urging me to accept the district youth office. Realizing I couldn't stall any longer, I opted to accept Mt. Zion. When I submitted my resignation the following Sunday, a deacon stood up and said if I left Milton, I would be 100% out of the will of God. He owned a dog named "Barko."

There was an anxiousness in making our decision, because any four of the opportunities seemed favorable. We prayerfully chose by faith because we walk by faith and not by sight. (II Cor. 5:7)

It wasn't easy to say no to the church folk at Mobile. And it wasn't easy to say no to our District Superintendent and Presbytery board. And probably worst of all it wasn't easy to part with a host of faithful Milton church members. I reminded them that someday when we get to Heaven, there would be no more partings ever!

A friend of ours told us about a trucker in Milton who went to central Florida each week to buy produce. He usually drove down empty. I contacted him and he agreed to move us to Plant City for $75.00. He even sent two men to help us load his semi. Amid sadness and tears we said goodbyes and found ourselves homeward bound.

When we arrived at the Mt. Zion parsonage, several of the church men met us, helped us unload and set up the furniture and gave us an overwhelming welcome. We would serve as pastors there for the next eleven years, from June 1954 until May of 1965, during which time many marvelous things happened. The first was the many souls born into the kingdom of God, including several of our relatives, and the next was the births of our three wonderful daughters.

Junell, overlooking Pensacola Bay
1954 – Expecting our first baby, Sandra

Ernest, in front of new sanctuary
under construction at Milton, Florida 1954

271

Sunday a.m. worship service – First Assembly of God Milton, Florida

Billy and Jane Raburn on their wedding day

Billy and Jane Raburn
with their son, Rodney

SIXTEEN

MT. ZION AGAIN

And they returned home again... Acts 21:6

I'll never forget the mixed emotions of utter elation and nervous anticipation that flooded my innermost being as the reality and prospects of being home again began to sink in. I recalled the warnings of Jesus about a prophet's lack of honor in his own house and hometown, (Mathew 13:57) and I assumed that may also apply to a home boy preacher. But a new challenge lay before me and I was determined to do my very best at it. The big burden burning in my bosom was to preach the Gospel of Jesus Christ not only to the community in which I grew up, but to my many relatives here as well.

The pastor who had preceded me, had led the congregation in plans to construct a new sanctuary next to the frame building built in 1933, after the first building had been burned by arsonists. This would now become my project. The congregants wanted to do as much of the work as possible, so I could clearly see that my mind and hands would be full, in addition to my other pastoral duties.

By then, we were also expecting our first child. We had been married five years and Junell, especially, was more than anxious to expand our family. This was one reason we had settled in Milton. Following failed efforts there, we had both consulted a doctor in Pensacola, Florida, who, after tests, said there seemed to be no reason why we couldn't have a baby.

On a trip home my dad had suggested my wife take Lydia Pinkham, a tonic that supposedly would aid pregnancy. She did, and whether it was this, our prayers, extra efforts or all three combined, I don't know. But in about February of 1954, Junell announced the good news that our first little one was on the way and would arrive in September. This was another totally new experience for us, coupled with a new pastorate, building a new church building and assuming a five weekday morning radio program I also inherited from the former pastor.

A new hospital had just been constructed and completed in Plant City hardly two miles from Mt. Zion. It was a combined effort of the community and churches, spearheaded primarily by the Baptists resulting in the name: "South Florida Baptist Hospital." The name prevailed, despite some dissension from the other church groups, who insisted that the project would not have succeeded without their help, which was true.

With the radio program, which followed the popular local morning news broadcasts, I soon was known again throughout the area. I took it upon myself to visit the hospital most every day. Jesus indicated the sick need a physician, Matthew 9:12, and I seized upon this action as an opportunity to minister.

I not only visited and prayed for my own constituents, but also all of those who called on me for a pastoral visit. Many of these did not attend church anywhere, and I became their "pastor of sorts." I then decided, as I read the daily lists of hospital patients, that I would also visit everyone I knew. This became a vital part of my life and ministry which afforded many wonderful opportunities to witness for Christ. Over the years, the outcome would mean several converts to Christianity, adding new members, not only to our church, but others as well. It also resulted in my becoming a counselor, a "marrying Sam," a preacher of many funerals and a referee for some family disputes.

Other opportunities to serve the Kingdom of God came with my involvement in the Plant City Minister's Association, where, over the years, I held the office of secretary once, vice president twice and president. I spoke in many area churches during community-wide services at Thanksgiving, Christmas, Easter and other special occasions.

I was elected as sectional secretary and then assistant presbyter for the West Central Florida area of the Assemblies of God. I later served as a District Officer by being presbyter of Section Nine, for nine additional years. I served as co-chairman of the Fellowship of Christian Athletes at Plant City High School and lectured at family-life classes on some occasions. I also served as a chaplain for the Boy Scouts at a special seminar where I spoke at the University of South Florida in Tampa.

Realizing my own lack of higher formal education, I later enrolled as a student at the University of South Florida in Tampa, selecting to major in psychology. While attending part-time there, I was elected to serve as president of Chi Alpha, which is the Assemblies of God college program. I also helped found the "Sons of Harmony" gospel quartet which later became "The Songsmen." With the former Saturday night youth rallies now gone, I participated in a Saturday night singspiration, holding one each month at Mt. Zion. With the new sanctuary complete, we could pack about 400 people inside and sometimes we would open the windows to accommodate an overflow crowd. It reminded me of the crowds we had in Andalusia, Alabama.

Having seemingly boundless youthful energies, the hectic schedule seemed routine. I designated a day a week for recreation, usually Mondays. The Plant City Golf and Country club let ministers play for free on Mondays, so I played with some of the ministers at times. But mostly, my recreation was fishing. With a dad, an uncle and cousins by the dozens, I didn't have to search for fishing buddies. Word soon spread about our bass catches and I found myself taking bankers, big-time businessmen and others, on fishing trips.

My wife said the Lord let her have her babies on Sundays so I wouldn't be off fishing when they arrived. Two were born on Sunday and she went into labor for the other two on Sunday and they were born on Monday. Our first, Sandra Kay, was born on Sunday morning, September 19, 1954. It was during the wee hours that Junell awakened me. There were sure signs that this was the real thing, so we made our way to the hospital.

The hospital called the Doctor and soon he arrived and periodically reported to me the progress, or lack of it! But just after daylight he announced that I was the father of a nine pound daughter. I announced our new arrival to the congregation just before I preached that morning. I returned to the hospital after church to see Junell and our big-little young lady. There were fifteen babies in the hospital nursery, a record at the time, and my Sandra was undoubtedly the prettiest. When the nurse brought her to the room, I got to hold her for the very first time. Wow!

How do you explain such an experience? Here is a new life, a gift from God, Solomon said in Psalms 127:3. And I was now awkwardly cuddling this bundle of joy in my arms. Junell assured me she wouldn't break as I carefully and anxiously tried to equalize my hands and arms under and around her. Then, I'll never forget the awesome feeling I had as I gave her back to Junell and watched them lying side by side.

Not long after Sandra's birth, we selected another Doctor as our physician. It was from a recommendation made by our Lakeland friends. This Doctor was married to their niece, was just starting out in his profession and shared an office with another prominent doctor. What a tremendous blessing he turned out to be through the years.

We would experience the awesomeness of birth three more times: when Sharon was born on Monday, August 10, 1959, and Phyllis on Sunday, November 17, 1963. Our baby son, John Mark, was born prematurely on Monday, September 19, 1960, and survived only four hours.

After two girls, we had wanted a boy the third time around. Back then, we did not know ahead of time whether it would be a boy or girl. But problems developed during the pregnancy of John Mark. He was born at just over six months and wasn't fully developed enough to handle life alone.

Our doctor came down the hospital hall where I was waiting and told me to talk with my God. "Being a minister, you should know how," he said. Four hours later, he told me the little boy had died. "I want you to make peace with God about this," he stated, "and remember, this is one way the Lord has of aborting that which is not able to survive properly," he concluded.

There were no words sufficient for expressing the strange emptiness at this time. As I embraced my darling spouse, we cried and prayed together, seeking consolation in Christ, and rehearsing the words of the Doctor. It was another new experience for us and hard to understand. We were clearly in a state of awe, both here in the hospital, and later at the graveside memorial service. I must admit that the prayers and support of our congregants, plus the compassion of our physician was a great comfort to us. When we did not get a bill from the Doctor, we inquired. He promptly stated, "I never charge when I lose a baby. Not for you or anyone."

Truth is, this doctor never charged me, as a minister, for any services he ever rendered to me. He said, "My services to ministers of the Gospel are free." He kept this pledge right on until he retired. On one instance, when I had gone to his office for something, he introduced me to the medical missionary ministry of a couple affiliated with another church organization. He had gone to the Yucatan peninsula on vacation, met these people, and spent the rest of his vacation administering medicine with them in the remote areas.

He said to me, "I have finally found some people who, for the first time in my life, I believe are true Christians. I want you to help me schedule some services for them in this area." At the time, I was serving as president of the East Hillsborough Minister's Association. I not only had one of the missionaries at our church for a service, but also had her speak at the monthly meeting of the ministers. Several of them also booked her for speaking engagements and support.

One day I was walking down a first floor corridor of the hospital near the emergency room and saw my doctor coming out. He quickly said, "Reverend, come with me." Back into the emergency room we went. Seated in a chair by the wall was a very distraught mother holding a dead two year old in her arms. "I've done all I can do," the doctor said. "Now she needs you!" I laid my hand on her shoulder and began to pray. Then, I tried my best to say something to comfort her, even though comfort is most usually not available from anywhere or anyone at such times.

About this time the emergency room door burst open and in came the lady's mother. She began to express her grief in a negative way. Rather than trying to console, she instead, began to accuse. "I told you before you ever dug that irrigation pit behind your house this might happen. More than once I warned and begged you not to create something that could cost you a child."

This was all I could take. I took her arm and led her outside the door into the hallway. "Please," I pleaded, "I know this is devastating, but recalling such now, makes bad matters even worse. Let's try to help the hurt, not intensify it." I was able to calm her down somewhat until her husband, the grandfather, arrived. I apprised him of the situation, told him the doctor couldn't revive the child. I suggested he try to keep his wife out of the emergency room. I went back in and stayed with the mother until her husband arrived, and the morticians came to get the child.

I guess I never realized the first time I viewed and toured the new South Florida Baptist Hospital what vivid memories it would later hold for me. This above related incident, the births of my four children, the births of many babies of our congregants and friends, the illnesses and deaths of many acquaintances and loved ones, the monthly ministers' meetings held at the hospital chapel, and several genuine conversions to Christ there, are among many.

Once I was on the elevator with a lady I did not know. Suddenly, the elevator stopped. The door did not open. I pushed the buttons. No response. I rang the emergency bell. Still nothing. The lady looked at me and said, "We are stuck!" With those words she collapsed onto the floor. I tried to revive her. No luck. I grabbed the door with my hands and braced and pushed with my feet until I broke the pressure and the door came open. The elevator floor was about one foot below the ceiling of the first floor.

I got down on the floor and cautiously stuck my head out, hoping the elevator wouldn't move upward. I looked both ways. No one in sight! Then I hollered, "Help! Help!" Two orderlies came out of a door down the hall. I said, "We are stuck and a lady with me has fainted." They observed the situation and one went for a ladder. He returned and we were able to slide the lady through the opening and down the ladder. By then, others were attracted and assisted the lady to the emergency room and helped me down the ladder. I went into the emergency room and in a few moments the lady opened her eyes. "What happened?" She asked. I said, "You and I got stuck on the elevator." She said, "I'll never get on an elevator again as long as I live."

One day I had gone into a ward to pray for a man who had relatives who attended our church. I was praying in a normal tone of voice, as I always did in hospitals, when the curtains suddenly parted and an irate doctor started screaming at me. He made several times the noise I was making. "Here I am working with a man who is bleeding and your "noise" just might cause him to die. Now shut up and get out!" I apologized, turned and softly told the man I'd come back later.

I went out the door, down the corridor and into the stairwell. I stood there shaken for a moment. I did not know the doctor and had only seen him a time or two at the hospital. At first, I thought of going to the hospital administrator, whom I knew well. Then I thought of the hospital Chaplain, a dear friend who worked with all the ministers and attended our monthly meetings there. Finally, I decided it would be best that I "cool down" before I did anything. I was really too upset to act. Had I been able at the moment, I might have foolishly desired, like the "sons of thunder" to call down "fire from heaven," upon that doctor. (Luke 9:54 and Numbers 11:1-3) How awful! How unchristian! The doctor's fury had taken control of me!

I waited for a few more moments, made some other visits, and then returned to the ward where I had been reprimanded. The doctor was gone, but the man with whom I was praying had his "dander" up. He said, "I'm not a Christian, Brother Holbrook, but that doctor stopped you in the middle of your prayer and that's not right. I'm going to report him to somebody." I said, "No, let me handle it."

I later discovered this doctor was new in the area, was very antagonistic toward any church, minister or anything that reflected religious faith. Other ministers had received the same treatment from him. The hospital administrator cornered him, reminded him the hospital was Christian-oriented and would stay that way. "Ministers," he told the doctor, "are just as important to the patients as are the doctors, and perhaps even more so!" After that, the doctor became very friendly with me and would smile and speak as we passed in the hospital hallways.

One morning just before daybreak, I was awakened with a sharp pain in my left side. In a matter of minutes it was so intense I was doing "cartwheels," hanging over the bedrail, moving everyway possible to try to get relief – but finding none. Having witnessed my dad and mother, and a congregant with similar pain, I began to realize I had a kidney stone, on the move. "Junell, get up and get me to the hospital as quick as you can," I pleaded. After what seemed like 30 minutes – she said it was ten – we hit the road none too soon for me.

Upon arrival at the emergency room I grew extremely nauseated to add to my dilemma. I asked the attending nurse for a pan. She went for one and returned – too late. I used the trash can and she let me have it! "Here's your pan! But you didn't wait! Now look what a mess you have made for me to clean up." So I let her have it right back. "If it hadn't taken you until forever, I wouldn't have done it," I yelled back. My carnal nature was alive and well, prompted, I'm sure, by my physical agony.

My doctor came, looked me over, asked a few questions, with me telling him what it was, and "Please give me something to ease this pain." He ordered a shot of Demerol. After 30 minutes, still no sign of a letup in the "torment," which is the word my mom used for "hell." It wasn't that bad I'm sure. Just almost! After another shot with increased dosage, in a few moments I began to feel relief. How good can good feel? They wheeled me to a hospital room where I slept for hours and hours. I resisted every time they tried to awaken me. But finally, on doctor's orders, I was aroused.

I was to strain the urine, and when the stone passed a couple of days later, it was so small you could hardly see it. It was about the size of a pinhead, with little spurs protruding outwards. I had seen a kidney stone lying on a surgeon's office desk some time before when I had taken a parishioner to see that doctor. The stone was the size of a small orange or tangerine and had been surgically removed from a man's kidney. When I had mine, I surely thought it must have been just as big – only to realize it was nothing in comparison. But the pain was big enough. It felt like someone had stuck a knife in my side and then just kept moving it around. No letup!

My oldest sister, Louise, had had two babies, and one kidney stone. She said of the two, she had rather have a baby anytime. An elderly doctor had attended my mom when she once had a spell with a kidney stone. I heard her say, "Doctor, I think I'm dying!" He returned, "No, Julia, you are too sick to die. You'll have to get better in order to die." We all laughed but my mother didn't think it was funny then, or anytime after.

Only a few months afterward, I suffered two more kidney stone attacks. Amazingly, when the stone wasn't moving down that small passageway the size of a thread, from kidney to bladder, there was no pain. But when it moved, so did you, doing whatever you could to try to get relief. The pain defies description.

On about the third morning of the second attack, the hospital chaplain came down to visit and pray with me. I said, "My brother, I can't get out of here and go home until I pass this stone. Would you please agree with me in prayer, that I soon pass it?" (Matt. 18:19)

He humbly bowed his head and asked the Lord, according to His will, to minister to my need and request. Immediately, upon his leaving my room, the urge came, then the straining process, and then the big little stone appeared. I ran out into the hospital corridor and saw the elderly chaplain hobbling his way along. I called to him and he turned and waited while I hurried to him. "Let me show you something," I said. He looked at the stone, never said a word, turned, and with big tears in his eyes trudged on down the hallway.

My cousin, Charles Raburn, who was by then pastoring the Gordon Street Assembly of God in Plant City, was amused when I told him, not only how painful a kidney stone episode was, but what kinds of physical movements one makes seeking any sort of relief. He laughed heartily when I tried to describe my particular gymnastics. Ere long, I was called to his hospital room where he was undergoing a similar attack. Describing his agony he agreed with my previous description of the physical response to a kidney stone attack. Both he and my dad had surgery for stone removal involving incisions that reached almost halfway around their body. So much for kidney stones! I hope and pray there won't be any more, ever!

I received a surprising phone call from the Turkey Creek High school principal one day. I was asked to be the baccalaureate speaker for the 1957 graduating class. I responded with a nervous "yes" and thanked the principal for the invitation. He said he was honored and delighted to have someone to speak who was also a graduate from Turkey Creek. I had graduated from there in 1946 and the class members I was to address were first graders at that time. It had been eleven years.

What could I tell a group of young adults that would inspire and challenge them to be and do their very best at this stage of their lives. This was before God became unconstitutional and was booted out of the public schools and the American national life. Scriptures could still be read in classrooms and the concept of the Ten Commandments could be taught as a moral compass. Prayers could be offered by Christian principals and teachers. Schools could still have Christmas and Easter programs and Bibles were still being distributed in schools by the Gideons and others.

At the time, I would never have dreamed that what has happened in our nation could possibly happen. So, I built my message after prayer and study, to reflect what God, Christ, the Bible and the church meant to me personally.

Amid all the activities, the church showed a slow, continuous growth pattern. The radio program also showed ratings, on several occasions, that equaled the noontime local news as the top listened-to programs on WPLA. Then the radio hierarchy decided to hire a P. R. (public relations) expert to give the station a "once over," with recommendations for increased listening appeal and thus more revenue. Guess what radio show was to get the ax? Mine! "No station should have anything religious," the expert said. "Religion is too divisive and costs you listeners," he stated.

But because of my program's good ratings and my close friendship with the owner, I was allowed to stay on. I was moved to the 5:15 p.m. spot after having broadcast at 8:15 a.m. for years. WPLA was a "daytime" station and signed on and off with the "sun," or daylight hours. In the long summer months the station would broadcast until 7:30 p.m. or later.

In order to keep my program time from constantly moving around to accommodate the last fifteen minutes of the broadcast day, I was given the 5:15 p.m. spot. With this arrangement I would only have to move to 4:45

p.m. during December and January, the months with the shortest daylight hours. The results? Can you believe prime-time, drive-home time?! I was told by one radio staffer that "Temple Vespers," my new program name, had absolute top listened-to-ratings according to the latest listener survey. I was grateful.

During this time, the issue of racial integration was making headline news everyday. In response, our minister's association invited the black clergymen to join our group. Some of them did. We held community-wide services in their churches and I preached for one of their revival services. Our fellowship was good. Despite my segregationist upbringing, I found myself reaching out to my black brothers and sisters in Christ. Acts 17:26 declares that they, just as us and everyone, were made of one blood by the creator.

I agree with a former Chaplain of the United States Senate who stated: "We can't do everything for everybody. But if we would put aside indifference and prejudice, we could do something for someone. Think what would happen if every affluent family did something for a needy family; if every white person took responsibility to relate to one black person; if every believer helped an unbeliever; if every man thought of himself as a committee of one to bring reconciliation and resolution to the social ills that are so deeply dividing our nation and our world! What if?" What a question to ponder!

During those busy years at Mt. Zion, our special Lakeland friends continued to contact us and we occasionally visited them. They seemed to like our company even though they seldom came to our church services. They were always exploring ways to further the Gospel of Jesus Christ. On one occasion, he loaned us money to buy a tent, some $800.00. Rev. Charles Raburn and I and several friends pitched the tent in several areas including locations in east and north Plant City, at Branchborough, near Zephyrhills, at Thonotosassa, and on the church grounds at Mt. Zion.

There were several converts in each of the meetings. We took a nightly offering for expenses and everything above these, we applied to the loan. We finished paying the loan in full when we sold the tent, which was later used to start a new church. One other time my friend loaned me a thousand dollars when I bought some cows. Every penny was repaid. The only time he ever gave me any money was once when he was in Alabama and one of his cows in Lakeland got out of the pasture.

The neighbors called him complaining, and he called me from Alabama and asked me to see if I could round her up and take her to the auction. Dad helped me. We found her in an orange grove across the lake from his house next to Southeastern College. It took some doing but we finally caught her, loaded her in our cattle trailer and sold her for $138.00. When he returned home a few days later, I carried him the check. He endorsed it, and gave it to me, he said, for all my trouble. These folks had a heart for the Gospel. They were always involved in assisting churches, not individuals.

They were generous supporters of missionary efforts in the Philippine Islands. Once when I had gone to the bank to co-sign a note with one of our missionaries to purchase an airplane to be used in Africa, we were turned down and my friend heard about it. He called me and offered to loan us $3,000, interest free, for the purchase of a used Piper Cub.

The missionary and I began an effort to find such an airplane. While trying out one in Kissimmee, Florida, the motor sputtered and quit on us at an altitude of about 1,000 feet. "I believe we may be out of gas," the pilot said. He turned on the alternate tank. It, too, was empty.

My heart moved up into my throat as the pilot began nervously trying to locate a place to make a "dead stick" landing. He spotted a pasture just east of Highway 17/92 on the south edge of town. As we glided downward and almost to the ground, suddenly there loomed a big canal we hadn't seen before. It looked for sure we would crash into the canal bank on the opposite side. In those tense moments, I felt I was surely about to depart this life. My past flashed before me, including some of my sins, which I hoped had been forgiven and forgotten, and covered by the precious blood of Jesus Christ.

I even visualized the newspaper headlines: PLANT CITY MINISTER KILLED IN CRASH WHILE TRYING OUT AIRPLANE TO PURCHASE FOR MISSIONARY. These split-second horror thoughts were interrupted by the sounds of the airplane engine restarting, carrying us safely across the big canal and then dying again, as quickly as it had come back to life. But, thank God, by then we were making a perfect gliding landing. A guardian angel, again? Whose, it didn't matter, mine, or the pilot's! What did matter was that we were safely on terra firma!

We hiked about a quarter mile to a big ranch house. The rancher was friendly, had high octane gas in his pump, filled a five gallon can and carried us back to the airplane. It cranked right up. He refused any pay and waved at us as we took off from his pasture and headed back to the airport. We soon discovered the airplane had a faulty gas gauge and the pilot had erred by not manually checking the fuel.

Another pilot at the airport, who was also an airplane mechanic, said the airplane engine probably restarted as we tilted downward to land, draining a little fuel to the engine and consequently taking us safely across the canal. Perhaps so, but I still contended it was a miracle, no matter how it happened. This plane was not purchased, but another was, with a fuel gauge that worked. And it was used in missionary work in Africa for a number of years.

In the meantime, some problems developed and the missionary was recalled from the missions' field by the Foreign Missions Department in Springfield, Missouri. I had stood good on the $3,000.00 note to my friend and I checked with him to see if any of the money had been repaid. It hadn't. I contacted Springfield, since we had informed them and got their OK for the loan in the first place, and in a few days they forwarded a check to me from the missionary's account that covered the full amount of the loan.

When I brought the check to my benevolent brother, he thanked me and told me that he would not have required me to pay the loan, even if there were no money coming from the missionary or Springfield. Over the years I spent several full days with him. We once rode up to his sand mine north of Polk City. He had built the road into the mine area and a General had purchased acreage along the road just off Highway 33. My friend complained, "I built the road, but they named it for the General."

Another time he called and asked me to help him buy a boat outfit. "One just like you would want for yourself," he said. We looked in Lakeland, Winter Haven and Auburndale. We finally took one out from Lakeland Marine, giving it a spin on Lake Parker. It was a 16 foot fiberglass boat with windshield, steering wheel, folding canvas top and 50 HP Johnson motor. What a beauty! He bought it, but never used it. His wife later told me it was a waste of money. He also toured me through the cement plant and showed me the concrete fence posts he invented for his pastureland near Polk City. Some are still there as of this date.

One day I was in Lakeland, on business for the church and I stopped by his office. He asked if I had time to ride around Lakeland with him. I agreed and he got into my car. We passed a "muck pond" where the soil was being extricated for use in aiding the growth of yard plants, shrubbery, lawns, etc. It was mostly sold to plant nurseries. He said, "See that muck pond? I could have bought it for $7,000. While I was trying to buy it for less, the owner sold it to this man who has now sold one million dollars worth of peat, muck and topsoil." As we drove, we discussed Oneonta and the dam projects once more. "I need an airplane to fly back and forth up there. If you will take flying lessons and get a pilot's license, I'll buy us an airplane," he said. I never did, and he never did.

He also later discussed with me the proposition of setting up a foundation so his estate would be used for the Gospel of Christ. "I want you to be in full control of it all," he said. I discussed this with Junell and being naïve and fearful about such a project, I declined.

I suggested a Christian attorney to help him with the project. I do not know if it was ever established. I was shocked not very long afterward when his wife called me and said, "Please come, and hurry." We went and discovered he had died instantly of a heart attack. I really lost a good friend at his passing.

I'll never forget a funny story about my grandfather, the late Rev. J. J. Holbrook, that my special friend told me. Granddad was holding church services in a rented store building in West Lakeland. These services eventually led to and played a part in the establishment of the First Assembly of God of Lakeland, later on.

Our friends had heard of a Pentecostal meeting being conducted by my dad's dad and found the location. This was in the early 1930's during the depression. About middle-ways during the sermon, they drove up in their new Austin, a compact car of that time. Everyone looked and some of the people actually got up and went outside to see the new car. Any kind of new automobile was rare in those days and always drew onlookers and admirers.

My friend said he heard my granddaddy say very loudly from inside the building: "Count on the devil to invent some new contraption to divert attention from God's Word!" I recalled that I remembered seeing the Austin myself at Mt. Zion. I must have been about six or seven at the time.

New sanctuary under construction at Mt. Zion Assembly of God
Plant City, Florida, about 1955

The Sons of Harmony Quartet
Left to Right: W. L. Porter, Joe Walden, Chuck McIntosh, Ernest and Leo
Gillman

The Sons of Harmony Quartet on a long play album recorded at Nugget
Studios in Tampa, Florida. The records were pressed in Nashville,
Tennessee
Front: Chuck McIntosh, Joe Hart Back: Ernest, Carl Sumner, Leo Gillman

WPLA front entrance

Ernest and James Sessions with a nice bass catch

Howard Barnes and Ernest with a bass catch from the Hillsborough River

SEVENTEEN

MT. ZION AGAIN – PART TWO

Believe on the Lord Jesus Christ and thou shalt be saved, and thy house...
Acts 16:31

There is no question that hospital visitation and the radio broadcasts were two major factors in my life and ministry at Mt. Zion. The radio listener numbers remained very high throughout the years. Many area businessmen became courtesy sponsors, sparing me from having to solicit support from the radio audience or my church members, whom I kept busy building the new sanctuary, a new parsonage and two educational buildings.

The radio format I used starting in 1954 became an "ear-catcher." In the 15 minute time-frame, I used a mixture of "one-liners" under the heading "Ponder this," two gospel songs, the latest religious news and a three to four minute sermonette. The manager of one of the "dime" stores said, "I listen to you because I know you will be finished in a very short time. I can't stand long sermons."

An auto dealership owner called and asked me to drop by his office. He said, "You have my mother as a radio-fan. He gave me a $100.00 check and then supported the programs as long as he had the dealership and beyond. He also furnished me "brass-hat" automobiles at near his costs during all those years.

A shut-in man sent for me. He told me how uplifting the program was to him. He said not to tell his wife, because she was not tolerant of any religion but hers, but he secretly gave me $50.00 toward the program. He passed away soon after that. I don't think I fully realized the impact of the broadcasts during that time, but testimonies have continued to come to me and my family members of many people whose lives were helped, changed or encouraged in the Christian faith, even to this day.

The total radio ministry time covered most of 1949, then spanned from 1954 until 2001 almost continuously on WPLA, WCIE and WTWB. It is

293

not unusual for people to recognize my voice and identify me even now, from having heard me but never having seen me.

By the way, when your voice is so recognizable because of years of radio ministry, it doesn't pay to let your carnal nature express itself verbally in public. Once I had had it with the telephone company. The phone kept cutting off over and again. After a delay of one, two or three days, the repair crew would come, "fix it," and it would be out again hardly before they left. After several times and weeks of this I let my anger do the talking. In the middle of a most heated complaint about the "super-sorry" telephone service I was interrupted by the telephone operator.

"Your voice sure sounds familiar," she said. "Aren't you radio Pastor Ernest Holbrook I hear each evening on WCIE?" I was speechless for a few seconds. When I found my voice, I admitted I was. "Oh, I enjoy your program so very much," she continued. I apologized for my uncontrolled outburst. This has happened to me more than once. My wife, who heard it, told me it was good enough for me. Imagine that!

Once while visiting an uncle of mine, who was also one of our church deacons, he told me the name of the man who spear-headed the burning of the church on Sam Allen Road. He was a familiar figure in the community and had become a member of another church. Unknown to me at the time, he had become a devout listener of my radio program. When he had become ill, a sickness unto death, he asked his wife to call me to see if I would pay him a visit. I told her I would and set a time to go.

In the meantime, I told my uncle of the surprising and unexpected request. My uncle said he expected I might get a confession of the burning, since the man was on his deathbed. I went at the appointed time and our visit was very cordial. He was bedfast, thanked me for coming and then began to tell me what a daily blessing my program was to him. "I'm at the point of death and wanted you to visit and pray for me before I pass on," he said.

It was a very touching moment as the man who allegedly had once planned our church burning was now weeping profusely while I was praying with him. But if a confession of the church-burning was at issue, it did not happen. In a few days I was notified of his passing away. One of his family members is now a Pentecostal pastor.

The hospital visitation, besides being commended as eternally rewarding by Christ Himself, (Matthew 25:36) and bringing encouragement to the sick as well, also resulted in several decisions for Christ, including some "eleventh-hour" conversions. Do I believe in "death-bed" conversions? Surely! Especially when I consider the thief on the cross; (Luke 23:43) the late-hour laborers; (Matthew 20: verses 6,9,12 and 15) and the amazing mercies of the Lord. (Psalms 136) My belief is also confirmed when I consider my own experiences with those who made complete surrender to the Lord evidenced by their testimonies and even facial expressions of peace with God.

The sad part, of course, is the loss of a lifetime of service to the Lord. Think of the wasted years! It is far better, both for now and eternally, to "Remember thy creator in the days of thy youth." (Ecclesiastes 12:1) Such can bring a repeat of Paul's testimony in II Timothy 4:6-8, arriving at death's door ready, having "fought a good fight, keeping the faith and finishing the race." The result: "A crown of righteousness…"

When I consider the many miles driven and hours spent at hospitals in Plant City, Lakeland, Tampa, St. Petersburg, Orlando, Gainesville, Ocala, Sarasota, Bradenton and other places like Dade City, Zephyrhills, Bartow, Sebring, Lake Wales, etc., I'm grateful for each privilege I had to minister to multiple cases of spiritual and physical maladies in the Name of the Lord.

One day I had gone to Tampa General Hospital to visit a congregant on the 7th floor, the ward for the mentally and emotionally disturbed. After the visit, on the way out, I heard a running noise behind me and turned around just in time to be enveloped in the arms of the pursuer. It was a beautiful young blond and we began going round and round, like we were close-dancing in the hospital corridor.

Actually, I wasn't dancing – I never learned how – I was holding on for dear life, trying to keep both of us from falling. Then, as we sort of got stabilized, she rumpled my hair, started unbuttoning my shirt and running her hands in my shirt pickets. I was trying to resist. Honest!

You would have had to see all this to believe it. About then, not a moment too soon, two orderlies who saw the commotion "rescued" me. They separated us and took her by both her arms. One called her by name and asked, "What in the world are you doing to this nice man?" "I was trying to find his comb," she said, as they apologized to me and led her away.

I couldn't help but wonder why such a young woman was in a place like this. There are so many pitfalls for children and young people, some caused by themselves and many, I'm sure, caused by others or by who knows what.

My heart and prayers go out to those who are victims of sin, Satan and misfortune; especially to children and young people whose lives have been misled and abused by adults. Jesus spoke of this in Matthew 18:3-7. Bad consequences for child-offenders!

Another time, I had been called and made an afternoon rush visit to the same hospital. At this time I was broadcasting live late in the afternoon five days a week. As I made my way back through downtown Tampa, it dawned on me that drive-home traffic was beginning. My watch showed 4:30 p.m. and my radio program was at 5:15. When I reached Interstate 4, it was bumper to bumper. As I finally emerged from the traffic-jam I was grateful for the Interstate and broke the speed limit all the way.

I exited Interstate 4 at about 12 minutes after 5:00. This was in north Plant City and the station was in south Plant City on what is now Jim Redman Parkway. In an emergency situation like this, one can expect catching every light red and getting blocked behind slow-moving cars whose drivers are going nowhere, as slow as possible. While stopped at a red light in downtown Plant City, my theme song began. It was titled "One Step" and went: "If you take one step toward the Lord, He'll take two steps toward you." A WPLA staffer had recommended it as a theme song for my "Temple Vespers" program.

I remembered it was about three minutes long when played fully through. Another traffic light and finally I was pulling into the parking lot and rushing into the studio just as it ended. I sat down behind the microphone, started talking as if all was perfectly normal. My good friend and broadcasting buddy made a fanning motion of his face as he saw me enter.

Later, he said he was wondering if he was going to have to "preach" in my place. Incidentally, on some occasions after this, he did fill in for me when I had to be absent from the studios, battling heart disease. And he did a splendid job, presenting gospel songs and devotional thoughts. But this day, as I sat down to the microphone, I motioned for him through the glass, to grab me a couple of songs. I usually arrived early enough to make the selections myself. He did it perfectly, and as far as I know, no one else ever knew what had happened. Whew!

Some months earlier, when I was still on the 8:15 a.m. time slot, I had an unusual experience. On the way to the station, I noticed some bubble gum in the car seat beside me. I had gotten it for my girls and had forgotten to take it out of the car. So I grabbed one, then two pieces and was still chewing away when I arrived at the radio station. I selected my songs and casually walked into the studio waiting for the time to begin. We usually played only about a minute of the theme song before the announcer introduced me. There was a red light on the studio wall above the door, and when it came on, my microphone was on.

This morning I waited for my theme. I didn't hear it, and the red light came on. At first, I thought my buddy was joking with me, pretending I was on the air. I sat chewing away, looking through the studio glass at him, and smiling at the "trick" he was pulling. But when I saw the sobering look on his face, I realized he wasn't clowning. I asked, (and this went out all over "radio land") "Am I on?" He nodded in the affirmative. The turntable used to play my theme song had malfunctioned and the red light did mean what it was intended to mean – that I was on the air.

I was so startled that it took a moment to come to reality. The first was the fact that my mouth was full of bubble-gum. I had actually added the third piece just before I got out of the car to go into the studio. I looked to the trash can on the floor beside me. It was a medium-sized metal can and was completely empty. I let go of the big wad and a "thud" resulted when it collided with the bottom. I'm talking about a humungous thud. It wasn't nearly as funny then as it was later when someone reminded me of it. The announcer called it the "bubble gum thud" that was heard all across the WPLA broadcasting area. I established lasting friendships with the WPLA radio station personnel and their families. Many of the courtesy sponsors remained faithful through the years.

With only a 250 watt A.M. station and located at the very end of the dial at 1570, I was astonished to have a regular listener in Wakulla, Florida, near Tallahassee. One morning around two a.m., while running test patterns, an engineer put on one of my radio tapes and a man called the station from New Hampshire to tell them he was listening to Temple Vespers with radio pastor Ernest Holbrook from Plant City, Florida.

But this all seems dwarfed by satellite uplinks and downlinks and computers, whereby about anything can be picked up from anywhere in the world. One day as I came into the WCIE studios in Lakeland, Florida, from which I had a weeknight broadcast for 20 years, the manager told me someone had just called from the state of Oregon who had been listening to our station. Radio and television beams can be transmitted and received from millions, perhaps billions of miles and more in space, which boggles the finite human mind, at least mine!

But none of this compares to a visit to earth, all the way from the Heaven of Heavens, by God Almighty, in the form of His Only Begotten Son Jesus Christ. And His message is one of love, peace and forgiveness for sinful humanity. He came from the Father and returned to the Father, (John 16:28) and He is now preparing a place in the Father's House for all who believe on him. (John 14:1-3)

This "Greatest Story Ever Told," is what I have tried to dedicate my life to tell, and I thank God for having given me the privilege of "Giving the Winds a mighty voice," (radio and television) to share such a marvelous hope. And I also want to thank Him for a host of friends and loved ones who have shared with me in spreading the "Good News."

The miracles along the way keep fascinating me as I ponder them in my closing years; miracles of divine protection in many near-disasters, miracles of finances, the list goes on.

While building the new sanctuary at Mt. Zion, the bank wasn't very cooperative. So, hoping we could make a showing for equity sufficient to merit a bank loan, we kept on raising funds and doing much of the church-building ourselves. However, we were always coming up short, which seems to be the story of my life. But, such situations have a way of putting you on your knees, which seems to remind you that the battle is the Lord's.

While in the bank one day, the bank president suggested I see how many men of the church would sign a note to be personally responsible for a certain amount of money so we could finish the sanctuary. This, if we could get twenty or so, along with a mortgage on the property and the signatures of the trustee board would give us enough capital to complete our work.

The response was adequate, with the exception of one person. He wasn't opposed to the bank loan; he just said he didn't want to be responsible personally for any amount. He asked what I was going to do. "Simple," I said. "First, we'll ask you to resign. Then, we'll call a special business meeting and elect someone in your place who will sign. He thought for a moment and then said, "Well, in that case I will sign."

Without proper budgeting, we were soon in a financial bind once again. We had not secured enough money to complete our project. A local businessman heard of our plight, paid off the bank mortgage and loaned us the extra amount we needed.

Amid growing pains, we kept stretching to the limit once more. If any extra funds came in above our necessities, we simply continued our plans for expansion. We began an educational plant, adding much-needed classrooms. An acre of property immediately behind the church became available and we purchased that. The former pastor's house on adjacent property was put on the market for sale and we bought that and then rented it out. We also purchased a front corner lot which would give us additional parking space. We soon started building a new parsonage on the back lot facing a side street. It caught up with us and we needed about another $4,500 to finish the new house. It was time to pray some more.

Into my yard one afternoon, one of the men from Ashford, Alabama, where I had held a very successful three week revival some five or six years previous, drove up and greeted me. "I hear you need some money to finish the parsonage. How much?" "About $4,500.00," I said. "You got it," he said, "at 4% interest." He had come down to bring a daughter to enroll at South Eastern Bible College in Lakeland. The bank wanted 6%, even if they would lend it. So, I told him I would consult the church board and let him know. He said he would be coming back in a couple of weeks to bring his daughter back to school. I wondered how he knew we needed money. I later learned a former member from his church, now at ours, had told him.

The church board agreed, I called the brother, and in two weeks, he drove up again. He got out, greeted me, opened the trunk of his car and took out two pasteboard boxes. In them were stacks of money. I saw bundles of twenties, tens, fives and even one dollar bills. He said, "You can count it if you want to, but it's all there, I assure you." He started getting into his car saying, "I've got to be heading home."

I said, "Wait, we haven't even discussed collateral! What about a promissory note, a mortgage on the house, something?" He cranked up while saying, "Nah! You said you'd pay me back and that's good enough for me." Off he went! No payment schedule, no nothing! I was standing beside two boxes full of money (this was a lot back then in 1956) and I couldn't wait to get the money to the bank the next morning. It took the bank teller quite some time to count it. It was all there!

We finished the new parsonage and moved in, rented the old one, which now gave us two rental houses for extra income. We were able to meet all our bills and took a nice step forward in overseas missions support. One of our own young couples had departed for an assignment in Africa and we became their main support.

Jesus had said, "Give, and it shall be given unto you; good measure, pressed down, shaken together, and running over, shall men give into your bosom. For with the same measure that ye meet withal it shall be measured to you again." (Luke 6:38) This has certainly worked for my family and me, and it also worked for our church. Someone noted that "givers" are the happiest people in the world. Much happier than "receivers only!"

Our quartet, the "Sons of Harmony", began to do quite well. We engaged a 13 year-old young man to play piano. Being very talented as well as a showman, he was a hit from the start. Our once-a-month singspiration at our church on each first Saturday night continued to attract overflow crowds. We usually invited a guest quartet or singing group to join us.

Soon we were singing at other churches, city auditoriums, or somewhere most every Friday or Saturday night. The original group decided to take a "tour." I called some pastor buddies and soon we were booked in Tallahassee, Milton, and Jacksonville, Florida, and Albany, Georgia.

After Tallahassee, we took the "beach" route to Milton. We stopped to swim at Laguna Beach near Panama City. A strong south wind was sending mountainous waves ashore and only two of us decided to tackle them. It took a mere few minutes, battling tons of water and dangerous riptides, that I made my way ashore after almost getting strangled. I called for the other member, but watched him take on a monstrous wave. He disappeared for too long. Finally, we saw him come up and return to the sandy beach. We wanted to complete our tour, not wind up a victim of nature's rampaging winds and waves. And Jesus wasn't with us (in person) to say, "Peace, be still." Many people have drowned along that stretch of beaches from deadly riptides.

We were well received each place we went. In every concert, we incorporated some comedy. One act was a piano duet that the pianist and I did. At the end of the musical number, he would slide my way on the keyboard and piano bench, and knock me off onto the floor. Then he would apologize trying to get me back on the bench, with me refusing. Finally, after a promise that he would never push me off again, I would get up, sit back down, and we would play again. This time, however, I would wind up pushing him off onto the floor. It's a wonder we hadn't gotten something broken in the process.

But our invitations at the end of our programs were all serious. Each of us would give a brief testimony of our faith and then we invited anyone to come forward to the altar that felt their need of salvation or had some situation they needed to pray about. We made ourselves available to pray with them. The response was very good as we witnessed numerous people receiving Christ or rededicating themselves to Him.

By the time we made our first long-play album we had a new bass and tenor singer. We named the album, "God is Love," the title of one of the songs. It was engineered and recorded in Nugget Studios in Tampa, Florida, and the records were pressed in Nashville, Tennessee. It was an exciting time!

One day my dad told me he wanted to set an orange grove. He offered me an equal partnership if I would help him as much as I could. We began to search for land from Brooksville to Wauchula. Sometimes we would go fishing and look at land tracts on the way, or on the way back. We wound up purchasing 120 acres at Masaryktown, some ten miles south of Brooksville, just about one-half mile off Highway 41.

With a mortgage on the property and our signatures, we were able to secure the land, a big tractor, disc, tree hoe, water tank, etc. The land had been cleared of trees so we began by planting it in watermelons. It grew some of the largest and prettiest I had ever seen. We made a bundle on the first crop and the second picking was even better. When we called the buyers of the first crop, melons had come in at Ocala, Gainesville and North Florida. No buyer wanted to come our way again since they could get them closer to their markets.

We finally managed to sell some of the second picking at ten cents each, and watched the rest rot in the field. But we cleared enough money to make a bank payment and plant the acreage in Hairy Indigo, a cover crop that would build up the soil and make seed, which was marketable. It would reseed itself, and we sold a considerable amount the next three years which we applied to principle, interest and 120 acres of small orange trees.

One hundred and twenty acres is a big parcel; especially when we had farmed ten acres of strawberries. We hired quite a bit of help to set the trees. Since my extra time was very limited, I wasn't of very much assistance.

Then came the big freeze of 1962. We banked each tree as high as we could. But many were killed despite our efforts. We reset and continued. I tried to give one or two days a week to the project during the most needful times and it was one day about ten a.m., while hoeing trees I suffered my first experience with angina. I suddenly was seized by the strangest feeling in my chest. I became very weak and could hardly breathe. My nephew and another worker helped me to the car. I drank some cool water, lay down in the seat for a couple of hours, and then went home.

I went to see the doctor. He examined me and sent me to the hospital for an EKG. At that time, the test results were sent to either Mayo Clinic or Johns-Hopkins for analysis. A week later I was called to the doctor's office. His nurse started to read my report, and then I saw a serious look on her face. She said to me, "You wait here. The doctor will have to give you this." Out she went and in came my concerns. How serious was this? Here I was in my mid-thirties, actually 33, with never a thought of more health problems, unless it was another kidney stone.

In a few moments, the doctor came in. He was looking at my papers. "Reverend, you seem to be OK, except you've got a very slow pulse – under 60." "What does that mean?" I asked. "It means you have to slow down your activities and pace yourself to your heartbeat," he replied.

He quizzed me about my schedule. When I finished, he said, you need 28 hours a day and 8 days a week for all you are doing. But you don't have it! Slow down or one day you'll find out the church, and the world, can get along quite well without you." I was shocked!

He advised me to set up a recording studio so I could record my radio programs at my leisure, rather that living under the daily pressure of meeting a time schedule at the radio station. He also admonished that I cut back some on all my projects: broadcasting, counseling, quartet singing and visitation to homes and hospitals. "Be sure to take vacations *from* preaching," he added.

I had been using all my vacation time to preach revival meetings. But this really was a slow-down signal. I sold the tent, stopped singing and preaching every Sunday morning at the prison at Zephyrhills and Sunday afternoons at nursing homes. I reduced my hospital visitation giving most attention to congregants in critical condition. "Let members of other churches have their own pastors visit them," one of my board members said. But the radio programs, for which I had such a burden, even on a five day a week basis, resulted still in me being a "Pastor" of sorts to many people in the area who didn't attend a church.

My phone rang quite often with calls from people I had never met. Funeral directors would call me to do funerals at the request of families who knew me only from the radio. Thus, I continued counseling, weddings and funerals, taking the opportunities to witness for Christ. The time spent on "outsiders" was often more than I was spending on my own congregants. But I was trying to serve the Kingdom of God to every extent possible.

One night I answered a knock at my back door. There stood a lady and three young children, all in tears. I had never met them, though they lived only a block away. After a brief talk and prayer, she asked if I would take a look at what a drunken husband had done at her house.

"His drinking has gotten worse and worse," she told me, while we walked across the block. As we approached the house, I could see the front screen door hanging sideways attached only by one hinge. The wooden door had been kicked in at the bottom. Inside, the furniture had been overturned, broken and scattered across the living-dining room area. The sheetrock at places was kicked in, revealing the 2X4 studs.

All around were broken beer and whiskey bottles. She showed me bruises on herself and the children, inflicted by her husband. I asked his whereabouts and she said he had left and was probably somewhere at a bar drinking.

I then asked how long this had been going on. "For several months," she said. "And only the last few weeks he has started beating the children and me. Then tonight, he did all this destruction to our house." I could see that she and the children were terrified. I asked if she had called the law. Her response was, "No, he said he would kill us all if I did."

I said, "You don't have any alternative. He might kill you if you don't." She promised she would. I then talked to her about her relationship with the Lord and church. She had none. I invited her to ours, had another prayer with them, and departed. They never came. They soon moved away. When I visited a short time later, the house was empty. A neighbor said she had taken the children and gone home to her mother, but she didn't know where.

I have known and experienced many similar situations and have often wondered just how many homes have been destroyed with alcohol abuse, as was this one. I once again thanked the Lord that I had been reared in a solid, stable home, with Godly, church-going parents, in a totally alcohol, tobacco-free environment, filled with loving care, discipline and plenty of good times together.

One afternoon, just after lunch, a bartender called me. He and his mother owned and operated a booze joint some nine or ten miles west of Plant City on Highway 92. The man said, "You don't know us, but we hear your radio program. My mother, who has run this business for years, is now very sick. The doctor says she is dying. She asked me to call you to see if you would come." "Yes, where do you live?" "In an apartment on the back side of the bar. Will you come here?" "Yes," I told him. "I'll be out in just a few minutes."

When I arrived, there were about three autos parked in front of the "joint." I thought it would be best, since I was a "teetotaler" and strongly advocated the same, in person, in the pulpit and on radio, to park in back, out of sight. I drove around back, but there was no door in back or on either side. Finally, I went around to the only entrance, the front door! It seemed the eyes of all the customers were glued upon me as I entered. I did not recognize anyone and apparently no one knew me. From behind the bar, the young man looked my way and said, "You must be Brother Holbrook." "Yes," I responded. "Please come this way," he said.

He motioned for me to come around behind the counter where he was standing. I passed many cases and bottles of all kinds of whiskey, wine and beer. He led me through a door about halfway behind the serving counter. From there, we entered a small kitchen-dining area and then into a bedroom where she lay. He introduced me to her, pulled up a chair beside the bed, and then returned to the bar. I could tell at first glance the lady was very ill. She managed a smile and graciously thanked me for coming to a place that was "off-limits" to me. She apologized for being a "barmaid," but said it was the only way she could make a living after her husband had died. "Now I am dying," she said. "I only have a few more days at most, and I'm afraid to face God. What can I do?"

I tried to comfort her as best I could. I told her that we are all sinners by nature, that God wants us to repent and turn from our sins, and to believe on His Only Begotten Son as Savior, and then make him Lord of our lives." She began to weep. I encouraged her to follow my words in prayer. She prayed the prayer of repentance, asked the Lord to forgive every sin, to cleanse her by Christ's precious blood and come into her heart and life as her Savior. To me, it was sincere and genuine. I sensed a miraculous change was happening within her. She began to smile and rejoice in the Lord.

She was amazed, she said, that it was so simple. "If I had known this, I would have become a Christian a long time ago," she said. "But I would have had to go into a different kind of business." I said, "Jesus Christ takes you just as you are, right here, right now. Let's worry about the business later." She didn't have to. As I recall, she died in the next day or so.

When I conducted her funeral service, I was glad I could give her testimony of repentance and salvation. It is so much easier at a funeral than when we fear so many die without any hope in Christ; (I Thessalonians 4:13) but what wonderful confidence for all who believe. (vv. 14-18) Truly, there is comfort in these words.

Radio broadcasting is not all fun and games; even religious programming. Since religious beliefs can be so diverse and consequently divisive, many stations refuse religious programs. The compliments, encouraging words and letters that come in the mail are always most welcome, but not all responses are complimentary or encouraging. Some are quite the opposite!

Once I read a religious news article about some groups who still practice polygamy in remote areas of the country. It so infuriated a local member that she called me and told me off, good fashioned. "We do not practice polygamy," she said, and whoever says we do are blatant liars, including you!" She also had some other choice words for me. She even demanded equal radio time to rebuff the newspaper news item I had quoted.

I knew her husband. He worked on a carpenter crew with one of my congregants. When I attempted to apologize to him for upsetting her, he didn't seem to be concerned at all. "She is always disturbed at most everyone about most everything," he said. "I wouldn't worry about it." Later, when I saw her with him at the supermarket, she half-way apologized to me for her outburst of anger toward me. I suppose a little is worth more than none at all. But she had been in defense of what she believed. Religious ties can be very strong!

Another listener turned out to be a tragedy as well. He came across my broadcast and promptly called and asked for a visit. I promised I would, in a couple of days, as time permitted. After a day, he called to remind me that I hadn't shown up at his place. He lived in the "Strawberry Trailer Square" in Plant City.

When I went the next day, I learned he was a widower. He had two children, both in New York, and neither would have anything to do with him. His neighbors treated him likewise. The church he had been attending was full of very unfriendly people who also wouldn't visit or help poor old him. I soon learned why.

Solomon said in Proverbs 18:24, "A man that has friends must show himself friendly." The very first visit I had with him, revealed to me why he didn't have friends, or, if he happened to make one, why the friendship soon ended. He was arrogant, demanding and downright obnoxious.

For Christ's sake, I tried to be a friend to him. He had suffered a stroke and one side was paralyzed. He didn't have an automobile and couldn't drive, even if he did. I hauled him to church, to the grocery store, ran errands for him, and even took him to the funeral home to plan his final services.

All this happened while I was broadcasting five days a week at 8:15 a.m. Early one freezing Saturday morning, he called and asked me to get some kerosene for his heater. He had run out, and couldn't get his fuel man or anyone else to accommodate him. But he said he knew I would. "I know I can count on my pastor friend, Ernest Holbrook, to help me out," he said.

At the time, I was still broadcasting live from the WPLA studios, but not on Saturdays or Sundays. Being still half asleep, and by habit, I drove right by his place, right through town, and arrived in the parking lot of the radio station. Then I came to myself. So I drove right back through town and right by his place again, and came to myself again, as I drove into my carport at the parsonage.

Junell heard me drive up and opened the door telling me I was wanted on the phone. You can guess who it was. "Here I am freezing to death and you are still at home," he stormed at me. "I'll be there in about three or four minutes," I said. This time I made it. I was then soundly lectured and accused of ignoring his desperate phone call, then rolling over and going back to sleep, leaving him to freeze to death! I did not have the heart to try to explain how my morning driving routine, combined with a couple of mental lapses had me driving past his trailer-home, twice.

The trip with him to the funeral home was a "shocker." The Funeral Home was relatively new, so I was not acquainted with the layout, not having yet conducted a funeral there. I drove in to what I thought was the entrance into the office to make plans for his funeral. There was no doorbell, so I knocked. I knocked some more and still no answer. Then I decided to try the door. It opened, only to "clunk" against something. The opening was only about 12 inches. I knocked again. Nothing! Then I pushed the door and it moved something inside another few inches, before it stopped again.

I stuck my head inside to find my face only inches from the face of a dead man lying in an open coffin. I closed the door and held onto the handle for a moment, trying to come to grips with reality. It took a little time to regain my composure.

I then returned to the car and got in. My passenger said, "Reverend, you're as white as a sheet. Did you see a ghost or something?" I said, "Something like that." Then we found the true front entrance, where we were greeted by the director, and planned the services. I felt for a while that I almost could have planned my own. He did pass away a few months after that. Just before he died, he kept telling me he had some "big" money laid up and since I was being so attentive to him, he would leave it all to me and nothing to his children, who didn't love or care for him.

I hate to say that this is one thing that probably kept me keeping on with him. Otherwise, I think in my humanness I might have told him where he could jump (in the lake, of course). But my carnal nature, despite my own suspicions, kept me trying to be the humble servant that "loves my neighbor as myself." He teased me about the money. He would call one day and say, "Come, and I'll give it to you today." He used it as a ploy to get me there. After I arrived, he would say he would wait until later. My suspicions were aroused about the promised money, anyway, since he had never offered a cent toward gas money for all the driving I had done for him.

But the day came when he finally handed me $1,800.00. It was confederate money! Then, he asked for it back. It might have been worth something as a collector's item, but I'll never know. His two children came to his funeral and disposed of his mobile home and goods. I don't recall as much as a "thank you" for the funeral or many months of service to him. But I wasn't serving for money anyway. It was "as unto the Lord." And I guess I shouldn't say it, but it was a blessed relief when he passed away.

I have always been a "new car" enthusiast. I generally traded every year. One year when I swapped my 1956 for a 1957 Oldsmobile, a church member, who was a widow, called. Her gossipy neighbor's son happened to be at the dealership when the transaction occurred. He went straight to his mother, who went straight to my member, who came straight to me. Her phone call "ordered" me to come to her house as quickly as possible.

She walked out as soon as I drove up, gave a quick glance at the new car and demanded I tell her how much I paid for it. I didn't tell her, so she told me! "My neighbor said her son said he saw the new car sticker price on the window. It was $5,100.00, and he said you laid down 51, one hundred dollar bills to pay for it.

I tried to explain to her that not one bit of cash was involved. My 1956 netted $4,200.00 and the balance I still owed on it, plus the $900.00 trade difference, was financed by GMAC. The whole deal was on paper, not paper money.

"Well, my point is this," she said. "If you can afford to pay over five thousand dollars for a car, surely you can pay for a poor old widow woman to have a bathroom put in her house." I felt my carnal nature trying to rise up. But I allowed the Sanctifying Presence, or something, to hold me in check about what I thought about saying to her.

I "turned the other cheek," took an offering for her at church, hired one of our church members who was a carpenter and helped him as much as I could to accomplish the project. When we finished, instead of "Thank you so very much," to us and the church folk, we were criticized because everything wasn't up to her expectations.

My experiences of total frustration with this lady, shall we call her, "Sister Centered Only in Self," covered several years. She was about as "centered-in-self" as was my trailer park friend. They were two of a kind! Since I, too, was guilty of the same thing, to a great extent, the controversy continued. But it was always easier to see their faults than my own! I wonder why.

It all began when I was an 18 year-old evangelist. Her home church, some miles away, was without a pastor. I had just started preaching and she put in, to put me in, as their pastor. Nothing would appease her until I agreed to go preach and "try out." I told her I was too inexperienced, too young and not interested. But I took her and my 14 year-old sister Joann to the Sunday services. Joann helped me sing, then I preached, then she "preached" to the church board that they should call me as their new pastor.

We went to her brother's house for Sunday dinner where she made a scene at the table that got all her brother's family upset. She then demanded her nephew cancel a Sunday afternoon date with his girlfriend so he could stay home and visit with her. "His old auntie, whom he only sees occasionally, should take precedence over any date," she said. But it didn't! And it's no wonder!

That evening after church, I informed the church board I had no interest in being a pastor and they thanked me for coming. On the way home, I was lectured for turning down such an opportunity for advancement in my ministry. She was older, wiser and could tell me what was best for me, if I would just listen, she said. I had to listen, until I delivered her to her front door! (Or the next time I saw her.)

The Wednesday evening services at our church included "testimonies." One night she was praising the Lord for protecting them when a train hit their truck. But she insisted the accident was her husband's fault. He was a very tall, quiet man, and was very "hen-pecked," some said. When she accused him, he jumped up and began defending himself. "How in the world could it be my fault when you were driving?" "But you told me I could beat the train across," she argued. By now the congregation was becoming very amused. He sat down and let her finish without further ado. I wondered what happened when they got home! At least he was still alive the next time I saw him. I did not check for bruises!

Her testimonies usually centered on her illnesses and many surgeries, and were laced with plenty of self-pity. At age 65, she declared we had all about seen the last of her. She would soon be going home to be with the Lord. She did, three surgeries and 29 years later, at the age of 94. A church member, who afterwards took it upon herself to see after this lady, told me she was "demon-possessed." I had never ventured that far in my analysis of her, but I sure had decided she was about as steeped in the carnal nature as anyone I had ever encountered.

My greatest anger toward her happened when she was hospitalized on 34th Street in Tampa. She let me visit almost an hour with her, and only informed me when I was leaving, that she had received a message to give me when I arrived. My dad had been taken unconscious, with a massive heart attack, to the Lakeland hospital.

I ran out of the hospital so angry I could hardly see straight. What I determined against her flooded my mind as I drove as fast as possible to the Morrell Hospital in Lakeland. Of course, I had to repent of it, as I always did, when overcome by my emotions. I sat by my dad's hospital bed in the hallway, since every room was full. After nine hours, he opened his eyes and said, "Hello, son."

He survived, and lived 18 more years. But my frustrations with this lady continued my entire time as her pastor. Each succeeding pastor inherited her, and her aggravating ways. I determined that I was not a good student in God's school, the part where "everything works together for good to them that love Him." (Romans 8:28) I couldn't see how in this case, and others, but surely they do!

One day after all this, she called me and insisted I drop everything and hurry to her house. So I obliged, went, and she introduced me to a neighbor winter visitor who was a stranger, and who told an even stranger story. At her home in the north she had been invited to a special meeting hosted by a couple of Christians who had had a visit by a group from another planet. (Or so they said!)

The visitors had arrived in their yard in a "flying saucer," and were "sheep of another fold," some of those Christ spoke of in John 10:16, KJV. Christ had visited their planet, died for their sins, everyone there got saved and Christ's millennial reign was in process. Sin was eliminated, perfect peace, health and prosperity was ushered in, technology boomed and heaven came to their earth. There were no doctors, no hospitals, no sickness, no crime, thus no jails, no wars, no courthouses, no judges, juries and lawyers. There was no aging, or dying, thus no funeral homes or cemeteries. There were automobiles and super highways, but no speed limits, no police or accidents. There were no divorces, no fights, no murders, nothing bad. Good prevailed. Joy was endless!

The lady went on and on, telling so many things I can't recall them all. But she concluded with this: "Right at this moment, people back home on that now heavenly sphere, can "zoom in" right on this living room scene and see us and hear what we are talking about. Actually, they can tune in on everything, anywhere and everywhere on this earth, and project it on their television screens in their living rooms. Their hopes and prayers are that the earth's people will all follow Christ, so this world will become as theirs."

With this, she said she had to go. After her departure, my problem lady member asked, "Well, what do you think of all of this?" I thought for a time and finally said, "These people have borrowed from some Scriptural descriptions of Christ's millennial reign on this earth some day (see Isaiah 9:6-7, 2:2-4, 35:1-10, 65:17-22, Revelation, Chapters 20,21 and 22, etc.), and have speculated what all might go with it.

"But, there is no scriptural proof concerning such a planet or redeemed people like this. This is something we have no way of knowing the certainty thereof. As far as I'm concerned, for now, this is all someone's fantasy. As far as them seeing us right here, right now, I'd say only God's all-seeing eye is "zoomed in" on us (II Chronicles 16:9, etc.) all because He loves all of us so," I concluded. "I agree with you one hundred percent," she said. At least we had agreed on something. We also agreed the "other sheep" mentioned were probably the gentiles. Us!

In the meantime, Junell's dad had passed away. After years of struggling with emphysema, he went home to be with the Lord. After a time, her mother had married another man who was very kind and humble. A couple of years later, he passed away where they then lived and ran a boarding house in Huntsville, Alabama. We had gone up for the funeral, but soon her mother called and asked Junell to come spend some time with her, assist her with boarding house chores and otherwise help her readjust her life in the loss of this husband. Sandra was in school, so Junell decided to take the train to Huntsville and I would come get her later. She would take Sharon, age five, and Phyllis, a baby in arms, with her.

We purchased the tickets and met the train in Plant City, where our passenger car stopped right by the Xcel and Plant City Grower's buildings. With the children so small, I carried the two suitcases aboard the passenger car while Junell took the two little girls. When I turned to get off the train, I heard "All aboard," from the porter outside. I encountered two ladies carrying multiple suitcases coming up the very narrow aisle, and could not get past them, as I felt the train began to move.

When I finally got to the door, I was going to jump from the now faster moving train, but was apprehended by the porter. I could not break his vice-like hold around my waist. By now, the train was rapidly speeding up. I frantically tried to pull loose, but he held on. "I can't let you jump from a moving train," he exclaimed! "But what will I do?" I asked. "I don't have a ticket." "You are going to get a 'free' ride to Lakeland," he said, "and then a 'free' ride back to Plant City. I'll see to it."

I looked out and saw that by then we were really traveling. "Can I go sit with my family?" I asked. "Be my guest," responded the porter. As I started up the aisle, little Sharon saw me and said, "Mama, here comes Daddy." "No, Sharon. Daddy got off the train." "But Mama, he's here!" I was, and I started explaining to my startled wife what had happened.

My cousin's husband worked at the Plant City Growers store. From the front of the store, he had watched the train-boarding scenario. He watched me kiss Junell and my little daughters' goodbye, then get on the train with them – and then, not get back off. He said to a co-worker, "Ernest kissed his wife goodbye, and then went with her."

311

When the train stopped in Lakeland, I bid my three loved ones goodbye once again, got off the train this time, and listened as the porter explained to a railroad employee what had happened. "I'll send him back on the next scheduled train," he told the porter. I waited around for about 30 minutes, and then asked when the next train back was due. "In about three hours," he said. So I decided I would call my dad, who lived only about ten or fifteen minutes away. He answered the phone, and I asked him if he would pick me up at the Lakeland depot and take me to Plant City. "Yes," he said.

In a few minutes he drove up, and our conversation was casual as we made our way to Plant City. Upon nearing our destination, he said, "It doesn't matter to me, but your mama wondered what you were doing at the Lakeland train depot and your car was in Plant City." I tried as best I could to relate the story of just what had happened. This incident, as well as many others in my life, was funny after the fact, but not so much so at the time of the occurrence itself. What a life, life is!

Ernest, Junell and Sandra (1954)

Sandra at age one

Smoky Mountain Vacation
Ernest and Sandra – 1956 Olds

Charles and Sally Ann Raburn
with sons Buddy and Johnny

315

Charles and Enrest with a few bass

Ernest and Uncle Jake (J.T.) Holbrook
with a few more bass

Robert and Ernest with even
more bass

Mt. Zion congregation about 1960

EIGHTEEN

MT. ZION AGAIN – PART THREE

I will shew thee my faith by my works... James 2:18

If a former high school classmate had determined that my life as a minister and pastor was humdrum, he and I surely had completely different points of view. In truth, I knew I was living the abundant life that Jesus Christ came to give, as recorded in John 10:10b.

There was absolutely nothing dull or boring during the second time around at Mt. Zion, from 1954 until 1965. Monotony could not have gotten in edgewise. And if "idleness is the devil's workshop," I was never in it because of the over abundance of fulfilling and rewarding activities. I was deeply involved in what I felt I was born to do and become. Doing the Lord's work and having lots of joy and fun doing it topped the list.

Then, the hope of eternal life with God and His Christ had replaced the once scary and uneasy feeling I had had of possibly being separated from the Almighty, eternally. Paul referred to it as, "The peace of God, which passes all understanding." (Philippians 4:7) Peter used the term, "Joy unspeakable and full of glory," in I Peter 1:8. And Christ, Himself had said, "My peace I give unto you; not as the world gives, give I unto you." (John 14:27) Who could ask for anything more?

But there was more, actually, much, much more! I had a home and family life, a spouse whom I dearly loved and who loved me in return, and three precious daughters who were darling little angels (most of the time). Watching our girls grow up was awesome. We played, took vacations together, ate together and sometimes cried together. The down side, seemingly, was that it passed too quickly, leaving us to wonder where it all went. I guess time seems not to register when it is filled up with so many good things. All in all, I suppose that most of the time I was too busy, but I hope not with the less important things. Even total involvement in church work should never be allowed to short-change the family life.

I enrolled as a psychology major at the University of South Florida, earning about 96 quarter-hours over a period of years. I sang regularly with the Sons of Harmony Quartet; I performed several weddings each year, officiated at multiple funerals and spent many hours in counseling sessions; I was on call 24 hours a day, seven days a week, never knowing what might "pop up" especially when the phone rang in the "wee" hours.

I averaged 30 to 40 visits per week to homes, hospitals, nursing homes and sometimes even to jails. I often ran errands for car-less congregants and outsiders, otherwise deprived of this world's goods. Include in this, time for prayer, Bible study, sermon preparation and other pastoral duties.

I tried to continue taking one day each week for recreation, mostly to fish and sometimes for golf. I even helped Dad in his cattle and grove business. There is and absolutely was no way my life could be spiritless or gloomy. No grass would ever be growing under my wheels! Or feet!

Warnings about "burn-out" from older fellow-ministers and the doctor was like water being poured on a duck's back. "Slow down, back off, reduce your schedule," were statements that did not register, until later! "I'd rather 'burn-out' for the Lord than 'rust-out' for the devil," was my motto, until my other parents, 'father time' and 'mother nature' began to call a halt to such a rigorous schedule.

I'll not forget when a lady congregant began to call me on the phone most every morning at 5:00 a.m., her getting-up time. I learned that a pastor must stay up with his "night owl" members, from 11:00 to midnight, and rise up with the "rooster" crowd, at 5:00 a.m. My phone was in the family room, about 40 to 50 feet from my bed. The 5:00 a.m. question was, "Oh, honey, did I get you up?" (She was 65, I was 35 and she always called me "Honey.") I always had an answer for her letting her know about late night calls to the hospital, or other things. She always so politely apologized: "I'm so sorry I got you up."

Day after day, or I should say early morning after early morning, she would call, and then apologize. The call was for no apparent reason, except I guess a "wake up – get up" call for me. There always seems to be certain congregants who make it their business to see to it the pastor stays on the ball and is never derelict in his duties. Some of this may be OK. But now, enough was enough.

I had a phone installed right beside my bed. At 5 a.m., the next morning, sure enough, the phone rings right beside my startled ear. "Hello!" "Oh,

Honey, did I get you up?" "No Ma'am! You didn't get me up this morning." (I was still in bed.) This continued for a few more mornings and I'd say "No, you didn't get me up!" The early morning calls soon stopped.

One day a knock came at the parsonage door. I answered to greet a tall, red-haired, middle aged man, with a very noticeably deformed right hand. He said he had moved into the area from West Florida (near Milton), and worked for the telephone company. In moving, his check had been delayed. He was Assembly of God, he and his family of six would be coming and paying tithes to our church. He named several ministers I knew from West Florida. So I let him have the fifty dollars for a deposit for electricity and phone deposits, plus a few grocery items. He would see me Sunday, and would pay back the money, as soon as his check arrived.

I never saw him again. Not until about five years later! We were by then living in the new parsonage around the corner and the doorbell rang late one afternoon. There stood a tall, red-haired man and as he introduced himself he shook hands, with his deformed right hand. I let him go through his "move" from West Florida. He was transferred to this area by the telephone company. He was Assembly of God and was looking for a church home for his family. One problem though! In the transition, his check had been delayed and he needed some money to make his deposit for telephone, electricity and for some food. (This time he needed about a hundred dollars.)

"If you need a reference, you can call pastor (so and so), and he'll vouch for me. And I bet you know some pastors that I know." He named a few I knew. I said, "You wait right here. I need to make a phone call to the Sheriff's office. While they are coming you can pay me the fifty you already owe me! Off the porch and zoom, he was gone! I certainly wanted to be a good neighbor and help out when I could, but it sure makes me hot under the collar to be "taken," as I have been several times. Where indeed, is that gift of discernment? Or is such as this really it's purpose?

I wasn't the only Holbrook preacher to get duped. My grandfather, Jessup, once owned a nice sorrel horse. A wandering family group, heading south for the winter, offered a very sturdy mule in exchange for the horse, which they said would pull their wagon at a faster pace. Convinced the mule would be a better farm-animal, granddad swapped and paid $25 difference.

A few months later, the same group, headed back northward, wanted their mule back. This time, they offered a beautiful pinto horse in exchange, but insisted it was worth another $25 difference. Since the mule had proven to be quite slow, Granddad forked over another $25. When the first rain came, the paint washed off and the pinto turned into his original sorrel.

At Mt. Zion, Junell always had something extra special to look forward to each Sunday morning – besides my sermon. It was a fresh bouquet of flowers sitting atop the organ she played, brought to her by a very elderly man. (Thankfully, he was much too old for me to be jealous of him.)

Among my many experiences as a pastor was this one: My phone rings, I answer, a distraught lady congregant says, "My husband has gone berserk, he has barricaded himself in, has grabbed and loaded his rifle and says he will kill anyone who comes here. Please come as quickly as you can!"

I had always hoped that if I was called on to die for my Lord that I would be ready. But I wasn't sure this would be the way it should happen. I thought about calling the Sheriff's office but decided against that. I went to the house, no one was harmed and the situation, brought about by a very traumatic incident on the job, soon was resolved in a tranquil manner. Whew! (again)

One morning a congregant and her adult son came to the church office. He was separated from his wife who was now living with her parents in North Florida. She had taken the children with her, a girl five and boy three. Their request: "Will you please take us to see about the children? We will buy the gas." I agreed, and we were off as soon as I could work things out.

When we arrived near the place, the son asked me to stop at the sheriff's office. Inside, he requested a deputy to go with him to get the children, whom he said she had deserted, leaving them with her parents. The deputy asked if he had a court order. "No." "Then there's nothing I can do. Does she have custody?" "No." "Then you've got as much right to them as she does. Go get them, if you can."

Despite having been misled, I headed down the country roads. They plotted their strategy. He would grab one, she the other and I would be the "get away" driver. Almost like a movie script! Upon arrival, the other grandmother came out with the two children close at her heels. The children ran, one to her daddy, the other to this grandmother. Once they were in their arms, he signaled me to start the car as they jumped in with the children. The other grandmother started screaming, "Put the children down." Then she turned and called her husband who was close by in the sugar-cane field. He came running with a machete in his hand. He started swinging it wildly as I spun out of the yard. He tried his best to slash a rear tire, but I evaded him, leaving him in a cloud of dust.

I looked in the rear-view mirror and saw both of them shaking their fists in the air. I could faintly hear her say she was calling the sheriff. I kept watching for a sheriff's car all the way home, but thankfully, there was none. Not long after, I learned this man also left these children with this grandmother. There were court hearings later, and he gained temporary custody, and this grandmother mostly reared them, not him. Thank God for grandmothers, but pity the children who are deprived of being brought up in their own homes with their own parents, in an atmosphere of love and mutual trust.

One morning at 2:00 a.m., I was awakened by a knocking on my bedroom window glass. Listening with apprehension, I discovered it was a church member. He and his wife had borrowed an outboard motor from a friend. They rented a boat at Louie Young's fish camp on the Hillsborough River at 301, near Thonotosassa, Florida. They drifted down-river for several miles to the old, now closed, Morris Bridge.

When efforts to fire up the motor failed, darkness soon set in upon them. They first walked the old dirt roadbed northward, which once went to Zephyrhills. Realizing it was probably the road to nowhere, they returned to the river, got in the boat and crossed over and began walking southward on the old roadbed. Finally, they came to the newer paved road and around midnight flagged down a newspaper carrier. They persuaded him to drive them back to their car at the landing. Then they came to my house to borrow my 3 HP motor to go back and get the boat. I said, "Wait until daybreak and I'll go help you." We went at dawn, managed to get through a pasture gate and drove to the river and boat. We took the old motor off and I told them I would run the boat back to the landing.

This couple was among our very close friends. They were a tremendous help with the church activities. We once went on vacation with them to Gatlinburg, Tennessee. He wanted to go horse-back riding across the mountain tops. I had had my fill of horses, having been bucked and thrown and kicked once, about seven or eight feet. I was bruised and stove-up for several days. Despite all this, I agreed to go with him anyway. We went to the mountain barn, paid the fee and were sent out to where the horses were tied.

"Which one of you will lead, since the trail is very narrow and one must follow the other," the attendant asked? I said, "It doesn't matter." "Oh yes it does! This horse will not follow any other. It must lead, or else." I agreed to mount the "lead" horse. Once we set out, the lead horse went so slowly, it was very boring. I did my best to speed him up, but my prodding didn't work.

When we came to a fairly wide place along the trail, my friend kicked his horse in the sides and came around the lead horse and me. The lead horse went absolutely crazy. He started bucking and then kicking the other horse in the side, and hitting my buddy's foot. A few feet from the incident the mountain sloped almost vertically, downward, who knows how far. After the near disaster, we put the lead horse back in the lead, and he led again, slowly, until the end of the trail, back at the stables. Not much to write home about, except nearly falling off a mountain and a very sore foot from a horse kick.

On the way back home from Gatlinburg, we stopped in the Great Smoky Mountain National Park when we saw a big bear with his head in a garbage can. We could see only his huge rear end protruding. This was before the park rangers secured the cans to prevent such. My friend grabbed his camera, ran down the slope between the bear and the wooded area to get a close-up snapshot. When the bear emerged, he (or she) looked first toward our car where we three were standing. Then the bear spied the would-be picture taker!

In a mad dash, it lunged at him. He took off so fast he was spinning on the ground like a cat chasing a mouse on a slick floor. The bear ran into him as he tried to make it back to the car. He finally jumped up on the car trunk lid and the bear turned and disappeared into the woods.

After the anxiousness of the moment, and realizing no serious injury had happened, it was time to laugh. We about "busted our sides." It was hilarious to us. Trembling and pale-faced the "bear chased one" tried to grin, but it was very obvious it wasn't all that funny to him.

He was from a large family. My very first wedding was for one of his brothers. They waited a few months until I could be ordained, in order to officiate at their ceremony. I married another brother "twice." The first time, at her home in Brewton, Alabama, during a revival I was preaching while on vacation in Crestview, Florida. The second time was when they renewed their vows on their twenty-fifth anniversary while pastoring the Church of the Open Bible in Pensacola.

This brother, along with my dad and I, were fishing Reedy Creek off Lake Hatchineha. Dad and I were "hauling" in the bass. He dejectedly lay down on the boat deck, slapped his hand on the deck and desperately said, "Lord, you know I love you just as much as they do. Please let me catch some fish."

His prayers accomplished nothing that day, but later on a trip to Arbuckle Creek, he beat me by four bass. I caught 74 and he caught 78. It was one of those days where you could hardly cast your bait without a bass latching on to it. We only kept our limit, 10 each of the biggest. The rest we released, not only to abide by the law, but to have more to catch, later on! Such a catch very seldom happens.

On a particular Sunday, we had a fundraiser for missions. Various departments of the church were involved and consequently, along with the dollars and checks, there were multitudes of coins: half-dollars, quarters, dimes, nickels, and the pennies that the Boys and Girls Missionary Crusaders had been accumulating for months. Later that evening after service, the secretary had rolled the coins and prepared the bank deposit after two of the deacons had counted it.

While counting and assembling the money in the church office up front, we had heard a noise outside. By then all the church people had gone except us. One deacon went outside to see if anyone was still there. The noise had come from outside the big office window. He returned saying he saw no one.

They all left and I was carrying the money bag back through the sanctuary, turning off the church lights as I went. Since the parsonage was behind the church, facing another road, I always went out the back side door where we had a concrete walkway that led to the back door of the parsonage. When I got to the front pew, I laid the very heavy money bag on it and went into the side room by the choir loft to turn out the final light.

As I entered the dark side room, I stepped on a person lying in the floor. He jumped up. He was a giant, towering over me, perhaps over six feet tall or more. He lunged through the door toward the money bag. How I did it, I'll never know. But as fast, or faster than I had moved while fleeing "Barko" in Milton, I ran around the big man, grabbed the very heavy money bag and swung several hundreds of dollars worth of coins at his head. I narrowly missed and out the side door he fled, with me in hot pursuit. I lost him as he crossed the road into the darkness. I called the sheriff's office and within minutes a deputy arrived. With his flashlight, gun and bully stick, "we" followed the tracks until we lost them in the woods.

It wasn't long after this I had to call the sheriff's office once again. I was mowing the churchyard one Saturday morning with a push mower, with a circular turning cutting blade. It was very powerful and would cut very high grass and pulverize most moss that had fallen from the oak trees. As I approached one big pile of moss, I started to "mow" through it, and then decided it might be large enough to tangle the blade and stall the mower. I stopped and removed the moss to discover 12 sticks of dynamite. I looked around at other moss, picking up several more sticks, which was what prompted this call to the sheriff's office once again.

I had friends in the sheriff's department. Several were "fans" of my radio programs. One of the captains told me to never hesitate to call him if I needed him or the department in any way. Today, I felt I needed the whole force. They sent my friend, who had previously stopped me twice for speeding.

When he arrived, he didn't know what to do with the dynamite. He called headquarters and talked to an explosives expert. He told him to put it in his rear floorboard, drive carefully and bring it to Tampa. He said it wasn't likely to explode. The deputy wasn't so sure!

I was listening as they talked on the two-way radio and I asked, "What would have happened if I had mowed into it?" "It probably wouldn't have ignited," he said. Then I asked if he would be willing to run my lawn mower over 12 sticks of it. He promptly said, "No!"

I helped put it in the trunk. "That way, at least it will be a little further from me," the deputy said. In a couple of days the newspaper stated that some teenagers had stolen the dynamite from a Powder Company which was using it to blast up stumps in a nearby pasture. Dynamite was discovered in several locations all around east Hillsborough County. Oh yes, my friend made it safely to Tampa with his powdered load.

One Sunday evening after church, we were preparing for bed. Junell checked the girl's bedrooms to find only Sandra and Phyllis. Sharon was missing. We searched the house over, but she wasn't there. "She was asleep on the front pew," Junell said. "I told you to bring her. Did you?" I hadn't.

I rushed back to the church. When I unlocked the side door, by the outside sentinel light shining through, I saw her standing in front of me, softly crying. When I picked her up, she almost choked me, grasping me so tightly. I thought, "This must be the way God wants us to cling to Him when He rescues us from our dilemmas."

Once when we were vacationing at Redington Beach, we were swimming in the motel pool. It had a big, curving slide. I coaxed Sharon into sliding down it, promising to catch her. At the last moment, I moved aside and let her splash in.

By the time I picked her up, I could see she had lost her trust in me. She refused to do it again, despite any promises I made. I felt terrible, betraying such childlike faith. Had I had the opportunity to do it over, I would have caught her, as I promised the first time. How very important not to "offend one of these little ones." (Matt. 18:6) The lessons from this scripture are so very important; especially as they pertain to misusing, abusing or even failing to "train a child up in the way they should go." (Prov. 22:6) We must "bring them up in the nurture and admonition of the Lord." (Eph. 6:4)

What a privilege and challenge we have as parents to recognize that children are a gift from God. (Psalms 127:3) And what an awesome responsibility to teach, train and discipline them in love and by Christian example. Each of our three girls is so uniquely different, yet so lovable and talented, and each very actively involved in church work today, bringing their children up in the ways of the Lord. Being a pastor for 44 years and having to help parents deal with rebellious teenagers, we are so fortunate that we were spared this worry with our three.

But the sad truth about many teenagers has been summarized by a syndicated columnist: "Teenagers have a certain affinity for bad behavior – for sin, for danger, for self-destruction, for outrageous acts and everyday rebellions. And American teenagers are blessed with a nation that offers a wonderful variety of fashions for being bad." A more recent newspaper article declares, the "deadliest driving age is 16!"

Ours is an environment conducive to drug and alcohol abuse, crime, murders, adulteries, same-sex sex, gangs and scores of other vices. Thank God, though, that the recent polls as of this writing state that 94% of teenagers believe in God, most say they never drink alcohol or smoke cigarettes or marijuana. Almost one-half say sex before marriage is "always wrong," and 54% of boys and 47% of girls say homosexuality is "always wrong." Pollsters concluded that, "Despite exposure to a culture that has dropped many of its inhibitions, in some ways, today's teenagers are as wholesome and devoid of cynicism as the generation that wore saddle shoes." I wonder?

I suppose anyone "always on call," as a church pastor is, can expect most anything, especially at night. One midnight I was awakened by the sounds of a racing motor in my back yard. We had poured a concrete slab for tennis, volleyball, basketball, etc., and it was situated behind the parsonage and church, was bordered by a high wooden fence on one side and the parsonage-church back yard on the other. Access to it in an automobile would have been difficult, especially at night. Anyway, an automobile was going in circles on the court slab, with the engine racing on and off. I grabbed my trousers and flashlight and ran out and tried to flag down the driver.

Upon seeing me, he stopped. I recognized him as a brother of a former neighbor when we lived at Trapnell. I also observed by the smell coming from within the car that he was very inebriated. (Another description: "just plain drunk.") I then asked, "How did you get in here and what do you think you are doing?" His answer was, "I'm looking for Highway 39!" I came back with, "Well, this isn't it. You shut this car down and I'll go call some of your relatives."

I called his sister, apologized for awakening her, and related the incident. She said she would come and take him home. I went back outside and he was gone. So I called her right back and told her there was no need to come. She thanked me and told me what a problem he was to all the family and himself – an alcoholic.

One morning a church member called and told me her son, who grew up in our church, was AWOL from the army, had been arrested in Tampa, and was in the brig at McDill Field. The McDill officials said they would release him if he would return to the base at Columbus, Georgia, and surrender. "Would you please go get him and take him?" she asked. "Yes, I will arrange to go tomorrow," I said.

The next morning the prison official released him in my custody and by mid-afternoon we were at the headquarters office at Fort Benning. I was introduced to a brigadier general as the guards carried the young man away.

The general thanked me for returning the soldier and asked what I knew about him. I told him he grew up in my church and once he entered the service was very unhappy. "All he wants is 'out'," I said. I learned this was not the first time he had been absent without leave. I inquired the possibilities of a discharge and urged the general to do what he could. "He will have to serve some time, and probably will receive a "dishonorable discharge," he said.

I asked if there was any way the dishonorable discharge could be avoided. "I'll work on it," he answered. "And I will do what I can to help him re-emerge into civilian life," I said. "It will be very difficult for him if he is dishonorably discharged," I continued. "Has he gone amiss in any other way?" I enquired further. "No, but that alone is bad enough, and twice is even worse," he concluded.

I left the general's office promising to write a letter in the soldier's behalf, which I did. After some months, the young man was released from the Ft. Benning jail, and released from the military without an honorable, but also without a dishonorable discharge. He did become a good citizen, a hard worker and a fine family man.

I guess the military is not for some people. I never served in the armed forces. When I turned 18 in 1947, the military draft had been put on hold. By the time it was re-instated, I was in full-time ministry. Because of this, I was classified 4D. And to keep this exempt classification, my district superintendent had to keep the draft board apprised of my preaching schedule. Had I stopped preaching, I would have been drafted. But this is not why I kept on in the ministry.

One of our scheduled evangelists was from "The Lone Star State". At age 21, he came from Texas and conducted a three week crusade at Mt. Zion. He had a new 1956 Olds Rocket 88. He liked to see how quickly it would go from 0 to 60 miles per hour. A road close by was newly paved and had few houses and little traffic. It was an ideal place to count the seconds. His took nine seconds, and my '55 Mercury took ten. This is not why I traded for an Oldsmobile. One second isn't much. It was because I liked an Oldsmobile and had a hankering to try something different.

He later became the pastor of a church in a near by city. He eventually moved the church and renamed it. After a few busy years of pastoring, relocation, building anew and continuing to conduct evangelistic meetings, his wife called me on the phone. "Brother Holbrook, He is way too busy. He goes day and night, never takes any time off and I'm fearful for his health. Would you please call him and suggest a golf outing, since he likes to play golf? And please don't tell him I called you!"

I obliged, and afterwards played several times with him. One day we were playing with two of his church members. When we reached the fifth hole, he was one under par. All of a sudden he said, "I forgot my radio broadcast. It's on in ten minutes." "You'll never make it," I said. "Take your clubs off the cart! I'll go to the clubhouse and broadcast over the telephone," he nervously exclaimed.

In about 35 or 40 minutes, he rejoined us. He said, "I've just preached 15 minutes about the greatest miracle I ever witnessed. Then, I won the club pro to Jesus." "Amen," we all echoed. But he never got his golf game back on track that day. He never managed even one more par, but did get acquainted with several doubles and even a triple bogey. As we parted, he said, "Well, sometimes you win and sometimes you lose. My greatest concern is to win with Jesus!" Amen, again!

Another of our evangelists was one that hailed from Louisiana. He conducted services for us long before he was well-known. His singing, piano-playing and powerful preaching was well received by our congregants and attracted several visitors. His wife, and four year-old son, accompanied him during the meetings.

Charles Raburn and I took him fishing on the Hillsborough River. It wasn't a very productive day but Charles and I caught a few bass. All he caught was an owl! I'm not kidding. Once when he cast his plug, an owl swooped down, grabbed it with its claws and got hooked. It tried to fly off and he kept trying to reel it in. Back and forth this went on until finally the owl pulled loose from the hooks.

Many years later when he sang at a funeral of a mutual minister friend, I asked if he remembered Mt. Zion and me. "Of course, I do," he said as he greeted me. "And do you recall catching an owl on a fishing trip to the Hillsborough River?" "Yes, and that is about all I've ever caught!" he answered.

One afternoon I came into the church where he was rehearsing for the evening service. He stopped playing and said, "I'm sick and tired of my piano style. It sounds too much like "honky tonk" playing. I am going to change, starting now!" Several years later, I attended a revival meeting he was conducting. We heard the same piano style from way back when. I thought, "Some things are very difficult to change!"

Once we had a "spontaneous" revival break out at Mt. Zion. Attendance surged, several people were converted and we conducted services every week-night, in addition to our regular Sunday and Wednesday services for six weeks. The protracted meetings gave the church a spiritual uplift that was very inspirational for the congregation as well as for me. A pastor can certainly use a "spiritual re-charge" occasionally.

I later learned that a young man from Nashville, Tennessee, had been converted and was entering the ministry. He conducted services at a neighbor church in Plant City. We visited the meetings and he and I became buddies right off. He wanted to see the Detroit Tigers play the New York Yankees during Spring Training, so I took him and his wife, to a game.

I soon scheduled him for a series of meetings at Mt. Zion. Of all the evangelists we ever had, none drew the crowds that he and his wife did. He was the son of a famous country singer and his wife was a daughter of country singers. Apparently this notoriety, along with their singing and his powerful preaching was a great incentive to many. Consequently, we had overflow crowds for four weeks and broke an all-time attendance record with 416 persons present the final Sunday morning.

We still enjoy so many of the recollections that come to us from those years while pastoring Mt. Zion the second time around. The work of the Lord, family life, and the many comical things that happened, all add up to nourish our memories and become conversation items from time to time.

Nothing supercedes the recall of genuine conversions to Christ and having assisted and observed the spiritual growth process of these individuals. Then, the many humorous things bring laughter again and again. Things that weren't so amusing at the time seem to get funnier as they are retold over and over. Like the "Little Liver Pills" episode and the many falls into the lakes and rivers.

Once Charles Raburn was reeling in a bass he had caught at Catfish Creek. He stood up in the boat to land the fish, our boat hit an underwater object and into the water he went with a tremendous splash. He totally disappeared. First, the fishing rod came up. It was still bent and bending, so I knew the fish was still on the line. Next, up came Charles, standing in neck-deep water. He hoisted the bass into the boat, then I helped him back in.

There were times in warm weather that we would jump into the creek or river to avoid being stung by wasps we encountered on overhanging tree branches. When a friend and church member who had moved from up north was fishing with me, he thought it was hilarious to see me plunge into the water rather than incurring wasp wrath. He later was sitting on the forward deck of my boat. I was planning with the 40 HP outboard wide open, trying to cross the very shallow "mud lake," on Arbuckle Creek. Ever been going 25 miles per hour on the water and come to a complete halt, in one split second? My friend went end over end across the water and emerged unhurt, but glasses-less. I later found them for him in the shallow waters.

I also found the glasses of our then District Secretary. We were fishing on a lake near Polk City, Florida, when I snagged a monster bass. The secretary stood up in the boat to net my catch and that was when he and the fish swapped places. He put my fish into the boat and he fell in the lake. It was over his head and he too, came up without his glasses. "I paid over $100.00 for those yesterday," he said. "We'll never find them!" But I jumped into the lake and kept feeling on the bottom until I struck pay dirt! He called it a miracle!

All in all, it had been and was a most wonderful life and ministry at the church where I had grown up and made the decision to follow in my Grandfather Holbrook and Grandmother Payne's footsteps in preaching the Gospel of the Lord Jesus Christ. But we could see the need for another transition as we stood at the crossroads after eleven more years at Mt. Zion. It was becoming more apparent all the while that we were nearing the end of the pastoring, preaching, building, hard work and fun and games we had enjoyed at this time and place.

I submitted my name as a candidate at a church some miles away. We visited, I preached and was elected. But in uncertainty, I declined to accept the invitation.

Not too long afterwards, our former district superintendent and by then assistant general superintendent of the Assemblies of God in our headquarters city of Springfield, Missouri, recommended me to the church in Tarpon Springs, Florida. One of his wife's relatives had started the church a few years earlier. She came to see us. Would we consider it? Yes!

We visited, preached and were elected. The following week I submitted my resignation at Mt. Zion. At first, it didn't seem real that we were really going to make a change. And if leaving so many friends and loved ones at Milton, Florida, had been the height of difficulty for us, it in no way compared to the crushing impact of departing Mt. Zion.

Memories began to flood my mind with pictures of the past few years. Here was the place my three daughters had been born scarcely two miles away at the South Florida Baptist Hospital. Here was where we had struggled through four building programs praying for miracles as we went. And here was family, relatives and friends who had surrounded us. Here were many converts to Christ we had helped win and nurture in the grace of God.

I looked at the huge church yard I had mowed so many times in the past and wasn't too upset at leaving that chore. I had learned that Tarpon Springs Assembly had a yard man! Even the parsonage we had built evoked memories. It was here we weathered Hurricane Donna in 1961. We could feel the cement block walls shake from the 110 mile-per-hour winds. Fortunately the only damage we sustained was from my brother-in-law parking his car on the septic tank lid, which broke and caved in. I hooked my car to his and pulled it out with him apologizing, not realizing what he had done.

The goodbyes were next. Even though Tarpon Springs was only some 55 miles away, it was "so-long" not only to church members, family and friends, but to our neighbors who lived around us. It was also goodbye to the radio personnel and ministry, the quartet, my fellow ministers in the East Hillsborough Minister's Association and to my too many fishing buddies. A very large part of me was being poured out, emptied, and left out! Reality was surely setting in as moving day moved upon us.

It didn't really help that one of my uncles came to help us load the big truck for moving because he was weeping, begging that we please not leave. "Is there any way you can reconsider and stay?" he pleaded. I told him I was sorry, but no!

A neighbor also helped us load and rode with us and helped us unload at the parsonage on Tarpon Avenue. We were now at the place we had to look forward, not backwards. Although we don't understand all the whys and wherefores about everything, it is certainly comforting to know God loves us dearly and is always working in our behalf to make things come out for our good, Romans 8:28, as well as the good of the Kingdom of God.

Mt. Zion – 1964

Evangelist Jimmy Snow and Ernest with the record attendance of 416 at
Mount Zion in 1964

Ernest and Junell with Sharon, Phyllis and Sandra (our little darlings)
about 1965

Children of Jessup and Nora Holbrook
Front row left to right: Bessie Holbrook Sullins, Janelle Holbrook Walden,
Pearl Holbrook Benner Back row left to right: Joel Thad (J. T.) Holbrook,
Audey Holbrook, Virgil Holbrook (My dad), and Elsie Holbrook Raburn

My family at a celebration of my parent's 50th wedding anniversary From the left: Ernest, Joann, Julia (Mom), Linda, Virgil (Dad), Ralph, and Louise

Aunt Mary (Holbrook) Miley

Pictures don't lie! A catch from Arbuckle Creek
with Crea Beauchamp (These are five we kept out
of over 100 we caught that day)

NINETEEN

FIRST ASSEMBLY OF GOD, TARPON SPRINGS, FLORIDA

Other sheep I have which are not of this fold . . . John 10:16

A new challenge! A new group of people to minister to, and they seemed to respond favorably to our family, our music and singing and my preaching. The church building was beautiful with a very attractive two-story educational edifice joined in back. A two-compartment office was as nice as I had ever seen. And the parking was paved and well lighted.

The congregation, many of which were elderly retirees, numbered about 60, including a small group of young people. This was about one-fourth the size of our previous group so surely there was room for growth.

And too, this was Greek country. I felt sure I would have considerable help with my Greek studies, the original language of most of the New Testament. Perhaps you can imagine how I felt when I discovered there was only one church member of Greek background and one other attender who was married to a Greek. And next, to learn the original New Testament Greek language was also "Greek" to them. Although the two could speak the Greek language, it had changed so much since Bible times that I could handle it better than them, with my helps!

But, there were the famous sponge docks and the renowned Pappas Greek Restaurant at the docks. There was some beach along the Gulf of Mexico here, but it was nothing like the not far away beaches at Dunedin, Clearwater and St. Petersburg. Downtown, there was Spring Bayou where every January the young men from a downtown church dive to retrieve a cross. The winner receives certain benefits and blessings. I couldn't help but think of the fellas who don't win and the accompanying disappointments. But I am glad that anyone who will come to Christ can receive His blessings, even without having to compete in chilly, January water. (John 6:37)

Junell had previously started back to college to further her education at the University of South Florida and Tarpon springs would be close enough that she could continue. I would baby-sit Sharon and Phyllis while doing my studying and office work the mornings she attended classes. Sandra was enrolled in elementary school which was close by.

The parsonage was also very nice and had a big back yard in which the girls could play. During the first few weeks I visited every church family and encouraged each of them to invite new people to the church. Things seemed to be progressing smoothly and before long I began to notice a steady growth as new families were attracted to the church. Among these were a couple of excellent soloists. One had sung with the Artie Shaw orchestra when he lived in the north. He surrendered his life to Christ in one of our services.

We were still getting settled in at Tarpon when we encountered a big surprise. I answered the new parsonage doorbell to be greeted by our friends from Nashville. They and a Canadian couple were in the area for a few days vacation. Before I hardly realized it, I was renting a scuba-diving outfit to accompany them to Weeki Watchie Springs. We first went to the mermaid show at the springs, then the boat ride on the river and finally to explore the river underwater.

With no previous experience or training whatever, and a few brief instructions from him, I found myself submerged and trying to "breathe backwards" or whatever it is you do with such an outfit. I did well for a brief time then suddenly panicked when the full realization of the moment set in. I struggled to surface in the middle of the narrow river and barely missed the churning propeller of a passing boat. Then and there I ended forever, I hope, my underwater exploration. This definitely wasn't for me!

Although the very clear river was fascinatingly beautiful beneath the surface, still, no pleading to return beneath succeeded. I sat out the continued episode. Then, and later, I was to learn of the abounding energies and continuous escapades of my Nashville preacher friend. His remaining days in the area were filled with one activity after another. When he left, he invited us to visit him in Nashville, and then go with them and the Canadian couple to Gatlinburg for a few days.

Since we had not taken a vacation thus far that year, I inquired of the Tarpon church folk and they gladly consented for us to go away a few days. We left on Wednesday, preached that evening in Jacksonville and drove the next day to Huntsville, Alabama, to visit Junell's mother. We arrived in Nashville on Saturday in time to go to the Grand Ole Opry.

We entered the back door where the stars come in and go out. The attendant recognized my minister friend, exchanged greetings and let all ten of us, his three, my five and the two Canadians, in free, and we walked in and sat down right on the stage. My daughters were thrilled beyond words, as we all were, and they got autographs from some of the stars.

After an exciting Sunday morning service at his new church, on the north outskirts of Nashville, we headed for the Great Smoky Mountains in eastern Tennessee. It was raining heavily and my host was an outstanding front seat, "back seat," driver. He was riding with me and Junell was with his wife in her car. Having just had a very bad auto accident, he kept cautioning me of the dangers of slick roads.

We arrived safely, stayed at a huge, old hotel and moved to a more economical, but new motel, the next day. We went sight-seeing all the rest of the day and night, and the next few days. I could hardly catch my breath trying to keep up with him, but it was really fun and certainly not boring.

We explored the surrounding mountains, rode the chair lift, went in almost all the shops, played golf at Pigeon Forge where the Gatlinburg course is located, played carpet golf at several places, went to Forbidden Caverns but balked at the admission price, went ice skating, you name it! What full and exhausting days!

The motel pool closed at 11:00 p.m., or was supposed to. One evening when we arrived back from going everywhere and doing everything, it was midnight and nothing would do my buddy but a midnight dip. "But the pool is closed," I said. "No problem," he said. "We'll climb quietly over the locked gate and swim in silence and no one will ever know." But I knew and remember even to this day every time I glance at my crooked toe. As I stepped into the pool my right foot slipped, turned under and resulted in a broken toe.

The girls had opted out of the late night dip and Junell opened the door to see me hobbling in, in pain. It took several aspirin tablets to help me get any sleep that night. To tell the truth, I was glad when the time came to head back home. This brief vacation had been so filled with going and coming and coming and going that I felt I needed to get home in order to catch up on my rest. With our goodbyes said we headed in three different directions - Canada, Nashville and Plant City! (No, to Tarpon Springs!) By years of habit, we almost missed the road that led to our new location. It seemed a little strange!

One night about 1:00 a.m., Junell and I were abruptly awakened by what sounded like gunshots outside. I got up, grabbed my clothes and as I opened the front door to go out to see what was going on I heard a voice over a megaphone saying, "We've got you surrounded, throw down your gun and come out with your hands up." Upon hearing this, Junell said, "Ernest, don't go out there. They are shooting at each other. You might get killed."

As I looked out the door, by the streetlights and flashing police-car lights, I realized the place was teaming with policemen. I quickly identified myself to the nearest one and he asked for my assistance concerning the layout of the buildings. "We've got a robber holed up somewhere around your church or house. We were called to a house a couple of blocks from here, where an intruder was in the house. When we arrived the suspect ran out of the house shooting at us. We returned the fire and chased him to here," he said.

He handed me a very long flashlight and we began looking behind shrubbery, the stairwells and shady areas between and around the buildings. All of a sudden, one policeman said, "I've just got a call and they've spotted him a block or two north of here." By then, we had emerged on the east side of the church in the paved parking lot beneath the street lights. The officer with me thanked me, grabbed the flashlight and joined three other police cars spinning northward. Just as he was crossing Tarpon Avenue, out came a man running between the church and educational building. I screamed to the policeman but he didn't hear me. The man ran between the church and my house and thinking about my family inside, I took off after him at top speed.

He crossed the road, and disappeared up the driveway of a doctor's house across from us. As I rounded the doctor's house I plunged into the darkness among his trees and shrubbery. I stopped dead still. I couldn't see a thing and the only thing I could hear was my heart pounding. It was beating so loud I wondered if the robber somewhere in this blackness could hear it too. And he had a gun. And the policemen were all gone. I thought, "What in the world am I doing here? This is police work and I sure don't want to make any headlines in the Tarpon News, like: "LOCAL PASTOR SHOT AND KILLED WHILE CHASING A ROBBER." My job was to save souls and nurture Christians, not capture thugs."

I eased back into the driveway, and into the lighted street area, hoping I wouldn't be shot in the back. It sure felt comforting to close the parsonage door and lock it behind me. Junell was anxiously waiting for me and our little daughters slept through it all. Needless to say, it took quite a bit of time for me to calm down and get back to sleep.

I called the police station the next morning and they had apprehended the man. It felt good to know he was behind bars. The sergeant told me this man had a history of breaking and entering and theft of houses and businesses. This time they hoped he would get several years in prison. So did I!

I walked across the street and inquired of the doctor and he hadn't heard a thing during the night. I told him where I had chased the guy into his back yard. We went out back and I was shocked to see an area filled with beautiful, huge shrubbery and bushy trees of different kinds, with any number of places a person might hide. Again I wondered in which bush or shrub the suspect could have waited and watched me. Or perhaps he had kept running. Anyway, I recalled I had decided I would let the police do the police work, if there ever was a next time.

I experienced something new for me in funerals at New Port Richey, which was a few miles north of Tarpon Springs. A neighbor of one of our church members had passed away and they had no pastor. They asked me to officiate. I met with the widow and planned the funeral. When I went the next day to the funeral home for the service, I was ushered in by the funeral director to a podium with no casket, only a picture of the man. It was sitting on a stool. I whispered, "Where is the deceased?" "At this moment his cremated ashes are being scattered over the Gulf of Mexico," he answered. "He was an avid fisherman and this was his request." Then, and ever since, I don't know why but I have such a strange feeling about cremations. One lady asked me what the Bible had to say about cremating a deceased person. "Not anything of which I'm aware," I told her.

We had two very successful revival meetings at the church. One was with a very talented songwriter as well as a good preacher. He and his wife were also an excellent singing duo.

The second meeting was with another young evangelist and his wife, whose parents attended our church and lived in nearby New Port Richey. The evangelist's father-in-law had been converted at our church. One evening, when they had all of us over for a meal at their home, the man told me how much wine and whiskey he had poured down the sink drain when he was saved. He had decided to become a "teetotaler," he said.

But he couldn't quit smoking – or so he said. He worked in Tarpon, and day after day, after work, he would stop by for prayer about his addiction to cigarettes. So, we'd pray and I'd give him testimonies of people like a cousin of mine in Plant City who had finally whipped the habit by a gradual tapering off.

One Sunday after church, though, he said to me, "Praise God, I haven't had a cigarette all week." He never smoked again after that. One afternoon as he headed home from work, he crossed the Anclote River Bridge moments before a sink whole swallowed up the bridge on the northbound lanes of Highway 19. A lady right behind him wasn't as fortunate. She plunged into the river and she and a small daughter drowned. He said, "Just think, if I had been a few seconds later, it would have been me. I am thankful, though, had it been me, at least now, I am ready to meet the Lord."

He later followed our newly-formed quartet, the Songsmen, everywhere we sang, and we would always ask him to sing for us. I lost a true devoted friend when this man died of a heart attack on Sunday, October 25, 1970. I preached his funeral at New Port Richey on Tuesday, October 27, and our quartet sang at the family's request.

There was an elderly couple in the church at Tarpon Springs, who, like so many others, had retired on the Sun Coast from the cold northern winters. He had been a police chief. He called his wife "Tootsie." One day after a pastoral visit with them, as I was leaving, I told him goodbye and I waved and said, "Goodbye, Tootsie."

The following Sunday, the secretary of our Sunday School asked me if I knew I had highly offended the Mrs. by calling her "Tootsie." I said, "No!" "Well, you did. She is very touchy about this so you'd better try to make it right." So I visited "Tootsie," and apologized several times. I'm still not sure if she accepted. She said, "My husband, and only my husband, can call me "Tootsie." You can believe I never called her "Tootsie" again. (At least not where she could hear it!)

One day the phone rang. "Get over here as quick as you can," the voice said! "It's my husband. Hurry!" I recognized the voice as she hung up. I wondered if he had had a heart attack, or had died, or what. This couple was also very elderly. It was about a four mile drive up busy Highway 19, but

I arrived in a very few minutes. They lived in a singlewide mobile home. I spied him on top of the house as I turned into their driveway.

"Get him down, get him down before he falls and kills himself," she screamed. I calmly climbed the ladder, assisted him with the repairs (leaky roof), then after some thirty minutes when we had finished, we both descended the ladder. She had not stopped fussing the whole time we were up there, and accused me of taking his side. He was 90 years old. Soon afterwards they were in an auto crash that crushed his right hip. After two or three surgeries and a lengthy hospital stay the wound would not heal. He would come to church and after the service show me his coat and trousers soaked in blood. He soon died from the infection and other complications associated with it.

There was a small but vibrant, lively youth group at the church. They wanted me at every service and outing. I spoke at many of their meetings and helped them plan social events. One day we all went to the Florida State Fair in Tampa. At that time, it was still located adjacent to the University of Tampa.

We ate Fair junk food, played many games, rode several rides (tame ones) and had a delightful time. Near going home time one of the young ladies asked if I would ride the "whatcha-ma-call-it" with her. It was one of the "wilder" rides. It had a compartment for two persons on the end of a shaft about 60 feet long, anchored in the middle. It turned every which way creating a mind-boggling, stomach-moving sensation. She wanted to ride it but was afraid. But with me with her, she would be safe she said, "Since I know God will take care of you, Brother Holbrook." I wasn't so sure!

Only seconds after it went in motion she was screaming for it to stop and let her off. She had not listened to my previous warnings as teenagers usually don't. And to make bad matters even worse, the thing stopped and got stuck with us on top, 60 feet high! And upside down! She said, "Pray Pastor, I can't stand this!" We were being held by seat belts and "uncomfortable" wasn't even a sufficient name for it. "Oh, my Lord, hurry, hurry," she kept praying. I joined her in prayer as time kept dragging on. Finally after what seemed about half an hour they were able to manually lower us to the ground where the rest of the group were anxiously waiting.

The young lady thanked the Lord and asked me to promise that I would never let her get on such a contraption as this ever again. I agreed and also promised myself that neither would I. She told her sisters she had an accident while up top, leaving her very wet. I didn't, I don't think.

I was invited and joined the Tarpon Springs Minister's group. Unlike Plant City, there were only five or six ministers. We had a nice Easter community service but only a very few people attended.

I recalled that a dear minister friend who had pastored in Plant City had come to Tarpon Springs to serve a church. He had planned to retire in Lakeland, Florida, after this pastorate. But he met a tragic death here. He drowned in Lake Tarpon in a boating accident. Instead of Lakeland, he "retired" in Heaven, which is far better. (Philippians 1:23)

The urge to return to radio invaded my mind. I wanted to make more friends and preach to hundreds or thousands, not just 80 or 90. I contacted the local radio station and was told a daily weekday time slot was available and at what price. I had no businessmen to be courtesy sponsors and when I made my appeal to the congregation, one lady pledged $1.00 a month. That was it. I tried to purchase recording equipment and that, too, failed. Needless to say, I never was able to broadcast to the Tarpon Springs area.

I suppose this contributed to a growing restlessness beginning to well up within me. I had gone from being too busy to not being busy enough. It was unlikely that I would make any inroads with the Greek community. Slowly, it was dawning on me that I was out of place.

I tried fishing and that too, failed. The waters in the Anclote River and Lake Tarpon were brackish, and that meant totally different approaches to fishing. I don't care for salt-water fishing and several hours on Lake Tarpon, area creeks and the Anclote River produced not a single strike.

One day, after a prolonged effort at fishing, I returned to find a flat tire on my car. In near 100 degree heat, I tried to jack my left front wheel. I had parked next to a white-washed wooden fence and had to turn the jack sideways to have room for the handle to work. As soon as I got the car lifted, it fell off the jack and rolled forward into the fence pushing the boards outward. I couldn't get the jack out because it was now wedged between the front bumper and the fence. People were coming and going but no one offered any assistance.

I went into the fish camp office and asked the attendant for help. "Sorry," he said, "I'm too busy! You'll have to do the best you can." Backing the car off the fence might have ruined the tire, so I decided I would take the jack handle and pry two boards off the fence. With them out of the way I was able to properly jack and change to my spare. When I finished I was soaking wet from head to feet from perspiration. I tried to renail the boards with the jack handle, which didn't work. I left them lying on the ground. I didn't tell the attendant. I figured he was too busy. After a few more attempts at fishing, I put my boat, motor and trailer up for sale and sold it pronto. This was another of my mistakes.

I searched for a golfing buddy but found none. My day for recreation was empty. At least I spent more time with my wife and growing daughters. Yet somehow, something was missing. And I was not handling the lack of fulfillment well at all. I began to realize that this was becoming a very serious matter. I had never experienced anything such as this before.

It was so confusing. I had only been here a few months, never dreaming such might happen. I could tell it was also affecting Junell. Since she always could see right through me, she sensed something was wrong and tried to encourage me. I became ill and was bedfast for an entire week. Staring at the ceiling for seven days didn't help. I decided then and there that I was going to overcome this thing one way or the other. I would busy myself in every way I could and trust God for the outcome. But why was it so difficult even to pray?

In the meantime, a steady stream of visitors from Mt. Zion didn't help one bit. Although I was delighted to see each one, each visit only brought back memories and was like adding fuel to the fire. Word soon got out about my despondency at Tarpon. A minister friend had been elected as District Secretary of the Peninsular Florida Assemblies of God. He consequently resigned his pastorate at First Assembly of God in Sarasota and immediately called for me to "try out" there.

Junell and I met with him, had lunch and looked over the parsonage and church facilities. I met with the church board who all seemed very enthusiastic about us considering the church. I told them I'd let them know. Before the week was gone, I phoned and told them I would not come to candidate.

Another pastor friend was leaving St. Pete First Assembly (now Suncoast Cathedral) to take another pastorate. He recommended me to the church. I was extended an invitation to be considered there. I had preached there with the Evangelistic Party in 1950. But again, feeling no inspiration whatever, after having preached a weekend there, I declined to be considered there also.

In the meantime, I received an invitation to candidate at an assembly in Georgia. Junell and I had had a tremendous three week revival meeting there in 1951. We accepted, preached two Sunday services, were shown a brand new beautiful parsonage and were carried to a fancy restaurant by the church board. In a meeting with the board before the evening service, they told me they wanted to construct a new sanctuary, start a daily radio program and organize a church choir and orchestra.

We had experience in all three of these proposed areas and the six-man board asked me to leave the room and wait outside. In a few short minutes, I was asked to come back in. All six voted to recommend me for pastor. The vote would come on Wednesday evening. They would call me immediately after the vote. Would I accept? "Yes!" Wow!

Junell and I headed back to Tarpon Springs Monday, feeling that soon we would be living and working in Georgia. There was no phone call Wednesday night, nor Thursday, Friday, Saturday or in one, two and finally three weeks. After three weeks I called the chairman of the board. He apologized for not calling me and informed me that he was no longer the board chairman, nor even a member. The entire board had resigned, and the church had split!

He said there was a group within the church that had hand-picked a minister they wanted to be their pastor. When the vote came, he and I split the vote exactly 50-50. After several ballots, no one would change their votes so both of us were discarded, the board resigned and many of the people left the church.

I could hardly believe what I was hearing. Everything seemed so right and it all had collapsed as it were, in a few moments of time. I shared the disappointing news with Junell, who like me, had surely felt this move would have been good for us. But it was not to be! God knows best. Goodbye, Georgia!

I visited my parents on occasions. I shared with them my desire to start a new church between Lakeland and Plant City, near the county line. It was precisely the location my pastor friend had urged me to think about when I served with him in Jacksonville. Dad and I, (mostly Dad), purchased five acres of property on the north Frontage Road, of Interstate 4, just west of the Hillsborough-Polk County line. I applied to start a new work promising the District I would not seek a single member from Mt. Zion, which was some seven miles away.

There were a number of members who had already left Mt. Zion and were visiting other churches. Some had stopped attending church anywhere, since we had moved. The area Assembly of God ministers turned down my request and the Presbytery followed suit.

By this time, my assistant general superintendent friend who had been alerted by some of the Tarpon Springs folks, got on my case. He came down to visit relatives. We all went out to eat at the then-famous Kapok Tree restaurant in Clearwater, Florida. He said, "Ernest, (he pronounced it Ernust), I always fast for a week so I can indulge myself on the steak, corn fritters and other goodies at Kapok." His wife's relative would always hand me the money to pay for all of our meals there. She said, "Don't tell anyone I gave it to you. Let them think you did it!" So, I did! But I think they knew.

Then came that "one on one" meeting with him that I knew was coming, and had hoped to avoid at all costs. "Ernest, the folk love you here at Tarpon Springs. The church is growing and you are winning and discipling souls for Christ, so I want you to promise me you'll settle down and quit trying to leave." "I'm sorry, I can't," I responded. "Promise me you'll give it a try and at least stay another year." "I can't promise!" "Six months?" "OK!"

The lady who was the church founder was a jewel. She was the main person behind the church effort. She had us over almost every Sunday for a splendid home-cooked meal. She let me buy gasoline from her pump located at her dairy, at her wholesale cost. She bought me a new suit and several new dresses for Junell. When we started on vacation, she gave me two credit cards. I felt bad, and actually only used one twice to buy gas. She too, really wanted us to settle down and forget the idea of moving.

I contacted the presbyter of the west central Florida area, sharing with him my desire to start a new Assembly of God Church at the Hillsborough-Polk County line. This was the beginning of a life-long friendship with him. He called a meeting of the Plant City area pastors to discuss my request. It turned out just as the others. They thought it best that I not be allowed to begin such an effort. Some of my closest friends suggested I resign from the Assemblies of God and start an independent church. I refused.

Then, as if out of the clear, blue sky it came! It was a telephone call from Lakeland, Florida. The newly elected superintendent asked if I was still interested in starting a new church at the county line between Lakeland and Plant City. I affirmed that I was. I tried to subdue my unbelievable joy.

"Well, make a new application and we'll see what happens," he said. I did. This time the Lakeland and Plant City pastors voted yes by a very narrow margin. After being sternly lectured by the superintendent and district secretary that I was not in any way to contact any Mt. Zion members, I was given the OK.

Any members that had left the church for good would be allowed to come, but none who were still attending. If any of these tried to come, I was to use all my influence to keep them at Mt. Zion.

My dad and I deeded four of the five acres to "Faith Temple Assembly of God," and I contracted with a builder to start my house on the one acre. It was a beautiful model home with three bedrooms, two baths and a double enclosed garage and utility room. I did some revamping, turned the garage into an office and family room with fireplace, and added a back porch with a utility room on the end.

All was set to go. Except the money! I went to the Hillsboro State Bank to borrow the then price of $11,450.00. This was 1966. With no credit records except car payments, and a new church with no members, I was turned down by the bank. The guys to which I had paid and never missed a car payment for many years refused me!

I went to Sunshine State Federal Savings and Loan. I had a friend there. This would be different and I could thumb my nose at the Hillsboro Bank. I was turned down there also. I was in shock. "No bad credit," I was told, but no good credit either. A then $5,000 car wasn't the same as a whopping $11,000 house. What was I to do? Junell was almost finished with college but she hadn't started teaching yet, and we were still strapped with college debts. Plus, we still owed money on the property.

The Tarpon Springs parsonage phone rang again. This time it was my only brother, Ralph. "I heard you wanted money to build a house and got turned down twice," he said. "That's the story," I responded. "Well, why didn't you ask me?" he asked. I stumbled and stuttered and awkwardly tried to come up with some kind of answer. "How much do you need?" I knew my answer would end it then and there. "I need $11,450 for the house, plus another $1,500 or so for a pump and well and I want to pour a slab for a future carport and another utility room," I tried to explain. "About $13,000."

"You got it! Come over and we'll fix the papers for a $13,000 loan at 6% interest, and as long as you can pay the interest, we won't worry about any principle, until you are able. In fact I won't even worry about any interest until you get things going." I wanted to shout "Hallelujah" and "Glory" to the top of my voice. I wanted to call the two banking institutions in Plant City and tell them to "take that!" Then I felt a tinge of guilt, so I dismissed my revenge against the banks and stuck with the "Praise the Lords!"

In the four months the house was being built, I arranged to rent a storefront at Winston in West Lakeland. All the while I was also trying to keep the whole matter from the church folk at Tarpon. It didn't work. The lady leader there cornered me and said, "I hear you are going to leave us anyway!" She, along with others in the church, put in to try to keep us from departing. We were being torn from within just as we had been at Mt. Zion and Milton, previously.

A call from our national headquarters in Springfield, Missouri, didn't help either. Yes, it was the assistant general superintendent again. After listening to his renewed pleadings, I reminded him it had been a little more than the six months I had promised him. He sadly agreed. It was difficult going against my church superiors, just as it had been in West Florida.

With 30 days to go on the new house, I submitted my resignation to a mostly tearful congregation. It had only been 18 months and now it was happening again, not only for us, but for the church group as well. I was hoping this move would put an end to heart-rending partings. I began the new church in full compliance with the district suggestions and things went well for us.

About two years later, I received a letter from the district secretary commending me for the splendid way I had observed the district's request and also informing me that I was no longer under any restrictions or probation.

In retrospect, I still cannot explain the trauma I experienced during the 18 months I was at Tarpon Springs. But once again I had found a "peace that passes all understanding," and was in a position and place where I could further concentrate on winning family members and others to Christ. One was my only brother and his family. This was worth the whole effort. And you can imagine that I had resumption of broadcasting on my mind as well as some fishing and golf!

My growing girls at Tarpon Springs, Florida
First Assembly of God
(Sharon and Phyllis)

TWENTY

FAITH TEMPLE ASSEMBLY OF GOD, PLANT CITY, FLORIDA

He removed from thence, and digged another well... Genesis 26:22

I had always been intrigued about the proposition of starting a new church from "scratch." My opportunity had arrived. It's a good thing I was age 37, with a vision for the future and boundless energy. Although I thought I had counted the cost, little did I realize the magnitude of the project.

As if having to work our way through the proper denominational requirements wasn't enough, we also had to locate facilities for services that had adequate accommodations. The empty store I rented was about 3 miles from the property location. I secured chairs, purchased a spinet organ, advertised in the Plant City – Lakeland, Florida, area and held the very first service with 67 persons in attendance. The date was October 23, 1966.

In a few weeks with an average attendance of about 60, we organized with the Assemblies of God, chartered as a non-profit organization with the State of Florida, received a sales-tax exemption number and purchased a new piano.

I set to work on the plans for a "first unit" building. It would measure 40' x 90' consisting of an auditorium with 100 plus seating capacity, along with a pastor's study, a church office, restrooms, kitchen, and 6 classrooms with folding doors between two of the rooms for youth group meetings. By faith I submitted the plans to 3 building contractors and we chose the lowest bidder, who included the provision that we could use all the volunteer labor we could get in order to cut corners on costs everywhere we could.

After estimating costs, Dad and I went to the bank that had refused to finance my house. I sat by Dad as he talked to the bank president, and requested a $20,000 loan. I was surprised to hear the banker say, "Yes, I think we can handle this." What would I have done without my dad and the rest of my precious family?!

This amount would pay the outstanding balance we owed on the property and with all the donated help we could get, finish the building - we hoped. The bank would take a mortgage on the property and building. They asked for all the church men to sign the note. (I wondered why not the church ladies also? Discrimination? Male chauvinism?)

We got the plans stamped for $150.00, our contractor secured the permit and by November 21st a friend had brought his bulldozer to scrape off the site. The whole five acres had previously been disked and planted in Bahia grass for cattle so all we had to do was bring the mower. Dad and Ralph donated a Farmall Cub Tractor to the future church for this purpose.

We started a visitation program one night each week. We canvassed the Winston and Northeastern Hillsborough County areas. Phone calls for pastoral visitation came rolling in and soon I was going to homes and hospitals as if I'd never missed a "stitch" during the one and a half years I was away.

On November the 18th, the folks surprised us with a "housewarming." Everything was happening so fast I could hardly keep up. So, I went fishing. I went to one of my favorite spots, Arbuckle Creek, once with Robert and Charles Raburn, once with my Dad and sister Louise, and once with my Dad and brother Ralph. This made 3 trips between October 27th and December 8th. We caught plenty of bass.

As was our custom, Mom's and Dad's immediate family gathered at the Varn's Rockin' V Ranch for Thanksgiving. All the families cook and carry food. We pray, eat, play softball and volleyball, and then make music and sing around the fire about dark. This all happens at a special picnic area near the backside of the vast 1800-acre Varn Ranch, provided by my sister Joann and her husband, Ed Varn. Out there it seems one is far away from everything—noise, traffic, and in general, "the madding crowd." This is a continuing tradition.

Amid all the hustle and bustle, the time was approaching when I had promised my Nashville minister friend I would preach a one-week revival meeting for him at Madison, Tennessee. He, like me, was in the early stages of a new Assembly of God church there. Actually, the services would run Wednesday night through Sunday night. Junell took me to the Tampa airport for the flight. She and the girls would not make this trip with me. I got seated beside an "atheist," and spent my entire trip to Atlanta discussing Jesus Christ, the Bible, the Church, etc. He had been deeply hurt at the behavior of some church people where he attended. He vowed he would never foot a church or believe in God again.

I kept trying to move the issue away from people to Christ himself, the Altogether Lovely One. He admitted he had nothing against Jesus, just those "hypocrites" who "play" church. By the time we reached the Atlanta area there was something wrong at the airport that prevented us from landing. We kept circling Atlanta for thirty minutes or more with the pilot making an occasional mention of the delay, without giving any specific details. Out our window we could see other airplanes circling.

By now, some of the passengers were getting a little tense, including myself, and I think my traveling "atheist" friend was too. I don't know if the "scare" played any part in his decision, but he promised me while we were finally landing that he would consider trying once again to look to Christ and overlook people. "Getting and keeping things right with the Lord helps us deal with what other people do," I told him. As we parted, I pointed upward and he smiled and gave a nod of approval.

The landing delay caused me to almost miss my connecting flight to Nashville. By running what seemed about a quarter of a mile, I barely made it through the gate to board the plane. Up and away we went to the northwest and soon the pastor was greeting me in the Nashville airport. He asked if I knew a certain lady star and pointed her out to me. She was about to board a flight to somewhere. She was a pop and country singer. I told him I had heard of her.

I was in for an exciting six days. First, we were off to eat a bite in a corner café near the church. A barbershop was next door so Pastor decided to get a haircut. He told me several of the Opry stars got their hair cut there. The barber never used clippers, only a comb and scissors. It took him about a full hour on each customer. He worked by appointment only, but we caught him at an open moment.

Then we stopped by the church, an edifice much like the one we were building at home. It was also a "first unit" structure, seating about 100 in the chapel area. Then we were off to downtown Nashville, some 15 miles away. It was about dark when we pulled into the pastor's house. It was situated next door to his famous country singer and guitar picker father. The big tour bus used for his travels was parked in the paved driveway between the houses. Later, I observed tour buses passing, showing visitors where he lived, along with other stars on down this same street.

The pastor's wife, daughter and mother greeted me upon arrival. I took a liking to his mother right away. She was a very pleasant, laid back, and friendly lady. Pastor had told me she seldom traveled with his dad on tour. She mostly stayed home and I soon discovered that she spent much of the time at her son's house.

The house was a very nice three bedroom, two bathroom home with a kitchen, nook, dining room, study and a large "empty" living room. Pastor said he would furnish his living room later when he was financially able. This room, carpeted in a beautiful red-maroon color, was used for his church youth group for prayer meetings, socials, and "horror movies." Being a friend of one of the owners of Channel 5 TV in Nashville, he had access to all the movies. He especially loved scary films such as *Dracula, The Wolf Man, The House of Wax, Frankenstein*—you name it. He thrilled at "scaring" his church youth and listening to the girls scream. He had a movie screen and 16 mm projector, which he left in the "living" room.

They showed me to my bedroom, a very lovely room with my own private bathroom. By then I was bushed from all the whirlwind of the day's trip and events and I was ready to collapse. They told me to "freshen up" and soon we would go out to eat. At 11 p.m., we were seated in a restaurant and finally arrived back home at 1 a.m. I died (slept), but woke up the next morning about 8 a.m.

I couldn't hear anyone stirring, but I arose, shaved and showered and went down the hall to the kitchen. No one was there. I went back to my bedroom and reviewed some revival sermon notes and around 10 a.m., went back to the kitchen again. Still, no one was there. I decided they were gone somewhere. I browsed around Pastor's office, looked through some of his books and then the phone rang. As I was about to answer it, it stopped ringing. Then I could hear the pastor talking from his bedroom at the end of the hall. I would be learning that the Grand Ole Opry Crowd, of which these folks had been such a part, stayed up nearly all night and then slept until noontime, or past.

I was certainly hungry when the Mrs. finally made it to the kitchen. We had coffee, toast, orange juice, and cereal. They said we would go out and eat before church. Pastor stayed on the phone much of the time. His mom came over and we talked, laughed and played games. We went out to eat again and, finally, church time arrived.

When the service was called to order, musicians and singers came forward to the front. There was an organist, a pianist, a drummer and two guitarists. And if I thought we had sung fast at places I had ministered or pastored, I had another thought coming. We would have been left far behind.

I tried to keep pace with Pastor leading, backed up by some Opry-connected folks. The Lord's praises were being sung fast and forcibly by these who surely seemed to be zealous for Christ. I preached with all my heart to some 70 or 80 folks and when I gave the invitation almost all of them moved as close to the front as they could and began kneeling on the floor, praying about as fervently as they had sung. I was deeply impressed at the sincerity and soul-searching. Not too many seemed in a hurry to conclude their prayers and by the time the service gradually broke up it was about 10 p.m. Just in time to go out and eat!

Home at last just after midnight and I hoped I would sleep later the next morning, which I didn't. But this time I had pre-arranged to prepare my own breakfast in case they again slept until noontime. Which they did! This turned out to be the perfect time in which to study, pray, and otherwise reflect on the remaining services. While experiencing what to me was a totally different way of eating, sleeping and working, I sincerely hoped that I could impart some spiritual truths and be a blessing while in Nashville.

The afternoon brought another "game" time with the girls. This time they told me they had gotten into graphology, otherwise known as "handwriting analysis." By carefully scrutinizing the manner in which a person writes they were supposed to be able to determine personality traits, characteristics, and so forth. For instance, if you write "downhill" you are a pessimist, if "uphill", you are an optimist and ambitious. If you write large, you are an ambitious, imaginative person and if you write small, you are a pedantic person, which is someone who majors on minors or who is narrow-minded, etc. It follows the pattern of psychoanalysis. I wrote rather large and uphill. There were a lot more considerations involved in the analysis, but I was glad when they turned to another game.

The next day Pastor suggested a boat ride. His father-in-law had a boat on a lake near Hendersonville, a part of the backwater of the Cumberland River. We started up the big outboard motor, which was mounted on a beautiful 16-foot watercraft, backed out of the boathouse and headed across the lake at some 35 mph.

359

Near mid-lake, a mile or so from land in any direction, the motor suddenly quit. Several efforts to restart it failed. While pastor was trouble-shooting the problem, I saw a small object bobbing on the water about 50 yards away. I then heard a faint call for help. I rowed toward a totally exhausted man and we pulled him from the water, apparently just in the nick of time to keep him from drowning.

He was so breathless it was several minutes before he could speak. He finally said he was on a picnic with his family when he decided he could swim across the lake and back. Realizing too late that he had miscalculated the distance across and being so far from land, he panicked. At the point of complete helplessness, in desperation he cried out to the Lord to save him.

And that was when our boat came out and stopped, close enough to give him renewed hope. He was trying to reach us when I saw him. Even more amazing, was the fact that the motor then cranked without further ado and we delivered him safely back to his family. He told them God sent us to rescue him and he couldn't stop thanking us and the Lord enough for a stalled outboard just at the right place at the right time. To him, it was a miracle! To us, too!

I'll not forget one message I preached. I had heard my preacher granddad Holbrook once say, "If you like music and singing, don't miss heaven, for there will never be any of either in hell." I took King David, sweet singer of Israel, as a text, told how he played King Saul's blues away on his harp and quoted various portions of his songs (Psalms). I also used the 150th Psalm and Ephesians 5:19, noting that Psalms here in the Greek is Psalmos, a sacred ode accompanied by the voice, harp, or other instrument.

I was in Nashville, headquarters for a church group that does not believe in having musical instruments in the church because they say it is not mentioned in the New Testament. I showed that it was mentioned in the Greek text and commended these congregants for singing and playing sacred songs. And I urged them to sing "clean" songs when they sang at the Opry or wherever. Then I concluded with the illustration my granddad had given about there being no music or singing in hell. I talked about Matthew 8:12 and other scriptures that tell of the outer darkness where there will be weeping and gnashing of teeth. The altar invitation resulted in almost everyone coming forward, kneeling and fervently praying once again. Some were seeking to be baptized in the Holy Spirit, including some of the Opry stars.

After the service, one of them came to me and thanked me for the sermon. "My whole life has been music and singing and I sure do want to go to heaven so I can sing and play and praise Jesus Christ forever." He admitted he had a drinking problem and was pretty high even then. But he and I spent extra time talking and praying about God's forgiveness through Jesus Christ and the power we have through the Baptism in the Holy Spirit to be witnesses for Christ with pure hearts and clean lives.

Friday evening brought a full church and some new visitors. Among them was a man invited to sing who was the cousin of a famous star and sounded much like him when he sang. Another was a young man who brought his Spanish-type guitar and sang a special number. After service, he demonstrated a special neck he had invented on his guitar that allowed for movement both forward and backward. It resulted in a "sharpening" or "flattening" of the strings, which gave it a sort of steel guitar sound.

I discovered one reason for which they both had visited the service. They were hoping for Grand Ole Opry connections. But I listened as Pastor told them he had cut loose from that sort of entertainment business and advised them to do likewise. We were invited to one star's house for a meal and this cousin was included. All he could talk about were his hopes to get on the Opry. And his famous cousin would not even talk to him about it, he said.

With no service scheduled for Saturday night, Pastor had plans for a full day of activities. He arose earlier than usual and we went next door to his folk's house. His dad was in his "office" which was also a first class recording studio. It was filled with musical instruments, music memorabilia and all of his hit records. It had pictures of various Opry stars and reflected in general the life of a successful Opry person.

Pastor had had a "run-in" with his dad a few days before our meeting. He told me about this, plus his dad's net worth, way back then. He owned stock in the Opry, radio station WSM, a downtown music store, a big record company plus other investments. Pastor predicted that his dad, who had refused to speak to him for several days, would "break down" and do something soon that indicated an apology, although he would never put it in words.

A little while later, he was phoned by his dad who asked him to meet him outside in the driveway. He responded and soon returned with a check for $10,000 made out to the church. "This," he said, "is my dad's apology."

He and his dad later made a long-play album entitled, "My Father's House." He sent me a copy.

We then took off for downtown Nashville, stopped by his dad's music store, then drove around the Ryman Auditorium, a building which once was the church of a great preacher. From there we went down Broadway, the location of a famous record shop and several restaurants where the Opry stars dine.

We went over the story about this outstanding preacher's encounter outside the old church. It was a Monday morning, and as he walked down the street an irate member confronted him. "I don't like what you said in your sermon yesterday morning. You were preaching directly at me." With this, he let go a haymaker and knocked the preacher down. The preacher got up, tried to think of what to do and thought of the Scripture where Jesus said in Matthew 5:39, "…Do not resist an evil person. If someone strikes you on the right cheek, turn to him the other also." So, he turned the other cheek and "wham," down he goes again. Lying once more on the sidewalk he thought, "Well, I turned the other cheek so what did Jesus say to do next?" He said he couldn't think of what He said to do next. So he got up, grabbed his walking cane and laid a good "whipping" on the man.

By now we were getting hungry so we parked in a city parking garage, walked to a "White Crystal" and ate several of their bite-size hamburgers. Then we took in a movie. Pastor loved movies and said he would like to be a movie producer. He did later advise a church member on the film, "The Gospel Road," and played the part of Pilate. He made three trips to Israel assisting in the film, which cost the member a considerable amount of money to make.

On the way home, he showed me a bridge in downtown Nashville that crosses the Cumberland River, where, when he was hooked on drugs and alcohol, he decided to commit suicide. But as he was poised to jump he lost his nerve. Instead, he fell on his knees right there, repented his sins, and received Christ into his heart and life as Savior and Lord.

While riding along, Pastor had the car radio on. He was listening to a Nashville country music station. A brand new song was being introduced. He pulled over and stopped on the side of the road to carefully listen to the words. He said, "I can tell you if it will be a hit or not." I asked how. "By an outstanding or very impressive line or phrase," he said. After the song ended he cranked up and drove off saying, "Yes, this song will make it to the

top, because of a certain special line. It's like 'Teardrops falling like rain,'"
He continued. "Catchy lines, phrases and similes often make a song go." I
realized from this, how strong the ties were that he had to the country music
world, having been reared in it. And as he predicted, this particular song
soon hit the top of the country music charts.

But his burden now was to win souls to Christ, and he said his connections
to the country music world would allow him to minister to country music
stars and their families. I was already aware of this as I noted various ones
who were attending the revival services. "These people are controlled by
managers, rigorous tour schedules and often get hooked on alcohol or drugs
because of this. They take 'uppers' to lift themselves and 'downers' to try
to rest, and soon they are in trouble. They especially need Christ and I'm
trying to tell them about Him," Pastor said.

After a short "breather," that evening we went to the Grand Old Opry.
The cousin, who was trying to get on the Opry, had asked to go and
accompanied us. Once again we came in the back entrance, got in without
tickets and were escorted right on the stage as before. All the stars were
coming and going right past where we were sitting.

I sat by the "cousin" who was still "itching" to get a shot at an Opry
tryout. Pastor's discouraging remarks on the subject had not made a dent in
his ambitions. When one star was introduced and began to sing, the cousin
began to criticize him. "Look at him," he said to me. "He has false hair (a
wig or hairpiece), false teeth, and a false (falsetto) voice. He's on the Opry
and I can't even get an audition." Poor "cousin."

We stayed until one of the pastor's church members had sung, and
arrived home about midnight. I was so exhausted I could hardly review my
sermon notes. My biological clock still hadn't adjusted to the eat, sleep,
wake up routine of Nashville's music row. But Sunday's morning and night
crowd filled the building and the services were very inspiring. When I gave
the invitation on Sunday evening, again almost every person in the building
tried to come forward! Believers and unbelievers alike came as close as they
could and were kneeling and praying everywhere. I observed an Opry star
and another man receive the Holy Spirit Baptism and heard them speak in
languages neither they nor I had ever heard or learned. It was amazing!

Since some were not Opry people, the crowd began to break up and by
about 10 p.m. we closed and locked the church and headed for a late-night
meal at a downtown restaurant. A number of the church folks were there and

it amounted to an extended time of fellowship around adjoining tables. But I was anxious to get home, get to bed, and then head home the next day to return to Junell, Sandra, Sharon, and Phyllis. And Faith Temple! It seemed a long time since I had seen them. Later, I returned to Nashville and taught an educational training course for the Sunday school teachers at this church.

On Monday, following the close of the revival meeting on Sunday night, the pastor and his wife decided to fly with me as far as Atlanta. Then they would go on to somewhere in North or South Carolina to sing and preach for a few days. Our flight was on a four-motored propeller airplane. As we approached Atlanta we got into a severe thunderstorm. We were told to fasten our seatbelts and none too quickly. The plane began to bounce up and down and sideways. I looked out the window. Amidst the rain and lightning it looked like the wing was flapping like a bird's. It also felt like it.

What a sigh of relief we felt as we passed through the storm and settled down on an Atlanta runway. Pastor called me a few days later and told me as they were trying to land in Carolina, the plane bounced and skidded off the end of the runway and gave them scare number two for the day. It was caused by the same weather system we had encountered earlier. Only a few days later, a plane similar to ours, maybe the same one, went down in a storm near Atlanta, killing everyone aboard. As I read about it I couldn't help but relive our experience over northwest Georgia.

Junell and the girls met me at Tampa International Airport about 10 p.m. How delightful to see them and head for home and get ready to plunge head long into the new church project we were starting. I found, however, that I would need a few days to recoup from the very exhausting time I had spent in Nashville. But I was grateful for the friendship and excellent hospitality afforded me by that Nashville congregation.

I managed to get in another fishing trip in December with two friends, to the Kissimmee River on the 22nd. The other days and nights were filled with hospital visitation, contacting prospects and going to court in Tampa, Florida, with a family for a custody hearing for their grandchildren. Their parents and a sibling had suffocated in their home from a propane gas leak. The children were awarded to their maternal grandparents, who later adopted them. They all became members of our church later.

I was asked to serve on a committee to raise money for the surviving children's future education. We met at the First National Bank in Plant City to organize the drive. Someone said they would see that it was publicized in the newspaper and on radio. The neighbors would solicit money in the Cork-Antioch neighborhood where the deceased family had resided. A Brandon gas station owner was present and volunteered to donate 1 cent per gallon to the fund for several days. And the two Plant City banks would be donor sites. I was asked to announce the project at half time at the high school football game. I did so and volunteers stationed at the exits told me they took up about $165.00. I don't know who was in charge of the money. I never saw any of it.

I waited for the committee to meet again. To my knowledge it never did. I contacted a banker and an attorney, the only members I knew, and they told me they had no idea who was in charge, or if there was another meeting. The effort apparently died. A few years later, when I was asked about it, I again sought information. The banker had passed away. His wife knew nothing of the fund, nor did the attorney or anyone at either bank. No one knew what neighbors had solicited funds in the community, who the gas station owner was in Brandon, or what happened to the money taken up at the stadium.

The president of the First National Bank and I searched the files at the bank and could find no record where anything had ever been set up in the children's or their grandparent's names. I finally found a neighbor who helped raise money in the community and he said what he got, he gave to someone and he had forgotten whom. I went to others, but could find no one else who knew anything about it. So I had to go to the family and share the strange news. Somebody somewhere had to know something about this, yet it remains a mystery to this day.

Soon, our building contractor began work on our first unit building. The basic work seemed to move along quite rapidly as the foundation, floor, walls, trusses, roofing, and a brick front with a cross attached made it appear that the building was finished and ready for occupancy. Far from it. Mostly volunteers would do the inside: partitions, electrical, central heat and air, sheetrock, floor tile and painting, but we hired a plumber. Naturally, things slowed but still moved forward.

I had not fully realized quite how much was involved. Both the building and electrical contractors let us buy materials at their contractor costs, saving us many hundreds of dollars. A carpenter friend and his dad led our men in laying out all of the partitioning. Two of our men took charge of the electrical. A cousin and a man we hired to help did the heating and air-conditioning. A Christian brother donated and supervised the laying of the tile assisted by another church family. Several others came night after night after work and on Saturdays.

I ran errands, picking up materials and helping in whatever project I could. As I watched and experienced the sacrifice of the men and women and observed their enthusiasm and excitement for the church-building project, I thought how wonderful it would be if every gospel effort had this much fervent support.

Slowly but surely, it all came together resulting in a beautiful, practical building for a beginning church. Being situated along Interstate 4 allowed it to be a spectacle, and brought other ministers to consider its likeness for their initial buildings. I drew and furnished plans for Crystal Springs, Tampa First Assembly, Turkey Creek Independent Church of God, a Church of Christ in Lakeland, and others at no cost to any of them.

When one attempts to mention names, invariably someone gets overlooked. So, suffice it to say that I owe a debt of sincere gratitude to the many loved ones who made it all happen and contributed so greatly to the kingdom of God.

We dedicated the building on Sunday, May 28, 1967, with 41 adult charter members, an average of 80 in Sunday School, and 100 in morning worship. Our Peninsular Florida Superintendent spoke in the AM service and the presbyter in the evening. We were doubly blessed as a member sang a new song she had written for the occasion entitled, "There's a New Church by the Highway." It was awe-inspiring.

This was a time of new and renewed beginnings. Totally immersing myself in church-related activities, I was able to reinstitute a seven day per week broadcast on WPLA, the Plant City radio station. I had sponsors in no time. I rejoined the East Hillsborough Ministers Association, helped start a new quartet, the Songsmen, was reelected to serve on the Assemblies of God Sectional Committee and became co-chairman of the Fellowship of Christian Athletes at Plant City High School. I also played on the church softball team.

A cousin set up a bookkeeping system for the church and soon we were conducting revival meetings, entertaining missionaries, training church workers and Sunday School teachers and cooperating with community benevolence projects. I preached at several of the downtown churches on special occasions.

In my "spare" time, I helped remodel my mom's and dad's house, redoing the inside walls and ceiling, and laying new carpet on the floor. I found a day now and then for fishing and golf. It was as if I had never moved away from the Lakeland-Plant City area. Gone were the unexplained days when I was struggling at Tarpon Springs. I felt ashamed and often pondered what had transpired there.

I added to my number of friends by broadcasting direct from the WPLA booth at the Strawberry Festival. This became an annual thing and besides, it afforded me a free pass to the festival. Thousands attend this winter festivity, usually held in late February and early March each year. Plenty of strawberries are on display and strawberry shortcake tops the list of foods available. There are all sorts of exhibits, arts and crafts, livestock shows, top singing stars, and of course, the midway, where the screams of the riders sound and resound across the area and into the night. But not mine!

How quickly a year had passed and we had recorded twenty-two new adult converts to Christ in our church. This did not count several who made professions in the hospitals or at our quartet concerts. After numerous tryouts, our Songsmen Quartet was formed.

At every concert where we sang, we continued to throw in a little comedy and always gave an invitation after each quartet member gave a brief testimony. After all, our group consisted mostly of ministers. Quite a few people received Christ as we sang at different churches and auditoriums. After each sing, if we got any money, we would stop at a restaurant and usually spend it all on the meals for the quartet families. What a splendid fellowship.

I suppose one of my greatest thrills was when my only brother, Ralph, who was ten years older than me, received Christ. Having been disappointed with some church goings-on as a teenager, he had abandoned the faith. During the war he was stationed with an avowed atheist and later expressed to us that perhaps he, himself, had become one. This so disturbed my saintly mother that each time Ralph came around she tried to force him back into the kingdom. He finally let her know that she needed to "lay off" and leave him alone.

This crushed her heart and she shared it with me. I told her that we would have to pray and commit Ralph to the Lord. One Sunday morning she was sitting on the third pew from the front. After the service started, Ralph walked in. He came past my mom and seated himself in an open spot just in front of her. I thought she was either going to faint, or shout! Invitation time came and Ralph came forward, wept his way to salvation through repentance and faith in Christ as his Savior and Lord. I baptized him and several others, including some from the First Assembly in Plant City, in Moore's lake at Dover, Florida, on Sunday, April 28, 1968. Not only was there joy in the presence of the Angels of the Lord, (Luke 15:10) but at the Holbrook house as well. Ralph's wife, whom we now call "Doc," had always said she would come to church if Ralph would. She did and still does. Their daughter was the first to come and led the way for her mother and dad.

The new "Songsmen Quartet" recorded its first long-play album, "Nashville Sounds of the Songsmen," in Nashville, April 11-12, 1968. It was produced by my Nashville pastor friend. This album featured Nashville union musicians, which greatly enhanced the sound of the quartet. We borrowed money from the bank to finance 500 records and to pay the producers, musicians, and studio costs. We had the money repaid in a few months.

One evening when our church softball team was playing another church at Turkey Creek, someone called me to come quickly. I ran over to the crowd to see my then 14 year old nephew lying on the ground with blood all over his face. He had been throwing and catching softballs alongside the playing field. Other youngsters, throwing a basketball, had hit him in the face at close range and split his head just above one eye.

I grabbed my handkerchief, applied it to the wound (you could see his skull), and rushed him to the emergency room at the hospital. The doctor on duty soon called him in. My nephew said so pitifully, "Uncle Ernest, please don't leave me." "I won't," I said. He clung to my hand as the doctor applied a foaming solution of some sort to cleanse the cut of all the dirt. Then he proceeded to put shots all around it, to deaden it, while he sewed it up. The gash was about two inches long and was gaping open about a half-inch wide. He then proceeded to sew the skin from the inside of the cut next to the skull. "Please keep holding my hand, Uncle Ernest," my nephew begged. Suddenly, I began to feel squeamish. The doctor looked at me and asked, "Are you alright?" I answered, "I'm not sure." "Hold on," said my nephew, gripping my hand more firmly. "Turn your head and look away," the doctor advised. I did, and soon after, things cleared up for me.

In these days I was "pastor" to hundreds of people, most of which never darkened the doorstep of the church, except for a few during a crisis. Some of these people had been followers of my preacher granddad Holbrook. Others claimed me because they would hear me on the radio and when the need for a minister arose, it was me, probably the only one they knew. I believe I was called on to serve as many or more "outsiders" than "insiders," marrying, burying, visiting hospitals, counseling, and "refereeing" family feuds. I sometimes wound up in the middle of a dispute and usually, before it was over, got clobbered myself, from both sides.

I was continually taking some courses at the University of South Florida in Tampa, but Junell's big day was her graduation, Friday, June 7, 1968. After the ceremony, I went with her in the reception line at the UC (University Center). The President and his wife were among the greeters, and when we reached them, the Mrs. looked at Junell, then at me, and exclaimed, "It is so nice for fathers like you to accompany your daughters on these wonderful occasions." I wanted to "correct" her but didn't have the heart. You can imagine what a "heyday" Junell has had retelling this through the years.

Two of our daughters also graduated from USF, Sandra and Phyllis. Sharon graduated from Florida Southern College in Lakeland. Both Junell and Sharon later earned masters degrees. Junell interned at Jackson Elementary and then taught at Springhead for 25½ years. We borrowed money on insurance policies, and even obtained a government loan to pay college bills. In fact, until Junell started teaching, we lived up everything we took in, and sometimes more.

It was at this stage, in our late thirties and early forties, that we realized Jesus Christ might not return in our lifetime and we might need something for retirement someday. Some of my minister friends opted out of Social Security but I stayed in. (For which I am now most grateful.) There were a few who said they didn't believe in it, others said they couldn't afford it and still others said, "If we live to be very old, there probably won't be any Social Security funds then." All the while, I was beginning to observe some of my elderly minister friends who had arrived at the place they could no longer minister, and had nothing with which to retire. No house, no savings, no Social Security, no insurance, no nothing. How sad, indeed!

This is when we began to get serious about "laying aside" as much as we could out of every payday. Our church denomination, because of meager fare, had not been able to provide retirement benefits for our pioneer pastors, missionaries, and evangelists. But becoming aware of this situation, they began to assist ministers with programs to encourage financial retirement planning. We were advised of government provisions like IRA's, 403B's, present and future tax-exempt parsonage allowances, and Social Security to aid the retirement years. Many churches now assist with financial retirement programs for their pastors along with the denomination.

When our sectional committee interviewed young ministers and their spouses, included in our admonitions were recommendations to enroll in Social Security, to purchase life and health insurance, to invest in tax-exempt savings accounts, and so forth.

I realize it was probably the same with young ministers as it was with me way back when. Older age and retirement seemed so far in the future that it was easy to think there will always be plenty of time and hopefully more money available later. It's no wonder some don't even try in the times when "outgo" often exceeds "income." Yet, it's amazing how much a few dollars a payday saved over the years adds up when interest is added.

Of course, first and foremost, we stressed the great importance of faithfulness in tithing. Tithing, basically, is the giving of 10% of one's income to the church. The concept began with Cain and Abel who brought offerings to the Lord. (Genesis 4) Abraham paid tithes to Melchisedec, priest of Salem. (Genesis 14:20) Jacob promised a tenth of his increase to the Lord (Gen. 28:22), and this pattern of giving to God continues throughout the Old Testament. Solomon cited the blessings of bringing one's "first fruits" to the Lord in Proverbs 3:9-10 and Jesus, himself, reiterated this in Luke 6:38.

I once heard of a church member who long ago was elevated to a salary of one hundred dollars a week. He faithfully brought ten dollars, plus offerings each week to the church. His company prospered and his salary rose to two, three, four, then five hundred dollars a week. Then, on it went to one thousand, two, three, and when it reached four thousand each week he came to the pastor. "Pastor," he said, "four hundred dollars is simply too much to give the church each week." So the pastor responded by asking the man if they should pray for a decrease in income, so he could pay tithes again. But the member didn't want that either.

I'm convinced that you can't out give God. Not that this is why we should give, but there are so many testimonies of the peace of mind that comes from the obedience of giving to Christ and His church. A consideration of the "earthmoving" machine inventor is one such example. He had repeated business failures until he took God for a partner and pledged 10 percent of his earnings. As he prospered, he upped the percentage of giving to 20, 30, 40, 50, and finally to 90 percent before he passed away.

And it's not just the amount given, but the proper amount based on the resources available. The widow's "two mites," perhaps worth a fraction of a penny, was more than the contributions of the "big givers," since she gave all she had, Mark 12: 41-44. According to Paul, quoting the Lord Jesus, "It is more blessed to give than to receive," Acts 20: 35b, and in II Corinthians 9:7, "The Lord loves a cheerful giver." Jesus promised a four fold blessing to givers, Luke 6:38. Again, Paul insists that one who sows bountifully reaps the same, as opposed to sowing sparingly and reaping sparingly, II Corinthians 9:6-8. The Old Testament warns that failure to bring tithes and offerings into the storehouse (church) amounts to "robbing" God, Malachi 3:8-9. I have always practiced tithing and giving additional offerings and I can testify of returned blessings in many ways and means of which I had never dreamed. When I reflect upon these, it most certainly seems miraculous, to say the least, and confirms numerous scriptural promises about giving.

With all my involvements, my college attendance and studies most often took a back seat. It was an "on again," "off again," proposition. When you achieve two years in seven or eight you should realize where your priorities are. Mine, of course, were the church and related activities, plus the family and some recreation. But, attending a secular college certainly opened my eyes to many anti-God, anti-Christ, anti-Bible and anti-Christian views. I was surprised at how many professors taught evolution as a "fact." Biblical accounts of the creation were constantly belittled and ridiculed. One philosophy professor referred to the Bible as a myth. He confessed he had once been a believer until he "learned" better. He said instead of God creating man, man created God, as a "prop" or "crutch" for his inability to otherwise account for all things. And to think our taxes pay for such as this!

I did gain the respect of some of my professors. One biology teacher particularly congratulated me on an article I wrote entitled, "True Science and the Bible Agree." He gave me an A+ and confessed to me privately that he needed to get back to his religious upbringing. The instructor of the "Marriage and Family" class, after discovering I was a minister, said it gave her courage to take a stand on certain issues in the course that were anti-

Christian. She said before the class, "The book says thus and so, but I don't believe it. I believe the Bible view on all of this!" Wow!

One day I was walking down a hallway on the way to class. I had my briefcase and I guess because of my age, about 40, a very attractive young lady sidled up to me and asked, "And which professor are you?" I'll never know why I did it, but I promptly responded, "I'm Doctor Holbrook!" I guess Freud would psychoanalyze it as my superego speaking from my id. I fully intended to tell her I was joking, but at the corner she turned one way and I the other. I never saw her again. I sometimes get letters addressed to Doctor Ernest Holbrook. I often keep them for a laugh. (Or is it an ego-booster?) The only "doctor" status I may have attained is one from "the school of hard knocks" and "blunder seminary."

This is in no way intended to be disparaging of the many men and women who have diligently applied themselves and earned college and doctorate degrees. Any person who will serve God wholeheartedly, remain humble and apply their wisdom and knowledge to the furtherance of the Gospel of Jesus Christ can be a tremendous asset to the Kingdom of God.

I think of Solomon and his God-given wisdom, Doctor Luke, a medical doctor who wrote Luke and Acts, and Paul the apostle, who wrote much of the New Testament. The more anyone has to use for God, the more God can use them. The more I learn, the more I realize how very little I know. And compared to God Almighty and His Christ, even the most learned and intelligent among us are really mostly dummies. (Job 9:10) What little I do know, I want to use for the glory and honor of God!

I am not given to the serious consideration of my every dream, or to follow every thought that crosses my mind. It is my understanding that certain foods we eat can result in various apparitions or delusions during the following snoozing hours. And who knows for sure where every thought comes from?

But when these "silent-voice" messages become so pronounced that one can't ignore them, it's time to take action to what extent possible. I can recall two specific instances where such occurred.

One was when such a voice in my mind kept insisting that I "stop the car," which, when I did, most likely prevented a serious accident. The other was in respect to a prayer I prayed to find a pair of lost glasses.

It was vacation time for this busy pastor and his family. I could hardly wait for the following Monday morning and the anticipated trip for two whole weeks to our favorite retreat areas in the North Georgia, North Carolina and Tennessee mountains.

With all my church obligations hopefully satisfied for the next couple of weeks, I decided to get an early start with a round of golf. On Saturday afternoon, I teed up at the Plant City Golf Course at Coronet, for an 18 hole round.

Since my light blue eyes did not take too well to bright sunlight, and especially the glare when driving, my optometrist had prescribed special sunshade glasses. I had just gotten them the day before, and was now trying them out of the golf course. They seemed to work perfectly.

On hole number 12, I pulled my tee shot to the right, right into a thick clump of myrtle-type trees and bushes. It was an area along a steep bank down to a phosphate pit some ten to fifteen feet below.

As I entered the very shaded area to search for my golf ball, I removed my sunshades. Making my way through the heavy underbrush, I recovered my ball plus several others. When I emerged from the dense area of some twenty to thirty yards, I reached into my shirt pocket to discover my glasses missing.

I hurriedly went back through the thick jungle-like area twice more hoping to find them, with no luck. As soon as I finished my round, I hurried back and searched again, still with no results.

The purchase price of these glasses had already reduced our vacation money by over a hundred dollars and now I had nothing to show for it. After the church service and lunch on Sunday, I returned and resumed my quest for the lost glasses.

I tried to retrace my previous steps through the very congested myrtle trees and bushes once again, but still there was no trace of the sunshades. I went through once again, and "ka-wham" came a golf ball. The golfers walked on by without a search, so I said, "finders-keepers," and pocketed their golf ball.

Running out of time and patience, I bowed my head and asked the Lord to help me find my glasses. Two words popped up in my mind, "look up." I silently responded, "Yes, Lord, I am looking up to you, now and always."

I made two more of the very difficult trips through the massive underbrush with those two words echoing through the grey matter, "Look up, look up." I gave up my search and headed back toward my car, but couldn't get away from the two words.

I turned around, went back to the thicket and began attempting to struggle my way through once more, stumbling, but looking up all the way. About halfway through the maze, I suddenly saw my glasses hanging on a tree limb some five or six feet above my head.

I climbed the tree, retrieved the glasses with a "Thank you, Lord," and began trying to figure how in the world they got up there. Regardless, I said, "Praise the Lord for the words, "Look up," which seemed to be an answer to my prayer, resulting in me finding my sunshades. I also thought about the psalmist who said, "I will lift up my eyes to the hills, from whence comes my help. My help comes from the Lord, who made heaven and earth." Indeed, it does! (Psalms 121:1)

Ernest holding the key to the first unit of Faith Temple Assembly of God
Plant City, Florida – Building completed in 1967

In the broadcasting studio of WPLA, Plant City, Florida

ERNEST E. HOLBROOK

CHURCH BY THE HIGHWAY

Words and Music

FAYE HALL

PROVIDENCE MUSIC COMPANY, LAKELAND, FLORIDA

Song written by Faye Hall
Sung at the dedication of our new facility

Album #2 recorded at Music City Studios in Nashville
Ernest, Jerry Ramsey, Jim Campbell, Jessie Barlow

Our new house next to the church completed in 1966

The Faith Temple Congregation – 1967

TWENTY-ONE

FAITH TEMPLE ASSEMBLY OF GOD, PLANT CITY, FLORIDA – PART TWO

... they that turn many to righteousness shall shine as the stars forever and ever...
Daniel 12:3

Once in a while, I would slow down enough to "smell the roses," to observe and enjoy the dearest things to me: my family, my wife and my three darling daughters. What a change (for the better) for me when I took a wife. I honestly don't believe there have been many marriages that have worked any better than ours.

I had dearly loved and cherished my parents, siblings, relatives and grandparents, but never to this degree. There aren't enough words to praise my life companion, Evelyn Junell Player Holbrook. Truly she made home and me happy. Certainly God had a hand in bringing us together. She was the perfect replacement for my mother, as a friend, cook and advisor. Plus fill a physical and emotional relationship par excellent.

And the girls! How uniquely different each one is. What a thrill to carefully watch each one after birth as they begin to grow, sit up, crawl, talk (Da-Da) and walk. They each cried in a different tone. There were times that we had to be up with them nights. I say we! It was mostly Junell. There were times she would awaken me and say, "I can't do anything with this crying young'un! It's your turn!"

Before the girls were old enough for school we used to vacation in the spring, usually May, before the summer crowds or prices were in full swing at our mountain vacation spots. When Sandra, our oldest, was about two, we spent several days in Gatlinburg, Tennessee. We ate at Tommy's restaurant across the street from the motel. Sandra spilled something on the table, seat or floor every meal. A young Indian girl, who was our waitress, took to Sandra and acted as though it was a pleasure to clean up after her.

One rainy afternoon, Junell wanted to explore all the unique shops up and down the main street. She asked me to baby-sit. Sandra started crying the second that Junell walked out the door. I tried everything I knew to make her be quiet. After two hours I gave up. When Junell finally returned, Sandra was still sitting at the door crying and holding one of her mother's shoes.

Junell started the girls on piano as soon as they were old enough to begin lessons. Sandra took a special interest and banged away, sometimes day and night, until our nerves were on notes, chords and discord's edge. But at age twelve, she took over as church pianist and has never stopped since. After teaching public school for nearly ten years, she is now teaching piano again, and directs a School of Music at the Plant City Church of God.

Once, our Superintendent told us we had one of the best church orchestras he had ever heard. With Sandra at the piano, Sharon on electric piano, Junell on organ, Sandra's husband Phil on guitar, Phyllis on clarinet, Phyllis's husband, Tom, on trombone, me on guitar and steel guitar, Alonzo Harrod on bass and different ones on drums (including my grandson, Phillip), we did have some good sounds.

Sandra and Phil once held union musician cards and did some backup sessions in Nashville and other places. Sandra has also written several songs. Her husband, Phil, was city manager for Plant City, Florida, for four and ½ years, after serving as director of planning and zoning and then community improvement services director for the twelve years prior to that. He is also retired as a Captain from the United States Coast Guard.

Their daughter, Farrah, is an accomplished singer and musician and is a music teacher at Cork Elementary School. (Another Cork stopper!) Her husband, Justin Moore (who is also a musician) recently graduated from USF with a degree in criminology and is currently pursuing a career in that field. They are expecting their first child (our first great-grandchild) this month. Sandra and Phil's son, Phillip, is also in the Coast Guard and we recently welcomed his new bride, Krystal Riling, who is a paramedic from Detroit, Michigan, into our family in February of this year. They are soon to be stationed at Cape May, New Jersey.

Sharon enjoyed spending time alone more than the other two girls who wanted to be in the middle of everything. She amused us early on with some of her first words that were, "Ock, T on," which interpreted meant, "Rock me with the television on." In high school she was involved in FBLA (Future Business Leaders of America). She later earned a B.S. in Business

Administration, and then an MBA. Her husband, Bob also has an MBA. They met while in school together.

Sharon had a 20-year career in banking and investments before "retiring" to be a stay-at-home mom to son Alex and daughter, Hannah. She is now in the process of getting certified to be an Elementary Teacher, and plans to begin teaching next year when Hannah starts Kindergarten. Bob manages large computer projects for a major credit card processor out of St. Petersburg. His team includes 20 computer programmers and systems analysts. He has worked in this field for 20 years. His son, Jonathan, from a previous marriage, won our hearts from the earliest acquaintance. Jonathan will soon graduate from high school and is learning to play the guitar.

Phyllis was the last born, after we lost the little boy, and she was a cutie and sweetie, as well. At church, she used to sit with one family, and then another, while Junell and I were up front carrying on the services. When Phyllis was age two, we were on vacation at Daytona Beach, and were swimming in the motel pool. One of the girls said, "Daddy, Phyllis is under the water." I dove in to find her swimming beautifully under water. I pulled her out. She pulled away and started swimming again. She had learned how to hold her breath under water, and pull and kick, across the pool beneath the water's surface.

Phyllis took an interest in golf when I used to hit balls in the back yard. We had a total of thirteen acres, twelve with the church, plus our one. We had plenty of room and she developed a beautiful, natural golf swing. Before long, she was beating me.

In high school, in addition to playing clarinet in the band, she won in golf three years straight. She also was in the top five girl golfers' group in the West Central Florida area, and tied for the top on two occasions. She played against one young lady who went on to pro golf on the ladies PGA tour for a time. Phyllis has a B.A. degree in Social Work, and is employed at a church preschool.

Phyllis's husband, Tom, is a correctional officer with the Polk County Sheriff's Department. They have two sons, Evan and Christopher, and a daughter Caitlin. Evan has become very skilled in flying remote controlled model airplanes. Chris shows talent in the artistic field. Caitlin, who excels in reading, was in the ninth percentile on the national reading test when she was in the first grade. I am thrilled that all my daughters and their families are actively engaged in the work of the church and the Kingdom of God. I'm so proud of all of them.

It hardly seems possible that my girls are all grown, gone, married, have families and occupations of their own. What a wonderful gift, the family, truly a little heaven on earth. My heart as a minister has been saddened on too many occasions, to have observed homes that are more of "a hell on earth," than anything else. God surely must have intended otherwise. His plan is still the best: one man, one woman, husband and wife, until "death do us part," and children, reared in a loving home with both dad and mom, who bring them up in the nurture and admonition of the Lord. But, I have been deeply impressed with many persons, who, despite experiencing broken homes, have been able to overcome the despair and emotional upheaval and go on to rebuild productive lives.

Junell and I are also very grateful for our sons-in-law Phil Waldron, Bob Franklin and Tom Conner. Of course, there are no grandchildren like ours: Farrah and Phillip, Jonathan, Alex, and Hannah, and Evan, Chris and Caitlin. Solomon put it well in Psalm 127:3 when he said, "Sons are a heritage from the Lord, children a reward from Him." (NIV) How wonderfully true!

In 1969, two special people in my life were called home to be with the Lord. One, as previously mentioned, was my successful business friend. He was a hard working man who made lots of money and used a good portion of it for the Kingdom of God. Junell and I sang at his funeral on February 15, in Lakeland, Florida. I was privileged to spend many hours and days with him.

Another giant of the Kingdom of Heaven was my very first district leader. He was the Peninsular Florida Assemblies of God District Superintendent when I went through all my stages of credentialing. He was an excellent banjo picker but stopped bringing it with him in later years. I often wondered why since he was so talented at it. I know I was a big disappointment to him concerning Tarpon Springs but he never mentioned it to me afterwards. He was still serving as one of the then four assistant General Superintendents when he passed away. His funeral service was held at Bethel Temple Assembly of God in Tampa, Florida.

The scriptures make it very clear that, "it is appointed unto man once to die and after this the judgment," (Hebrews 9:27) but the next verse tells of the sacrifice of Christ for our sins and the hope of eternal salvation for all those who are looking for His second coming. What a privilege to have our sins forgiven so we can welcome Christ's return acquitted of all our wrongdoing!

1969 was also the year of the first "break-in" at our church and home. When I arrived at church one morning I discovered both the secretary's and my office doors had been forced open, the door jambs and trim riddled. Then we found a rear window screen had been removed, the window broken making way for the thief or thieves. Gone were my tape recorder, turntable and microphone all of which were used to tape the radio broadcasts. Gone also was the church adding machine, typewriter and a few dollars of change from the secretary's desk drawer which had been pried open. From the chapel area, the robbers had taken my Gibson and double-neck steel guitar and amplifier and the quartet P. A. set.

A "camera clause" addition to our regular church insurance policy covered the losses and soon the insurance company had replaced some of the stolen goods and paid the difference. We repaired the screen, broken window, and the damaged door jambs, locks and trim as best we could.

Since our church secretary was only part-time, Junell by then teaching at school, Sandra and Sharon in school and Phyllis in preschool, I was alone at the church and the office in my home much of the time. As a security precaution I would bring all the new musical equipment to my house next door to the church.

Most every Thursday noon I would go to First Assembly in Plant City for a delicious "home cooked" meal for $3.00. It helped their church projects and allowed fellowship with the pastor and other ministers and friends who were there. On this particular day I was away from the house from 11:45 a.m. to about 1:30 p.m. Upon returning home, I drove into my carport which was situated on the rear of the house and I could see that the double french doors were standing wide open. I knew I had left them locked since the church robbery had only been about two months before. I entered the house to find all the equipment and musical instruments gone again, as well as a beautiful braided oval rug from the family room floor which a church family had given us for as a house-warming gift.

My heart sank as I looked through stuff scattered all through the house. Drawers from chests and dressers were pulled out and dumped in the floor, bedspreads and mattresses had been pulled off the beds and cushions from the living and family room chairs were scattered around.

So I made another call to the Sheriff's department and insurance company. We went through the same process once more. These were two of some 24 break-ins we had at the church and parsonage, and my house, over the 28 years we were there.

I, more than once, thought of the scripture where Jesus, in the Sermon on the Mount said, "...lay up for yourselves treasures in heaven, where neither moth nor rust doth corrupt, and where thieves do not break through nor steal." (Mt. 6:19-21) Thank God there won't be any stealing in heaven. Thieves aren't allowed!

It surely seems we had more than our share of robberies. Words are difficult to find to describe the feeling of entering one's house or church to discover almost everything turned upside down, inside out and numerous things missing.

From such frequent association with the law enforcement officials, we learned there were many gangs involved in such thefts. They would spot a potential robbery site, scout it out, learn the coming and going habits of the occupants, strike at the most opportune moment and be gone in a matter of a very few minutes. They would transport the stolen goods over state lines to purchasers there, get a load of stolen goods there and bring them back to sell here.

There was a young man attending our church who was learning to play steel guitar. He was in a music store in Tampa looking to buy a double-necked steel guitar. My doorbell rang the same afternoon. It was he and his dad. He exclaimed, "Brother Holbrook, I have found your steel guitar!" He explained that a week previous he had inquired at this music store for such an instrument. They told him to come back in one week and they would have one. And this day he had gone back, only to recognize it was the one I had had stolen from the church previously.

Even though we had already settled with the insurance company, the next day I went to the same music store. I not only saw my steel guitar, but the amplifier, the Gibson guitar and the quartet P.A. system. This was from the first robbery. I went outside to a pay-phone, called and got the detective who was assigned our case. He was there in fifteen minutes. We went into the store and the manager came to wait on us. I told him what all I was interested in (everything that I recognized from the theft). Then the detective identified himself, told the manager this was "hot" (stolen) merchandise and would take all of it to the Sheriff's office.

The manager went into a rage. "I bought all this stuff fair and square and you are not taking any of it," he roared. The detective said, "O.K.! Then I'll take it, and you!" He decided to let us take all the equipment without him. Outside, we loaded all the goods into the detective's car. He told me this wasn't the first time stolen musical items had been found at this store.

"We may have enough to put him away this time," he said. He called me later and said the manager got two years and a hefty fine. He had also owned a music store in another Florida city where stolen goods had been found. By the way, I did notice on the double-necked steel guitar, when I was helping the detective load it, a sticker from the other music store.

Another 1969 memory standout was the moon landing. On July 20, 1969, we had invited two church couples over to watch the televised event. Neither had television sets. Two astronauts landed on the moon's surface while another orbited it. Once outside the landing module, one of them said, "One small step for man, one giant step for mankind."

Wow! What a spine-tingling, emotional, and mind boggling achievement. And we had watched it "live" from the moon. All except one Brother. He said as he was leaving, "Brother Ernest, I hope you don't believe all this stuff. This was all made up in Hollywood." I don't think to his dying day he ever believed that man actually went to, or landed on, the moon. "God wouldn't allow it," he said.

By August of 1969, I had drawn the plans for phase two of our church building program. It would be a 45' X 95' sanctuary that would comfortably seat 250 plus. (On special occasions we counted up to near 500. At my dad's funeral on September 19, 1971, 465 people packed the sanctuary, the choir area, aisles and 50 were in the small balcony. At a 15 year-old boy's funeral, high school students and adults present totaled near 500.)

I carried the plans to the same gentleman who had finalized and stamped our first unit plans. He worked in the Hillsborough County office where plans were submitted and approved. He re-drew the plans to county requirements and had an architect friend who reviewed and stamped them for us. These were the days before such strict laws and requirements for buildings were mandatory, the kind that now can cause one to become a nervous wreck. The building would consist of a cement floor, tiled and carpeted, four 16 feet-high by 45 feet wide laminated trusses on 16 feet centers, a 3" X 6" tongue and groove varnished cathedral ceiling of northern spruce and modern antique brick walls inside and outside with a 4" airspace between, and a decorative front.

Again, our contractor friend would pull the permit and we would do most of the work ourselves. Contractor prices for materials would once more be available from the building and electrical contractors. What a blessing and what cooperation from Christian contractors who would donate time and profits for the church. It's a good thing I was still quite young and energetic since this would be a much greater undertaking than the first structure.

With a new sanctuary in the making, we were always looking for ways to raise money. Someone suggested "pecans." We were approaching Thanksgiving and Christmas, so it seemed to be an excellent time to go for it. I went to Moultrie, Georgia, in my brother-in-law's pick-up truck. The new crop pecans were excellent and our folk took them wherever they worked and they sold like hot cakes. I parked on the South Frontage Road of I-4 just east of the citrus plant. In no time at all mine were sold and we all celebrated a highly successful "pecan" campaign. We decided to do it again! A big mistake! We didn't leave "well enough" alone! Where was that gift of discernment, once again? Or how about common sense, whatever that is?

Early the next week, I once more engaged my brother in law's pick-up and made my way back to Moultrie. I had called ahead and the warehouse crew was waiting and had me loaded quickly with a "double-portion" load. I passed the agricultural inspection station on I-75 heading south, and realized it said, "All trucks stop for inspection." I had already passed it, but decided I had better stop. I backed up carefully along the road shoulder.

Fearful of being fined for backing up this way, I decided to stop and walk back. I tried to explain my failure to stop (ignorance, not used to driving a truck, etc., since I had not stopped the first time either). The officers were busy with the inspections of the incoming semi-trucks and trailers and looked at me as if I were a little off upstairs.

Finally, one man, who seemed to be in charge, looked down the side of the interstate to where the pickup truck, loaded and stacked with bulging burlap sacks, was parked. He ordered another man to go with me to see what was going on. On the way he asked what I had on the truck. I said pecans. He wanted to know what business I represented, the legal requirements attached to such sales, papers of the transactions, etc., etc. I showed him the only papers I had, a receipt from the pecan broker, made out to the name of our church. I did not tell him this receipt reflected all the profits from our previous sales, re-invested again hoping for twice the profits.

He opened a couple of the sacks, retied them, felt of a few of the other bags and then asked me to once again tell him what this was all about. With cars whizzing by on the interstate and big semi-trucks and trailers struggling by to gain speed from the inspection stop and re-entrance onto the freeway, it was difficult to hear. Raising, then lowering, then raising my voice again, trying to explain, he finally waved to me to go on. "Should I stop with such a load as this if I come through again?" I shouted as he walked back. He turned and gave me an answer that I couldn't hear for the noise. His facial expression seemed to indicate, "I hope not!"

By then, I was wishing I hadn't stopped at all. And if I had only known what I did, and didn't have, in those pecan bags, I would have wished I had never gone to Moultrie, or heard how much we could contribute to our church building fund from pecan sales. One-half of the pecans were from the previous year's crop (or even perhaps the year before that) mixed in with the new crop. We didn't know this until we had sold nearly all this "new load." The calls started coming in. We replaced pecans for bad ones only to have more people call back that complained about the rotten replacements.

You can guess by now that this ended our "ventures in Georgia Pecans" and I doubt we broke even in dollars, plus we were out for all our efforts, bagging and driving. All because of a "crooked" pecan dealer! I'm sure most everyone has been "taken to the cleaners" in what appears to be quick and easy ways to made some money. The saying, "If it sounds too good to be true, it probably is," should have been included in the Proverbs, or somewhere in the Bible.

Perhaps the greatest education we get is the one earned from the school of experience. Some of the candid advice we got from older ministers, and then gave to the younger ones after us, was, "Everyone makes mistakes, but learn from them! And don't keep making the same ones over and over!" This rule of thumb is practical not only for ministers but for everyone.

My appreciation and friendship with an automotive dealer continued through the years. Besides his helping me with automobiles we had splendid fellowship. He was a member of a famous evangelist's board of directors. I attended several of the evangelist's crusades with him and first met one of our outstanding ministers when he was a member of the team in a city-wide crusade in Plant City at the High School Auditorium. It proved to be one of the area's best religious campaigns with full cooperation of most of the Christian churches. An unusual unity prevailed as these groups prayed and worked in harmony to promote the Kingdom of God and Christian evangelism.

I first met another well-known minister in January, 1970. I had been hearing about him for many years from various friends of mine in the ministry. I booked him for a series of preaching services. He had pastored a large Assembly of God church and then served several years as a District Superintendent. He traveled alone, so in order to have more money available for his support, we kept him in our home, rather than in a hotel or a motel. This would be the first of what turned out to be five revival meetings we had with him.

He had a unique nickname, one that about everyone used, and was a very delightful person. He favored some of my relatives on the Holbrook side of the family. He was in his upper 60's and had an almost full head of wavy white hair, which he shampooed every day. After church he donned his robe, grabbed the newspaper and began to work the crossword puzzle. He only wanted to play golf about five times each week. He said, "Why, I played nine holes almost every weekday morning, even back when golf was a sin."

Another minister had vociferously declared golf a sin in several of his sermons. One person he had in mind when pontificating this awful worldly evil was none other than my new found friend. The same critic was an avid hunter and often took his bird-dogs in his station wagon with him, even while visiting and preaching at churches in his district and elsewhere.

Once, when visiting a minister who golfed for recreation, upon seeing the minister's golf clubs, he sarcastically asked, "Why, my dear brother, what are those things?" The minister quietly answered, "My dear brother, these are my bird dogs."

Even with my busy schedule, and the nightly meetings, I managed to take this preacher golfing a few times. Back then, the city of Miami, Florida, sponsored an "International Clergy Golf Tournament" every May. I took him to one of these. We played at the city-owned Mel Reece course right across the street from the Miami International Airport. It was a very difficult course and had a way of humbling even the best of golfing ministers or anyone else that played there. He thoroughly enjoyed it even though he and

I both, "hit the ball lots." In golf, the least amount of strokes, the lowest score, wins.

Several of my golfing minister friends played the Miami tournament each year. At night, we would eat at some exotic restaurant, usually Chinese, Spanish, Mexican, etc. With my very delicate stomach I had to be very careful. Most of my preacher buddies laughed at me and said it was all in my mind. I said, "No, it's in my stomach!" One evening at a Mexican eatery they met their match. Seven of us were sleeping in adjoining hotel rooms with the door between the rooms opened. They kept me and each other awake most of the night visiting the bathrooms. I thought, "Who's laughing now?" I was, but they were disturbing my sleep!

The Miami clergy tournament was one of the best in which we participated, followed by the Georgia Preachers' Tournament at Calloway Gardens at Pine Mountain, Georgia. (There were others at Perry and Statesboro, Georgia, as well as at Santee and Myrtle Beach, S. C.) One year, as we headed for Miami, we passed three National Guard units on their way to Liberty City, where race riots had broken out. Once in view of the city, we saw the smoke rising from burning buildings. Liberty City was located on the north side of the golf course, and police and other law-enforcement officers were everywhere. There were none at our hotel, but when I went to another to pick up a couple of buddies, the "sharpshooters" were stationed atop their hotel with their binoculars aimed at Liberty City.

This signaled the beginning of the end for this tournament. With a normal group of some 150 minister-golfers at each tournament, the number dwindled to near one-third the next year. The following year there were only 36 golfers and that was the last one.

The year Liberty City was burning, I was playing the 16th hole at the Mel Reece course. There was water all the way down the left side of the hole and a high fence down the right side separating the golf course from the city tennis courts. A group of six black men were working along the fence under the big eucalyptus trees.

I had pulled my ball into this area, as did many golfers, avoiding the water on the other side. When I went to play my next shot, I thought I would sort of tease the men by saying, "I wasn't trying to hit you, honest!" Wrong thing to say! In fact, I suppose most anything said would be the wrong thing.

They all stopped working and looked at me as I drove up in the golf cart and made the above statement. I observed the frowns on their faces so I spoke further, "Do you fellas play golf?" "____, no!" one returned. "We have to work, so you "honkies" can play." I decided I had better hit my shot and move out of there, since I was quite a ways from the other three ministers in my group.

On another day, Robert Raburn and I were playing along the expressway on the south side of the course on hole number 15. One of us, probably Robert, had hit his shot through the fence into very thick high grass and heavy underbrush under the trees that fronted the freeway. We smelled an awful odor, spied a wooden slatted carton with what looked like a dead body in it. We reported it to the golf course manager and he ignored it. We then called the police. The one who answered the phone said, "So what? Do you know how many get killed in this city every night? We won't even bother to go look."

That, along with everything else associated with this tournament in Miami is probably why it wasn't the end of the world for us when it got cancelled. On our very first trip down there, the motel owner where we stayed greeted us with a gun. "Just for protection," he said, as we nervously paid him. This is one reason why we went to a big hotel after that.

Speaking of golf, we often played the course at St. Leo College west of Dade City, Florida. I played there many Wednesday afternoons with a minister friend. I took my evangelist there, and for the first time in his life, he made a "hole in one." When we turned in his score card and told the "brother" who ran the course, he didn't even know what "a hole in one," was. My friend said, "I play golf for over 40 years, make my very first "hole-in-one" and you don't even know what one is?!" He sent his scorecard, endorsed by me and the brother, to the maker of the golf ball he was using. They sent him a dozen free balls and their congratulations!

The evangelist was a very personable, loving, compassionate preacher. His love for God and people was very apparent in his sermons, illustrations and altar invitations. Numerous people responded to his pleas for salvation, rededication and service to God and man. All this was why we had him back four more times for revival services.

He was preaching for us during the first moon landing by the astronauts. He had been invited to speak at our nearby College chapel service. On our way over he had picked up our newspaper. The headlines, in big bold letters read: "Man on the Moon." When he took the pulpit, he showed the headlines, and then announced his subject, "God on the Earth." Then he preached Jesus Christ, God incarnate in the flesh, crucified for our sins, resurrected for our justification. What a living example of the ministry he was to younger ministers like Robert and me and so many others.

He suffered a heart attack soon after our last meeting with him and passed away after by-pass surgery failed. Robert Raburn and I were asked to serve as pallbearers at his funeral at the First Assembly of God in Memphis, Tennessee. The Pastor conducted the service and Robert and I rode with him in the mortician's limo to the cemetery. Just before we reached the burial plot, we passed a beautiful golf course adjacent to the cemetery. Pastor told us that this was where he and our departed brother played golf when he was home between meetings. "And this is where he told me he wanted to be buried," Pastor concluded. I can truly say my life was enriched by my association with this wonderful man.

At the time we began to build the new church building, a neighbor pastor was in the process of constructing a recreation building. Since it was similar to our proposed structure, we shopped together for building materials and were able to save many dollars with a double order of laminated trusses and 3" X 6" tongue and groove decking.

We dug the foundation troughs including the 4' X 4' holes for the laminated beams support. We installed the steel, called for inspection and this is where the "fun" began. The county inspector had never seen or heard tell of a building like this. He wanted to know what the eight 4' X 4' holes were for. We tried to explain but failed. We finally had to arrange a meeting of the draftsman and engineer, who stamped the plans, with the inspector, who, finally, reluctantly gave an OK.

With donated labor, the project was very slow. But, eventually, we managed to erect the front and back walls which would give us a place to temporarily attach the trusses until we could install the 3" X 6" tongue and groove decking. Next came the "big" day, the erection of the huge beams. As I left the house for the project, Junell asked if I knew what I was doing. I answered, "Sure," as if it were an everyday happening. "Just you watch," I said. "I'm afraid to," she returned.

The laminated trusses had arrived a few days earlier and were lying on the ground, each in two pieces. Upon erection, each piece would be joined together at the peak and each base secured in a steel "saddle" situated on top of each 4' X 4' foundation. Precise measurement was required since the steel saddles would be anchored by huge steel bolts in the concrete bases.

One member had brought his dragline and several men had taken off from work. A nearby pastor also joined us. He had built a similar structure in another city earlier. I reminded the crew about what the builder of the trusses had said, that to let one fall onto the concrete floor would result in it 'exploding' into fragments since it was glued together under pressure.

This warning provoked concern on their countenances. We attached the cable and up in the air went half-truss number one. While it was held with the dragline, we secured the base and attached 2' X 6's to the back cement block wall. He turned it loose and it held steady. Whew! Then the other half! It joined perfectly.

Up went the next and the next and finally the last. With each securely nailed to the other and to the front and back walls, we "rested" from our success and took pictures. Only one steel saddle had been off about an inch, but the beam flexibility took care of that.

Another congregation in Plant City had also recently finished a similar church building and warned us not to arrive at the "decking stage" in June, July or August because of the heat. But there was a delay in the shipment of the northern spruce decking and instead of coming to Plant City we were notified it was on a side track in Dade City. Since it would take several more days (or weeks) for the railroad to get it to us, we decided to haul it ourselves.

We managed to beat most of the summer heat installing the decking, but we still had the two outside brick walls to be finished. While some of our church folks and I laid one side, another member hired a crew to do the other side. Finally, the building was enclosed!

Then, another round with the inspector began. He wanted a solid 2' X 1' concrete lintel with four continuous steel rods run atop each side wall to support the weight of the roofing. "But the roof is supported totally on the laminated beams and the front and back walls," I told him. He disagreed. "We would have to cut into each laminated truss to pour such a lintel," I argued. "Such would greatly weaken the trusses." Once again, I had to engage my draftsman and engineer to persuade him. Once again he grumbled as he signed the inspection.

Then, with the outside complete, came the next challenge, the inside. Another member and I spent endless hours putting several coats of sealer and satin varnish on the cathedral ceiling and laminated trusses. We had rented scaffolding and night after night when we had finished our other labors we would work until 12:00, 1:00 or 2:00 a.m. Tired wasn't a proper word for it. Total exhaustion better described it. But what a work of art it was when it was finally finished.

We then built the platform, the side rooms and the balcony, and installed the baptistry, lighting, tile and carpet. The pews arrived on time and at long last, 14 months all total, we were finally ready to occupy and then dedicate our own member-built worship center. Our first service was held on Sunday, July 18, 1971. We dedicated the building on October 24th.

For several months, a member had left his dragline sitting beside the new building. Since the church was located alongside Interstate 4, passersby would often ask me how long it would remain there. "As long as he wants it to," I would answer. A lady and her young son passed by every few days and would have a little "bet" on whether it would still be there. One day they passed and it was gone. I don't remember who won the last bet.

During the extended construction time of the new church building, life went on as usual, with church services, radio programs, hospital visitation, and everything that goes with it. The Songsmen Quartet was in concert somewhere almost every Saturday night. On June 8 and 9, 1970, we recorded our second long play album this time at Monument studios in Nashville. This one, "Wonder of Wonders," was titled after a song written by our quartet pianist.

We were guests on Channel 5 TV in Nashville and a big music company offered to publish our songs and promote our records if we would agree to go on the road full time. A gentleman offered to buy us two new travel buses and be our manager if we would travel full-time. We seriously considered it but I was the first to back out. I did not want to leave my church or be gone from my family that much. I told the quartet that baritone (my part) would be the easiest to fill. But one by one, they decided not to pursue the road. The Quartet did appear for a weekly program for three months in the fall of 1970 on Channel 44 in St. Petersburg, but fell one sponsor short for the second series.

After the church construction we decided it was time for a vacation. So we loaded up July 19th, took off, spent the night in Graceville, Florida with some of my wife's relatives, the 20th in Shreveport, Louisiana, the 21st in Amarillo, Texas and the 22nd in Canon City, Colorado. The next day we crossed the mountain pass through Monarch, then on through Gunnison, Montrose, and Delta and to Cedaredge, where my brother Ralph, and wife Lauredo, had a summer home. We rented an apartment on Grand Mesa, a sort of flat-top mountain 10,000 feet above sea level. On the way up we saw a sign: Colorado Assemblies of God Youth Camp.

For the next four days we lived next to heaven (literally). We hiked up a small mountain where Sandra lost her sweater. We returned and searched for it twice, finally deciding perhaps a bear had gotten it. There was still snow in the shady places and one day it snowed for several minutes (July 24th). We turned up the heat at night, covered with several quilts and still stayed chilled.

On one day we fished for rainbow trout (caught a few small ones) and on another day we went to Land's End. The drop-off went straight down a mile or two! There were several signs warning visitors to keep their dogs on leash. "Why?" I asked the park ranger. "Because they will chase the chipmonks who jump over the edge and cling onto the grass, vines or weeds and the dogs fall a mile or more." Enough said! Along one area the updraft was bringing water up into our faces sufficient for a good sprinkling. We also saw about a dozen deer running in one group.

On Sunday, we watched a pastor from Denver on television and then went to First Assembly in Grand Junction. They announced the attendance at around 800. It was an outstanding service and sermon in a beautiful sanctuary. With thanks and goodbyes said to Ralph and Lauredo, we took leave to head home by another route.

From Grand Junction, we took Interstate 70 through Rifle, Vail, and through the Rocky Mountain State Park. Junell kept looking over the edge of the road which dropped downward almost forever and wanted me to move away from the edge. But I couldn't because I was already on the center line. We found lots of snow at the Alpine visitor's center area and took pictures.

We headed for Cheyenne, but discovered that so had about everyone else, where some sort of big rodeo was to take place the next day. There were no rooms available anywhere. We finally found one in Denver and the next day traveled up Pike's Peak, which Junell did not like going up or down any better than she did the park. Our girls seemed to relish all of it.

From there we took in Dodge City (Gunsmoke) and then Springfield, Missouri, the headquarters of the Assemblies of God. Then we went down through the Ozark Mountains and on to Nashville, Tennessee, for a weekend visit with our friends there. Pastor again took us backstage at the Grand Ole Opry and this time a star gave my girls an autographed long play album.

He sold over a million copies of the single's hit, it thus becoming a "gold" record. He later told us it had been the only song from which he had been able to make any money, which was still uncollected because someone had sued the owner of the song. Their lawsuit claimed the song was stolen from them. I don't know how that ever came out but we still have the album.

On Sunday we discovered the new sanctuary had been completed, a school had been started and among their congregants now were numerous Opry stars and their families.

Pastor preached a powerful sermon and I noticed a well-dressed man rise from near the back of the sanctuary and respond to the invitation to come forward and receive Christ. After service, we learned the man was the president of one of the biggest record companies in Nashville.

From Nashville, we went to my favorite vacation spot, Gatlinburg, for a few days, then on down to North Georgia to Cumming where we visited with relatives of the Holbrook and Bramblett families.

But, as always, it was good to get home again, to enjoy the new church sanctuary and get Junell, Sandra, Sharon and Phyllis ready for school. Junell taught almost 26 years at Springhead Elementary School and had our youngest daughter, Phyllis in one class she taught.

But a sad event was awaiting me in September. My dad checked into the hospital with a bleeding ulcer and passed away on the 17th. We had his funeral on the 19th in the new sanctuary. What I had feared so long had finally come to pass. A massive heart attack at age 57 and a series of minor strokes that followed, kept me expecting that call that finally came at his age of 75 years. I thank God for those extra 18 years.

With Dad's death, I lost one of my best and dearest friends. We spent many happy hours together fishing, building churches, working in strawberries, the dairy and the orange grove. Several times we fell in the lake or creek or river and always had big laughs on each other.

This particular summer had also brought us some wonderful news concerning our relatives. Upon hearing that Robert Raburn's son, Terry, and daughter, Caren, had entered the ministry, we invited them and their cousin for a youth revival at our church. Their singing, music and preaching brought back memories of the time some 24 years earlier when Robert and

I, and Charles soon after, started in the ministry as teenagers. And now a new generation was following suit. How thrilling!

Young people and adults alike were challenged and blessed in the services and it is noteworthy how encompassing their ministry is even to this day. Caren attended Continental Bible College in Brussels, Belgium and married Eric Laursen from Sweden. They have since served as evangelists and pastors in Europe.

Terry married Athena Register and their ministry encompasses evangelism stateside, missionary work in Lebanon and also pastoring Mt. Zion, my home church, where they authored the book, "Under the Guns in Beirut." Terry served as presbyter of our section then youth director of the District. From there, he moved to Springfield, Missouri, to serve as National Youth Director for our denomination. Then, he served as national Education Secretary before becoming superintendent of the Peninsular Florida District of the Assemblies of God.

Charles and Sally Ann Raburn also have a minister son, Johnny, who along with his wife, Gail, pastors Clair Mel City Assembly of God, a church that was pioneered by Charles and Sally Ann. Other Raburn ministers include Hellen and Vester Raburn, Jr., daughter and son of the late Rev. Vester and Jewel Raburn. What a wonderful family of Raburns who love and serve the Lord.

Another project at Faith Temple that turned out to be a great ministry was our church sign. A minister friend, who worked with us for quite some time, had donated hundreds of dollars worth of shrubbery for our church including the huge, beautiful palm cluster out front, which the Interstate 4 expansion took later. He also helped us locate and purchase a sign that not only identified our church name and affiliation, but had capacity for changeable messages.

When we weren't having special announcements of various services or church activities, we posted "sentence sermons" and witty sayings every week. Hence, thousands of passersby each day and night on Interstate 4 would see scriptural quotes like: "The meek shall inherit the earth;" "Blessed are the peacemakers" and "In the beginning – God created the heavens and the earth," etc.

Other sayings included: "If your outlook is dark – try the uplook." "Dirt thrown is ground lost;" and "Seven days without prayer makes one weak."

At Christmastime we often used: "Hitch your wagon to a star – the star of Bethlehem."

Immediately, we began to get personal compliments and phone calls commending these messages as a blessing and people who passed daily wanted us to change the sign every day. Over the years these testimonies were numerous and encouraging. Thus, we learned a busy highway always brings opportunities for service to God, Christ and the Bible.

Ground-breaking for new sanctuary – Faith Temple Assembly of God,
Plant City, Florida
With shovels left to right: Ward Crawford, Ralph Holbrook E.O. Homan,
Lester Crawford, Raymond Holbrook Standing on left: Rev. Sammy
Mizell
Standing on right: Pastor Ernest Holbrook

The first half-truss goes up!

The laminated trusses take shape on the new sanctuary

It's time to add the bricks!

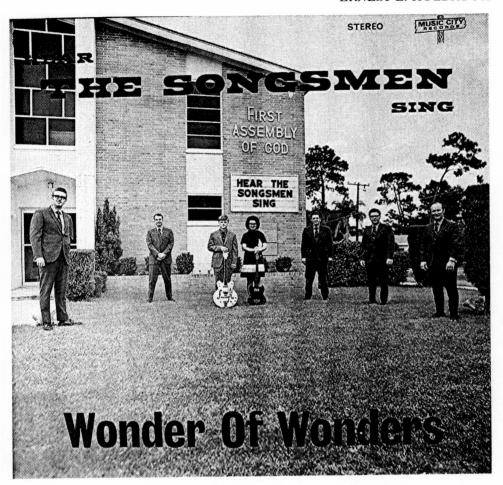

Album #3 recorded at Monument Studios in Nashville
Picture taken in front of First Assembly of God in Lakeland, Florida
From left: Jim Campbell, Chuck McIntosh, Phil Waldron, Sandra
Holbrook, Joe Hart, Jessie Barlow, Ernest Holbrook

Sheet music to "Just Over the Hilltop"
Written by Ernest Holbrook

Junell, the Pastor's wife, mother of our three girls
School teacher at Springhead Elementary School
Plant City (Springhead) Florida, for 25 ½ years

Phyllis and Ernest overlook the sky-high #12 hole at the
Gatlinburg Golf Club
(It is 150 yards long and 150 yards high)

TWENTY-TWO

FAITH TEMPLE ASSEMBLY OF GOD, PLANT CITY, FLORIDA – PART THREE

... endure hardness, as a good soldier of Jesus Christ... II Timothy 2:3

The 26 years and 8 months I served as Pastor of Faith Temple were also a time of periodic attacks of angina pectoris. I was under the constant care of a cardiologist and I did a lot of praying to Doctor Jesus. For years I observed a pretty strict diet, walking and exercising regularly. Every time I experienced chest discomfort, my doctor at Watson Clinic in Lakeland, gave me another stern lecture about being too busy and not taking adequate time off.

I tried to explain that pastoring a congregation of 200, plus another 200 or so adherents who claimed me as their minister, was quite time-consuming. But I also told him I tried to take one day off each week to either fish or play golf and took a two or three week vacation each year. "This is not enough," he insisted. "You need two days off each week, plus three additional days each month and six weeks of vacation each year."

I thanked him for his concern and wondered if he understood what pastoring a church involved. There had to be time for prayer, Bible study, sermon preparation, preaching and teaching, training courses, revival meetings, youth programs and services, missions planning and evangelism outreach, home, hospital, and jail visitation, counseling sessions, weddings, funerals and always the unexpected incidents. Plus radio broadcasts, quartet singing and a number of other things I felt I had to be involved in.

But each doctor visit, I would vow to do better, while realizing time off was hard to come by and longer vacations were very expensive. The church was mindful of the situation and the official board extended my vacation time to six weeks per year, which I never did fully take. They also provided additional help for the pastoral process. Being close to Southeastern Bible College we were able to engage several young ministers and their wives

407

and families from time to time. A total of some 35 served with me over the years.

These young people were all a tremendous asset, not only to our church but to the Kingdom of God as well. Several were interns from Southeastern Bible College and spent numerous hours with me in practical pastor training. Most are in active ministry somewhere today. A professor from Southeastern College once told me that my intern program was the best the school had. I was grateful for the privilege. Three interns became military chaplains, two have doctorates and teach at Southeastern College, some are successful pastors and one is deeply involved in radio and television ministries. Others have served in district offices and others are missionaries.

Besides all these, I had a hard-working, devoted group of church members including those from my own family. Having one's immediate family, plus several other blood relatives and others who were faithful year after year, not only made pastoring pleasant and much easier, it inspired me to give it my best. I have very few regrets, except my own failings and shortcomings from time to time. But I give the honor and glory to the Almighty, His Christ and the Holy Spirit for their presence and guidance these 56 years of ministry.

It seems I had a special calling to do radio ministry and hospital visitation. I was always jotting down thoughts for radio sermonettes, religious news and catchy "one-liners". It seemed a magnetic-like force tugged at me to visit the sick. Some of our constituents were military or had relatives who served in the military, so much of my hospital visitation was at the Veterans Hospital in St. Petersburg, Florida, and later at Tampa.

One of my congregants had a father who was at Bay Pines in St. Petersburg for several years. Often I would take him (the father) riding around the area to help break the monotony. One day as we headed for Madeira Beach we saw a man on a motorcycle chasing a young lady across a shopping center parking lot. He jumped off, knocked her down and started beating her with a big, wide black belt.

I abruptly turned into the area, jumped out of my car and demanded the man to stop. In anger, he turned on me and was attempting to strike me with the metal-studded belt. But for an interruption by a siren of an approaching police car, I probably would have been clobbered too. Thank goodness the policeman happened by at the perfect moment. My passenger said later, "Reverend, I'm very sick and weak, but I was about to wade in and try to save you!" The young lady was a "run-a-way" according to the man, who said she was his "rebellious" 15 year-old daughter. We left the scene with the police in charge.

One Sunday morning, just as I had ended my sermon at the correctional and work-release prison at the county line, I put my guitar in its case, gathered my Bible and songbook and was heading out the door. Suddenly an alarm sounded and I heard the clanking of metal bars as they all automatically locked shut, including my exit. No one was nearby with a key so I went to the office where the sheriff's lieutenant who was in charge was on the intercom conferring with other officials about an "uprising" and also a fight in some part of the several compartment facility.

I said, "Listen, lady, I'm due at church momentarily and I need to get out." She paused and angrily responded, "No one is getting out until we get this settled." I waited and listened as the two-way radio exchanges continued. She got up to leave the room. I followed her out the door and again pleaded to be let out. And once more she said, "I said no one is leaving for now."

I said, "Ma'am, I come here every Sunday morning voluntarily and uncompensated, to sing, preach and counsel. I've even married one couple here and carried two others to church with me several times. I'm due at church and I want out of here now or else I'm going to report this to your superiors!" With that, she grabbed her keys and promptly let me out the front door. I did not see her there anytime after that.

Wedding bells for my three daughters came in a span of nineteen years: Sandra to Phillip Waldron on November 17, 1972, Phyllis to Tom Conner, June 17, 1988, and Sharon to Bob Franklin, October 20, 1991. It was a happy, yet scary occasion as I "gave them away" and also performed the ceremonies. Our sons-in-law are just like sons and we love them all dearly.

In May 1973, a church member and I flew to the Bahama Islands at invitation from Robert Raburn, who at the time was pastor of Evangelistic Temple in Nassau. We drove to Miami Beach on Friday and took Chalk Airlines. It was a small sea-plane and we landed at Bimini right in the middle of a political upheaval. Our airplane was surrounded by soldiers with machine guns and rifles. We were herded into the small air-terminal building. Our suitcases were turned upside-down and searched. About as quickly as the soldiers had arrived, they suddenly departed with orders that no one was to leave the building.

With their absence of about an hour, my friend said, "Let's go outside and walk around." I was reluctant but went along. We had walked down the street about 50 yards or so when here comes a jeep-load of the same soldiers stopping us again, bawling us out and ordering us back into the building. But soon, the pilot said we were cleared for take-off. It felt good to be airborne from there.

We next landed at Cat Kay and then as we headed for Nassau, encountered a big thunderstorm. The pilot said, "Hold on and buckle up! We're going down under this thing!" We began flying what looked like ten feet above the water (the pilot said 25 feet) and I felt I could have made a few casts into the clear blue waters below if I had had my rod and reel. I also thought about us being in "the devil's triangle," but we soon passed by the bad weather.

As we came to Nassau, we flew down the long harbor and under the bridge that leads to Paradise Island. The Raburns were waiting as we "waddled" out of the water and up the cement ramp, like a wet duck. We stayed in the home of a congregant who treated us royally. We toured the Island and visited a couple from Plant City, Florida, who were serving as assistants to a missionary effort there. They were glad to see someone from "home," they said.

On Saturday, we went through the downtown markets where all sorts of food and merchandise were on display out on the streets. At the 50 foot deep harbor we watched men dive for coins as tourists tossed in quarters and half-dollars. The water was so clear you could almost see to the bottom and the divers would catch the coins in their mouths.

All the vehicles were driving on the wrong side of the streets and all of a sudden as we walked the sidewalks we began to see several people we knew from Lakeland and Plant City. A local quartet had sponsored a cruise ship out of Miami to the Bahamas and they had docked in Nassau.

We went over to Paradise Island to one of the "Las Vegas," "Atlantic City," types of gambling establishments. It was filled with gamblers at the wheels, tables, card games and slot machines. Suddenly a voice said, "Brother Holbrook, what are you doing here?" I responded to one of the quartet singers, "What are you doing here?" We both justified ourselves as non-gambling "visitors only." We observed a lady in a neck brace playing two slot machines. She played one, then the other and kept repeating the same. He asked, "Brother Ernest, do you suppose she broke her neck looking from one machine to the other?" I said it looked that way.

The Sunday services were great. I preached to a full house at the big church and afterwards we ate out at a famous restaurant with the Raburns, some missionaries and a neighbor pastor from Tampa. On Monday we boarded Chalk to head back to Miami. We were anxious when we landed at Bimini. We let off and took on a passenger and cargo there, and thankfully, no soldiers appeared.

Back home, our next project was to build a parsonage for our assistant pastor. Again we used voluntary labor hiring only a minimum of workers. It was a beautiful ranch-style home with over 2400 feet of living area and an oversized double garage and screened back porch. Our assistant pastor moved away before he was to move in and the church leaders moved us into it and arranged a "swap" with us and our house, as a ten-year bonus. What a wonderful surprise!

We arranged to let a congregant move in a single-wide on the church property, where he lived several years and helped us with the Quartet, church music and activities, and the mowing of the property. He later married and both he and his wife are devoted friends.

In late 1975, our lead singer in the Songsmen Quartet approached me about land area for a radio tower. My mom agreed to give a 99 year lease on seven acres on the east part of her property, the part she planned to leave to me. Our singer had liked my radio format and asked me to become a part of the new radio station which he and his church brought into being. It became a very popular 100,000 watt FM station and my program was broadcast each Monday through Friday evening at 9:45 p.m. for 20 years from 1976 until 1996, when the station was sold to Moody broadcasting. I titled the program "Temple Vespers," the same name I used on WPLA for many years.

I served as a radio board member most of those years and listener surveys gave us "significant recognition" and more than 7500 listeners each evening. I later broadcast on another radio station until September, 2001. A constant hoarseness brought about a cessation to a 45 year-long series of radio ministry broadcasts. It was very difficult to see it end.

In 1976, we decided at doctor's orders, to take a prolonged vacation trip. From June 13th until July 9th we made a loop southwest to midwest to northwest, north, northeast and back southward. The trip was as follows: Milton, Florida, to visit friends; Vicksburg, Mississippi, to the Civil War battlegrounds and monuments; to Tulsa and a religious university there;

to Carlsbad Caverns, El Paso and Juarez, Mexico; to the Painted Desert, Petrified Forest and Holbrook, Arizona.

In Holbrook, Arizona, I looked for Holbrooks and found none. The town was named after a Civil War Captain Holbrook who camped with his troops there, but apparently no one ever lived there by the name of Holbrook. We met some friends from home at the Grand Canyon, tried to hit golf balls across the narrower end (he did, but I didn't), toured the Navaho Indian Reservation and Arches National Park in Utah; spent some time at Grand Mesa and Cedaredge, Colorado, with my brother and his wife. We later took the guided tour of a big religious group's headquarters in Salt Lake City. From there, we headed toward Idaho.

We ran out of motels in northern Utah but finally found a sign of one in Snowville, a very small community in the middle of nowhere. The motel office had a light and a sign that read: Go north about 2 miles to a house with the porch light on, on the right. A man followed us from there back to the motel. I inquired if he had a medium-soft bed since a hard bed put my back in spasms. He threw down 12 keys and said, "Take your pick." He had 12 rooms.

The entire motel must have been 50 years old or more, was run down and after checking three or four beds in different rooms, I decided they were all bad. Our friends took the room next door to the one we chose and when he took a shower, the water ran into our shower floor and room.

Walking back to the office to return the other keys I groped in the darkness and was suddenly approached from behind. I turned around to hear a lady say, "Oh, my god, you're not who I was expecting to meet me here." I sure wasn't, and I tried to watch her return to a car parked further in the dark.

During the mostly sleepless night we heard other vehicles arrive, men arguing and threatening each other. It seemed the lady who mistook me had arranged to meet a man and her husband had caught her there with him. Finally, the noise subsided and the vehicles left. I was glad the husband had not arrived when I was in the dark with his wife. Can't you see what the next day's headlines might have said?!! "FLORIDA MINISTER KILLED BY ANGRY HUSBAND WHO CAUGHT PREACHER WITH HIS WIFE."

We arrived the next day in Mountain Home, Idaho, and preached and sang at five services there with our former assistant pastor. We toured the Air Force base, picnicked up the mountain range north of Mountain Home, soaked our feet in different hot springs and had a marvelous time. From there we went to Yellowstone National Park and enjoyed the boiling "paint pots" and the geysers, including "Old Faithful." Our Lakeland friends left us just before we got to Yellowstone and headed back to Florida on another route.

We spent the night in Cody, Wyoming, and then traveled to Mt. Rushmore. While sitting in the restaurant I kept seeing something move on top and around the stone images of Washington, Jefferson, Lincoln and Theodore Roosevelt. The girls couldn't seem to see any movement, so we went to the paid telescopes and discovered mountain goats roaming about the 60 feet high heads located atop the 6,200 feet high mountain.

We toured the Corn Palace in Mitchell, South Dakota, continuing through Iowa, Illinois, Indiana, Ohio, Pennsylvania, New Jersey and finally to Staten Island, New York, where Sandra and Phillip lived while he was stationed at Governor's Island in the Coast Guard. Phillip, Phyllis and I tried golfing on a Staten Island golf course and incurred a tremendous thunderstorm that literally almost blew us away. We struggled to get back to the clubhouse, soaked to the bone. Once I grabbed Phyllis to steady her and her pull cart in the violent winds.

The storm moved away quickly and we went to a fireworks display over New York harbor that evening. It was spectacular, celebrating our nation's 200th birthday and Independence Day, as the "tall ships" were gathered into the harbor. We were involved in an almost two-hour traffic-jam trying to return to Phil and Sandra's apartment. People there apparently were prepared for it and began to get out of their stalled cars. Some were playing cards on top of their cars. Others were tossing footballs, softballs, or playing other games in and around the vehicles.

The next day we rode the ferry across the harbor, by the Statue of Liberty and landed in lower Manhattan near Wall Street where Sandra worked. We walked up and down and around the crowded streets and shops and once I observed a man who apparently was dead drunk lying on the street. He resembled my late dad. The crowds walked around and over him as if it were routine, which I guess it was. Heart sickened by this and other similar sights, I was grateful it wasn't my dad, but I surmised he was probably someone's dad.

From New York, we came through Maryland, Virginia, West Virginia, and Tennessee where we spent a night in Gatlinburg, my favorite "away

413

from home" place. It was good to be home after 27 days. It took a few days to wind down and re-enter the everyday routine of pastoring.

I engaged a famous songwriter to conduct a singspiration and found he enjoyed golf as much as I did. In fact, on a later engagement, he and I were on our way to Lakeland to play golf when we watched the space shuttle go up and then explode, falling down in pieces. It was a sobering sight to know several of our astronauts, including a schoolteacher, were killed on the ill-fated mission.

I helped coach the Plant City High School girl's golf team where Phyllis played three years. It gave me the privilege to play free at Walden Lake and several other West Central Florida courses. Phyllis competed in the Greater Tampa Junior Girls Golf Association.

An aspiring young minister attending Southeastern College, who worked with our Royal Rangers, disappeared while hiking at Table Rock State Park near Greenville, South Carolina, while home for the Christmas and New Year's holidays. The search for him lasted several weeks. My son-in-law, Phillip Waldron, helped mobilize some military personnel in the area to aid the search. Finally, it was abandoned and hope for finding him was gone. But the young man's father wouldn't give up. He called me from Greenville and said, I've taken off from work and will search every day until I find him.

But it was a fisherman on the park reservoir who found his body floating about six weeks after he came up missing. His death was ruled accidental since he was found in the water below some very high, slippery, steep cliffs. No foul play was apparent. It seemed he slipped and fell to a watery grave heavily dressed with boots and coats for cold weather. I assisted with his funeral on Monday, February 18, 1980, in the Washington Avenue Baptist Church in Greenville, accompanied by a couple of students from Southeastern College.

I helped Sandra and Phil build a house on a lot I gave them near the radio tower on Knights Station Road, after he retired from active duty with the Coast Guard. Their place became a hot spot for break-ins by thieves, just as our house and church along the interstate was. I'm glad such will not make it into Heaven else I guess they would try to steal the walls of jasper and streets of gold. (Matt. 6:20 and Rev. 21:18-21)

On October 8, 1987, I lost another dear friend and uncle. He was my dad's youngest brother, a very faithful church worker, deacon and a top notch fishing buddy. I netted a ten pounder he caught on Arbuckle Creek and once when he, Dad and I were fishing up Marion Creek off of Lake Hatchineha, we watched Dad set his hook in a bass. It pulled tremendously heavy and my dad said, "How will I ever land it?" When he got it to the boat, it was a one pound bass wrapped in seven or eight pounds of grass.

In 1989, we buried two more special people. One was my cousin from Frostproof, Florida, who revived the Payne family reunions which continue annually to this day. On October 2nd, it was my long-time friend and pastor in Jacksonville, Florida. 1989 was also the year our church began plans for a larger sanctuary. But this time I insisted we hire a building contractor from start to finish, which we did. We continued fund-raising as the planning progressed.

This was also the year the radio Training Network began. With help from a Christian businessman, a minister friend was able to found a new Christian radio network which has now grown to about 12 stations and numerous translators. I was invited to serve on his radio advisory board and have until this day. We began with the Joy FM, 88.1 in Sarasota, Florida, and His Radio, 89.3 FM in Greenville, South Carolina. The Joy FM also broadcasts over 91.5 WLPJ, in New Port Richey, 96.7 in Brandon, 96.3 in north Lakeland, 106.1 in south Lakeland, 98.7 in Auburndale and Winter Haven, 90.7 in Sebring and 89.5 in Lake Placid. We later added stations in Ocala and Crystal River. In Springfield, Missouri we have "The Wind" FM, at 88.3.

In Georgia, we have WVFT, 93.3, in Atlanta and Manchester, also WFDR 1320 AM in Manchester, WAFJ, 88.3 in Augusta and a translator in Statesboro, and another FM station in Savannah. We also have an FM station in Roanoke Rapids and AM stations in Raleigh, North Carolina, and Spartanburg, South Carolina. Our format features light contemporary Christian music and singing, prayer requests from listeners, and free announcements for churches. We involve ourselves in community projects like blood drives, etc. We appeal for disaster relief around the world and the radio audience always responds wonderfully. Kosovo, the Central America floods and Angola prison in Louisiana are a few mentionables.

On Tuesday evening, June 26, 1990, I had ridden Phyllis's bicycle over to the church office. On the way back, about 10 p.m. as I pedaled the some 200 yards, I was gripped with a very deep chest pain. Nitro-stat did not bring relief as it often had before. Junell rushed me to the Lakeland Regional emergency room. A continuous flow of liquid nitro finally brought an easing of the pain about four a.m. The wife of one of our ministers was my nurse. She said, "Brother Holbrook, I've got nothing else to do, but attend you." This was very comforting.

I had learned that one of our members had also been admitted to the emergency room at the same time. They told me the next morning that she had been moved to Shands Hospital in Gainesville, Florida. I underwent a treadmill test, and then a catherization. My cardiologist told me that evening that two heart arteries were blocked 100%. He recommended by-pass surgery, as did another doctor who was consulted. They said the surgery suite was available the next morning as was a surgeon. They came in and asked if I wanted the surgery done. I could hardly believe my own ears as I said, "Yes, let's do it!"

I had smelled something alcoholic from the surgeon and after he left, I asked my doctor if he was sure about recommending this doctor. "Yes," he said, "he is one of our very best!" I slept off and on (partly sedated I suppose), but about four a.m. the next morning, they began prepping me for surgery. All of my chest and stomach area was shaved, I was hooked up to intravenous whatever's and so forth. I was only slightly aware of being rolled to surgery. I remember my family saying goodbyes (goodbyes?) and that they would be waiting for me. (Here, or in eternity?)

It seemed I was in the darkest midnight. And a voice, which I recognized as a woman's, was saying to me, "Mr. Holbrook, your surgery is all done and you did well. You did very well." She further tried to waken me but I didn't want to be awakened. Later, a man's voice interrupted my "unconscious" state by trying to get my response. I faintly heard Junell's voice and the voices of my daughters but I wanted to sleep, sleep, sleep. But they didn't want me to sleep. It was time to wake up!

Where was I? Was it day or night? Various voices were trying to carry on conversations with me. I felt helpless. When I fully awakened, it was daylight, and our District Superintendent and one of his sons was standing by my bed. They left after having prayer with me and an orderly came in and told me it was time to remove the big tube that was in my throat down into my stomach. He said, "Hold steady, this may sting a bit." With a snatch, it felt like he pulled me inside out. I said to him, "If I were able, I would knock you across this room." I (jokingly) meant it, too.

Back home after eight days, I would at times nearly "climb the walls" for the two months of recovery time. But I was still alive with hopes of being well again and they had told me that our church member did not make it and they had already conducted her funeral. My niece let Junell and me stay a week at her condo at Daytona Beach. While there, I was able to get off the "heavy" pain killers which could very quickly become addictive. I began preaching the Sunday morning services after eight weeks.

When the hospital and doctor bills starting coming, the insurance company (we were on my wife's school insurance) refused to pay one procedure listed as a "balloon" process used during the surgery. It cost just under $1,000 and both the hospital and clinic wrote the company insisting it was a necessary procedure that literally revived me after I had almost died on the operating table. The insurance company still refused, stating it was not necessary. We were very disappointed and I was out the $1,000 plus another $8,000. The total bill ran over $33,000.

We let the contract for the new sanctuary and it was so nice not to have to rally a group of volunteers and work myself nearly to death. Besides, I wasn't able anyway. It was enough to round up three 10,000 gallon tanks to store water for the new sanctuary in case of fire, since we weren't on any city or county water hookup. The restrictions and requirements had multiplied several times over as we faced the HRS, county and state stipulations and Swiftmud, the Southwest Florida Water Management District.

We were required to dig a huge retention pond with an overflow, fill up an old well with cement ($400), plant so many trees and native shrubbery and were told exactly where each tree and shrub would go. I was shocked when they required planting a couple of small oak trees right under beautiful big trees already there.

Swiftmud and the HRS had a dispute with each other and refused to negotiate, which held up the entire project. It took quite a bit of "shuffling diplomacy" to iron out the issue. I have no problems with some requirements to protect adults and children but I thought many of the stipulations were totally insane and unnecessary. The pastor of a neighbor church had been in a building program and when he heard we were starting, he called me and said, "Get ready to backslide, because the county, state and Swiftmud will cause you to!" Afterwards, I learned what he meant.

But we finally finished and dedicated the new sanctuary Sunday, October 18, 1992. It was still a very busy time for me and my recovery from the bypass surgery wasn't doing too well. I discussed retirement with my wife but we were afraid we couldn't make it financially. I guess this is the concern of many people who face this time of life.

And yet, retirement for us both seemed almost inevitable, considering my health problems and her weariness from teaching school 25 ½ years. As with all the other decisions we had faced together, we would retire by faith. We knew that the Lord who had never failed us would surely be with us at this critical juncture of our lives.

On April 7, 1993, I submitted my resignation to the church, promising to continue until they could elect a new minister. Junell gave her retirement notice to the school board to be effective at the end of the present term in June.

After receiving over 100 resumes, the next pastor was chosen. On June 27, 1993, we held our farewell services at Faith Temple. Amid much sadness and mixed emotions, we said goodbye to so many friends who had stood by and supported us for so long. A new chapter in our lives awaited us.

We bought a building lot at Bloomfield Hills in North Lakeland and began plans to move away from the church where we had lived ten years on the east side and eighteen years on the west. It was a strange feeling to be "free" from all the years of pastoring. I continued to serve as presbyter until 1995.

In the 26 years and 8 months we were pastors of Faith Temple we recorded 639 decisions for Christ, received 412 members, baptized many of these in water, first at Moore's Lake in Dover, Florida, and later in our church baptistry, experienced many being baptized in the Holy Spirit, dedicated numerous babies and helped train several young ministers. Our records also show as of this date that I performed 303 weddings and officiated at 490 funerals during my years of ministry.

But it was all coming to an end. Like Paul seeking for his "thorn in the flesh" to be removed, which it wasn't, I besought the Lord many times for healing sufficient to continue preaching the gospel. It too, wasn't to be, and I prayed for grace to handle retirement. It was given to me even though I still had a battle facing it. In a recent year, representatives from three different churches sought me out as a possible pastor for their congregations. That too, wasn't to be. And I struggled physically to continue the radio ministry until September, 2001. I had to leave visions and adopt dreaming. (Joel 2:28b)

What would I do if I should get able again? Probably start a new church and obtain another gospel radio program. But it's likely to be unlikely! But, "I can dream, can't I?"

Sanctuary number two completed at Faith Temple

The three crosses beside Interstate 4 between Plant City and Lakeland,
Florida

An effective road sign

Meet the Pastor

A view of part of the congregation at a Faith Temple worship service

A church where the Cross lights the way!

My favorite announcer and Master of Ceremonies: Dick Shiflett

The Songsmen Quartet in Action
Left to right: Jim Campbell, Jessie Barlow, Ernest and Joe Hart

The Faith Temple congregation about the early 1970's

Sandra weds Phil Waldron at Faith Temple (Nov. 17, 1972)

Building a parsonage

A scene from a Payne Family Reunion at Irwinville, Georgia in the 1980's
Left to right seated: Canty Payne, Virlin Payne Chandler, Pearl Payne
Wright, Julia Payne Holbrook, Leola and Clyde Payne

Members of the Payne Family – Front row left to right: Dewey Payne, Essie Payne Clifton, (Little) Phillip Waldron, William Clifton Second row: "Bo" Clifton, Larue Payne Clifton, Helen Payne Culbreath Back row: Sandra Holbrook Waldron, Junell Player Holbrook, Farrah Waldron, Ernest Holbrook (Mid 1980's)

Junell, Phyllis, Sharon and Ernest in front of the old James Thomas Payne family house east of Ashburn, Georgia (1970's)

Grave marker of Pollard Payne (My great, great, great grandfather) This was found in a wooded area beside Highway 19, north of Ellaville, Georgia. (1786-1856) It was discovered by Paul and William Payne and moved to Mt. Vernon Cemetery in Schley County, Georgia.

Robert and Ernest at the Chalk Airport in Nassau, Bahamas

Junell receives her Master's Degree from
the University of South Florida

Our three grown up angels (1980's)

Rev. and Mrs. James Gilbert
Some of our favorite people

Sharon weds Robert (Bob) Franklin at the
house of Ernest and Junell Holbrook
(October 20, 1991)

Phyllis weds Tom Conner at Faith Temple
(June 17, 1988)

The Ernest Holbrook Family in 1992

Front row left to right: Evan Conner, Tom Conner, Phyllis (Holbrook) Conner holding Chris Conner, Junell and Ernest Back row: Phillip Waldron, Sandra (Holbrook) Waldron, Phil Waldron, Farrah Waldron, Bob Franklin, Sharon (Holbrook) Franklin, Jonathan Franklin

Miami Clergyman's Golf Tournament

The Big – Little Golfers at the General Council Tournament in Haines
City, Florida
Left to right: Jim Campbell, D. J. Burrell, Ernest (the short one) and
Weldon Gosnell

437

Ground-breaking for third sanctuary at Faith Temple about 1990
Left to right: Randy Phillips, Ernest, Rev. Ray Schultz, Willie Julian, Ray
Slocum, Dick Shiflett, Vernon Calhoun and Raymond Holbrook

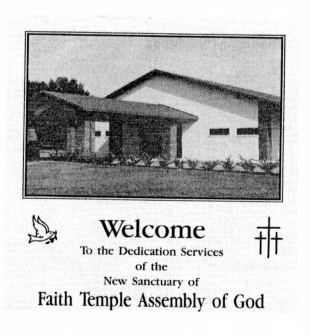

Welcome
To the Dedication Services
of the
New Sanctuary of
Faith Temple Assembly of God

438

New Sanctuary Faith Temple Assembly of God

TWENTY-THREE

RETIREMENT?

*Remember your creator before the years come when you shall say,
I have no pleasure in them. Ecclesiastes 12:1*

There is a saying that I have heard numerous times and especially since I have arrived at this time of life. It goes like this: "Ministers don't retire." The implication is that they shouldn't or mustn't, since their work is always needed and of eternal consequence. I have had a few gentle and some mild repercussions when I have mentioned that I am a "retired" minister. The whole truth is that I have only retired from pulpit preaching, church pastoring and radio broadcasting. But for a physical ailment that prevents me, I would probably still be doing all three.

This does not mean I have retired from working for the Kingdom of Heaven. It simply means I have shifted my field of labors to some other areas of Gospel proclamation. Pastoring or preaching is certainly not the sum and substance of Christian ministry. There are many other facets. What about the layman's ministry? Try to imagine a church without someone to attend faithfully and support with prayers and finances. What about loving and serving people? This is one of the cardinal indispensables of the Kingdom of God.

The scriptures reveal that God's primary business is people. He created us, came and died for us and now continually intercedes for us. All four gospels cite the "famous last words" of Jesus Christ. We call them "the Great Commission," which leaves no question as to Christ's final instructions for His followers. They are to evangelize the whole world. I should say, "We," rather than "they." And retirement after any fashion does not alter this!

It seemed very strange to move from a leadership role to that of layman. I have had to search and find my niche from a congregant's standpoint and continue to serve the Kingdom of Heaven in every way possible.

441

Early on, a Tampa pastor invited Junell and me to work part-time with him. I had officiated when his and another church congregation had merged some months before. So for about three years we assisted in the music program and served in an advisory capacity while the combined church moved to its present location. Having just completed our new sanctuary at Faith Temple, we were able to offer some pointers now and then as the beautiful new sanctuary, complete with offices, educational facilities and social hall was constructed and completed there.

The old church had sold before we were ready to move out. We rented a club building at a golf course. The lease was also called early on this facility leaving us to worship under the oak trees for three Sundays at the new location. It was in the springtime and was cool enough in the shade for the services. There was only one incident. During the pastor's sermon one morning I heard a "plop" and a couple of squeals. A snake had fallen from one of the oak trees. Needless to say, it was not allowed to remain in the service. It evoked memories of the biblical story of Mother Eve in the Garden of Eden. This pastor and his wife were wonderful people to be around and to work with. Every now and then, he and I were able to get in a round of golf.

As we began plans to build our new house away from the church, we did some research on home financing and I remembered how I had fared previously at a couple of banks. I surely didn't wish to go through this again some 28 years later. My brother Ralph, and I, had gone into a business venture so I still owed him some money on my house. He found out we wanted to move and offered to transfer the mortgage to the new location. Plus, he said he had some extra money I could use until I sold my present house.

We figured, and were still some $20,000 short (my middle name). My stepfather-in-law heard of it and offered to loan me the $20,000. Wow! We were ready to start with the house plans. My niece, her husband, and son, who own Dynagraphics, offered to do the house plans free of charge as a retirement gift. Soon, we had engaged a home-builder to construct our new house. The very thought of it all was so exciting. We were told the project would take around four months.

I went to the hardware store, purchased a "For Sale by Owner" sign and erected it out beside the interstate. I had the place appraised and was shocked at how soon several people were stopping to inquire. No one knows how long it will take to sell a house but with immediate prospects like this, I told Junell if we sold now we would be "left in the cold," with no place to go. So I removed the sign.

Two months before the projected completion date I re-erected the sign and in a couple of days a family with no money and no credit "claimed" our house in prayer. I told them I appreciated their faith and respected their prayers but I had to have money to apply to my new house. In another couple of days, with this family coming every day hoping a miracle would happen and move them in, another couple from Orlando stopped by. After a brief look around and inside, she sat down at the counter and said, "God showed me a set of curtains and there they are hanging in your dining room. She looked at her husband and said, "This is it. I want this house." You can't argue with God! Her husband didn't either. He said, "OK," and they gave us a nice deposit.

We told them it would be about two months before we could get into our new house. "No problem," they said. "We'll have to arrange financing, even though we are already pre-approved. It will take a few weeks." All was seemingly going well, when along they came and paid us in full. I said, "But we are still about a month away from our place being finished. "No problem again," they said. "We will extend our lease where we are and you can call us and let us know when you are ready."

Thinking all was well, I relaxed, but they called and said their landlord wouldn't renew their lease, except for another six months. "We have about ten days to be out of here." I called my building contractor and he said he would do his best to finish in two weeks. I hoped that maybe we could squirm by. That is, until in nine days, the buyers drove up in a huge, loaded, rented truck and said, "We are sorry, but we have to have everything out by tomorrow. We are going to move in with you!"

We had already transported some things into our new garage and big utility room out back. I had this garage stacked about half full of stuff. I helped the new owners unload their load and asked if I could hire him and his truck to "move" me. He said he would at "no charge." I called, got permission to stack things in the new house in the areas that were finished. In some rooms we placed things away from the walls that hadn't yet been painted. By getting permission from the new owners, we left a few things for another week after they had already occupied the house. My middle daughter Sharon, and husband Bob had a spare bedroom so we moved into it for a week. Whew! And I had assumed "retirement" would be easy. And moving into our "dream" home would be a breeze. It was more like a tornado.

Finally, we lay down in our new house. I awoke during the night "lost." From the sentinel light outside-which was in the wrong place-and the faint light shining through the window-which also was in the wrong place-I tried to collect my bearings. Again it seemed strange after 19 years, 29 all total, to be driving home by a different route. But I suppose this is a good way to keep from getting "bored" with the usual routes and happenings.

The driving distance to Tampa was quite a bit longer from our relocation, so we told the pastor we would have to find a place to worship closer by. They did not want us to leave, but we felt we should, and we began to attend Mt. Zion, my home church. We helped with the music and worshipped there about a year and a half. From there we once again began to "shop" for a new church home. We visited several places looking for another Faith Temple which we have not found.

We are doing something occasionally that we have never been able to do before. I used to call it "church-hopping," which I was always against. It is interesting and we are discovering some great preachers and church programs. But I still do not recommend it, except for special times. Everyone needs a church home and pastor.

I still serve on the Advisory Board of Directors of the Radio Training Network headquartered in Lakeland. We now have about 15 Christian Radio stations with numerous translators which pick up our stations and beam them into other communities. We continually expand as opportunities become available.

Not long after we stepped down from pastoring, I lost my "sainted" mom September 2, 1993. My brother, Ralph, passed away November 4, 1994. My oldest sister, Louise, died May 26, 2000. These were three very important people in my life and at each passing, it seemed a part of me passed with them. The many years we traveled life's road together brought me special enrichment from each relationship. I certainly do have "Precious Memories" of the very many ways their lives touched mine.

Mom was always the sure anchor of my life after Dad left us. She was there for me whatever came or went. I had no greater supporter of my ministry than she. Louise let it be known that she thought I was the best of ministers. In some ways she was like another mother instead of an older sister. My brother, Ralph, was an untold helper to me and the church. What greater brother could I have possibly had? And I am blessed with two more lovely sisters and many nephews and nieces. I can hardly keep up with their offspring as our family continues to expand! I have several special in-laws, some of which have greatly supported my ministry efforts. To them I will be forever grateful.

While they were living and working in Springfield, Missouri, Terry and Athena Raburn had more than once invited us to visit with them. In the spring of 1995, we had decided to go to Branson, which is some 25 miles south of Springfield. I called Terry and he insisted we go stay with them a few days and he would take us to Branson.

We were to meet them at their home on Wednesday afternoon when they got off from work about 5 p.m. On Tuesday afternoon we were already in the Ozark Mountains and were looking for a motel. A Ford Taurus began following us fairly close through the mountainous curves. At first opportunity it passed us. A lady was driving and the man began to wave back at us with both hands. I told Junell he was trying to tell us something. I looked into the rearview mirror to see if the car was smoking. It wasn't. I checked the gauges. Everything seemed OK.

I looked to see if perhaps the gas lid had been left open. It was closed. Maybe a tire was slack. But if it was, I hadn't felt it. I looked and the man was again waving both arms at us. I couldn't figure what was going on.

When I had the chance I pulled up even with the Taurus, telling Junell to ask them what was wrong. Nothing was wrong. It was Terry and Athena! They were returning from a wedding in New Orleans, decided to take a different route home and lo and behold came up on us totally unexpected in the middle of nowhere. We stopped at the next filling station and they told us the story.

First, they had observed a Florida tag on the car ahead. Next, they noticed it was from Polk County. Next, Terry said to Athena, "That is Uncle Ernest and Aunt Junell." They just had a hard time getting us to recognize them. We drove on to Springfield and were entertained royally by them for five days. They took us all around Springfield, gave us a tour of our Assemblies of God national headquarters and publishing house, drove us through both Evangel College and Central Bible College campuses, took us twice to Branson where we took in the Japanese fiddler, Shoji Tabatchi, the "Bald Nobbers Show" and the old-fashioned "dime" store, one much like our old McCrorys when I was a lad. We were amazed at the many theaters at Branson.

We said our goodbyes to Terry and Athena, not realizing that they would become our next district superintendent and first lady. What a thrill to note the progress and promotions God had for them. A couple dedicated to the cause of Christ from "Under the Guns in Beirut," to the leadership of the Peninsular Florida District Council of the Assemblies of God. Terry also serves as a General Presbyter for the denomination.

On our more recent vacation trips, twice we have attended the Sunday school class taught by a former President. He is an excellent teacher and we have followed with great interest his humanitarian achievements through "Habitat for Humanity," as well as other charitable efforts and peace negotiations throughout the world. I said to him, "Mr. President, I thought surely you would win the Nobel Peace Prize for your successful efforts to bring peace to Israel and Egypt." He smiled and sort of shrugged. His recognition as such did not come until the year 2002. He and his wife made a picture with Junell and me, and our grandson, Evan Conner.

Sometime back, while visiting relatives in West Florida, I went with another minister to a viewing at a funeral home. I was re-introduced to a certain lady who attended my meetings some 50 years previously. She had not recognized me and expressed shock at how much I had aged. "You used to be good-looking," she said. I tried to figure a way to be nice to her in response, without inviting her to take another look at herself in the mirror.

Additional medical problems cropped up for me in 1996. On Friday, December 19, I had surgery for a hernia in the lower left side of my stomach. I was in the hospital at 5 a.m., had the surgery and was back home again the same day by about 5 p.m. I thought of the difference when I was operated on in 1951 for a rupture in the lower right side: In the hospital about 11 days and the total doctor cost was $150.00, and hospital costs at St. Joseph's Hospital in Tampa, $345.00. The 1996, one day cost was near $10,000.00. Thank the Lord for health insurance.

In June 1999, our three daughters and their families gave us a 50th wedding anniversary party at Faith Temple social hall. It was a wonderful occasion with a gathering of close friends and relatives and the beginning of 50th wedding anniversary celebrations for a number or our friends. I had forgotten how many couples got married around the time we did in 1949.

On December 2, 1998, my wife's stepfather, Dallas Boyce passed away. It ended a marriage of some 27 years and we had already realized that Junell's mother, Cassie, had been doing some very strange things. A doctor's examination revealed the beginning of Alzheimer's disease. After trying to keep her ourselves, the stark realization of putting her in a facility faced us. It was very difficult but a definite necessity to help preserve our own health. We have watched her deteriorate in mind and body ever since.

After a series of chest pains, I went for a checkup at Watson Clinic in Lakeland. A stress test and pictures revealed some problems. It had been nine years and two months since my quadruple bypass surgery. The doctor recommended another catherization and on Monday, August 2, 1999, I went to Lakeland Regional Hospital. Having visited congregants and other friends there hundreds of times, it always seemed strange to be the patient myself. It turned out to be a one-day event and having gone in at 6 a.m., I was back home by late afternoon.

The tests revealed three of the four bypasses were still working fine, but the attending physician told me that one bypass had, in error, been grafted into a completely blocked artery. It never had worked and never would. This explained why I never stopped having angina pains even after the bypass surgery in 1990. My former doctor had always been puzzled by the chest pains since the by-pass surgery should have eliminated them. And this was probably why, after preaching on Sundays, I struggled with chest miseries every Monday and Tuesday until I was finally forced to retire.

And the unexpected keeps "popping" up. Junell began to have difficulties with her eyes. Finally, several tests showed signs of Macular Degeneration, first in one eye, then the other. She has the "wet" kind which is the worst. We had to sell her car since she could no longer see to drive. And add to this, the fact we lived quite a distance from our daughters. In 2002, we bought a house in South Lakeland just two miles from Sharon and Bob and two and one-half miles from Tom and Phyllis. We sold our house in Bloomfield Hills, moving away from our many dear friends there.

But now with two daughters so close, it is comforting plus we get to help with the grandchildren more often. You know what I mean, spoil them! As of this writing, our eight range in age from 3 to 27 years old. Quite a span! I was privileged to perform the wedding ceremony of my oldest granddaughter, Farrah, to Justin Moore, December 19, 1998, and my grandson Phillip's to Krystal Riling this past February 7, 2004.

On September 20, 2002, I suffered another heart attack, spent six days in the hospital, received a stint and defibrillator and am now the recipient of several kinds of medicines. The medical bill this time was about $97,000.00. Medicare and our supplement paid most all of it, thank the Lord! Junell also has osteoporosis to add to the aging happenings that make their unwelcome abodes in our so-called "golden" years. But, thank God, we can still worship Him, go to church, walk, eat, help with and enjoy the grandchildren and our friends and relatives.

Even though we often laugh about it, when it is not really all that funny, we are amazed at how unprepared we have been for the various aches, pains and maladies that have come to pass. My personal experience with my aging grandparents and parents, relatives and congregants, should have sent some strong signals about what "surprises" we might have been in for.

It happened with my eyes way back at age 42, when after reading the Christmas story at church by candlelight, my vision became somewhat impaired. A trip to the optometrist brought a very simple statement: "You have come of age," (for glasses). An additional shock was when an EKG was ordered for me at about age 33. It introduced potential heart trouble, diet and exercise and a "slowing down" of activities. (Except I didn't slow down!)

Somehow all these things are supposed to happen to other people, not me. But I had seen what had happened to my dad, my brother, my aunts and uncles and congregants. The big heart attack in 1990, at age 61, and the quadruple bypass surgery just didn't get through to me. I could still vision recovery, strength, vitality and whatever else it takes to take on life after these "roadblocks." I am discovering, though, that my body cannot perform what my mind can still envision. The "want-to" is curtailed greatly by the "I can't" reality.

All these changes, some drastic, taking place in our lives and "earthly houses" (bodies) are also accompanied by so many other changes all around us. Our tendency is to embrace ever more tightly the traditional and resist the contemporary both in and out of the church. This is what presented such a problem in our search for a "new" church to attend. I've talked to several other "old-timers" who have the same problem.

A minister friend of mine was visiting a church recently where all these new approaches to worship were taking place. After standing and singing songs projected on the wall for near 45 minutes, one old-timer was overheard saying to another: "Since we don't use them anymore, perhaps we could sell our songbooks to our senior citizens for souvenirs." The response was: "Yes, and maybe we should put our pews up for sale, since we don't sit anymore!"

At a district function some time ago I had stood until bone-weary, while choruses were being repeated multiple times. After what seemed almost an hour, I asked a former district superintendent who was standing just in front of me, if such prolonged standing was required in order for a person to be saved. He nonchalantly answered, "Yes!" I laughed and promptly sat down, and he, seeing me do so, followed suit. I told him we would have to "repent" from our "back-slidden" condition. The seat felt comforting to my "aging" bones.

In "self-defense," I thought about what Acts 2:2, KJV, said of the 120 persons in the upper room on the day of Pentecost. They were "sitting" when the Holy Spirit came. Of course, I don't know how long they kept sitting after the "outpouring."

One cannot, however, say that "retirement" life and the "aging" process is uneventful. Almost every day brings about something "new." A new doctor's appointment. A new prescription. A new war. A new disease. A new terrorist attack or threat. And to think Solomon said in Ecclesiastes 1:9b, "There is no new thing under the sun." He insists that everything that happens has already been. I'm not so sure. There are some mornings I awake, arise (when I'm able), only to discover another new ache or pain very frequently. There is more time to do things and less capability to perform. We could travel more but interstates filled with speeding autos, intimidating semis and road rage lessens our desire. There is more time to sleep but the ability to sleep often takes a leave of absence!

Breakfast time now brings a different sort of conversation: "How was your night dear?" "How well did you sleep?" "How do you feel this morning?" "Why the grunting and sighing?" Your call for sympathy for your own miseries is often drowned by the response of your spouse's, which are as bad as or worse than your own. Retirement and aging. What wonderful and not so wonderful experiences!

Based on our knowledge and exposure to the problems of aging, and vowing to never be as cantankerous and miserable-acting as some elderly people have been and are, we press forward towards further aging, hopefully, with dignity and the least possible fanfare. We certainly hope to deport ourselves worthy of the toleration of our children and grandchildren. For behold, if we live long enough, most, or all of Ecclesiastes, Chapter 12, verses 1 through 7 will be fulfilled in us: years of little pleasure, failing eyesight and hearing, fear of heights, sleeplessness and certainly, sooner or later, our trip to our eternal home with our bodies returning to dust and our spirits returning to God.

But who knows, we might even be living when Jesus Christ splits the eastern skies and "the dead in Christ rise and we which are alive and remain are caught up together with them in the clouds to meet the Lord in the air." Either way, we shall ever be with the Lord. (I Thessalonians 4:13-17) These are comforting words (verse 18) and behoove each of us to make our calling and election sure. (II Peter 1:5-11)

All in all, it has been a most wonderful life and I can say in all truth, "I'm glad I lived."

Ernest – in the middle of a sermon
Faith Temple third sanctuary

Ernest, Robert and Charles
A celebration at Mt. Zion in Plant City, Florida

Celebration at Mt. Zion in 1997

Ernest and Junell – 50 years of ministry

My granddaughter Farrah Waldron weds
Justin Moore (December 19, 1998)

Terry and Athena Raburn (1999)

Terry Raburn honors Ernest and Junell at their 50th wedding anniversary celebration at Faith Temple (June 1999)

Our family at our 50th wedding anniversary
Front row: Evan Conner, Ernest, Alex Franklin, Chris Conner, Junell, Caitlyn Conner
Back row: Farrah Waldron Moore, Justin Moore, Sandra & Phil Waldron, Phillip Waldron, Sharon and Bob Franklin, Jonathan Franklin, Phyllis Conner (Tom Conner-absent)

Ernest, Junell, Merle and Robert

Ernest, Junell and Athena Raburn
Ernest's 50th Anniversary of Ordination
Ft. Lauderdale, Florida in May, 2002

Proclamation

WHEREAS, on behalf of the Board of City Commissioners and staff of the City of Plant City, it is with great pleasure that I take this opportunity to congratulate you on your retirement from the active ministry of the Assemblies of God; and

WHEREAS, you have given joy and comfort, as well as guidance, to the citizens of the Plant City area since 1949 as senior pastor of Mt. Zion Assembly of God Church and subsequently Faith Temple Assembly of God Church; and

WHEREAS, your faithfulness not only as a minister of the gospel but also as a friend to everyone, cannot be expressed in words or deeds, but only in the hearts of the many people you have touched; and

WHEREAS, since the 1950's, your regular radio program, "Temple Vespers", on WPLA Radio and WCIE Christian Radio, has provided the means for those persons unable to attend church to have their spirits uplifted and to have someone to call their "pastor".

NOW, THEREFORE, I, GEORGE K. COLLINS, by virtue of the authority vested in me as Mayor of the City of Plant City, Florida, do hereby recognize the Reverend Ernest Holbrook as

"THE RADIO MINISTER"

in the Plant City area and we thank you and your family for the sacrifices of your time and talents as you have ministered to the citizens of the City of Plant City and our best wishes are extended to you in your future endeavors. As you always say on your radio program, "Good Day and May the Good Lord Richly Bless You".

IN WITNESS WHEREOF, I have hereunto set my hand and caused the Great Seal of the City of Plant City, Florida, to be affixed this 25th day of June in the year of our Lord nineteen hundred and ninety-three.

CITY OF PLANT CITY, FLORIDA

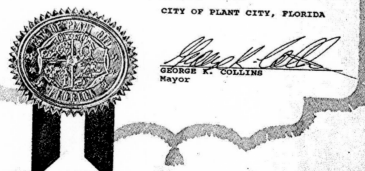

GEORGE K. COLLINS
Mayor

460

ADDENDUM

Husbands, love your wives, even as Christ also loved the church... Ephesians 5:25

*Train up a child in the way he should go and when he is old,
he will not depart from it... Proverbs 22:6*

*He was wounded for our transgressions, He was bruised for our iniquities, the
chastisement of our peace was upon Him; and with His stripes we are healed...
Isaiah 53:5*

*Thus it is written, and thus it behooved Christ to suffer,
and to rise from the dead on the third day... Luke 24:46*

*The kingdoms of this world are become the kingdoms of our Lord, and of his
Christ;
and He shall reign forever and ever... Revelation 11:15*

Next to my relationship to God and His Christ, those most dear to me have been my family members and close friends. As a child, it was my parents, siblings, grandparents and nearest relatives. The family and home memories stand tall as I recall them from time to time. Indeed, my childhood had all the ingredients of a well-rounded upbringing. Who could ever forget good home-cooking, home-made ice cream, cakes and pies, fishing, hunting, and swimming? And I certainly can't overlook the hard work with its blisters and rewards, plus an occasional spanking to keep me on the "straight and narrow" way. And greatest of all, was the nurturing I received in the church, the Bible and the Lord.

Then, comes my dear, darling wife. Who can possibly, adequately describe in words the life-long loving companionship of a spouse? She unquestionably has been and is my very best friend. Early on, she proved to be gracious, industrious and a remarkable companion. None has stood by my ministry more faithfully than she. And who could ask for a more devoted mother for our daughters? Her dedication, nurturing and tender loving care is unsurpassed in this and every area requiring faithfulness.

And next, are my three precious daughters. I'll never forget the first sight of them as they entered the world. Or the first and later times that I held them. Junell used to bathe them in the evening, apply sweet-smelling baby powder and then bring them to me as I sat relaxed in the recliner. She would ask, "Do you want to hold something precious and sweet?" Wow! Did I ever!? After this, came the thrill of their embrace as I would come home from a day's activities. It was like a heavenly breeze encompassing me.

What greater rewards than watching them grow up, sharing their uniqueness and togetherness at the table, playing games or taking vacations? And you wouldn't dare to miss any of their school programs until finally you are watching them walk across the stage in cap and gown. And before you hardly realize it you are giving their hands in marriage, wondering all the while where the time went. And thank God for sons-in-law who are all tops!

Then comes the grandchildren and even great-grandchildren, if you can hang on that long. The spoiling process is for grandparents, who then send them home for the parents to try to undo what has been done. And they seemingly grow up more quickly than did your children, because you aren't with them every day. Again, you are wondering how time eluded you. The song, "Sunrise, Sunset," resounds its haunting memories as also does, "Old Pappy Time is Pickin' my Pocket, I can't seem to stop it."

Hindsight says I should have taken more time with family and other special people. Still, I am eternally grateful for the privilege and opportunities afforded me to live and experience my loved ones. Truly, "the abundant life" has been mine in both the natural as well as the spiritual realm. I couldn't have asked for anything more.

Most of all, I am extremely grateful to Jesus Christ, the Only Begotten Son of the One and Only Almighty God. What a tremendous price He Paid for our redemption. It is impossible for us to fully comprehend the agony of spirit, soul and body that Jesus endured to free us from the power and penalty of sin. What a sacrifice on our behalf. Perhaps we'll understand it better by and by. But we know it is by and through Him that we have this marvelous abundant life.

With Paul the Apostle I can certainly say, "I have finished my course," and I hope I have "fought a good fight" and "kept the faith." I do thank God and His Christ for blessings way beyond what I deserve and I'm grateful as I face the transition, for the hope I have of eternal life, because of Jesus Christ's love for me.

We used to sing a song titled: "It's an Unfriendly World to Me." And for the born-again Christian believer, this world-system has gotten even more unfriendly as time goes on. For me, this results in a yearning for the time when "the kingdoms of this world are become the Kingdoms of our Lord, and of His Christ; and He shall reign forever and ever." (Revelation 11:15)

No longer will God, Christ, Bible-reading and prayer in public be unconstitutional in this or any nation in the world. For Christ will Himself reign and many people will say, "He will teach us His ways, and we will walk in His paths." (Isaiah 2:2-3) Wars will come to an end. (Verse 4) There will be peace at last. (Isaiah 9:7) For "In that day shall there be upon the bells of the horses HOLINESS UNTO THE LORD..." (Zechariah 14:20) It seems a befitting prayer would be: "Lord, hasten the day!" (Rev. 22:20b) And, "Thy kingdom come, thy will be done on earth as it is in heaven." (Matt. 6:10)

After redemption has been complete, eternal judgments done and Christ enthroned, myriads of the redeemed of all nations and all the ages, will join the four and twenty elders, innumerable angels and those sealed of the tribes of Israel, and will bow before the Lord and loudly proclaim, "Blessing, and glory, and wisdom, and thanksgiving, and honor, and power, and might, be unto our God forever and ever. Amen!" (Revelation, Chapters 4-7)

I'm most certain there will be those, along with my granddad and me, who will say, "I'm glad I lived; because now I'm alive forevermore with Christ the Lord and all our loved ones!" Amen and Amen!

Ernest and Grandson Evan Conner in front
of the White House in Washington, D.C.

Junell, Ernest and Evan with former
President Jimmy Carter and his wife
Rosalyn at Maranatha Baptist Church in
Plains, Georgia

Radio Training Network Board – Rev. James L. Campbell, President
Left to right: Rev. and Mrs. Jim Campbell, Mr. and Mrs. A. J. Davis, Mr. and Mrs. Dean McGinness, Ernest and Junell, Rev. and Mrs. Phillip Lykes, Mr. and Mrs. Joe Christian and Mr. and Mrs. Mike Howard

The Holbrook Campground near Cumming, Georgia

Campground tabernacle

A gathering of our family in July 2003

My Grandson, Phillip Waldron, weds Krystal Riling Feb. 7, 2004 at Plant City Church of God

From left: Bob, Sharon, Hannah, Jonathan and Alex Franklin, Evan, Chris, Tom, Caitlin and Phyllis Conner, Krystal and Phillip Waldron, Junell and Ernest Holbrook, Sandra and Phillip Waldron, Farrah and Justin Moore

A gathering on March 7, 2004 to celebrate Ernest's 75th birthday (March 8, 1929)

From left: Janette Walden, Junell, Joe Walden, Ernest, Joann Varn, Raymond and Joan Holbrook

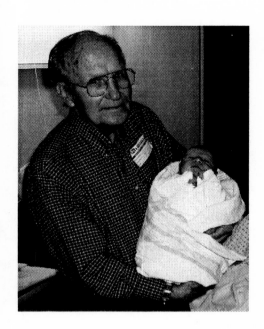

On March 24, 2004 Ernest and Junell welcomed their first great-grandchild, Jacob Benjamin Moore born to Justin and Farrah Moore.

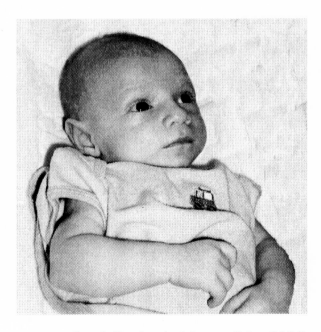

Jacob Benjamin Moore (May 2004)

positive, uplifting music!

2000 & 2001 Dove Award
"Station of the Year"

88.1
Sarasota
Bradenton
St. Petersburg

91.5
Tampa
Clearwater
New Port Richey

96.7
Brandon

96.3/106.1
Lakeland
Winter Haven

98.7
Auburndale

90.7/89.5
Sebring
Lake Placid

88.1
Ocala

90.9
Crystal River

Listen "LIVE" Online
www.thejoyfm.com

WLFJ • 89.3 FM
Greenville, SC
Spartanburg, SC
Anderson, SC

WLFJ • 660 AM
Christian Talk
Greenville, SC
Spartanburg, SC
Anderson, SC

WLFA • 91.3 FM
Asheville, NC

WMBJ • 88.3 FM
Myrtle Beach, SC

WLFS • 91.9 FM
Savannah, GA

103.7 FM
Hendersonville, NC

91.9 FM
Toccoa, GA

91.1 FM / 91.9 FM
Charleston, SC

90.9 FM
Boone, NC

www.hisradio.com
Listen Live Online

HIS RADIO NETWORK

472

RADIO TRAINING NETWORK

James L. Campbell, President

P.O. Box 7217 • Lakeland, FL 33807-7217
5015 South Florida Avenue, Suite 104 • Lakeland, FL 33813-2043

863-644-3464 FAX: 863-646-5326
E-mail: gosrad@aol.com

The Wind *fm*

2550 S CAMPBELL AVE STE 100
SPRINGFIELD   MO 65807-3540

 ERNEST HOLBROOK MINISTER

2208 Chesterfield Cir. Lakeland, FL 33813-5837

Ph. (863) 647-9941 Email: Eholbrook2@aol.com

RTN Radio Training Network • 35 stations & translators

• THE JOY FM •

Sarasota 88.1 • Tampa 91.5 • Brandon 96.7 • Lakeland 96.3 & 106.1

ABOUT THE AUTHOR

"I'm Glad I Lived" is an autobiography of the life and times of Ernest Eugene Holbrook. Born to Virgil Ernest and Minnie Julia Payne Holbrook on March 8, 1929, he grew up as a farm-boy in the Plant City and Lakeland areas of West Central Florida, U.S.A.

From early childhood, he worked with the family on small truck-farms where the principle winter crop was strawberries. Other farm products included a variety of vegetables. As soon as each family member reached the proper age, they were assigned certain chores, which included tending the horses and cows, mowing the lawn, and working the crops.

Church attendance played a significant role for the family. Ernest's adolescent years were greatly influenced by his parents and grandparents who had strong religious convictions and ministries. He learned to sing and play guitar as a youngster from his older sister and brother and by listening to records on the big "graphonola" (phonograph).

Being somewhat talented in this realm led to opportunities for a possible career in the country and western music field. Decision-time concerning this and the ministry presented a major challenge, with advisors abounding on each side of the issue. The final choice, however, had to be made by one person only, Ernest himself.

He chose the ministry and began preaching at age 18, in 1947. He traveled as an evangelist for some four years, then pastored more than 44 years at four different churches. He founded Faith Temple Assembly of God at Plant City, Florida, and continued as senior pastor there for almost 27 years.

His radio ministry, "Temple Vespers," spanned most of those years on stations WPLA, WCIE and WTWB. On June 25, 1993, the Mayor and City Commissioners of Plant City proclaimed him "The Radio Minister" of the Plant City, Lakeland area.

He has been an ordained minister of the Assemblies of God since 1952. He presently serves as a board member of "Radio Training Network" with headquarters in Lakeland, Florida. This non-profit organization operates numerous Christian stations and translators.

Ernest's life, with its highs, lows and everywhere in-between, is vividly portrayed in this fast-moving drama that includes romance, laughter, fantasies, realities and much, much more.

This author's hope for this offering is that it will not only amuse, but otherwise entreat the reader to a sincere introspection. If any lifetime or eternal benefits can be accomplished in any person, then the multitude of hours and efforts will be well-rewarded.

Printed in the United States
20560LVS00002B/121-213